ADVANCE PRAISE FOR *THE NEW MORE THAN TWO*

"*The New More Than Two* is a true game changer in the field of nonmonogamy theory and education. Rickert and Zanin have crafted a smart, thorough, compassionate book that tackles many issues, including topics that others shy away from such as misconduct and abuse. This book is useful for beginners and veterans alike and offers practical tools to nourish any kind of relationship."

—Tristan Taormino, author of *Opening Up*

"Eve and Andrea's desire to present this current edition as a resource that is practical, compassionate, conscientious, aware, educational, kind, and loving can be felt on every page, in every word. I am beyond excited to discover how *The New More Than Two* impacts me as a more mature nonmonogamous person and that it exists as a resource to aid a new generation of nonmonogamous persons.

—Evita "Lavitaloca" Sawyers, author of *A Polyamory Devotional*

"At last, an update to a classic! It's wonderful to see this edition cover intersectionality and touch on more nuance and diversity within nonmonogamy. I'm so excited to recommend this book to anyone interested in nonmonogamy, even those who've been practicing for years."

—Michelle Hy, nonmonogamy educator, *Polyamorous While Asian*

"This is essential reading for anyone who wants to date humans and not be an asshole, whether you practice polyamory or not."

—Rachel Lark, writer, musician, and creator of *Coming Soon: A New Rock Musical*

"Essential reading, not only for those who are (or wonder if they are) nonmonogamous, but for their friends and families, and ultimately for anyone who wants to think carefully and deeply about what it means to love and respect one's partner(s)."

—Carrie Jenkins, author of *What Love Is (and What it Could Be)*, *Sad Love* and *Nonmonogamy and Happiness*

"*The New More Than Two* validates the immense courage it often takes to begin—and continue—one's ethical nonmonogamy journey. This is a powerful new addition to the library of ethical nonmonogamy and should be considered essential reading!"

—Andre Shakti, educator, producer, activist and polyamory pundit

"There are so many complexities to consider around nonmonogamy, and this book does a truly great job of covering many bases extremely well."

—Lola Phoenix, author of *The Anxious Person's Guide to Nonmonogamy*

"Rickert and Zanin accomplish a tricky task, discussing an often-misunderstood topic in a direct but respectful manner. Without holding nonmonogamy up as superior to monogamy, they offer their readers a glimpse at the reality that nonmonogamy can hold as much joy and fulfillment for some as monogamy does for others."

—Race Bannon, author of *Learning the Ropes: A Basic Guide to Safe and Fun BDSM Lovemaking*

"While *More Than Two* was always highly regarded, it was time for an update to adjust for the way the landscape has changed in the last decade. *The New More Than Two* more than meets the need."

—Kevin A. Patterson, M.Ed, author of *Love's Not Color Blind* and the For Hire series

"Eve and Andrea have done something truly remarkable in taking what was good from the original edition and updating it to create a nonmonogamy resource for a new era, one that is full of wisdom, kindness, awareness, compassion, empathy, and useful practical information."

—JoEllen Notte, author of *The Monster Under the Bed* and *In It Together*

"Whether your nonmonogamy is flavored more like relationship anarchy or polyamory, whether you are solo or multiply partnered, whether you're asexual or allosexual, there is quality information here that will help you navigate love in all its forms."

—Kitty Stryker, author of *Ask Yourself* and *Say More*

"In *The New More Than Two,* Eve and Andrea have revitalized the original, making it a new essential book. Never preaching or condemning, they explain, examine, and explore in dialog with the reader. They reach out welcoming hands, saying not to be afraid of this lifestyle and that you can do it."

—Cooper S. Beckett, author of *My Life on the Swingset* and co-author of *The Pegging Book*

"When the first version of *More Than Two* came out, many referred to it as the poly Bible. I like to think that we've all collectively learned a lot since then, and it's nice to see a new incarnation of this book that has grown with us. May we all continue to learn and grow, and keep noticing what is best for our own hearts, minds, and souls."

—Tikva Wolf, creator of Kimchi Cuddles comics

"*The New More Than Two* is a much-needed expansion on the original: a maturation, an improvement that is not just information, but heart and soul come to fruition. Rickert and Zanin have given us the compassionate update that nonmonogamy, and the world, needed."

— Zach Budd, LMSW, consent educator

"*The New More Than Two* keeps the practical throughline that made the original effective and unique while adding even more depth and compassion. While we all carve our own paths, *The New More Than Two* is an indispensable guide through the terrain of nonmonogamy.

—Shay Tiziano, author of *Tying & Flying* and *Creating Captivating Classes*

"*The New More Than Two* doesn't try to be a manual, a course, a quick reference, or a casual read, but it somehow reads as all of those and more. It's deeply rewarding to dive in and see the complex and nuanced details and decisions about some of the most important parts of our lives given clarity, giving everyone more options and more power to make decisions and create relationships and community."

—Dylan T. Thomas, co-host of *Life on the Swingset*

"*The New More Than Two* is for anyone who wants to practice conscientiousness and kindness in their connections with others. The practical, actionable advice for nonmonogamy flows intuitively from the thoughtful prompts for self-reflection."

—Eli Heina Dadabhoy, blogger at *Heinous Dealings* on The Orbit network

"A beautiful deconstruction of how fairy tale mononormativity shapes our expectations for connection, with deep insight into more expansive ways of relating. Whether you're new to exploring or looking for a sound refresh, this book is ready to walk you down the enriching and well-trodden pathways to opening up."

— Leigh Cowart, author of *Hurts So Good*

"Get ready to engage in honest discussions about difficult subjects without cheerleading or boosterism. *The New More Than Two* is both warmhearted and clear-eyed. Recommended for existing practitioners and those curious about getting started."

—Marcus McCann, author of *Park Cruising*

"Eve and Andrea take readers on a journey beyond conventional relationship norms, offering practical advice, personal anecdotes, and thoughtful reflections on navigating multiple intimate connections. With warmth and wisdom, they challenge societal norms, offering a roadmap for creating fulfilling, ethical, and sustainable relationships."

—Laura Antoniou, author of *The Killer Wore Leather*

"*The New More Than Two* leaves no stone unturned in offering guidance for weathering the highs, lows, and in-betweens of nonmonogamy. Monogamous folks will find a lot to value here, too: insights into growth and change, building trust, communication skills, and real talk about abuse, all written with great empathy and awareness of our very human vulnerabilities. A classic relationship book for everyone."

—Mo Daviau, bookseller and author of *Every Anxious Wave*

"The authors of *The New More Than Two* have seamlessly incorporated important topics such as decolonization into their riveting discussion of nonmonogamous structures and values. This is the *More Than Two* for a new empathetic and radical audience."

— Mainely Mandy, video essayist

The New More *than* Two

ALSO BY EVE RICKERT AND ANDREA ZANIN

Post-Nonmonogamy and Beyond
by Andrea Zanin

Nonmonogamy and Betrayal
by Eve Rickert

MORETHANTWO.CA

Foreword by Dr. Kim Tallbear *and afterword by* Nalo Hopkinson

Eve Rickert & Andrea Zanin

The New More *than* Two

A Philosophical Reimagining of the Classic Nonmonogamy Guide

THORNAPPLE PRESS

THE NEW MORE THAN TWO
A Philosophical Reimagining of the Classic Nonmonogamy Guide

Thornapple Press
300 – 722 Cormorant Street
Victoria, BC V8W 1P8 Canada
press@thornapplepress.ca

Our business offices are located on the traditional, ancestral and unceded territories of the lək̓ʷəŋən and W̱SÁNEĆ peoples. We return a percentage of company profits to the original stewards of this land through South Island Reciprocity Trust.

Thornapple Press is a brand of Talk Science to Me Communications Inc. Talk Science is a Certified Women Business Enterprise, a CGLCC CERTIFIED 2SLGBTQI+-owned business, and a Certified Living Wage Employer.

Cover illustration by Eugenia Zoloto, © Thornapple Press 2026
Cover design by Brianna Harden
Interior design by Jeff Werner
Copy editing by Heather van der Hoop
Proofreading by Hazel Boydell and Alison Whyte
Index by Maria Hypponen

Body typeface set in Maiola by Veronika Burian.

Library and Archives Canada Cataloging-In-Publication Data
Title: The new more than two : a philosophical reimagining of the classic nonmonogamy guide / Eve Rickert & Andrea Zanin ; foreword by Dr. Kim TallBear and afterword by Nalo Hopkinson.
Names: Rickert, Eve, author. | Zanin, Andrea, author. | TallBear, Kimberly, writer of foreword. | Hopkinson, Nalo, writer of afterword.
Description: Series statement: More than two essentials ; 15 | Includes bibliographical references and index.
Identifiers: Canadiana (print) 20260146633 | Canadiana (ebook) 20260151092 | ISBN 9781997702252 (softcover) | ISBN 9781997702269 (EPUB) | ISBN 9781997702276 (PDF)
Subjects: LCSH: Non-monogamous relationships. | LCSH: Sexual ethics. | LCSH: Intimacy (Psychology)
Classification: LCC HQ980 .R53 2026 | DDC 306.84/23—dc23

10 9 8 7 6 5 4 3 2 1

Printed and bound in Shenzen, China, by Reliance Printing.

MIX
Paper | Supporting responsible forestry
FSC® C102842

Authors' note

What's in a name, anyway? Well, a lot, as it turns out—particularly in the age of the algorithm, to say nothing of the quirks of online bookselling, book review sites, library cataloguing conventions and more.

The book *More Than Two: A Practical Guide to Ethical Polyamory* was published in 2014. In 2024, one of the original authors (Eve) and a new co-author (Andrea) collaborated to reimagine the book and create an almost fully rewritten successor. In keeping the same main title (also now referenced in the name of a series Eve curates, More Than Two Essentials), we hoped it would serve as a familiar signpost for readers who knew the original and, like us, were hungry for something that kept the best of it, but reconceived the rest in the way it needed to be a decade later. We signalled that difference with the rest of the main title—*Second Edition*—and the subtitle, *Cultivating Nonmonogamous Relationships with Kindness and Integrity*. To help people find it, we had it catalogued as a second edition of the original, for which Eve had acquired full copyright.

Sadly, this approach confused the heck out of our robot overlords and caused a range of publishing and publicity headaches. Lots of people couldn't wrap their heads around the idea of a new "edition" as anything more than a cosmetic touch-up. Our new book was catalogued with its predecessor at libraries and on a number of popular websites, reviews were merged, authorship was mixed up, and all of this proved impossible to fix.

So when it came time to issue the book in paperback, we decided to tweak the title once more to help solve those problems. And voilà! *The New More Than Two: A Philosophical Reimagining of the Classic Nonmonogamy Guide* was born, issued as a standalone work rather than an edition of anything else. The text is the same as the 2024 hardcover, aside from a handful of minor corrections (we're both editors; we couldn't help ourselves) and the new afterword by Nalo Hopkinson.

Do you need both of these newer books? Content-wise, probably not. But if, like us, you're a bit of a collector when it comes to nonmonogamy books, well, we certainly won't stop you from adding this handsome green tome to your shelf (or, for that matter, tracking down the 2024 hardcover, if you're starting with the paperback). Really, though, as with so many things, it's what's on the inside that counts.

As always, thanks for reading.

Eve and Andrea
February 2026

To Kelly and Shelly

I am listening now with all of my senses, as if the whole universe might exist just to teach me more about love.

ADRIENNE MAREE BROWN

Contents

Foreword

"Nonmonogamy is not utopia," write Eve Rickert and Andrea Zanin in *The New More Than Two*. I laughed; no kidding! Yet, they also write, in nonmonogamous relationships "You have more of everything you get from romantic relationships—more companionship, more advice, more joy, more love." Rickert and Zanin are clear about the benefits and challenges of living nonmonogamously in a society that has been set up to prohibit or inhibit, at every legal and social turn, open, accepted nonmonogamous relating.

Rickert and Zanin are experienced nonmonogamists; Zanin is now "post-nonmonogamous." The authors write in supportive voices that many readers will find edifying, whether one is a new or experienced nonmonogamist, a monogamous reader, or even someone like me, who after a decade of practising solo polyamory, now calls myself "more-than-monogamous." I have expanded my relationship focus beyond both monogamy and nonmonogamy as I focus on not putting human loves into a hierarchy over the nonhuman relations that sustain my body and soul. For example, I recently coined the term *poly-river-amory*, both playfully and seriously as I became post-nonmonogamous like Zanin and also recognized the profound influence of my multiple river loves on how I have always related to human loves. Rivers are both here and away, both committed to place and always travelling. I do not have more than one human sexual/romantic love now, but I continue to consider all of my relationships according to values and practices that exceed the restrictions of normative monogamy and family, and the ideals of compulsory sex, marriage, settlement in place and the relationship escalator. (You may need the glossary near the end of this book to read this foreword, too!)

Rickert and Zanin focus on relationships between more than two *humans*, but there is much here for this poly-river-amorist, and for so many of you diverse humans with your bountiful relationship desires. The authors question not only compulsory monogamy, but also the compulsory alignment of sex and romance with coupledom or more than coupledom. While emphasizing how to manage nonmonogamy and how or why to choose it or not choose it, *The New More Than Two* also supports more than two relationship possibilities, monogamy vs. nonmonogamy. The authors help their readers see past restrictive patriarchal, colonial and capitalist ideas about how love and family are "supposed" to look.

When I began writing *The Critical Polyamorist* blog in 2013, I knew that I was experimenting with polyamory until I could forge a language that better captures, perhaps Indigenizes, more-than-monogamous relating. I started the blog as an Indigenous Studies scholar and as a Dakota woman in search of relationship possibilities grounded in age-old Dakota extended kinship practices and also in newer possibilities that resist settler-colonial norms related to sex, marriage and family. I live in both Canada and the United States; I study both countries in which Indigenous and all people have been railroaded into relationship forms that benefit the settler-colonial state with its private-property fetish. The United States and Canada, in order to facilitate settlement and expansion of their borders, scripted stories about how love, romance and family are supposed to work. At the same time, both countries made illegal Indigenous and other diverse family forms. Settler laws governing land ownership, private property and inheritance went hand in hand with the development of new norms of compulsory monogamy, marriage and heterosexuality. Even when breaking past some of the limits of heteropatriarchy in how we make love and family, many of us still find ourselves bound within heavily scripted, mononormative, propertied and hierarchical bonds in our relationships of many kinds.

In place of dominant and oppressive-for-so-many relationship norms, Eve Rickert and Andrea Zanin offer abundant possibilities that not only disrupt those norms, but better meet the desires, needs, skills and life conditions of the individual humans who are trying to love and relate as best we can in this challenging world. For those of you who are nonmonogamous, you will find practical advice and reassurance in this book. You may also feel challenged to do better. The same goes for those of you who are monogamous, but who want to push against mononormativity. And for those of us who are post-nonmonogamous, even poly-river-amorous like myself, or who are out there forging new languages and ways of loving and relating, there is learning for us too in these pages. I wish you all good reading and good relating.

KIM TALLBEAR
Amiskwaciwâskahikan (Edmonton, Alberta)
and Los Angeles, California

Another world is not only possible, she is on her way. Maybe many of us won't be here to greet her, but on a quiet day, if I listen very carefully, I can hear her breathing.
ARUNDHATI ROY

Eve's Preface and Acknowledgements

CONTENT NOTE: This chapter discusses sexual assault, domestic violence, child death and residential schools.

There was nothing particularly remarkable about that October morning in 2014. But in the mental play of my life, it stands out as a sort of intermission between acts, a clear moment between "before" and "after," though I wouldn't recognize it until years later. That threshold is marked in my memory by yellow maple leaves, morning mist on a lake, the smell of fall and of mountain soil, and a dream I wasn't ready to wake up from.

I had just spent two months on the road promoting *More Than Two: A Practical Guide to Ethical Polyamory*. With my co-author of that edition, I'd driven over 7,000 kilometres in a camper van, stopped in dozens of cities and spoken to thousands of people. Our itinerary often involved speaking in one city in the evening, driving several hours to the next, camping on public land overnight, and then speaking again the next evening. Other times, we'd drive for days through the desert or mountains between events.

I remember it as one of the most idyllic times of my life. Wrapped up in a sense of purpose, warmly received at every stop by people eager to hear our perspectives, convinced we were making the world a better place. The whole thing still feels unreal, suspended in a sort of crystalline bubble in my mind.

That morning, it was coming to an end. We'd given our last talk in Montana, driven through the next day, and camped at a state park just east of Washington's Snoqualmie Pass. The next leg of the journey would bring me home. While my co-author slept, I savoured the last few peaceful hours. I showered, made coffee, sat for awhile in the morning silence...then opened my phone.

Who the fuck is Jian Ghomeshi?

I'd become a Canadian citizen just days before the start of the tour, and my assimilation was far from complete. The name and face of the then-beloved host of CBC Radio's Q had been unknown to me until that morning. The day before, Ghomeshi had made a tearful Facebook post announcing he had just been fired from his job at the CBC, claiming he was being blacklisted for disclosing his participation in consensual kink. Later that same evening, the *Toronto Star* published an article detailing allegations by four women that Ghomeshi had engaged in nonconsensual punching, choking and biting, among other things, during dates, and had sexually harassed a colleague.

I fell down the rabbit hole. Ghomeshi had defenders who believed his kink-shaming story, but women were speaking up, saying he'd long had a reputation in Toronto as a bad date, and pointing out how his Facebook post smelled like someone trying to get ahead of a story.

Later that evening, Andrea Zanin, a blogger I'd admired ever since their post the previous year on "the problem with polynormativity," published a piece called "poor persecuted pervert?" examining the allegations with a lens that was both survivor-centric and kink- and sex-positive. That post would go viral, be republished by *Ms.* magazine, and lead to Andrea's sudden mainstream visibility. Through those two blog posts, and a series of threads leading through our professional lives and the website formerly known as Twitter, within a few months the two of us would find ourselves together in a Toronto bistro, where I have another vivid sensory memory of another moment that proved itself, in retrospect, to be a turning point: a beautiful meal, and several hours of surprisingly (for two people who'd just met) deep and connecting conversation.

The allegations against Ghomeshi broke three years before #MeToo exploded across social media. But things were changing. Ghomeshi employed all the strategies used throughout living memory by dangerous men—and they didn't work. But beyond that, the tone of the media coverage was different, and not just in how it handled allegations of sexual assault. As Andrea would describe to me later, the kink element just... wasn't really a thing. There was no ick factor. Even in national publications, there was a tacit acceptance that Ghomeshi's misdeed was his handling of consent, and not his interest in BDSM. Even the fact that he'd tried "I'm just being kink-shamed!" as a defence at all (and many people bought it, at least until the *Star* article came out) showed that ideas about kink and consent were filtering into the mainstream.

Do you remember 2014? Like, really remember it? It's dizzying to think of everything that's happened in the last ten years. It was before #BlackLivesMatter became a household phrase; before the 2015 report of Canada's Truth and Reconciliation Commission, which sought to force the country to finally confront the horrifying legacy of residential schools in Canada; before the 2016 US presidential election and the visible rise of fascism across the Americas; before the COVID-19 pandemic; before the siege of Gaza.

By the time Andrea and I connected over brunch in early 2015, the first tiny ends were beginning to show of the threads that would eventually, dramatically, unravel my entire life. Of course, I didn't know that then, either. But many other things were about to unravel, too, around the world.

Nothing ever really changes all at once, of course. A lightning strike begins days or weeks before, with changes in the atmosphere that may begin hundreds of miles away. Earthquakes may be decades or centuries in the making, as tension builds between tectonic plates. The same is true of human lives, relationships and societies: Ruptures, upheavals and revolutions never happen spontaneously (even when they feel that way), but are always preceded by years or decades of dissatisfaction, tension, learning, organizing and quiet change, building under the surface.

If the fall of 2014 had been an intermission, by the summer of 2021 the curtain had fallen on the following act. I was living in a different city, recently divorced, still in COVID isolation, trying to pick up the loose ends of my life and weave something new. That summer there were no peaceful dreams or mists on mountain lakes. There were orange flowers under orange skies, and row upon row of children's shoes.

So-called British Columbia was on fire. Animals were dying by the billions in record heat. And across the province, ground-penetrating radar investigations were finding first hundreds, then thousands, of "anomalies" beneath the earth on the grounds of former residential schools, believed to be unmarked graves of children who'd died there. 215 in Kamloops. 40 in Sechelt. 159 in Williams Lake. 160 on Kuper Island. It seemed more were found every week.

The Indian residential school system had operated in Canada for well over a century—the last one closed in 1996—and was an integral part of the colonial effort to assimilate Indigenous people by eliminating their culture and language. Hundreds of thousands of children were taken from their families, forced to have their hair cut and clothes changed, forbidden to speak their languages, and subjected to psychological, physical and often sexual abuse. Thousands died—maybe tens of thousands; statistics are poor. Thousands are still alive today as adults. (Lest the Americans reading this be tempted to feel superior: You had these schools too. The guiding principle of "Kill the Indian and save the man" came from one of the American founders of the system.)

In Canada, where the country at large has finally, in the last two decades, begun to grapple publicly with the legacy of residential schools, orange has become the colour of reconciliation. That summer, when the news of unmarked graves began to emerge, I picked marigolds from my garden and brought them to the steps of the legislative building, where people had piled shoes, flowers, candles and teddy bears in a makeshift memorial to the lost children.

I still don't really know how to talk about that summer. I don't want to talk about yet another white woman's awakening to something so many millions of others already knew in their bones, generations deep. I've been a leftist, and an activist in various forms, all my life, and I like to imagine that I am better informed than most people of my background about the kind of world we live in. But like so many privileged people, I knew without really knowing. I was able to intellectualize, observe and empathize with the suffering of the world and critique the monstrous systems that generate it, all while floating a bit outside it all.

I didn't learn anything particularly new that summer, but I did learn how to *feel* some things that I perhaps had long known.

One of my teachers that summer was an episode of the podcast *All My Relations* that talked about love: specifically, how one of the main purposes of the residential school system had been to destroy love. How generations of stolen children had grown up not knowing love, never hearing "I love you" said to them, and came home to their communities unable to express it to their own children. How recovery from the damage of colonization had to include relearning how to love.

That podcast wasn't talking to me, or people like me. I am a white, Christian settler, the eighth generation of my family on this continent, and my ancestors were not the victims of genocide or slavery—they were its perpetrators. But what I came to understand then was that my ancestors had passed down a wound to me, too. My privilege, the relative ease with which I move through the world, comes at a price, and that price is paid with my heart and my soul. This was a bargain made hundreds of years before my birth, and I was taught to pay the price before I could ever understand it. Love had been taken from me, too. These systems, settler colonialism and capitalism, rely on all of us interacting through a lens of power. They rely on the destruction of relationships with each other, with the earth, with ourselves. If we all felt empathy, compassion, connection, love—really felt them, all the time—the system couldn't survive. So it starves us of those things, early on. We're not ever supposed to even know what we've lost.

That summer, while the world burned, I experienced a profound, wordless grief beyond anything I can remember. I grieved for the children, for the lost languages and stories, for the planet, for the past and the future, for myself. And slowly that grief turned into a rage so hot I sometimes felt it alone was capable of burning the world.

What we have lost is incalculable—in terms of ecosystems, biodiversity, cultures and languages, and human lives, of course. But also, less tangibly, in terms of the things systems of domination have demanded we kill off in ourselves so that we will sustain and tolerate those systems.

We have all been robbed of love. It's on us to find it again—or to reimagine it.

Everyone on this planet today is living through a global unravelling: of societies, ecosystems, empires, and stories about who we are and how we should live. What will come next? Will we live in the world of the most dire sci-fi dystopias? Or will we, somehow, build something better?

Nothing ever changes all at once. Ghomeshi's career was over; his comeback attempts would fail. It was tempting to think things were slowly getting better. But backlash was inevitable. In a criminal trial in 2016, the defence used tried-and-true strategies to attack the credibility of his accusers, and this time, it worked: Ghomeshi was acquitted.

Then in 2022, millions of people revelled in the "global humiliation" campaign waged on social media against actress Amber Heard as she defended herself against a defamation suit brought in the United States by her celebrity ex-husband. According to the findings of a UK judge 18 months earlier, that ex-husband had beaten, kicked and sexually assaulted Heard and ripped hair out of her head, all in a context of verbal and emotional abuse and coercive control. Despite the overwhelming evidence Heard had to back up what was ultimately a depressingly typical account of experiencing domestic abuse, the North American public seemed all too ready to swallow her abuser's account of her as a liar and manipulator of *Gone Girl*–level proportions.

I am less concerned with the fates (or careers) of dangerous celebrity men than I am with the way society, from the press to the justice system to TikTok influencers, treats the people they harm—and what that says about all of us. These high-profile cases are a symptom. The disease is the system, and the system is all of us: how quick we are to dehumanize, how easily we turn on one another, how readily we seek power, how reluctant we are to give it up.

I know I will spend the rest of my life trying to heal the wounds, in myself and others, passed down from the generations before me, and then re-enacted and re-experienced in my relations with so many wounded others. I know I will never live to see the different, better world so many are trying to create. So what do you do with that kind of knowledge?

I'm taking a page from Lauren Olamina, the imperfect protagonist of Octavia Butler's *Parable of the Sower*, on how to survive an apocalypse: You learn what you can, then you teach what you know. And we survive together.

It was also in 2021 that I realized I needed to rewrite *More Than Two*. The original, which had sold close to 200,000 copies, had helped many people—but it was flawed to begin with, and by the time it was seven years old, my thinking (and that of nonmonogamous folks in general) had moved beyond it. But I didn't know how to start such an undertaking. Diving back into the manuscript meant coming face-to-face with too many of my own wounds, in ways I was not yet prepared for.

By the time I acquired the rights to *More Than Two*, in January 2023, Andrea and I had developed both a friendship and a long-standing working relationship, through my role as a publisher and theirs as an editor. As someone also aligned with my values in nonmonogamy (and much of life), they were a natural choice to help me revise the book. As the collaboration developed, it became clear they should be my co-author. This book could not have existed without them. While the bones of the original are there, we've revised every bit of it, and added significant new content.

The book you hold in your hands now is the culmination of ten years of unlearning and relearning, grief and heartbreak, unravelling and breaking and remaking. It's a triumph and an apology, an attempted righting of past wrongs and a prayer for the future, a tiny—and, I hope, humble—contribution to the vital project of love.

So many people today are trying to reimagine love. Or to reclaim it, or both. Much as I fear what the future holds, I am grateful to live in a time when this is happening, and for the many opportunities to learn. I owe a great deal to the incredible minds (and hearts) of those whose work have influenced me over this past decade. There are too many to name, but a few worth mentioning are adrienne maree brown, Alexandra Stein, AV Flox, Carrie Jenkins, Charlie Jane Anders, Chelsey Rhodes, Danya Ruttenberg, Estelle Ellison, Heidi Priebe, Jessica Fern, Kai Cheng Thom, Kali Tal, Kate Manne, Kelly Hayes, Kim TallBear, Kitty Stryker, Leila Raven, Mia Mingus, Monica Byrne, Nora Samaran and Shelly Deforte.

I am also thankful for my anchors, especially Shelly, Zach, Kat, Dan and Wayne, for never letting me forget who I am.

But more than anything, I owe my gratitude to the underground: to the whisperers, the whistleblowers and the secret-keepers, the tellers of stories—stories as nourishment, stories as medicine, stories as survival, passed quietly through the nodes of a global network that is always there, but that you only find when you really need it. The ones who know that you always answer *that* message, always take *that* call. The ones who name names; the ones it's not safe to name.

We survived.

Thank you.

I love you.

EVE RICKERT
Lekwungen and W̱SÁNEĆ territory (Victoria, BC)
June 2024

Andrea's Preface and Acknowledgements

I read the original *More Than Two* when it came out, and reviewed it on my blog at the time. I had a lot of praise for its focus on ethics, and some criticism for the things I felt it left out. Never would I have imagined the flow of events over the ensuing decade that would culminate in me co-authoring the book's second edition.

When Eve first asked me to help out, I was honoured. I knew the project was one of great significance to her, and since my initial role was as an editor, I devoted myself to fixing the things she wanted fixed and making her voice shine. As an editor, my job is to enhance, polish and clarify an author's voice, not to insert my own. If someone else's book sounds like me, I've done a bad job!

When Eve first mentioned the possibility of being co-authors, I was resistant. As her friend, I wanted her to have the experience of making it entirely hers—kind of like how if someone goes through a tough divorce, you might support them as they settle into their new solo apartment. I was also skeptical of the notion that I'd have anything of value to add. But as the project developed, and our conversations about it deepened, it became clear that my own voice might have its place after all. So my first thank you goes to her: for trusting me and making space for me to join my voice with hers. Making *The New More Than Two* has been an incredibly rich and rewarding collaborative project, and I'm grateful for the opportunity to contribute to it and learn through it.

Speaking of learning... my own trajectory has happened over the same timeline as Eve's, but with different milestones. The Ghomeshi affair that Eve details in her preface was significant for me, of course, but in a very different way. When it occurred, I was struggling with debilitating chronic pain from what turned out to be the regrowth of a rare spinal cord tumour for which I'd previously had surgery. After my blog post went viral, the mainstream media suddenly saw me as a source on BDSM and consent, and the interview requests came fast and thick.

I remember being interviewed for a TV show, leaving the studio, and taking a call from another journalist in the car as my then-partner drove me to the pain clinic. There, I sat on an examination table awaiting my weekly set of nerve block shots, in which a doctor inserted a long needle through the holes of my sacrum and shot carbocaine directly into my spinal nerves. I nearly passed out on the table, as I did every week; I sipped a juice box to revive myself a bit and limped back out to the car to go home and talk with another journalist. Numbness was bliss, but it only lasted a few days. The urgency of speaking out on consent—trying to make it clear to the public that you can consent to kinky fun, but assault is never okay—was a welcome distraction from my own grinding, intractable pain.

The intensity of the contrast between the topics I was suddenly talking about on national news and the reality of my everyday life was... a lot. It highlighted the schism that had grown for me in the previous few years between the focus I'd always had on sexuality and relationships—in my studies, my community-organizing work, my personal life—and the reality that, living in my body with all its troubles, I couldn't actually enjoy my sexuality very much at all.

A few months later, I had a second major spinal surgery, followed by radiation treatment, which prevented the remnants of my tumour from regrowing again but threw the rest of my health into chaos, leading to many years of agonizingly slow recovery. Almost everything about my life fell to pieces in those years, and the rebuilding has been painstaking and imperfect.

Meanwhile, as Eve has so clearly described in her preface, the world has been on fire, literally and figuratively. I started out, in my tender youth, as a lefty feminist queer, and the last decade of world events has both deepened my despair and strengthened my convictions. At times, it has brought me into deep cynicism and a sense of voicelessness: With so many awful things happening in the world, at what has seemed a steadily increasing pace, what could I possibly say about sex and relationships that wouldn't just seem hopelessly out of touch? So instead of speaking, I have listened and learned: through school and social media, books (so many books) and community gatherings, news stories and work projects and everyday life. Tending plants, teaching myself to cook new foods, relearning my body. Deepening some friendships while grieving others; listening to what solitude and silence have to teach.

The disability justice theories I'd learned about in grad school met up with my own bodily experience, which forced me to drop out, but that's only part of it. When Black Lives Matter disrupted the Toronto Pride parade in 2016, I watched my community split in ways I hadn't foreseen, with people I used to respect taking the side of police over Black queers. Meanwhile, those same police dismissed the community's reports of a serial killer preying on gay men; two years later, he would finally be caught, after murdering eight. (The killer and I had multiple friends in common on social media. It felt very, very close to home.) I read about conspiracy theorists in the news, thinking it was terrible, but feeling safe on the other side of the American border. Then, for weeks in the spring of 2022, a convoy of far-right anti-vax conspiracy theorists in borrowed trucks blighted the streets of Ottawa—and later, Toronto, too—with their hateful messages and ceaseless honking, which I could hear from my own living room: not so far away after all.

I read books by Indigenous writers and learned about decolonization and the long history of genocide against Indigenous people, and then watched as debates raged among different generations of my relatives when the name of our colonizing ancestor, Egerton Ryerson, was removed from a local university along with his statue. I watched a global pandemic sweep the world, shut down our systems, and kill or disable people in my community, mostly the ones who were already most marginalized: elderly and disabled folks, trans people, people of colour. And then I watched my province reelect the premier whose slow responses had cost countless lives and who, to this day, is intent on screwing over the nurses who helped save so many. I watch Gaza burning on the news, while catching the first whiffs of this year's crop of wildfires, carried into the city on the spring breeze. Turning on my new air purifier feels like a microcosm of the whole situation: an act of self-preservation within my four walls, necessary but nonetheless available to me through privilege, while the larger problem is just so, so much bigger.

These, and the many other things I've seen, experienced and learned in the last decade have not, for the most part, been about intimate relationships or sexuality, which was my previous area of focus. I'm glad I started out as an editor on this project, because if Eve had started out by saying "Let's write this book together!" I probably would have demurred for imagined lack of having anything useful to say. It wasn't until I got into the material that I started to perceive the connections between this other scope of learning and nonmonogamy. The way that we are, at every moment, faced with choices about who to care for and how, about what boundaries to draw and what trust to extend, about what kind of people we want to be and what kind of world we want to live in.

My thanks go to the people who've been with me in this learning. If we've had intimate or intellectual conversations, been vulnerable with each other, turned to each other in hard times and good times, fed each other, checked in, expressed love and care—then I have learned from and through our closeness, and I am grateful. My thanks also go to the countless people whose wisdom I've learned from who'll probably never know it: the writers, thinkers, journalists, storytellers, scientists, entertainers, filmmakers, teachers, scholars, poets and speakers whose ideas and expertise have shaped my thinking from a distance.

The world might be burning, but I am glad you're all in it.

ANDREA ZANIN

Tkaronto (Toronto, Ontario), on the traditional territory of the Mississaugas of the Credit, the Anishnabeg, the Chippewa, the Haudenosaunee and the Wendat peoples

June 2024

The universe is made of stories, not of atoms.
MURIEL RUKEYSER

Introduction

It's a story as old as time—or so many have been told. Two people meet, they date, they fall in love. They pledge sexual and emotional fidelity, start a family and settle down to live happily ever after, the end.

Stories like this can offer a comforting view of relationships: True love conquers all. Everyone has a soulmate, just waiting to be found. Once you've found your soulmate, you will live happily ever after. Love is all you need. There's no need to work hard at understanding yourself or your needs, no need to keep working on your happiness once you've found it. Even queer people, who may be alienated by the heteronormativity of such fairy tales, can end up mentally switching out the genders but retaining the concept as a template to pursue.

Turns out, though, this story isn't really all that old. This view of relationships was, until recently, a relatively fringe position, globally speaking. In Canada, where we live, it mostly showed up in the last 200 years or so, imported by European colonizers and imposed on the Indigenous populations as one of many strategies used to break down their families and social structures, "assimilate" them into European culture, and turn them (and their families) into productive units of capitalism. Of course, diverse relationship structures practised by newcomers—both those who came by choice as settlers, and those brought here forcibly and enslaved—also had to go. This imposition of the monogamous couple as an organizing unit of society, and as the only acceptable form of relationship, is called mononormativity. You might also hear it called compulsory monogamy, and it's backed up by its siblings, heteronormativity and the gender binary. Its younger cousin, amatonormativity—the twin ideas that these monogamous relationships should be based on romantic love and that romantic relationships are the "best" and most important kind of relationships, the ones around which we should organize our lives—showed up even later, really starting to dominate only in the last century or so.

We don't have to follow the story created by mononormativity, amatonormativity, and the social and political pressure to marry and have children. For starters, even if we do pursue that path, it often doesn't work out the way we're told it will. Plenty of marriages end in divorce; some of these splits are acrimonious, some amicable, most somewhere in between. Blended families are common (and their emotional and practical logistics can have a lot in common with some of the challenges we face in nonmonogamy!). Career paths and educational pursuits can lead partners to live separately or in long-distance relationships, whether temporarily or in the long term. The ongoing housing affordability crisis is inspiring many people to try new living arrangements, such as sharing a home purchase among several adults. One spouse often dies long before the other, leaving the remaining person to create a new life on their own. People discover new things about their sexual orientation, gender or other aspects of themselves, which can profoundly change the nature of the relationships they committed to before knowing these truths. Caring for elderly parents or other loved ones can add new dimensions to a nuclear family's living situation; in many cultures, it's normal and expected for multiple generations to live under one roof.

Even if you choose to embrace the idea that romantic relationships (and the pursuit of happiness) should define your life, you probably know that "happily ever after" is a myth. People, unlike characters in fairy tales, are not static. We live, we grow, we change. Healthy, supportive romantic lives require not just continual reinvestment but constant awareness of the changes in our partners, our situations and ourselves. Our partners don't owe us a guarantee that they will never change, nor do *we* owe anyone such a guarantee. And as we change, so do the things we need.

Before we get anywhere near nonmonogamy, these and many more trajectories provide a wealth of alternative endings and next chapters, even for those who start out following a mononormative story. People have been creating other relationship structures—and telling other stories about how we should live and love—for as long as we've existed. Nonmonogamy as we're discussing it in this book—an egalitarian kind focused on consent and sometimes called consensual or ethical nonmonogamy (we'll get to that later)—is just one of these options, and not a particularly new one.

Nonmonogamy can feel threatening because it upsets our fairy-tale assumption that the right partner will keep us safe from change. It introduces the prospect of chaos and uncertainty into what's supposed to be a straightforward progression to bliss. But relationships don't usually work that way even if they're monogamous. A healthy relationship must be resilient, able to respond to the changes and complexity life brings. Nor, as philosopher Carrie Jenkins has written, should happiness even necessarily be the point of life. In her books *Sad Love* and *Nonmonogamy and Happiness*, Jenkins argues that such an idea is very much a creation of white, capitalist (mostly American) society, and that it is *meaning*, rather than happiness, that defines a life well-lived—and good relationships.

The relationship fairy tale also carries other hidden falsehoods. For instance, it promises that one person will always be able to meet all of our needs. The idea that nonmonogamy addresses this situation has its own problems (more on that later), but it's still unreasonable to expect one person to be everything. And even the basket of "needs" that we are supposed to bring to the table in a romantic relationship—as opposed to having some of those needs met by kinship, friends or community, for example—represents a fairly recent invention of (mostly) white, Western, capitalist, individualist culture.

If we accept the fairy tale, we may feel shaky and insecure whenever reality doesn't live up to our expectations. We may imagine that if we are attracted to more than one person, something is wrong. And if our one true love is attracted to someone else, we may feel like a failure. After all, if we do everything we're supposed to do, then we should be enough for our partner, right? And if our partner loves someone else, that means our love isn't good enough, right?

The idea of The One, the "love of your life," is seductive. In reality, it's perfectly possible to have more than one love of your life. Over the last century, society has mostly come to accept that long-term relationships and marriages often don't last forever, and that it's possible to fall in love again after a devastating breakup, divorce or loss. In this respect, sequential "loves of your life" are pretty common. In nonmonogamy, we understand that multiple loves can happen at the same time, too.

Misconceptions about nonmonogamy

Some common responses to learning about nonmonogamy as an option range from "Woohoo! Endless orgies!" to "I don't buy it. This is just a fancy way of saying your partner lets you cheat." For anyone who imagines that being nonmonogamous means sleeping with whomever you like, whenever you like, without having to consider others' feelings, we have some bad news: Nonmonogamous relationships do not mean that anything goes. They require far more listening, discussing and self-analyzing than you might expect. And if you start out with a vision in your head of what they'll look like, you may be disappointed.

You might end up with one partner, or you might even be single (it's possible to be nonmonogamous and have no partners at a particular time). You might have fewer partners over your lifetime than someone who has many monogamous relationships in a row; nonmonogamous people can be very picky indeed.

For those who imagine that nonmonogamy is a fancy word to excuse cheating, we also have bad news. Cheating is violating trust by breaking the agreements of a relationship. If having multiple partners does not violate trust, then it's not cheating, by definition. Betrayal, not sex, is cheating's defining element. (A person can move from cheating to nonmonogamy, though it's a road fraught with peril; we get into that in chapter 17.)

Some people imagine that a multiple-partner relationship situation has no boundaries at all, but if this is you, think again. Many kinds of nonmonogamous relationships exist; each has its own agreements. But all require trust, respect for everyone's boundaries and compassionate behaviour.

Despite the images of free-love compounds that occasionally garner the media spotlight, nonmonogamy usually does not mean living in a commune or an intentional community. Not all nonmonogamous people live with multiple partners, or with any partners, for that matter. Nor is nonmonogamy all about couples seeking thirds.

Nonmonogamy doesn't necessarily suggest a taste for orgies or kinky sex. A good percentage of people into kink, BDSM and sexual exploration of various kinds are also some form of nonmonogamous, and vice versa—but it's a Venn diagram, not a circle. Plenty of nonmonogamous people aren't into group sex and don't have a cupboard full of butt plugs and whips. That being said, the overlap does mean that some people come across the idea of nonmonogamy through their pre-existing interest in BDSM, Leather or kink, or within the communities that gather around these practices and identities. And some people who start hanging out with a nonmonogamous crowd encounter its kinky members, who then introduce them to new ideas about pleasure and pain. The important thing is to not assume that because someone is into one, they must be into the other. The only way to find out what people are into—sexually or relationship-wise—is to ask them. Also, don't feel pressured to become a sexual adventurer just because you're interested in multiple relationships! Vanilla is a popular flavour for good reason.

A lot of the focus of this book is on relationships that could be described today as polyamorous, meaning having multiple loving, often committed, relationships at the same time by mutual agreement, with honesty and clarity. We have a few reasons for this focus. The first is simply that it's a kind of nonmonogamy we both have a lot of experience with. Also, closer or more committed multi-partner relationships are often the ones that require the most navigation of the deeper emotions and practical conundrums that can arise, thus requiring a how-to manual such as this one. Finally, polyamory is the flavour of nonmonogamy most often represented today in the North American mainstream. The word, from the Greek *poly*, meaning "many," and the Latin *amor*, meaning "love," was coined in the early 1990s by Neopagan author and artist Morning Glory Zell-Ravenheart, and for a couple of decades, she and her contemporaries were the most visible elements of the late-20th-century North American resurgence in nonmonogamy.

These kinds of nonmonogamous relationships come in an astonishing variety, just like the human heart. There are vee relationships, where one person has two partners who aren't romantically involved with each other; triad relationships, where three partners are mutually involved; and quad relationships of four people, who may or may not all be romantically involved with one another. Larger configurations exist as well. Quite common are open networks, where each person may have several partners—some of whom may be involved with one another and others not. Relationship networks tend to be loosely structured and often don't have an overall hierarchy, although local hierarchies may exist in some parts of the network.

Even deeply emotionally intimate, attached or committed relationships can span a spectrum of entwinement and even exclusivity. A nonmonogamous relationship can be closed, which means the people in it agree not to pursue additional partners. When a group of romantically connected people agree to exclusivity, it's called polyfidelity (or polyfi as an adjective). Or one or more of the people in a nonmonogamous relationship may be actively looking for new partners. A nonmonogamous person might have one or more primary partners and one or more secondary partners, or they may recognize no rankings. They might even have a group marriage, sharing finances, a home and maybe children as a single family. Or they might live alone while prizing their autonomy, friend network and solo time, but still engage in bonded relationships involving varying kinds of commitments.

Some people imagine that nonmonogamy involves a fear of commitment, but nonmonogamous folks, on average, probably fear (or desire) commitment in about the same proportions as monogamous people. Commitment in nonmonogamy doesn't mean commitment to sexual (or emotional) exclusivity. Instead, it means commitment to the type of relationship that people agree to have together. In more attached relationships, that might include a commitment to being there when your partners need you, investing in their well-being, building a life with them (whether or not it's under the same roof), creating healthy relationships that meet everyone's needs, and supporting one another when life gets hard. Unfortunately, society has taught us to view commitment only through the lens of sexual exclusivity, which diminishes all the other important ways that we commit to one another.

Many parts of this book are still relevant for people engaging in more casual connections—and of course, even deeply committed polyamorous folks often also engage in casual sex, swinging, comet-style relationships, occasional BDSM play partnerships, and other less entwined forms of nonmonogamy in addition to attached relationships. But you will notice we default toward discussion of the deeper kinds of connections.

About this book

Who are we to be offering advice to others? Where does our perspective come from? We're both longtime members of a variety of nonmonogamous, queer and kinky communities, sometime community organizers and educators, advocates for relationship choice, and people who have been living in different flavours of nonmonogamous relationships for most of our adult lives. We're not therapists or researchers. We're also not experts on nonmonogamy. While knowledge about modern nonmonogamy, both scholarly and experiential, has proliferated in the last few decades, we believe there *are* no experts—just an increasing number of people with varying viewpoints and sources of information. We are two of those people.

Eve is a white, queer, Gen X, cisgender woman who first heard about polyamory when she was twelve, from a First Day school teacher (that's Quaker for Sunday school) who challenged her assumptions about monogamous relationships and introduced her to the concepts of primary and secondary partners. In high school, her social group flirted with nonmonogamous ideas and practices, but didn't have any frameworks or mentors to explore them under that name. She was even very briefly in something like a triad, which lasted about a week because none of the three had any idea that could even be a thing. After high school, Eve's own relationships started out monogamous, though she had friends who were not. In her late twenties, she and her husband opened their monogamous relationship. Since then, it's been a two-decade journey through brief flirtations with swinging and hierarchical polyamory, through egalitarian kitchen-table poly as part of a sprawling polycule, to relationship anarchy and solo, parallel polyamory—and for now, voluntary singlehood, with a focus on close friendships, community and cats. During that time, she has blogged, organized local polyamorous groups, spoken at gatherings, led workshops, and for the last ten years, published books on nonmonogamy. She's also been involved in grassroots anti-abuse work and volunteers locally supporting survivors of sexual assault and as a community member in restorative justice processes.

Andrea is a white, nonbinary, middle-aged queer who discovered nonmonogamy when they found the queer and kink/Leather worlds in Tiohtià:ke (Montreal, Quebec) in 1999, at age 21, having long wondered where they could meet people who shared their inclinations. At that time, queers were fighting for marriage equality, and lots of them—often the very same people—were also engaging in all manner of creative relationship structures and sexual and romantic explorations. Andrea finally felt right at home and tried (almost) everything, from group sex to BDSM to bathhouses to hands-free orgasm workshops. (But not marriage.) They dove into polyamory in 2001 with their first serious girlfriend and were actively nonmonogamous in various arrangements for some 15 years, including spending the better part of a decade in two consecutive triads. During this time, Andrea did an independent undergraduate minor in sexuality studies, and later a master's in women's and gender studies with a focus on queer and Leather history, and then began a PhD in the same area. They also blogged, taught and wrote about sex, nonmonogamy and kink through numerous venues and did a lot of community organizing. Eventually, health problems (a rare spinal cord tumour that caused severe chronic pain and disability) took over much of their life and shifted their focus toward treatment and long-term recovery. Now temporarily able-bodied once more, for the past many years they've been post-nonmonogamous—a somewhat ambiguous state in which they're still a strong advocate for people's right to define and build their relationships as they see fit, including through nonmonogamy, but they are not actively involved in multiple relationships. They recently wrote a book called *Post-Nonmonogamy and Beyond*, also from Thornapple Press.

Throughout this book, we draw from our personal experiences—some of our own, some we've witnessed among the countless people we've encountered along our respective journeys. Unless otherwise stated, the examples we give are fictionalized or composite accounts. Everything we suggest comes from what we have observed to work. The things we recommend you avoid are things we have observed, over and over, to cause strife. We're not criticizing the people doing these "bad" things, unless they act with malice, and we're not holding up the people doing the things that tend to work as perfect nonmonogamous role models you should emulate (though sometimes, maybe, you might want to). All we're saying is, if you're choosing strategies to help you get where you want to go, the ones we suggest here are the ones we've observed to be most successful in the long term.

While this is an advice book, it's also part polemic. We talk about both best practices and mistakes, sure, but in the time we've both been around, we've also seen a lot of cruelty, selfishness, exploitation and outright abuse, and we have some feelings about it all. While we do our best to be compassionate to those doing their best to pick out a path among some very difficult terrain, we have little patience for bad actors. Our lefty (if you hadn't noticed yet) political leanings also heavily influence our approach to both relationships and ethics, and vice versa. And so do our privileges, primarily as white, educated, sometimes able-bodied settlers in Canada. Obviously not everyone sees the world as we do, and you may not agree with everything you read here. That's fine: We're here to share what we've learned with the intention of helping others, not to issue directives from on high. If what you find here serves you, use it. If it doesn't, that's okay too. Look at some of the other wonderful resources listed in the back of this book to find what meets your needs.

Themes in this book

As you read this book, you will see several ideas come up again and again. Strong relationships of any kind tend to have certain things in common.

The first theme is *trust.* Many problems in any relationship, but especially in nonmonogamous relationships, come down to "How much do I trust my partner?" Having such trust is often more difficult than it sounds, because internal emotions such as insecurity or low self-esteem can affect how much confidence you place in a partner's love. As well, sometimes partners behave poorly—because nonmonogamy reveals a pre-existing set of troubling ethics or personality traits you didn't previously see, because they are unskilled and so do some damage as they stumble, or because they're genuinely bad actors. (We'll get into that more later.)

The second theme is *courage.* Many approaches to nonmonogamous relationships require confronting socially imposed norms and your own fears, and that takes courage. When many people think of courage, they might think of a group of land defenders facing down a militarized police force, or a whistleblower exposing a corrupt or abusive government department—extraordinary acts of bravery in the face of danger. The kind of courage we mean is a more personal, ordinary thing: talking about your feelings even when you're afraid; taking accountability for harm you've done even when it challenges your stories about yourself; giving a partner the freedom to explore new relationships even when you fear being abandoned; challenging yourself to step outside your comfort zone even when you aren't sure anyone will be there to catch you. Courage is important when tackling anything that's new and unfamiliar, that your family or loved ones might misunderstand or judge, or that goes against the mainstream notions you've been taught since birth and requires you to unpack and examine things you took for granted.

We want to add a caveat here, though, which leads to our third theme: *discernment*. At every step of your journey, it's also important to stay connected to your own instincts, sense of self and values. Sometimes, fear is telling you there is real danger and you shouldn't continue. Sometimes, you shouldn't push through your discomfort—it means you really, genuinely don't want to (or shouldn't) do a thing. Sometimes, as you explore, you hit a boundary and realize that a new idea doesn't actually work for you, and your original position still suits you just fine. So while it's great to be courageous, it's also useful to retain a sense of discernment about how to employ that courage. We discuss this more in chapter 4, among others.

The fourth theme is *ethics.* We believe it's important for everyone to have clear values and to live by an ethical system that they understand and can articulate. In chapter 2, we discuss approaches to ethics in nonmonogamy and outline our own values and ethical systems, which underpin this entire book. And while there's room for plenty of diversity within the realm of values and ethics, we believe some baseline values need to be present in order for nonmonogamy to work, such as honesty, integrity, and treating people with compassion and respect, no matter what role they play in our lives.

The last theme we often return to is *empowerment.* We believe that relationships work best when all the people involved feel empowered to help shape and guide their relationships, to advocate for their needs, and to feel that they have a hand in the outcomes.

Nonmonogamy, like any worthwhile endeavour, is a journey. We hope to give you some signposts to help you along the way, but nobody can make the journey for you. It is up to you to navigate your way toward relationships rooted in kindness and integrity.

Nonmonogamy jargon

As nonmonogamy has become more visible in mainstream society, it has developed its own vocabulary. Much of that vocabulary has emerged specifically within nonmonogamous circles and communities, but it's been disseminated widely online and through books, TV shows and podcasts. Folks in nonmonogamous relationships will talk about *compersion*, a feeling of joy at the happiness of a partner in a new relationship, and NRE, for "new relationship energy," which is the giddy, honeymoon phase of a newfound love. You might hear someone talk about *wibbles*, or minor twinges of jealousy. A *hinge* is someone with two or more partners. A *metamour* is your partner's partner. A *polycule* is a group of people who are affiliated in various ways through the bonds of nonmonogamy but aren't necessarily all partnered with one another.

All this lingo can create a certain amount of confusion. After all, the idea of nonmonogamous relationships isn't new; people have been doing versions of nonmonogamy since the dawn of time. So why all these new words?

New terminology arises where old terminology doesn't fit. These terms have evolved to give contemporary nonmonogamous people a way to discuss the joys, challenges and practical situations they encounter that might not have direct corollaries in monogamy. We have tried to be careful not to overload this book with jargon, but if you get lost, there's a glossary in the back.

We've also made some broad shifts in our use of language in this rewrite of *More Than Two*. We've moved away from defaulting to the term *polyamory*, instead using the broader term *nonmonogamy* unless we're referring to a specific style of nonmonogamous relationship. As the popularity of nonmonogamy has spread, it's become clear that many people shift among various relationship configurations and styles over time due to circumstances, preferences, stages of life and more. Or they may do more than one style at the same time. For example, a person might have a long-term nesting relationship with one partner and a long-term commitment to another partner, and have flings with additional people while travelling. *Nonmonogamy* allows us to speak to people across the spectrum of flexibility and change over time in a way that does not insist on rigid categories.

We're also making a shift from talking about sexual and romantic relationships to talking about intimate ones, which is more inclusive of the full variety of relationships that can be part of nonmonogamy, as well as relationships where one or more people are on the asexual or aromantic spectrum. It's also more appropriate when discussing relationship anarchy, which can encompass closely bonded but nonsexual and non-romantic life partnerships, as well as other relationships that don't neatly fit into a mould.

Finally, we're avoiding the condensed label *poly*, except as part of widely used compounds such as *solo poly*, *mono/poly*, *polyfi* and *polycule*. Over the last decade or so, various folks who identify as Polynesian—some of whom have also identified themselves as polyamorous—have made repeated requests for polyamorous people to be more mindful of using the abbreviation *poly*, which many Polynesians also use among themselves. While these requests have mostly focused on titles and hashtags online, to allow the different communities to more easily find each other, we've found it's easier, and just feels a bit more respectful, to get into the habit of spelling out the full word every time. Some people also like using the short form *polyam* instead, which has the benefit of being unique to polyamory. While Eve sometimes uses this term, we're not using it in this book—though we encourage you to use what feels good to you. Whatever you choose, please be mindful that those who use the abbreviation *poly* are sharing it with other groups.

Part 1

Laying Your Foundation

We're about to offer a framework and tools for building a nonmonogamous foundation. We hope these tools will benefit you even if you ultimately decide not to pursue nonmonogamy. We start by helping you explore whether nonmonogamy is really for you and by discussing some of the assumptions many people need to unpack when they're newly discovering nonmonogamy. Next we dig into values and ethics, including the importance of having a clear ethical system when you're engaging in nonmonogamy. This is where we set out the axioms that shape our overall approach in this book. Finally, we discuss the difficult topic of abuse: what it is, how it can show up in nonmonogamy, and some of the ways you can deal with it if it arises in your own relationships or those of the people in your circles.

I happen to believe every story is a love story if you catch it at the right moment, slantwise in the light of dusk.

ALIX E. HARROW

1 Choosing Nonmonogamy

Relationships nourish us in myriad ways. Mononormative societies teach only a handful of paths that intimacy and love, particularly romantic love, can take.

These relationships are expected to follow a specific trajectory that we call the "relationship escalator," a concept popularized by Amy Gahran in her blog *Solo Poly* and her book *Stepping Off the Relationship Escalator*. If a relationship doesn't follow that path, there's something wrong with it.

Same-sex relationships are pushed to ride the escalator, too, just with two women or two men. This is known as homonormativity: the idea that same-sex relationships should follow the same norms as heterosexual ones, including marriage and kids. Meanwhile, nonbinary people, asexual and aromantic folks, and people of various other identities are pushed to take on binary genders and normative relationship desires so they can get on that escalator with everyone else. In fact, that pressure can even sound like "If you don't become more normal, nobody will ever love you and you'll never find a spouse!" While lots of people resist these norms in lots of different ways, they still hold a great deal of power in our lives. They're encouraged by laws and policies, promoted in the media and entertainment, and pushed on many people by well-meaning friends, family members and colleagues ("When are you two gonna tie the knot?"). People can choose these relationship forms and be very happy in them. But they're not for everyone.

This cookie-cutter way of looking at relationships is so ingrained that people often try to hang onto it even when they discover nonmonogamy. Sometimes they intentionally limit the shapes of their relationships—and sometimes this works out okay, but often (as we'll discuss later) it doesn't.

Sometimes folks try to follow an escalator trajectory with multiple people: They start by searching for two or three live-in polyfidelitous partners, or some other predetermined form of nonmonogamous relationship, instead of letting each relationship take the shape that best suits it, based on what each person wants, needs, values and offers, and how things develop over time.

As nonmonogamy has become increasingly well-known to the mainstream in recent decades, it's developed some of its own norms. Andrea coined the term *polynormativity* in 2013 to refer to the one kind of nonmonogamy for which mononormative society has made a little space in the standard blueprint, like a little optional side room tacked onto a house. This kind of polyamory starts with a couple opening up, is always hierarchical (i.e., there's one primary relationship and other secondary ones), involves a lot of rules, and—in terms of media representation—usually looks like a white, heterosexual-ish couple with a girlfriend on the side. We'll come back to this later, but we're mentioning it here because we think it's important to challenge the notion that nonmonogamy automatically avoids an escalator approach to relationships.

One of the amazing things nonmonogamy offers is the freedom to negotiate relationships that work for you and your partners. The possibilities are not always obvious, even for people who have lived nonmonogamously for years. For example, there's sometimes no need to break up a relationship if something (or someone) changes. Maybe you can keep a connection and reshape it in another way. You can build relationships that are free to develop however they naturally want to flow. It helps to recognize that love itself is malleable and ever-changing. Its intensity and nature vary, and this variability influences its flow, its mutable forms.

Are you nonmonogamous?

For some people, whether they're nonmonogamous or monogamous is obvious; for others, it isn't. Many people feel that nonmonogamy is an intrinsic part of who they are, like hair colour or sexual orientation. A person who feels inherently nonmonogamous can identify that way even if they have only one relationship, or none, at a given time. Eve likes to borrow terms from biology: obligate and facultative. *Obligate* means something is required, like how cats need to eat meat; *facultative* means you can adapt to different conditions but tend to do better in certain ones, like how dogs will eat just about anything to avoid starving, but will only really thrive when they have meat in their diet. Perhaps you'll find you're a panda, requiring highly specific conditions and suffering outside of them—or maybe you're more like a crow, able to adapt and flourish in just about any environment.

Some people embrace nonmonogamy because they see it as more honest than monogamy, which often requires denying attractions to other people. Other folks see nonmonogamy as a way to shed the assumptions about property and control that have long gone hand in hand with monogamy. Many people find that nonmonogamy most closely aligns with their political beliefs, or view it as part of reclaiming ancestral cultural practices lost through colonization, enslavement or migration.

Whether you want to be nonmonogamous is just one part of the decision. You also have to think about what *kind* of nonmonogamy is right for you. Deciding whether more committed forms of nonmonogamy, such as polyamory, are a good fit requires deciding whether the things you want from life, and the personal ethics you bring to the world, align well with having multiple honest romantic relationships. For instance, a desire for sexual variety without romantic attachments might point to swinging, sex parties or hookup apps as a good fit. A desire for multiple romantic relationships without openness or transparency might mean some self-work is in order.

Nonmonogamy is not right for everyone. It is not the next wave in human evolution. Nor is it more enlightened, more spiritual, more progressive or more advanced than monogamy. Nonmonogamous people are not automatically less jealous, more compassionate or better at communicating than monogamous folks. What we critique in this book is the aforementioned mononormativity: a socially prescribed life path that's reinforced through everything from cultural representation (films, songs, TV shows) to insurance policies and laws on things like marriage, parenting rights and more.

We believe relationships that are deliberately, intentionally constructed are more satisfying, and more likely to support a meaningful life, than relationships whose shape is determined by default social expectations. It is absolutely possible for a monogamous relationship to be built by careful, deliberate choice. Many people are content in exclusive relationships, and that's fine. Being with only one partner doesn't necessarily mean simply following a social norm. It's pressure of any kind that's the problem here, not people's individual relationship choices. So if you decide that nonmonogamy is not a good fit for your life, that's okay. Don't let anyone—including yourself—push you into it.

For many, it can be useful to think of nonmonogamy as an outgrowth of a certain set of beliefs. Rather than asking, "Am I nonmonogamous?" you could ask yourself questions like "Are the tools and concepts of nonmonogamy useful to me?" or "What is my commitment to relationship choice, and how do I want to embody it in my life?" Even if you decide you don't want multiple relationships, the things we talk about in this book may be valuable to you.

Why be nonmonogamous?

The best way to understand why someone might be nonmonogamous is to ask, "What do people get out of intimacy in the first place?" A quick answer might be "People are more likely to thrive when they're in connection with others." Humans are social animals. We do better when we share our lives intimately with others. We're built for it. As complicated and messy and unpredictable as romance is, for many of us, its rewards are fantastic. Indeed, most of us feel driven to seek out people who see us for who we are, who share themselves with us, who love us.

For many people, establishing a romantic relationship switches off this drive. The task is done, the race is won; there's no need to find new partners. But for some, being in a relationship doesn't flip off that switch. They remain open to the idea of new connections and more love. Alternatively, maybe they're not currently in a romantic relationship, but they're open to starting more than one at the same time—whether by getting involved with a pre-existing couple or polycule, or by starting brand-new involvements with more than one other single person, together or separately. Or perhaps they start dating someone who's nonmonogamous and suddenly find themselves intrigued...whether by the idea itself or by someone in particular. (This is one way that a vee can become a triad!) Nonmonogamous people engage in multiple romantic relationships, and love others who do the same, because doing so enriches the lives of everyone involved. Loving more than one person at the same time is not necessarily an escape from intimacy; in fact, it can be an enthusiastic embrace of *yet more* intimacy.

Be aware, of course, that for some people, nonmonogamy is appealing because it's a framework within which they *can* actually have less-intimate relationships. That's not necessarily a bad thing! It can work out great as long as everyone involved is clear about what's going on, fully consents to it, and isn't just hoping the other person will change their mind and want to get married in a couple of years. For example, a person who's highly focused on their career for the moment might enjoy a low-stakes relationship in each of the various cities they visit for business travel—each of them a sort of "long-term long-distance low-commitment casual girlfriend," as Ken says in the movie *Barbie* (substitute your gendered or non-gendered term of choice). Some folks who understand themselves as solo poly might want a few different non-nesting relationships because they like connecting with people but prefer to maintain a high degree of overall life independence, even if they date in their home city and aren't overly preoccupied by their career or schooling. A third example: Someone might be allosexual, meaning they desire sex and seek it out (possibly with multiple partners), but aromantic, meaning they don't experience romantic love (we talk more about romantic love on page 24). A fourth: Someone might be polysaturated, with one or more serious partnerships and no desire for additional ones, but still enjoy the freedom to date casually or hook up at play parties or other sex-focused events. A fifth: A person might have married themselves and be committed to raising their child as a single parent, but still enjoy hiring a babysitter once a month so they can spend time as the "jam in the sandwich" with a couple they've dated on and off for years. All these and more are totally valid reasons to engage in nonmonogamy without forming deep or life-entwined kinds of attachment with each person involved.

Nonmonogamous relationships, particularly those of the more entwined variety, have practical benefits. More adults in a family often provide greater financial freedom and security. Some nonmonogamous folks combine living spaces, incomes and expenses, which increases everyone's financial flexibility. Even nonmonogamous people who don't cohabit or share expenses gain many things from mutual support among multiple partners. If you're having a bad day, there are more people to comfort and help you. If you're having a problem, you get more perspectives. You have more of everything you get from romantic relationships—more companionship, more advice, more joy, more love.

Being nonmonogamous can also be fantastic for your sex life. Sex is a learned skill, and the human sexual horizon is vast. Whatever your tastes, however ingenious your imagination, the range of sexual experience is so great that someone, somewhere, is doing something you'd love to do that would never occur to you. Each time you invite another lover into your life, you have the opportunity to learn things you might never otherwise have learned...often, things you can bring into your existing and subsequent relationships. Nobody is so creative that they have nothing to learn from someone else.

It's also very common for couples experiencing desire discrepancy to open their relationship as a way to help reduce conflict about sex, thinking the higher-libido partner can get their needs met with other people and alleviate pressure on the lower-desire partner. Unfortunately, in a relationship that began as sexual, it rarely turns out to be quite that simple. In chapter 20, we discuss the challenges that can come up in nonmonogamy in cases of desire discrepancy between partners, and other sex-related difficulties.

Downsides of nonmonogamy

Authors such as Sarah Carter, Kim TallBear, Stephanie Coontz and Carrie Jenkins (all listed in the resources at the back of this book) have written about how compulsory monogamy—and later, amatonormativity—in North America has served as one prong of colonization and capitalism. In other words, our current system has a lot riding on our implicit acceptance of these norms. So it's not surprising that people who take a different approach to their relationships are often met with pushback at multiple levels: social, legal, financial and more. And one way that people deal with criticism and pushback is to get defensive. In some ways, that's a good thing; alternative life choices sometimes really need to be defended! But it can also cause people to present an excessively rosy picture of how it all works. The world of nonmonogamy is home to many activists, cheerleaders and salespeople vaunting the merits of these relationship styles. That means much of what you will hear about nonmonogamy focuses on the benefits rather than the costs. This book tries not to provide that one-sided view. Nonmonogamy is not utopia. Only you can decide whether the benefits are worth the costs at every point along your journey—and that balance may shift for you over time.

Nonmonogamy is complicated. When you have more than two people involved in your romantic life, things get complicated fast. Keeping more than one relationship going at the same time is not for the faint of heart. Problems can occur in any relationship. Personality conflicts can arise, and all sorts of things can go wrong. In nonmonogamous relationships, there are more opinions being offered, more people's feelings to get hurt, more personalities to clash, more egos to bruise. Navigating a disagreement or problem in a nonmonogamous relationship configuration requires outstanding communication skills and good problem-solving tools, which this book aims to help with.

For some people, the fact that many nonmonogamous relationships are more complicated than many monogamous ones is "proof" that nonmonogamy is wrong. This argument is nonsense; many relationships are complicated, such as those involving blended families, or between people of different religious faiths or cultural backgrounds. Would any reasonable person say these relationships are also "wrong"? At the end of the day, the best measure of a relationship isn't how complicated it is, but rather how much meaning, fulfillment, creativity, intimacy, support and love it brings. Sure, nonmonogamy can be complicated—but for many people, it would be much more difficult to follow a conventional path that doesn't feel right for them.

You will grow—whether you want to or not. Nonmonogamous relationships offer many opportunities for growth, some easier than others. Whether that belongs on the list of "good things" or "bad things" depends a lot on how you feel about personal growth. You may hear some nonmonogamous people sighing about AFLE or AFOG: "another fucking learning experience" or "another fucking opportunity for growth."

Nonmonogamy is not safe. As polyamorous therapist Jessica Fern wrote in her groundbreaking book *Polysecure*, nonmonogamous relationships are inherently insecure. Without the external support of a relationship escalator and mononormative structures, you have to build security from within, and most people aren't equipped to do that. Many people try to replicate the default structure provided by mononormativity by placing strict controls on the form their relationships may take or the level to which they may grow. This approach pretty much never succeeds; it merely replaces one kind of pain with another. Nonmonogamy can increase love and connection, but it also increases the odds that you'll be hurt.

Nonmonogamy means giving things up. When your partner has another partner, there will be times when you will lose something, even if it's just time and attention. Any relationship needs attention in order to thrive, and no matter how close you may be to your partner's other partner—indeed, even if you and a partner share a lover—there will be times when a relationship requires one-on-one focus. It is not always possible to schedule things in such a way that you always get everything you want.

Nonmonogamy changes things. This idea comes up throughout the book, but especially in chapters 14 and 16. The short version is you cannot open your heart to multiple people and expect your life to be unchanged. There will be disruptions, and you will not always be able to anticipate or control them. All relationships are subject to change. Even seemingly idyllic nonmonogamous relationships don't necessarily last forever, any more than perfect-seeming traditional marriages do.

People don't always get along. Just because someone loves your partner doesn't necessarily mean the person will mesh well with you. It's easy to say "I will only date people who like my current partners" (or in extreme cases, "I will only date people who are romantically involved with my current partners"), but in the real world that's not always practical. You can't coerce people to like one another, and in consensual relationships, it's not ethical to make your love contingent on how the person you love feels about someone else. Sometimes, the best you can do is to agree to be civil toward one another.

You might hate it. Some people genuinely want nonmonogamy, do years of inner work, and still find that they're in pain all the time, having panic attacks and nightmares, and just generally miserable. That could be because they have a partner or polycule who are mistreating or even abusing them—we'll talk about abuse in chapter 3—but it could also be that nonmonogamy is just fundamentally incompatible with the way their nervous systems work. This isn't a failure; if this describes you, it just means you've learned something important about yourself and your needs, and maybe you'll take something from the process into your next (exclusive, hopefully lifelong) relationship.

Being flexible

Let's say you're seeing nonmonogamy as a way out of the rigid forms you were taught that relationships had to take. It's exciting! You get to customize everything about your relationships! Time to get planning, right?

Sort of. The vast potential in nonmonogamous relationships can be misleading. A relationship can be many things, but it also has built-in constraints. It's constrained by what you want—and also by what each of your partners wants, and what their partners want, and the inherent range of potential intimacy in each partnership. It's constrained by outside factors, such as the health, financial status and existing life obligations of each person. And it's subject to every individual's personality characteristics and attachment styles, how compatible these traits are, and how each person changes over time. These same factors affect how relationships work whether you're on the escalator or not.

Also, just because you want something doesn't mean that it will satisfy everyone the way you hope. People often have mismatched expectations, desires and skill sets, even if they love each other very much. If you go into any relationship thinking you can make a person fit your plan, you are fairly likely to be disappointed. You might want a nesting relationship, but that doesn't mean the next person you date is going to be the right person for that level of commitment. Pushing them to become the perfect spouse might just kill the sweetness of the lighter connection you started with. And you might be really enjoying your freewheeling singlehood, but sometimes that's exactly when Big Love shows up and asks you to shift gears. That means you may either need to rethink your priorities or have a bittersweet "the one that got away" story to tell in your elder years.

Nonmonogamous relationships come in enormous variety, so they encourage flexibility in ways that escalator relationships don't. Flexibility does not come naturally; it can be difficult to cast off a lifetime of ideas about how relationships should look. Because we're typically shown a limited number of relationship models, it's sometimes overwhelming to try to understand just how many ways relationships *can* work.

Something people often end up saying, after a little bit of experience, is "When I started exploring nonmonogamy, the things I thought would be important and the things that turned out to be important were very different." It's tempting to plan out how you want your life to look and then search for people who fit the plan. But you can't look at a person and predict what a relationship will grow into; relationships have a tricky way of zigging when you expect them to zag. Nor can you really predict how you're going to react to the wide variety of novel situations nonmonogamous relationships will confront you with. Sure, it's important to communicate what you want in your relationships up front—but it's also important to remember you're not ordering a relationship from a catalogue. Leave space for your relationships to grow, and try to adapt if they grow in ways you didn't expect.

Defining partnership

What is an intimate relationship? What separates one from an ordinary friendship? Does a relationship that involves no sex or romance still count as intimate?

A simple, glib answer would be that an intimate relationship is anything the people in it say it is. That's certainly true at one level, if not particularly useful. It's helpful to consider the elements of what we might call a relationship, both to help people in a relationship communicate with each other about what their relationship is, and also because most of us desire some social recognition of our relationships, and that means communicating with others about what our relationships are.

Amatonormativity has taught many people that romantic love is an essential component of any "real" relationship. Two people feel romantic love for one another, and it's a relationship, end of story. If they don't both feel it, then it's something else. But not all intimate nonmonogamous relationships include romantic love, and some people—aromantics—don't experience romantic love at all. And even for people who feel romantic love for one another, nonmonogamy offers ways to explore new forms that love can take, including non-romantic kinds of intimate relationships. That's before you get into what romantic love actually *is*, which might be even more challenging than defining partnership itself. There have been many whole books on the subject; one that we recommend, from a nonmonogamous perspective, is *What Love Is* by Carrie Jenkins. She argues that romantic love is "ancient biological machinery embodying a modern social role," the latter shaped by the stories many people have learned about it. Within the modern, colonial worldview, nonmonogamous love has not been considered real love—but until recently, neither was queer love. Both perspectives are changing, but the stories many people have learned about love shape what they can imagine, and even what they feel. Romantic love is an important part of the picture for many, but it's not the whole story.

It's also important to consider what intimacy itself means. Some people use the word as a euphemism for sex, of course, but that's not what we're talking about here. There are various types of intimacy, and these can exist in many different kinds of relationships. One good description of intimacy we've heard comes from attachment theory scholar, coach and educator Heidi Priebe, who describes intimacy as a mirror. Your intimates are people who see you at a deep level and reflect you back to yourself. You may experience different kinds of intimacy with different people, who are each able to reflect back different parts of yourself. You may trust some people with your traumas and fears, and others with your ambitions and dreams. Physical intimacy can mean someone you feel safe to be physically vulnerable with, whether that's by sleeping unclothed, giving or experiencing pleasure, or co-regulating (using closeness to an attachment figure to calm your nervous system). If you're neurodivergent or live with mental illness, intimacy can mean having people you don't need to mask with. Disability justice advocate Mia Mingus has also written about access intimacy, the experience of having one's access needs deeply, effortlessly seen and understood without the need to explain them.

For many people, sex is a defining element of what makes someone a partner or not, though this criteria is far from universal and excludes many real partnerships. Many people on the asexual spectrum, for example, have nonsexual intimate relationships, and it's incredibly common for relationships that start out as sexual to eventually become nonsexual—with varying degrees of agreement and comfort by the partners in those relationships. We'll discuss these issues at much more length in chapter 20. For now, we'll just say that while it's helpful to know if you consider sex essential to your intimate relationships, it's also important to recognize that for many, many other people, it isn't, for a variety of reasons. Nor does the end of sex in an intimate relationship necessarily need to mean the end of that relationship, especially in a nonmonogamous context. In addition, nonsexual physical closeness can be an important part of many relationships, and the human need for touch can be met in a wide variety of ways, both inside and outside relationships (intimate or otherwise).

Another element that may or may not be present in a relationship is attachment. We're using *attachment* here in the sense of attachment theory, where it refers to a deep physiological bond we develop over time with someone we regularly co-regulate with. People need consistency and availability from their attachment figures in ways they don't tend to require from non-attachment-based intimate relationships, and a threat or rupture to an attachment can create a uniquely painful physiological response, which Jessica Fern refers to as primal panic. Attachment-based relationships can be secure or insecure based on the behaviour of the people within them. Also, you can have attachment needs in friendships (see the book *Platonic* by Marisa G. Franco for more on these types of relationships).

Based on early experiences with caregivers as well as later experiences in relationships, people develop different unconscious strategies for engaging in attachment-based relationships. Researchers generally group these strategies into four attachment styles: secure, anxious-preoccupied (or just anxious), dismissive-avoidant (or just avoidant), and fearful-avoidant (also called disorganized, though this term is falling out of favour). We're not going to go into these styles in depth—for that, we recommend *Polysecure*—but we will occasionally loosely reference attachment styles in this book, where relevant.

People can also form varying kinds of entwined life partnerships that don't necessarily include all the elements of an escalator relationship. You might decide, for example, to form a chosen family with a couple of close friends, move in together, and commit to supporting each other for life. You could also have a closely bonded life partnership with someone you never live with. Aromantic and asexual thinkers coined the term *queerplatonic* to refer to committed, bonded relationships that don't involve sex or romance, and may or may not include other escalator markers such as cohabitation.

Kim TallBear has described how many Indigenous communities have systems of kinship and relationships that long predate settler notions of coupledom and the nuclear family. Instead, they are based in "a sense of community that *exceeds* rather than *fails to meet* the requirements of settler sex and family." She writes,

> Many Indigenous communities still exhibit a framework of extended kinship where responsibilities are more diffusely distributed, where we work as groups of women (or men, or other gendered people ideally) to share childcare, housing, and other resources. In my experience, our ways of relating often seem to contradict the monogamous couple and nuclear family.

Relationship anarchists have come up with various metaphors to evoke the idea of co-creating your own relationships from components that you each want to share rather than fitting into a pre-designed mould. One of these ideas is the relationship smorgasbord, which lists numerous potential elements of a relationship and invites people to choose from among them. The smorgasbord was created and iterated collaboratively by members of Vancouver Polyamory and several polyamory- and relationship anarchy–related Facebook groups. However, this metaphor only stretches so far, because not every facet of a relationship is independent from every other facet. Not all attachment or intimacy involves sex, for example, but for many people, sex very often leads to attachment and intimacy. (And for demisexuals, for example, attachment and intimacy often lead to a desire for sex.) We tend to think of nonmonogamy as more like cooking, where you can choose the kind of meal you want to make, but you have to work with the available ingredients, and not everything is going to go well with everything else.

We recommend the aforementioned book *What Love Is* by Carrie Jenkins, along with her more recent books *Sad Love* and *Nonmonogamy and Happiness*, for a much deeper philosophical dive, from a nonmonogamous and essentially relationship anarchist perspective, into what makes up relationships—and the stories we tell about them. In *Sad Love*, Jenkins introduces the concept of eudaimonic love, which treats love as a shared project of meaning-making. You might also check out the book *Redefining Our Relationships* by Wendy-O Matik, a nonmonogamy classic that also challenges you to think deeply about what relationships can look like for you. And the book *The Other Significant Others* by Rhaina Cohen examines various kinds of non-romantic partnerships and life-entwined relationships that people choose instead of or alongside their romantic ones.

Very strictly speaking, the only things that set nonmonogamous relationships apart from monogamous ones are sex and romantic love, because having sex or falling in love with someone other than one's partner is implicitly a violation of the monogamous contract. But mononormativity, at least as we know it in the white North American context, usually also prescribes that many or all of the other elements we've listed above—intimacy, attachment, nonsexual physical touch, various forms of life-entwinement and care commitments—are also off-limits with others when we are in a monogamous relationship. (Just consider the recent idea of "microcheating" that's appearing in various online articles. It includes things like texting with a co-worker or staying friends with your exes. Yikes!) Adopting a nonmonogamous framework makes room for all these variations, not just sex—and so can expand the possibilities for our friendships, too! Going forward in this book, when we talk about intimate relationships, we're talking about relationships that include some combination of these elements, but ultimately, what makes something a partnership is up to you and your partners.

How many partners?

It's possible to be single and nonmonogamous. It's possible to have only one partner and be nonmonogamous. If your intention is to remain open to the possibility of multiple intimate relationships, you are nonmonogamous, regardless of your current relationship status. Indeed, if nonmonogamy is part of your identity (for some people, it is; for others, it isn't), you might be in an exclusive (closed) relationship with one person and still be nonmonogamous.

Is there a "right" number of partners to have in order to count as nonmonogamous? No. Is there a "right" number for *you* to have? Maybe. There is certainly some maximum. There's a saying among nonmonogamous people: "Love is infinite; time and attention are not." It's debatable whether love is infinite; in practical terms, it probably isn't. But time and attention definitely aren't. Different people have different constraints on the time and attention they can offer, and different relationships require different amounts, so some people can maintain more romantic relationships than others before they become, as the term goes, *polysaturated*.

There is, especially, a pretty firm limit on the number of attachment-based relationships a person can cultivate securely. In an interview, Eve asked Jessica Fern and David Cooley, the authors of *Polywise*, what that upper limit seemed to be, based on their experience with clients. For the overwhelming majority of people Fern and Cooley had worked with, it was only one or two. On very rare occasions, a person could sustain a third secure attachment, but only when the previous two attachments were many, many years (or decades) old and rock-solid. While you can certainly try (and many people do) to have more attachment-based relationships, you are likely to have a very hard time making all those relationships secure, and your attempts to do so may end up negatively affecting *all* your attachment-based relationships. It's best to be realistic about what you can really commit to, based on your existing relationships and your life circumstances, when you begin exploring a new connection.

The number of partners you have room for can change. Some situations, such as starting a new job or caring for a baby or toddler, consume tremendous amounts of time and emotional space; it's normal to feel that you don't want to start a new relationship until more space opens up. On the other hand, you may meet someone who so upends your ideas about what you wanted that you are willing to rearrange parts of your life to create space for them. We discuss this kind of disruptive relationship on pages 261–264.

Frankenpoly

Because different people have different needs, and nonmonogamy allows us to distribute our need eggs into more than one relationship basket, it is possible to maintain a relationship in a nonmonogamous setting that otherwise might not survive. Stable nonmonogamous relationships can exist, for example, between people with mismatched sex drives or no interest in sex at all. The same thing can happen when one partner is more sexually adventurous than another and wants to explore being tied up or spanked, or some other kink that leaves the other cold. Maybe one person really likes ballroom dancing, but the other has two left feet. One person may have a deep religious conviction not shared by the other. Nonmonogamy offers an opportunity for different relationships to meet different kinds of connection needs.

The danger here is in seeing other people as need-fulfillment machines. When a need isn't being met, that need can feel bottomless, and it can be tempting to go out searching for a person to fill it. People have come up with different terms for this situation, such as *Frankenpoly*—stitching together the perfect need-providing romantic partner out of bits and pieces of other people—and *Pokémon polyamory*, after the idea that you need to collect a complete set of different kinds of partners.

When you begin to look at people in terms of which of your needs they can meet rather than as whole people in their own right, you objectify them (and not in a fun way). A person you're with only because you get some need filled when you insert time-and-attention tokens is not a full partner joining you on the journey of life. That's not to say that any attempt to have different needs met by different people leads this way. Such people can, of course, be intimate partners in their own right, valued for reasons beyond helping meet a given need.

Some needs, though, don't exist independently of the relationships you're in. Needs for intimacy, understanding or companionship are often attached to the *people* you are in a relationship with, or to your baseline needs that remain the same within any relationship. For example, you might need direct communication, physical affection and some minimum amount of quality time with any partner. Just because one partner is very affectionate doesn't mean you've had your fill and stop wanting touch from another partner; just because you have great dates with one person doesn't mean it's okay if another person rarely wants to get together. And needs in attachment-based relationships, especially, tend to be quite consistent across relationships, and must be met in *each one* of them if those relationships are to be secure.

QUESTIONS TO ASK YOURSELF

Rather than telling you what you should do, throughout this book we ask a lot of questions to help you figure out what is best for you. To start with, here are some questions that can help you determine what is most important to you in relationships and whether nonmonogamy might be a good match for you:

- Have I ever felt romantic love or intimate attraction for more than one person at the same time?
- Do I feel there can be only one "true" love or one "real" soulmate? Where did I learn this belief, and how committed am I to it?
- How important is my desire for multiple intimate relationships? With the right person, could I be satisfied in one intimate relationship for the rest of my life?
- Why do I have intimate relationships? What do I get out of them?
- What do I consider essential, indispensable elements of an intimate relationship?
- Are there specific kinds of relationships that I know I am looking for? Kinds that I know I don't want?
- What do I bring to the table for others?
- If I want more than one intimate partner, what degree of closeness and intimacy do I expect, and what do I offer? Do I want different degrees of intimacy in different relationships?
- How do I define commitment? Is it possible for me to commit to more than one person at a time, and if so, what might those commitments look like?
- If I am already in a relationship, does my desire for others come from dissatisfaction or unhappiness with my current relationship? If I were in a relationship that met my needs, would I still want multiple partners?
- What are my needs in relationships? Which of my needs are attached to specific people, and which can I meet more generally?
- Do I have a vision in my head about what my nonmonogamous life will look like? Am I prepared for it to look differently?
- If my relationships change, is that okay? Can I accommodate change, even unexpected change or change I don't like? What kind of changes would cross my personal line of what's acceptable?
- When I visualize the kind of relationships I want, can I leave space for partners to shape the relationships to their needs?
- What would happen if I were to connect with someone in a way that differs from how I or my current partners want my nonmonogamous relationships to look?
- How do I feel about the possibility that my current partners (if any) or future partners will develop other partnerships?
- If I'm asexual or aromantic but still interested in intimate relationships, does nonmonogamy seem like an option that could solve some of the issues that make it difficult to find relationships that fit me?

What are we sowing into the world when we speak?
KELLY HAYES

2 Finding Your Compass (or, Don't Be Mean)

Nonmonogamous folks have long struggled to find acceptance for ourselves and our relationships. As a defensive move, nonmonogamous people started to use the word *ethical* to differentiate nonmonogamy done with the agreement of all partners from cheating.

This strategy was exemplified by one of the earliest nonmonogamy guidebooks, *The Ethical Slut* by Janet Hardy and Dossie Easton, and over time the word moved into the general lingo, with acronyms such as ENM for ethical nonmonogamy or CNM for consensual nonmonogamy.

In some ways, the word "ethical" is useful shorthand for "I'm not cheating on my partner." But it's also problematic in its own right, because there are lots of ways to be unethical—cheating is just one of them. Many of the most common forms of nonmonogamy present serious ethical issues that deserve real consideration. And no one is immune to messing up and falling short, even when they're doing their best. Just because someone tries to live by their own ethical systems doesn't mean they always succeed—and not everyone has a well-thought-out ethical system in the first place, even if they have good intentions. (More on ethical systems shortly.) As nonmonogamous folks, we need to find a balance between defending ourselves to a mainstream that doesn't get how nonmonogamy could possibly be okay and being able to honestly appraise our own practices to make sure we're treating others well and minimizing (and repairing) harm.

We also have to acknowledge that not everyone has good intentions. Some people just don't care that much about how their actions affect others, even if they can learn enough jargon to make it seem like they're on the same page as everyone else. Others go further than not caring: A tiny percentage of society is made up of people who are genuinely predatory, and they do a disproportionate amount of damage by deliberately gaming any system they come across and exploiting and harming people as a matter of course. So even if we build communities and gatherings around the idea of ethical nonmonogamy, some percentage of the people in those communities and spaces will inevitably fall into one of these groups: not caring about the harm they do, or even relishing it. We discuss this more in the next chapter.

On a different note, various thinkers and writers in the realm of nonmonogamy have challenged the logic behind using the word *ethical* on the grounds that it implies that nonmonogamy is inherently *un*ethical unless we specify otherwise. It's a reasonable critique; after all, nobody says "I'm an ethical lesbian" or talks about doing "ethical kink," even though 2SLGBTQI+ and BDSM/Leather/kink communities, identities and practices have long been condemned as sinful, sick, violent and otherwise wrong—much like nonmonogamy. Each of these groups of people have had to do plenty of self-defence in order to fight demonization. And while their strategies haven't always been perfect, they also haven't chosen to use the word *ethical* to try to redeem their image. In addition, people certainly don't say, for example, "I'm an ethical math teacher" or "I do ethical rock climbing on the weekends." These things are presumed not to require any qualification. Shouldn't nonmonogamy be seen in the same way?

In a way, these criticisms come at the issue from two opposing angles. The first asks us to admit that nonmonogamy (even assuming we're not talking about cheating) is not necessarily ethical by definition, so we shouldn't make big claims like that. The second asks us to assume that nonmonogamy *is* in fact ethical by definition, so much so that we shouldn't have to specify. In both cases, the solution seems to be to just stop saying "ethical nonmonogamy."

Some folks have chosen to use the term *consensual nonmonogamy* instead, to avoid the issues with the word *ethical*—in fact, for about five years, this was how Eve identified herself—while others feel the same critiques apply. After all, we don't have to talk about "consensual monogamy," so why do we have to qualify our nonmonogamy?

Terminology shifts over time, as we discussed in the introduction. We're not personally attached to the terms *ethical nonmonogamy* or *consensual nonmonogamy*—or for that matter, to the idea of avoiding them. However, no matter your preferred terminology, we think it's important to consider how to do nonmonogamy while following a clear ethical system. When you set aside the expectations of mononormativity, you're also implicitly setting aside its assumptions about morality. Just like how you no longer have a template for what your relationships should look like from the outside, you also don't have clear prescriptions anymore for how they should operate internally. Some folks try to transfer monogamous ethics into a nonmonogamous setting, and they usually find it doesn't work so well. Others go the opposite direction and imagine that anything goes, as long as everyone is at least nominally consenting. This approach, too, has caused untold amounts of harm. We think that anyone who wants to break away from the prescribed ethics of the dominant society—which is great!—also has an obligation to think really deeply about what they're using in its place.

What are ethics?

We're not going to talk about ethics as the study of moral philosophy here; neither of us is a philosopher in the formal or scholarly sense. For us, a practical definition is more appropriate. So we propose the simple idea that ethics are a tool, a set of principles, that can help guide behaviour. Whatever ethical system you develop for yourself, or adopt from an outside source, its purpose is to help guide your decisions toward "right" and away from "wrong."

Sometimes the difference between the two is really easy to discern—either because your ethical system is very detailed and rigid, or because a situation is so black-and-white that there's just one possible "right" choice. Of course, real life is full of situations that aren't black-and-white and that challenge you to discern what the right choices are. This is why it's helpful to put some careful thought into your own ethical system so that it's able to flex to meet the realities of everyday life while being clear enough to provide you with consistent guidance.

Some people source a lot of their ethical system from their culture or from a religion they were raised in or joined later in life. Others base it on an institutional code of conduct, such as athletes who believe in good sportsmanship on and off the field, or martial artists who live by the codes of their practice. A lot of people cobble together their personal ethical systems from multiple sources: the way they were raised, plus things they've read, heard or experienced that combine to form an overall approach to life. A bad experience can lead you to think, "I hate that someone did this, and I commit to never doing it to anyone myself." A good experience can have you thinking, "That feels right. I want to do things that way." You might want to emulate a mentor or a character in a story you loved, or take to heart a proverb, quote, poem or line from a book. Some people like having detailed systems with go-to rules for most situations, while others prefer holding a few core principles.

For example, in her book *Hello Cruel World*, veteran trans writer and performer Kate Bornstein promotes a deceptively simple ethical system summed up in a single sentence: "Don't be mean." She explains it as follows:

> Over the course of this book, I will be giving you permission to do anything you want to do—anything at all—short of killing yourself. I don't care if it's illegal, immoral, fattening, self-defeating, whatever [...] as long as it isn't mean to anyone.
>
> Being mean triggers shame and regret, not to mention bad karma. Shame and regret are nature's way of telling us to forgive ourselves for whatever we just did, apologize and make amends for it if we can, and try to do better next time. That's how we learn to be kind as we keep on in life's journey. No one is perfectly kind, compassionate, and generous. But you can live a kinder, more compassionate, and generous life by following just one simple rule: DON'T BE MEAN. Anything else goes, anything at all.

The genius of this system is that "don't be mean" actually has some massive ramifications as a guiding principle once you start to think about it, including implications for how you treat yourself. And it raises fascinating questions about what is and is not mean. In a sense, this one simple principle invites you to create a more robust and complex ethical system to better explain what exactly it means in practical terms in your own everyday life.

While we don't want to be prescriptive about what values should be important to you, we also don't think everything is relative. If a person's ethical system consistently makes it possible for them to harm others without accountability, then we'd say it's a bad system. And if a group's ethical system consistently results in harm, whether to people within the group or people outside it, then it needs an overhaul, or maybe needs to be tossed altogether. Consider the values taught in pickup-artist subcultures, which often teach men to manipulate women and disregard their lack of consent. Think about the many cults that are supposedly about self-improvement but that ask members to give all their money and time to a leader and cease contact with family and friends. Or look at so-called conversion therapy practices—carried out at sleepaway camps, within religious groups and by individual counsellors—which purport to be about healing, but are deeply rooted in homo- and transphobia and aim to force trans and queer people to become cis and straight. (Spoiler: It doesn't work, and it can destroy their lives.) Proponents of these systems say that what they're doing is right and good, and they may even believe that with their whole hearts. And we disagree.

A concept from the field of cybernetics can be useful here: "The purpose of a system is what it does." In other words, no matter what the stated intentions, if a system's result is consistently harmful, then that system is harmful. And if a harmful system doesn't change, then that's fundamentally the same as if it were *designed* to harm. Intentions count, but results count more.

We also reject a wholly individualist approach to ethics, or one that stops at considering effects at merely the level of dyad (meaning any two-person relationship), family or polycule. The way people view and treat each other is deeply, intricately shaped by the systems we live within, to the point where it becomes difficult to even imagine what other possibilities might exist outside that system. Mononormativity, amatonormativity, heteronormativity and the gender binary weren't just made up for no reason; they exist to uphold systems of domination, namely colonialism, capitalism and patriarchy. These systems rely on disconnection to function. Haíłzaqv author Jess Housty ('Cúagilákv) sums up this idea:

> The way western society interacts with the world is often rooted in disconnection, in dissociation. We think we are architects of the order of the world, that our needs are the higher needs. This kind of thinking is so firmly embedded in my broader social context, and when it creeps into my thinking, I have to remind myself: think like an ancestor.

Or, to paraphrase Mia Mingus, capitalism requires the breaking of relationships.

Just as that systemic disconnection ripples downward and inward into your most intimate spaces, in turn, the beliefs that drive your actions in close relationships also drive your interactions with the world at every level. And these small actions, iterated billions of times at scale, reinforce the systems that create the beliefs that...you get the idea. Author adrienne maree brown refers to this interconnectedness as *emergence*: "In the framework of emergence, the whole is a mirror of the parts. Existence is fractal—the health of the cell is the health of the species and the planet."

We believe that if we're to really rethink and disrupt the mononormative paradigm that has so limited the ways we relate to one another, we must necessarily confront these other systems and consider how their stories, too, have affected us. And in turn, if we are creating new relational ethics, we have a responsibility to ensure that they, and the actions that result from them, do not reinforce these systems, and instead do their tiny part to actively disrupt them.

"The personal is political" is a saying that emerged from the feminist movement in the early 1970s, and we think it applies to nonmonogamy as well. Right now, people who are writing, speaking and teaching about nonmonogamy, giving interviews and appearing in reality shows, are actively involved in creating culture. But so are those who are simply rethinking mononormativity in their own lives: When you make new decisions about how to do your relationships, that, too, is (emergently) part of creating culture. The ethics you bring to your intimate relationships are deeply connected to the broader ways you move through the world. As brown's sister, Autumn Brown, has said, "The fundamental unit of change is relationship." And it really does matter how you—to paraphrase Octavia Butler—shape that change.

As the world faces cascading global crises brought on by the same systems that create such profound disconnection at intimate scales, many brilliant people have been thinking and writing about the kinds of interpersonal ethics that could collectively remake our world in a more connected, resilient, sustainable and loving way. We're not going to try to perform any grand synthesis here, but we want to encourage you to read widely as you explore your own thinking. We have been inspired and influenced by writers from the fields of Black feminism, prison abolition, transformative justice, decolonization, trauma and resilience studies, queer and trans thought, and much more, including all the writers mentioned in this chapter. You'll find many of their works, and others, listed in the notes and resources sections at the end of this book.

So how do you take these huge ideas and turn them into an ethical system that helps you make everyday decisions? That's the work of a lifetime, really. As you learn over time, you can revisit your system, overhaul it as needed or just tweak it on a regular basis. Ethics is a huge topic, and we can't hope to fully do it justice here. The main message we want to get across is that we think that having an ethical system is important, and so is being able to explain its basics to others with whom you're in relationship. And for that, it can also really help to figure out and name your values.

What are values?

Think of values as the building blocks of an ethical system, or the components of the machinery that make it all work. Another way to understand their relationship would be that values are what you think is important, and ethics are what you do about that—the system of personal rules you follow. In her book *Ecstasy Is Necessary*, Barbara Carrellas explains:

> Your values are essential to who you are. They are the core organizing principles you use to live your life. Your values are like the operating system on a computer, constantly running in the background of whatever application you might be working in. They influence every choice you make and every interaction you participate in.

You may already be able to list your values. Perhaps you're part of a faith, community or practice that sets out its values explicitly, and if you agree with them, that might give you a head start. Maybe you can identify the values set out by your family or the culture you were raised in, and put them on your list, if they resonate with you.

For example, in her book *I Hope We Choose Love: A Trans Girl's Notes from the End of the World*, Kai Cheng Thom describes (some of) the cultural values she was raised with:

> I'm not a big believer in justice. That skepticism extends to the notions of accountability, restorative justice, transformative justice, and most of the related terms that have taken hold in social justice culture—though I do very strongly believe in integrity, honesty, and personal honour. "Integrity" is a word you hear used fairly frequently in social justice circles, but honesty and honour, as I know them, are values that come to me through my Chinese family and upbringing. Honesty, in my family, means saying what you mean, even if it is unpopular. Honour means acting in a way that your ancestors would be proud of, even if it requires personal sacrifices to do so. However, "honour" is not a word you hear very much in social justice community, and I feel its distinct lack as an influence on activist conduct.

Sometimes being part of a faith, community, practice, culture or family actually teaches you values that you *don't* find useful, or that you disagree with, which can help you determine, by way of contrast, what values you *do* hold. You may be able to hold this tension and manage it in ways that allow you to keep participating. Or such a disagreement may create enough tension, either within yourself or in social contexts, that it leads to a rupture of some kind. In that case, you might leave a community, cease a practice or end certain relationships. As you change over time, you may later revisit these decisions; if you've stayed involved, you might find that the gap keeps widening, and the tension you used to be able to manage becomes unbearable enough that you have to leave. Or, if there was a rupture, you might later reassess the situation, soften your stance and rejoin in a different capacity, rekindle a connection or find that you can accept certain differences with more grace.

If you're not sure what exactly your values are, it's worth taking a little time to think about this question in a deliberate way. Barbara Carrellas provides a couple of exercises to that end in chapter 2 of her book. You can also do a quick online search for keywords (such as *exercise* or *quiz* and *personal values*) and you'll find any number of tools and quizzes, though these are likely to come from a limited perspective. Even if you can rattle off your list of values at the drop of a hat, it's still worth doing an exercise or two to help you consider and challenge them; you might end up reaffirming them, but you might also drop or reformulate some, or add new ones you hadn't yet put into words. Very few people are given a predetermined set of values and go through their whole lives without questioning them or shifting them along the way. The point isn't to follow any one specific process here, but to explore and come out with greater clarity.

Why are your values important? Because they inform how you make choices in your life. Taken together, they provide a structure or system that can help you to either make those choices more consistently over time or to improve the kinds of choices you make to lead to greater meaning and belonging, and less suffering, for yourself and the people around you. This consistency in turn builds trust—both your trust in yourself and others' trust in you. And it also helps you set boundaries around what kind of things you'll do and what kinds of behaviours you'll accept from others. Therapist Sander T. Jones explains this well in their book *Cultivating Connection*:

> A boundary on my own behavior is a limit *based on my values* that helps determine both my behavior in the face of pressure from other people and the behaviors I will allow myself when struggling alone with a difficult situation.…A boundary is also a limit we enforce on the behavior we will allow other people to direct toward us or inflict upon us.

Jones encourages you to find an appropriate balance between limits on your own behaviour and self-compassion; you need to recognize the limitations of your own power while also striving to hold yourself to the standards you could achieve. They also explain that values-based boundaries help you to strengthen and clarify your personal identity and to avoid actions, people and situations that are damaging to your self-esteem and self-respect. (We talk about boundaries more in chapter 9.)

(Some of) our values

We've each got our own set of values, and we have each developed fairly in-depth ethical systems. The same values that shape our approach to nonmonogamy also come into play when we choose what to eat, how we use social media, or how we approach our professional work. We're going to take a moment to set out a couple of the key values that underpin our approach to nonmonogamy, because you'll see evidence of them in a lot of what you read from this point forward.

The first one is *kindness*. What does that mean? In a social media post that went viral, Jordan K. Green wrote, "The East Coast is kind but not nice, the West Coast is nice but not kind." Green went on to add, "Niceness is saying 'I'm so sorry you're cold,' while kindness may be 'Ugh, you've said that five times, here's a sweater!' Kindness is addressing the need, regardless of tone." We're not here to debate coast-based cultural differences, but Green is getting at a useful point: Kindness isn't just about sounding like you care about someone, it's also about choosing actions that concretely demonstrate that you care, that you recognize another person's fellow humanity. And when you think about it like that, it becomes clear that kindness is a sort of umbrella value that encompasses and interconnects with a whole lot of other values. For example, it's hard to demonstrate that you care if you haven't bothered to find out what a person wants, needs or finds meaningful. So that means part of kindness involves values like curiosity and listening. And if you believe that people all deserve to have agency over their lives, and that everyone should hold the same basic rights in relationships, then the kind thing to do is to always be honest with them, even on topics where that might feel uncomfortable—that's the only way they can be full partners in decision-making about their lives. Of course, part of being kind is also about being respectful and considerate of people's feelings, boundaries, bodies and dignity; that means you have to find ways to be both honest and compassionate in how you express yourself and what actions you choose to take. Kindness also encompasses generosity, meaning the willingness to share what you have with others, offer them the benefit of the doubt, and proactively consider their needs and desires.

It would take a long time to list all the concepts that can fall under the umbrella of kindness; we're just listing a few of the basic ones. To sum it up simply: Kindness, for us, involves the full package of values and actions that demonstrate our regard for others' inherent worth as human beings.

The second value is *integrity*. To get a sense of how important this value is to us, consider that Eve has a tattoo based on this quote from the graphic novel *V for Vendetta* by Alan Moore: "But it was my integrity that was important. Is that so selfish? It sells for so little, but it's all we have left in this place. It is the very last inch of us. But within that inch we are free."

What exactly does it mean to act with integrity? Some people define *integrity* as essentially the same thing as honesty. Others see it as consistency of action, or consistency of action with belief. But the root of the word *integrity* means "whole." Focusing on integrity, for us, means an intense focus on the present moment: What am I doing *right now*, and is it in alignment with my most authentic self? If in ten years I were to look back at myself and the choice I am making in this moment, would I like the person I see?

Integrity, for us, describes the practice of not only having an ethical system but sticking with that system even when, and perhaps especially when, we're confronted with difficult, painful situations—or situations in which compromising our ethical system would present us with immediate gratification, material reward or an easier path. Integrity means living by our ethical principles in a consistent way, not only when it's convenient or simple. We think that sticking to our ethical principles and living in accordance with our values is a way of achieving a kind of wholeness, in the sense of keeping ourselves consistent over time and not shifting based on whims, outside influences or the promise of rewards. It's making decisions we can stand by, not because we can always guarantee it will work out the way we want but because we want to be able to look back and feel comfortable with how we acted. Integrity doesn't mean never changing; it means holding on to consistent principles and committing to constantly doing the work of figuring out how they apply in everyday situations and whether they need to shift, deepen or clarify in order to address and accommodate the complexities of the situations in which we find ourselves.

We each have a set of values that are important to us beyond the big ones discussed here. For example, in life in general, Andrea values information, which for them means they'd always prefer to know all the facts of a situation (including the emotional aspects!) than to make snap judgments or be "spared" from the "burden" of knowledge—even if they don't particularly like what they learn, and even if the timing is inconvenient. They also deeply value co-creation, meaning the idea that relationships (intimate and otherwise) should be fundamentally collaborative and shaped by the people involved in them; together, two or more people can draw on a wealth of skills, ideas, resources and knowledge and combine them in ways that can never be achieved if they're each left alone to make decisions, come up with plans or solve problems "for" each other. Finally, they value integration, which for them means that given the opportunity, and when appropriate, they would always prefer to connect rather than separate, to harmonize rather than compartmentalize. This value applies to things like identities (it's one of the reasons Andrea is very out of the closet in every aspect of their life), relationships (yes please to lunch with the metamour!), and even scholarship (interdisciplinarity all the way).

Eve's values are heavily shaped by her upbringing as a Quaker, through which she was steeped in ideas of nonviolence, simplicity, honesty and the conviction that every person is an expression of the Divine. As an adult, her values have also been influenced by ideas from progressive Judaism—which in many ways align closely with Quakerism—such as community, accountability, and intergenerational and global responsibility, as well as by numerous writings from the transformative justice and prison abolition movements, which also centre the inherent worth and dignity of every person and the importance of addressing harm. In intimate relationships, she places a high value on individual empowerment and choice, balanced with commitment and relational responsibility, including—outside contexts of abuse—responsibility for repair, both within relationships and after they have ended.

Right and wrong nonmonogamy?

One of the things you'll hear a lot is that "there's no one right way to do nonmonogamy." This is true. There are many ways to "do nonmonogamy" that give you a decent chance of having healthy, fulfilling, meaningful relationships with low conflict. But when people say "there's no one right way," it sometimes seems like they mean there are no bad ways to do nonmonogamy. We disagree. There are plenty of choices likely to lead you and your partners into pain, stress, trauma and tears. There are ways to do nonmonogamy that shift most of the emotional risk that comes with any intimate relationship onto one person. There are ways to do nonmonogamy that reliably cause suffering.

It seems pretty fair to say that approaches that are likely to cause pain to you and others probably aren't very good strategies. We are even comfortable calling such approaches "bad" ways of doing nonmonogamy—though choosing a flawed strategy doesn't necessarily make someone a bad person. Everyone is struggling to meet the same basic human needs. People make mistakes because they're trying to solve a problem, and many of the less successful approaches to nonmonogamy tend to promise quick relief—but come with insidious, hidden costs.

So what does it mean to apply your ethical system to nonmonogamy, given that you're going to make mistakes, hurt others, be buffeted by your emotions and fall down sometimes? Going by the values we set out in the previous section, we think it means that you need to be willing to look at and take responsibility for your actions and their effects on other people. If you're presented with evidence that you're causing harm, or that what you're doing won't achieve what you and your partners want, you need to look for ways to change this. In making decisions, you need to consider the well-being of *everyone* involved, not just some of the people.

We think it also means that you need to be willing to have the kinds of discussions that permit an honest analysis of the way you're choosing to do nonmonogamy, without getting defensive or accusatory. After all, you're learning. If you're not willing to assess the path you're on and whether it's taking you where you want to go, you're likely to end up in some pretty messed-up places.

Our assumptions about you

If we're going to talk about things like nurturing healthy relationships, we need to make some assumptions about your intentions and the kinds of relationships you want—such as what we mean when we use the word *healthy*. Nonmonogamous people are a diverse bunch, and we can't speak to the full range of those backgrounds, choices, needs and expectations. Even so, we need to work from *some* assumptions to provide useful advice, and we think it's helpful to name those assumptions. We assume that you:

- seek, like most people, to engage in relationships because you value love, connection and belonging.
- want your partners to engage in a relationship with you, and specifically a nonmonogamous relationship, of their own free will.
- want your partners to feel loved, cared for and secure in their relationships with you, and want to feel loved, cared for and secure in your relationships with them.
- value honesty in your relationships, which we define as, at minimum, everyone involved with you being aware of the other people you're involved with.*
- accept that all long-term relationships will contain conflict, but want that conflict to happen safely and be generative (that is, ultimately lead to a deepened understanding of one another).

Among other things, then, we're assuming that you're not among the kinds of bad actors (or careless actors) we mentioned earlier—though you may run into them, and they're likely to try to twist our and others' advice as cover. That's another reason we're listing our assumptions: because when in doubt, you can come back to them and ask yourself if you—or a person you're interacting with—seem to be acting with these intentions. (Please see chapter 3, on abuse, for more on this.)

Accepting and honouring these assumptions will lead in a natural way to caring, supportive, open relationships. When we talk about "good" ways to do nonmonogamy, we're talking about strategies that, in our experience, seem most often to lead people toward these kinds of relationships. When we talk about "healthy" or "good" relationships,

* Some nonmonogamous people engage in a structure called "Don't ask, don't tell," in which the people involved don't talk about their other relationships or even mention they exist. We discuss this approach further in chapters 10 and 14.

we are talking about relationships that move toward these values more often than they move away from them.

Strong, ethically grounded nonmonogamous relationships are not a destination, they are a journey. Nurturing such relationships is like walking toward a point on the horizon: You move toward it or away from it with each choice you make, but you never actually arrive. Sometimes you'll make a choice that takes you farther away, but that's okay, because you can always make another choice and start moving again in the direction you want to go. (Notice how this is just as true for monogamous relationships!)

For your journey in nonmonogamy, think of this book as a compass, not a map. There is no magic road to contentment or fulfillment in nonmonogamy. That said, as we emphasize over and over, the compass directions we've seen that lead to strong, vibrant relationships are courage, honesty, willingness to accept responsibility for your own emotions as well as the effects your actions have on others, respect for both the autonomy and needs of others, and compassion, humility and empathy.

Our axioms

An axiom is a statement that is taken as a fundamental premise, without the need for further explanation. All of us have premises that we accept as self-evidently true, whether we articulate them or not. Here, we set out the two axioms that underpin the ethical ideas we're sharing in this book. These axioms don't capture the entirety of our own respective personal values and ethical systems, but they do form a foundation for them, and we refer back to them numerous times throughout this book.

- Other people are real.
- The people in a relationship are more important than the relationship.

These axioms might sound simple, but they are not necessarily easy.

AXIOM 1: OTHER PEOPLE ARE REAL

Axiom 1 is inspired by a quote from Irish-British novelist Dame Iris Murdoch: "Love is the perception of individuals. Love is the extremely difficult realisation that something other than oneself is real. Love, and so art and morals, is the discovery of reality."

It's easy to assume that all the other people sharing this world with you are reflections of yourself—some more true to the original than others, perhaps, but all of them essentially similar. The reality is different. Human beings are a varied lot. Whatever values you hold, whatever truths seem obvious and self-evident to you, there are people for whom those values are entirely alien and those truths opaque. Everyone takes different paths through life—sometimes very different.

You will encounter crucial moments every day when you need to actively work against your natural tendency to stereotype and project, or you risk harm to your relationships, your communities and your societies. As Rabbi Danya Ruttenberg has written, "Much harm is caused when we regard others as objects, or in transactional ways, and forget to behold their full humanity—to see them as complete human beings whose concerns and feelings matter as much as our own." In other words, you need to work to remember, every day, that other people are real—as real as you are.

This is harder than it sounds. Because what this means is not just that you need to remember that the people you're dealing with are all multifaceted humans with complicated histories and rich inner lives. It also means that you need to remember that their stories are just as important as yours—not just subjectively, in their own experience, but objectively, in terms of what those stories can tell you about reality.

Forgetting that other people are real sometimes means you assume that other people's experiences are similar to yours and other people's perceptions of the world are like yours. Psychologists have a name for this: the typical mind fallacy. This is the error of believing that other people are more like you than they really are—or that you are more like everyone else than you really are.

You don't, at least yet, have the means to place yourself behind another person's eyes to see the world as they see it. Even if you could, the experiences you accumulate over your entire life will shape how you react to the same things. At some point, you must accept on faith that your experience is different, and that there are limits to how well you can hope to understand another person.

It's imperative, then, to acknowledge the experiences of other people, and not try to define their experiences for them. This process begins with listening. And listening begins with understanding that other people are better experts on their lives than you are.

It's easy, when you're confronted with someone who describes a drastically different experience of the world, to reject it. The world doesn't really work that way; you've had an entire lifetime to prove it! They must be exaggerating, or perhaps making it up to cover for their own inadequacies. Right? This is the "I can't imagine it, so it can't be real" problem.

When you hear people tell their stories, and their stories don't align with your experiences, it can be hard to believe them—especially when your experiences are shaped by things that are completely invisible to you. To combat this difficulty, you must accept that your own experiences may be the norm for *you*, but that doesn't mean they are the norm for everyone. You might have advantages you aren't even aware of. You might make assumptions that aren't true, without realizing you're doing it. Other people might face problems you never have to face, in ways that are so subtle you don't even know they exist.

You can create bridges with other people—and try to understand them—by stepping outside your own assumptions and listening to what others say, even when what they say seems unlikely or just plain weird to you. This can be uncomfortable. It might mean having to admit that you're wrong—about another person's character, motivations or experience, or about the way the world is in general. It might sometimes bring you face-to-face with the notion that you might not have the same problems other people do because of structures and patterns that benefit you at the expense of other people, but are completely invisible to you.

The purpose of this kind of seeing and listening is not to make you feel guilty or ashamed, but to be more aware, to understand other people better, and perhaps even to choose not to participate in those structures and patterns once you start to see them.

This is an important practice in everyday life. We're mentioning it specifically in the context of intimate relationships, and nonmonogamy in particular, because intimate relationships are one of the places where people are often most closely confronted with the need to try and see each other clearly—and where the failure to do so can have the most painful consequences. Your assumptions about what a good relationship looks and feels like, what things people want and need in relationships, and many other things (what is sex? what is intimacy? what is cheating? what is love? what is loyalty? and so on) generally emerge from your life experiences, and for this reason, your assumptions may be very different from those your partners hold. That's challenging enough in monogamous relationships, but nonmonogamy multiplies the number of contrasting perspectives that may come into play on these big questions. The more you can remember that other people are real, the easier it will be to create sufficient space for each person to express their desires, needs and emotions, and the better equipped you'll be to try and co-create ways to see, meet, respect and satisfy them.

AXIOM 2: THE PEOPLE IN THE RELATIONSHIP ARE MORE IMPORTANT THAN THE RELATIONSHIP

Axiom 2, of course, does not mean that relationships aren't important. And it doesn't mean that you should never make personal sacrifices for the benefit of a relationship. But while for the long-term benefit of a relationship (or a partner), it is often necessary to make sacrifices of time, short-term gratification or non-essential desires, it is never a good idea to sacrifice your *self* for a relationship. We discuss this concept further in chapters 4 and 5. And while individual wishes do sometimes need to take a backseat to collective well-being, it's important to remember that relationships exist *to serve the people in them.* If a relationship stops serving the people in it, it's not doing its job. Thus, axiom 2 is, like axiom 1, *always* true (that's why it's an axiom). Even though the people and the relationship need to serve each other, the people are always more important. Always.

In practice, these axioms mean that relationships are consensual, and people are not need-fulfillment machines. People cannot and should not be obligated to remain in any relationship; if a relationship ceases to meet the needs of the people in it, that relationship can end. People are not commodities; relationships based in a compassionate ethical system recognize the humanity, needs and desires of each individual involved.

Consent, agency, honesty and responsibility

Our ethical systems contain several important, intertwined ideas that need a bit more elaboration because they are fundamental to the kind of nonmonogamy we are espousing: *consent, agency, honesty* and *responsibility.* (You can probably see a number of ways these ideas connect to the values of kindness and integrity we discussed earlier.)

Consent is about *you:* your body, your mind and your choices. Your consent is required to access what is yours. The people around you have agency: They do not need your consent to act, because you do not own their bodies, minds or choices. But if their behaviour crosses into your personal space, then they need your consent. It's important to note here that ideas about personal space—in essence, an extension of one's self—are highly culturally specific. As one trivial example, in many cultures and families, it's completely normal for people to take bites of food from each other's plates without asking. Try this in a group where it's not normalized, though, and people will be completely shocked at such appalling and disrespectful behaviour. With people you don't know well, it's important to get familiar with the cultural norms you're dealing with—maybe not to follow them yourself, but at least to help you understand others' behaviour. With people in your intimate circles, it's important to get on at least broadly the same page about where you believe you end and they begin, and what the collective space between you looks like. It can also be helpful to talk to your partners about how they came to these beliefs.

Most people will, over the course of their lives, encounter situations—perhaps at work, in their families of origin or on the streets—where they have to put up emotional walls and accept a loss of control over their lives, their minds or even their bodies. But you should never have to do that in your intimate relationships. This may seem obvious, but it's actually a radical idea.

If you want to do a deep dive into your own beliefs about consent—both how you honour your own and how you honour that of others—you can check out *Ask Yourself: The Consent Culture Workbook* by Kitty Stryker, a journal-style workbook filled with prompts that you can consider for yourself or discuss with your intimates.

Honesty is an indispensable part of consent. Being able to share, to the best of your ability, who you are in a relationship is critical for that relationship to be consensual. You must give your partner the opportunity to make an informed decision to be in a relationship with you. If you lie or withhold critical information, you remove your partner's ability to consent to be in the relationship. If your partner has casual hookups that weren't negotiated in your relationship, they may be breaking an agreement, but they have not (yet) violated your consent. If they then have sex with you—or engage in other forms of intimacy, including emotional intimacy—without telling you about the hookups, they have violated your consent, because they have deprived you of the ability to make an informed choice.

It's especially important to communicate things that might be deal-breakers or might be threatening to your partner's emotional or physical health. Your partner deserves to have a choice about how they want to participate in a relationship with you, given the new information. Examples of these kinds of potential deal-breakers might be sexual activity with others, drug use, the acquisition or use of weapons, and violent impulses or behaviour—but your knowledge of your partners and what is important to them should guide you here. Anything you know or suspect might be a deal-breaker should be disclosed. You can't force someone to make the choice you want them to make, and if you lie or withhold information, you deny them the ability to know there was a choice to be made.

When people talk about dishonesty, it's often in the context of uttering falsehoods. By the simplest definition, a lie is a statement that is factually untrue. But there are other kinds of lies. For example, consider someone who cheats on their partner and says, "I'm not lying, because I'm not telling them that I'm being faithful!" In truth, that's lying—the person is concealing information that, if their partner knew about it, would have changed their assessment of the relationship. We think the same goes, for example, at the beginning of a relationship if a nonmonogamous person doesn't disclose their other relationships to a new partner on the grounds that "we haven't agreed to exclusivity." The same goes for things like disclosing your nonmonogamous status on dating apps. If you know that the other person thinks you're single or exclusive and wouldn't be dating you if you weren't, you have a responsibility to proactively disclose. When we talk about honesty in this book, we do so from the position that a lie of omission is still a lie.

Sometimes, when confronted with the notion of a lie of omission, people say, "Not mentioning something isn't a lie. I don't tell my partner every time I use the bathroom, and that's not lying!" That brings up the idea of relevance. An omission is a lie when it is calculated to conceal information that, were it known to the other party, would be materially relevant to them. Failing to tell your partner how long it took to brush your teeth isn't a lie of omission. Failing to tell your partner you're having sex with someone else is.

Agency is also intertwined with consent. Many people have been taught that if they are empowered to make their own choices, to have agency, they will behave selfishly and hurt others, so they must surrender some of their decision-making power to external authority—which may include a partner or partners. This idea permeates society, but also seems to inform how people build their intimate relationships. Without engaging in a debate about whether people are fundamentally good or bad, it's important to look at your partners and ask yourself if you respect their ability to choose—even if a choice hurts you, even if it's not what you would choose—because they can't consent if they do not have a choice.

Empowering people to make their own choices is actually the best way to have your own needs met. Communicating your needs, and equipping others to meet them, succeeds more often than attempting to restrict or coerce another into meeting them. (We talk more in chapter 13 about what we mean by "empowerment.")

Finally, you always have responsibility to others. Your responsibilities grow in concert with the amount of intimacy and vulnerability you invite, encourage and accept from others. You have greater responsibility to your lovers, partners and friends than you do toward those you have not cultivated intimacy with, and this book primarily deals with that kind of responsibility, but you are surrounded by people (and other living things) toward whom you have responsibilities. In daily life, or all relationships, these people could include your coworkers, in-laws, stepfamilies or neighbours; in nonmonogamy specifically, it could include your metamours and ex-partners. Mononormativity often assumes that you have no responsibilities toward your exes. Queer folks have long rejected this assumption, and increasingly, nonmonogamous folks are doing so, too. And mononormativity certainly doesn't support the idea that you might have responsibilities toward anyone else your partner might be involved with! But functional nonmonogamy requires that you think beyond just the needs of a couple. As Nora Samaran writes in *Turn This World Inside Out*,

> In a healthy community, most human interaction takes place in this relational area in between closeness and complete stranger. The idea that we have relational responsibility only to those humans we love, and no responsibility toward anyone else, is destroying the very fabric of human connection in Western societies. Disconnection is not our physiological reality.

As nonmonogamous communities have moved toward more flexible models that prize autonomy and flexibility, some have arrived at a hyper-individualist, even capitalist approach wherein everyone is responsible for their own feelings, anyone can walk away at any time, and people are perceived to have no, or almost no, responsibility to others, even their closest intimates. This framework has been called poly libertarianism, and to be quite honest, a lot of it was encouraged by parts of the first edition of this book. We believe that while some of these ideas are rooted in good principles, when they are not balanced with responsibility, they can lead to a lot of harm. "You're responsible for your own feelings" can be used to deflect responsibility for the effects of someone's actions when they behave in ways that are thoughtless or cruel. Threats to leave a relationship can be used as emotional blackmail or to maintain the upper hand in a nonconsensual power dynamic.

Author and activist Kitty Stryker summed up the dangers of this approach in a 2015 article titled "'Radical Self-Reliance' Is Killing People":

> The attitude that everyone is an emotional island and that no one's behaviour affects anyone else, that we can all completely manage our own needs independently, that taking care of other people is at best a hassle and at worst a threat, is fucking bullshit. It's emotionally abusive and it actively hurts people. It pits partners against each other.
>
> Having to continually feel like I have to earn my partner's love by being "good, giving and game", which so often means not having boundaries (or having the "right" boundaries) puts me in a situation of constantly second guessing myself. How far am I willing to push myself before breaking up is the only option? Am I just being jealous and I should challenge myself, or am I actually needing to trust my gut? Is this a question of us having our freedom and independence, or is this a question of just blatant disrespect? Whose needs are being met, and at whose expense?

To be fair, the shift that led people toward poly libertarianism was in many ways a reaction to polynormativity, the rigid, hierarchical, rules-based system that predominated for a couple of decades. And while we critique the colonial and capitalist worldviews that reinforce the disconnection that underlies the harms Stryker is naming, we also want to resist idealizing other systems and cultures. For example, while many more collectively oriented cultures have much to offer in terms of the importance they place on community and belonging, they can also (just like many individualist cultures, to be sure) be deeply patriarchal and homophobic. They may also place a low priority on—or be actively hostile to—ideas of consent and self-determination.

We don't believe there is a perfect system. The important thing, for the purposes of this book, is to remember that these values—consent, agency, honesty and responsibility—may often feel in tension with one another, and part of the work for people who want to behave ethically is to constantly think about and talk with each other about how to keep them in balance, for themselves and others, and then take action accordingly.

A relationship bill of rights

We've talked about the idea of "right" (as opposed to "wrong"), but what about *rights?* Rights are a cornerstone of many systems of ethics. At various points in history, the notion of rights has emerged within various cultures and systems of thought all over the world, but it rose to prominence in particular after World War II with the Universal Declaration of Human Rights, signed in 1948. This notion has since become key to Western liberal democratic thought—the basic system we, your authors, were raised in, and one that's informed most of the social justice activism we've seen in our lifetimes. So it's perhaps not surprising that we think rights are important.

However, rights aren't everything. Among other things, the notion of rights-based activism has been criticized for its inadequacy in helping everyone achieve freedom, and for the ease with which it can be co-opted to serve a conformist agenda. So we're not saying that "rights" is a perfect framework for thinking about how to do right by each other. Among other things, a lot of the actions you might take to make the world around you better, including your intimate relationships, are more about generosity, kindness and a recognition that everyone is interconnected—not about rights, which are a much more limited set of ideas. (Does a tree have a right to grow? Do you have a right to cut it down? These aren't the questions we should be asking if we're trying to collectively mitigate climate change and take care of the planet.)

However, a rights-based system is still useful insofar as it's familiar to a lot of people and can offer insights into how to be good to each other. Rights aren't everything, but they do provide a useful starting point. For this reason, in our own ethical system, choices are *not* ethical if they infringe on another person's rights.

That said, it's common to hear the word *rights* used when the speaker actually means "things I really want." In relationships, a right often means "something I expect" or "something I feel entitled to," such as "I'm your legal spouse, therefore I have a right to end your other relationships if they make me uncomfortable." Or "My partner and I have children together, so I have the right to decide who my partner can become involved with."

You have the right to want what you want. You do not, however, have the right to *get* what you want. For rights, a higher bar needs to be set. So what *is* a right? Here, we come back to the idea of creating culture. The rights you agree on—in your relationships, in your polycules, in your communities, and at larger scales—are, in essence, statements of values, and they define the kind of person that you aspire to be and the kinds of collectives you want to create. At a personal level, being clear on what you believe are your relationship rights can help you set boundaries, find people who are compatible with you, leave unhealthy relationships and better understand how you want to treat your partners. As long as you remember that your partners (and metamours) have all these rights too!

Eve developed most of the Relationship Bill of Rights for the first edition of this book by drawing from numerous other writings on rights from a wide variety of perspectives. It has since been released into the public domain. We have made a few changes to the version in this edition in light of our current thinking, and we encourage others to adapt and build on it as well.

YOU HAVE THE RIGHT, WITHOUT SHAME, BLAME OR GUILT:

IN ALL INTIMATE RELATIONSHIPS:

- to be free from coercion, violence and intimidation
- to choose the level of involvement and intimacy you want
- to revoke consent to any form of intimacy at any time
- to be told the truth
- to say no to requests
- to hold and express differing points of view
- to have influence and seek compromise
- to feel and communicate your emotions and needs
- to set boundaries, including concerning your privacy needs
- to set clear limits on your commitments
- to be able to rely on others to honour their commitments to you, and for them to be accountable if they cannot honour them
- to seek balance between what you give to the relationship and what is given back to you
- to know that your partner will work with you to resolve problems that arise
- to choose whether you want a monogamous or nonmonogamous relationship
- to grow and change
- to make mistakes
- to end a relationship

IN NONMONOGAMOUS RELATIONSHIPS:

- to decide how many partners you want
- to choose your own partners
- to have an equal say with each of your partners in deciding the form your relationship with that partner will take
- to choose the level of time and investment you will offer to each partner
- to understand clearly any conditions that will apply to a relationship before entering into it
- to co-develop or, at minimum, have the freedom of whether or not to agree to any new conditions that will apply to your relationship after it has begun
- to discuss with your partners decisions that affect you, and to have them consider those effects on you in their decisions
- to have time alone with each of your partners
- to enjoy passion and special moments with each of your partners

IN A NONMONOGAMOUS NETWORK:

- to choose the level of involvement and intimacy you want with your partners' other partners
- to be treated with courtesy
- to have relationships with *people,* not with relationships
- to have plans made with your partner be respected; for instance, not changed at the last minute for trivial reasons
- to be treated as a peer of every other person, not as a subordinate, even when differing levels of commitment or responsibility exist

Of course, if each person in a relationship has all these rights, there are plenty of occasions when different people's rights might seem to come into conflict. If everyone has a right to decide for themselves whether they want a monogamous or nonmonogamous relationship, for example, what happens if one person wants monogamy and one person wants nonmonogamy? That right *doesn't* give one person the right to unilaterally open (or close) a relationship. It does mean that some hard conversations are in store, to see if one or both people can compromise, and if not, to consider whether they can really be compatible as partners. (We discuss this particular case more in chapter 17 on mono/poly relationships.) After all, both partners also have the rights to seek compromise, have influence, have their partner consider the effects of their actions on them, and end a relationship. These rights will usually involve some interplay—among each other, and among the different rights of different people.

And don't forget, it's not just about rights: you also have *responsibilities* to people you are in relationship with. When you knowingly invite someone to place their trust in you, to be vulnerable with you, to share intimacy with you, and especially to attach to you, you have a responsibility to treat those gifts with commitment, consistency and care.

When it's hard to treat others well

Embracing nonmonogamy may well expose you to a great deal more uncertainty and change than people in monogamous relationships experience. Every new relationship has the potential to surprise you. Every new relationship might change your life. And that's a good thing, right? Picture your best relationships. Can you think of any truly awesome relationship that didn't change your life in some important way? The first time you had a long-term partner, did it change things for you? The first time you fell in love, did it change things for you? Every person you become involved with stands a good chance of changing your life in a big or small way. If that weren't the case, well, what would be the point? The same goes for your partners and the new people they become involved with—and when their lives change, so will yours.

Change is scary for a lot of people, and so preparing for nonmonogamous relationships in many ways is about assessing and improving your ability to handle change. Even just *thinking* about it, taking a deep breath and saying, "Yep, I know my life is about to change" is a huge step toward preparing yourself to live nonmonogamously.

In some cases, for some people, circumstances may make change even harder than usual. For example, if you've just had another big change—a new job, say, or a big move, or a marriage or divorce, or a new baby—additional changes might cause you a lot more stress than they otherwise would. In these situations, it's common for people to try to limit the amount of change that nonmonogamy can bring.

A very common example is couples with young children. For example, let's say a couple has two very small children, one of whom is just a few months old. The new parents are under intense stress, as often happens in such situations. To try and cope, the couple puts into place a lot of restrictions to control each other's relationships. These restrictions cause a lot of pain for one person's other partner, who is deeply in love but finds their relationship unable to grow and who may be expected to perform services such as babysitting for the couple in order to continue to have access to their relationship.

In situations like this, it's easy to fall back on the idea of "putting the children first." Clearly, parents need to be able to live their lives in a way that allows them to care for their children's needs and provide loving, stable homes. But too often, this need is used as an all-purpose shield to deflect any analysis of how one couple's behaviour might be affecting their other partners, or how it might be damaging their other relationships. Anything that looks like criticism can be framed as attacking the couple's right to care for their children.

Make no mistake: Kids change things. They did not choose to come into the world, or choose the people who care for and make decisions for them. Only slowly and painfully, over many years, are children nurtured into agency and personal capability, with the ability to think and plan, to learn and make rational choices, to develop judgment and individual responsibility, and to consent or withhold consent.

When children come into a home, for the first time there are truly immature people present, making childish and selfish demands that have real moral legitimacy and must be dealt with. You have a choice about how to deal with these issues, but you can't ignore them. Children add a categorically different new dynamic to the mix and, especially when they are very young, significantly subtract time and attention from adult matters. But that doesn't mean you can use their needs as emotional blackmail or to excuse unethical behavior in the adults around them.

Acting in accordance with a robust ethical system means applying that system to your behaviour with everyone—partners and children. Children are not an ethical Get Out of Jail Free card; it's possible to be both a responsible parent and an ethical partner.

Remember also that not every time in your life will be a good time to add new partners. If you have young children and you simply can't stand the idea of your partner having other partners without, say, instituting a hierarchy, you and your partner might agree to wait until your children are a little older before you start new relationships. If you (or a partner) are struggling with anxiety, insecurity, depression or other issues that leave you (or them) sobbing under the covers when the partner is with someone else, you could go to therapy and learn some coping strategies, or avoid nonmonogamy altogether, instead of bringing someone into your life but surrounding them with metaphorical barbed-wire fences to keep them from getting too close. If you are dealing with a recent betrayal, you might want to work with your partners on building trust before testing that trust by investing in someone new.

We'll get to the question of choice ownership in much more detail later, but for now we just want to stress that if a particular relationship decision is unethical under your ethical system, don't make excuses for it by saying, "But I have to because..." Try reframing the situation. Instead of looking for partners who will let you treat them poorly, who will let you compromise their agency or keep them at arm's length, ask yourself if you are in a position to seek new partners at all. Put another way: Look at yourself and the relationships you have and ask what you need to do, individually and collectively, to enable you to have relationships that will let you treat everyone well.

QUESTIONS TO ASK YOURSELF

To explore more about your own values and ethics, consider some of these questions:

- What kind of values did I learn growing up? Who did I learn them from? How do I feel about those values now? Are there values I no longer agree with that still affect my choices?
- Who are some people whose values, ethics or actions I admire? Why? In what ways do I seek to emulate them in my own life?
- What are some values-related words that resonate with me, and why?
- How do I want my intimates to feel in their relationships with me?
- How do I want to feel in my relationships?
- What kind of value do I place on principles like autonomy and interdependence, self-reliance and community, and how do I balance them?
- What do I want people to remember about me when I am no longer in their lives?

Never be cruel. Never be cowardly.
THE TWELFTH DOCTOR

3 Abuse

CONTENT NOTE: This chapter discusses the topic of abuse, both in general and within nonmonogamous relationships. It does not include graphic descriptions of abuse or stories about abuse.

It might seem odd to put a chapter on abuse right near the beginning of a book about nonmonogamy. But we think it's important to put this information right up front, because ordinary relationship advice (as well as relationship therapy) tends to be useless, counterproductive or outright harmful in situations of abuse.

If you are being abused, trying to use some of the advice in this book could make things worse—or the person or people abusing you might try to use it to control or shame you. We don't want that. Abuse can also show up in nonmonogamy in some special and insidious ways. So we want to equip you as best we can to discern when you're just having a hard time and when a situation has become toxic or abusive—and thus when you might need a different kind of help than what's in these pages.

Before we even start talking about what abuse is, we want to make something really clear. And that is: If you're feeling harmed in one or more of your relationships, it doesn't have to meet the technical definition of abuse to be not okay. Sometimes, people can get caught in wondering whether something they're experiencing "counts" as abuse. It's almost as if there's a flowchart in their heads, where a "yes" would lead them to a certain set of actions and a "no" would lead to others. But there are three problems with that.

First, people's understandings of abuse have shifted a lot over time, and they continue to evolve based on the work of advocacy and support groups, changes in laws and legal systems, new research and scholarship, cultural movements, advances in the fields of psychology and trauma treatment, and lots more. For example, in Canada, it was perfectly legal to rape your spouse until 1983, and the Labour Code didn't require workplaces to have policies against sexual harassment until 1985. In 2019, England and Wales became the first jurisdictions in the world to designate coercive control as a crime. Those are just a few examples of legal shifts; there are many more. And the law is usually many steps behind the culture at large—or sometimes out of step entirely. So depending on what system you're turning to for definitions, you might end up coming to conclusions that don't track with your lived experience.

Second, the representations of abuse that we most commonly see can be misleading. For instance, it's easy to show a picture of someone with visible physical injuries, but a lot of abuse is far more subtle and harder to represent in a photo. News articles and TV clips about abuse often focus primarily on situations that involve extreme and frequent acts of physical violence, because those are the types of abuse that are most likely to come to the attention of a reporter or writer. Recent documentaries, such as the several series and movies about the NXIVM cult, have dramatized psychological control and abuse that mostly didn't involve physical violence but was still quite extreme. But a great deal of abuse doesn't look like the HBO-worthy cases—and it's still just as real. So if you turn to films, TV and the news to figure out whether you're experiencing abuse, you might not recognize your own situation in those representations at all, and you can easily end up convincing yourself that what you're experiencing doesn't count as abuse or isn't really "that bad."

Third, and perhaps more importantly: *It's the wrong question*. Whether your experience technically falls under the umbrella of "abuse" is not the most useful question to be asking—or at least, it's not the only question or the most important one. Rather than asking yourself, "Is this abuse?" consider asking yourself questions like these, which can apply either to a person or a group:

- Does their behaviour cross a line for me in terms of how I'm willing to be treated?
- Do I feel afraid of them, or intimidated, browbeaten, belittled, disrespected, manipulated or objectified?
- Does this relationship feel like a test of how much unpleasantness I'm willing to absorb or how hard I'm willing to defend my boundaries or stand up for myself? Do they badger me and try to wear me down when I state a boundary?

- Do I have to walk on eggshells around them, or twist myself into a pretzel to avoid setting them off in some way? Am I constantly bracing for the next conflict, the next attack? Are they constantly angry with me or on the verge of anger?
- Am I never really sure they are telling the truth or giving me the whole story? Do I leave conversations with them feeling confused or disoriented?
- Are they malicious or mean-spirited toward me? Do they set me up to fail, or mock me or humiliate me?
- Do they play mind games with me—twisting my words to mean things they don't, reinterpreting events to cast me in a bad light, accusing me of things I haven't done, or otherwise bending reality to justify being upset at me?
- Do they respect my privacy, my relationships with friends and family, my work or school commitments, and my decision-making power in my own life?
- Do they punish me or threaten me if I do things in a way they don't like, or talk to people they don't want me to talk to?
- Are they contemptuous of me? Do they act as though I'm a burden or a chore, or unworthy of their time and attention, or as though my existence is an annoyance to them?
- Do I feel drained and exhausted from trying to manage the unpleasantness that comes from being with them? Do I lose focus at work or school, cancel plans with friends and family, or do a poor job taking care of myself or others because I'm feeling so sad or upset about the way they are treating me?

The answers to these questions won't necessarily tell you whether you're in an abusive relationship or polycule. But they can still give you some clarity on whether the situation is a positive, strengthening force in your life or a negative and harmful one, as well as whether the other people involved are likely to be your allies in improving things.

Of course, you may also read the questions above and recognize some of your own treatment of others. If you have a conscience, it can feel just as awful—or worse—to realize you've been mistreating someone close to you as it does to realize you've been mistreated. While we're not going to let you off the hook, we do want to say that it doesn't make you irredeemable, and it's never too late to do better. People engage in harmful behaviours for lots of reasons, and these behaviours can be unlearned. But you do need to be able to recognize when you've been causing harm, take accountability and be willing to take steps to change. And it *also* doesn't give anyone carte blanche to treat you poorly in return. In fact, it's common for abusive people to use their victims' own mistakes and even poor behaviour—no one is perfect, after all—to convince the victims they deserve the abuse, or brought it on themselves. So while it's important to take responsibility for your actions, if you feel like you're being punished for some transgression, instead of feeling like you're on a team to make the relationship better for everyone, that's a red flag.

Relationships aren't supposed to hurt. They're supposed to lift you up and nourish you, not cut you down or drain you. Partnerships are supposed to make your life better, not worse. They are supposed to be loving.

A digression about love

In her book *All About Love*, bell hooks makes a bold statement: "Love and abuse cannot coexist." She arrives at this assertion by working from a definition of love proposed by M. Scott Peck in 1978, who writes that love is "the will to extend one's self for the purpose of nurturing one's own or another's spiritual growth." And he specifies that love is "an act of will—namely, both an intention and an action." From there, hooks writes: "When we understand love as the will to nurture our own and another's spiritual growth, it becomes clear that we cannot claim to love if we are hurtful and abusive.... Abuse and neglect are, by definition, the opposites of nurturance and care."

She goes on to explain why this definition of love might be hard to accept:

> For most folks it is just too threatening to embrace a definition of love that would no longer enable us to see love as present in our families. Too many of us need to cling to a notion of love that either makes abuse acceptable or at least makes it seem that whatever happened was not that bad.

In other words, no matter how intense a person's *feelings* are, if their *actions* are harmful and destructive, *it's not love*. But especially (though not only) if you were raised in abusive, neglectful or otherwise dysfunctional families, it can be really difficult to embrace an understanding of love that makes no room for abuse. It can be really difficult to accept that a person who treats you poorly is *not actually loving you*. You might have to rewrite your stories about your past, or rethink the ones you're living in right now. Accepting that love and abuse cannot coexist can be *really costly*, emotionally and materially. It can be psychologically challenging to wrap your head around this idea.

This is one of the many places where courage is a useful tool. That doesn't mean fearlessness. It just means taking a deep breath, examining things *as they are* and not as you'd like them to be, and making decisions accordingly.

None of this is meant to imply that people can't make mistakes or occasionally do hurtful things within an otherwise loving relationship. But when those things happen, which is inevitable, being loving means the person who caused harm or hurt apologizes, makes a genuine attempt to repair things in a meaningful way, and then refrains from doing the hurtful thing again.

This brings us back to the question of defining abuse. There are useful definitions, and we will get to those in a moment. But rather than asking, "Is this abuse?" we think a better question to start off the flowchart in your head is, "Is this relationship loving?" And by that, we mean:

- Does this relationship support me and bring me joy?
- Do I feel relaxed and at ease with my partner?
- Do I have room to make mistakes with my partner and be given the benefit of the doubt?
- Do I trust my partner to tell me the truth?
- Is my partner generally kind to me?
- Does this partnership nurture my growth, spiritual or otherwise?
- Do I feel like my partner and I are on the same team?

These questions can all be applied to polycules, as well. If you combine the answers you got to the first set of questions in this chapter with the ones you get here, you might get a perspective on whether the partnership in question is a good one for you—regardless of whether or not you think it's abusive. If it *is* abusive, this will cover it. And if it's not, but you discover that it's also not loving, well, maybe you'll make different decisions about how to move toward your own well-being once you've determined that.

It might also be worth thinking about the definition of love in terms of how it connects with an overall project to build what Kitty Stryker calls "consent culture." For her, consent culture is the goal, and it's the opposite of rape culture, which is the context that allows abuse to thrive. In her consent culture workbook *Ask Yourself*, Stryker writes, "I want to encourage people to think critically about their own lives and experiences, to think about where they could be choosing informed consent instead of our society's encouraged values of entitlement, dissociation and pushing yourself beyond your own limits."

In a way, this formulation acts as a society-level counterpart to the question "Is this relationship loving?" But it also comes right back down to interpersonal relationships. Does a loving relationship include non-negotiated entitlement, in the sense of assuming you can do things to your partners without asking and receiving a clear yes, or that you can disregard your effects on your partners? Does it require you to dissociate in order to get through what you're doing together? Does it require you to push yourself beyond your limits? We'd say no to all these questions: They don't fit into bell hooks's understanding of love. And if you understand yourself as a person who wants to build a consent culture, what better place to start than with your own relationships?

Definitions of abuse

The term *abuse* is commonly used to refer to two main concepts: coercive control and toxic behaviours. These concepts are both worth explaining. They aren't one and the same, but they do overlap. This is important because the slippage between them can make some discussions (and even your internal thought processes) confusing.

COERCIVE CONTROL

Some people use the term *abuse* when they're talking about coercive control and related harms as part of an ongoing pattern. In a report to Canada's House of Commons, scholar Carmen Gill defined coercive control as follows: "Coercive control encompasses acts of both coercion and control through the use of force, deprivation, humiliation, intimidation, exploitation, isolation, and domination. This is done to produce a victim's obedience, ultimately eliminating their sense of freedom in the relationship." In *The Globe and Mail*, Gill elaborates, referring to partners who engage in

> power games ... it's gaslighting, lies, blaming, cruelty, intimidation—all those things that we don't necessarily recognize as a form of violence [under] the Criminal Code of Canada. (...) It's isolation from friends and family. Restricted access to money or food or medicine. Damaging property, or hurting pets. Degrading comments. Barrages of text messages. Monitoring social media.

Coercive control may or may not come with direct physical violence; it is abuse regardless. But a pattern of physical violence almost always occurs within a context of coercive control. The important thing here is to recognize that coercive control encompasses emotional and psychological abuse, as well as other kinds, such as financial abuse and stalking, and that all of these are real forms of abuse whether or not they include physical or sexual assault. Patterns of coercive control may also extend to control over another person's perceptions of reality itself—insisting that abusive incidents never happened or were the other person's fault, for example, or trying to convince someone they are mentally unwell in order to get them to accept another person's control over their decisions. This is, of course, what we call gaslighting, and it is both an abuse tactic and a form of abuse in itself.

The nature of coercive control is that one person is deliberately skewing the power dynamic to instill fear and obedience in their partner. It's very rare that a person exerting coercive control will relinquish their power willingly; they are systematically undermining their partner's ability to self-advocate. This is generally the kind of dynamic we're talking about in this chapter when we use the term *abuse*.

For the sake of safety, rather than thinking about ways to fix the relationship, the person on the receiving end of this kind of harm might want to invest in building an escape plan: storing important documents at a friend's house, saving up money and choosing a strategic moment to move out while the abusive partner is away, for example. People experiencing coercive control are often in the greatest danger of being assaulted or even murdered right after they escape, as the abuser attempts to regain control by any means necessary. People experiencing abuse often know this to be true, which is why they often don't leave until they're prepared and ready—which can be difficult to achieve when they're being coercively controlled. (This is one of the many reasons "Why didn't they just leave?" is such an ignorant question!)

We'll discuss these dynamics further and provide resources later in this chapter.

TOXIC BEHAVIOUR

The second main way people use the term *abuse* is when referring to toxic and harmful behaviour more generally. People may exhibit toxic behaviour of many kinds, up to and including physical violence, outside a context of coercive control. For example, a person might make a belittling comment to their partner or lie to them about something.

They may engage in emotional blackmail, like guilt-tripping a partner or threatening to end a relationship if they don't get their way. It's even pretty common to engage in gaslighting, like when someone feels ashamed of something they did and tries to minimize it, even when they know how bad it was. And while that behaviour may be anything from unpleasant to a deal-breaker, if it's not part of a pattern of nonconsensual domination enforced against another person, it wouldn't be considered coercive control. Similarly, if a person assaults someone on the street, that's a criminal act, but it's not coercive control, because it's not part of an ongoing pattern of intimidation within a relationship.

When someone displays toxic behaviour, it may be possible for the people involved to work through it, if the person displaying the behaviour is willing to change and the person or people receiving it are willing to forgive. For example, if someone insults others, lies or cheats, while it might cause deep hurt, they might be able to resolve the problem through conversation or therapy, and it might never reoccur. Despite the instance or instances of toxic behaviour, the power dynamic between the people involved might remain relatively egalitarian. And it might be possible to repair the relationship rupture or breakdown caused by the harm. The strategies you might want to employ to resolve this kind of situation could include clear boundary-setting; communication exercises; individual, joint or family therapy; targeted skill-building or anger management courses; and so on. The fate of the relationship depends on each person's decisions about whether to stay or leave, to change or remain entrenched.

It's also entirely common for people to engage in toxic behaviours toward each other. This could be because neither of them has ever learned healthy relating, one could be reacting to the other, or they could be setting each other off in particularly explosive ways. Some people call these relationships "mutually abusive," but we agree with domestic violence prevention organizations that such a thing doesn't exist, because abuse (as coercive control) always involves a one-sided power dynamic. People being mean to each other can be awful, and certainly counts as toxic behaviour, but because it's mutual, it's not coercive control. Finally, it's also common for victims of coercive control to use toxic behaviours in self-defence, or to adopt some of the tactics of their abusers as survival strategies.

Some toxic behaviours might be instant deal-breakers—actions that make you decide to end a relationship right away, before they can possibly escalate to a pattern. For example, if someone hits you once, you might decide to leave immediately rather than stick around to give them a second chance or an opportunity to repair things. Or if someone makes an insult that crosses a major line for you, and you feel it was deliberate and malicious—or it simply hurts you so much you don't feel you can trust them again—that might be a relationship-ender: They don't need to repeat it for it to be sufficient grounds for you to leave. This is completely reasonable. Nobody should feel they have to tolerate or forgive harmful acts that cross their boundaries, even if they happen only once. It is totally valid to say, "I don't want to be with a person (or in a polycule) who could or would ever do that," and end things on the spot. You do not owe anyone a second chance once they have harmed you.

Putting them together

Neither coercive control nor toxic behaviour are acceptable in any kind of relationship, intimate or otherwise. Even in the absence of coercive control, toxic behaviour can certainly be considered abusive, and one or two instances of toxic behaviour might in fact be the starting point for a coercive control dynamic. Such behaviours may be the red flags or warning signs of the beginnings of a pattern of harm. A pattern always starts somewhere, after all; abuse rarely shows up all in one shot. It escalates once a person is already feeling attached and has something to lose by leaving.

If you're experiencing toxic behaviour from a partner, but it hasn't crossed a clear line for you, this is where your sense of discernment becomes extremely valuable. Difficult times happen in every relationship; over time, you'll always discover things you don't like about your partners, or have experiences where you'd like them to have behaved better. But remember, a lot of abusers get away with their abuse by making their target question their own perceptions or experiences. And unfortunately, some abusers are very skilled manipulators who are invested in making sure their victims remain under their spell. Are you giving them the benefit of the doubt and being compassionate, or are you being manipulated into letting someone cross your boundaries? It can be hard to tell.

Remember, too, that abusers aren't necessarily following some sort of grand plan or playbook; their behaviour may stem from all kinds of sources, but only a small percentage are predators in the strict sense of knowing exactly what they plan to do ahead of time and finding someone to do it to. For many abusers, whether they engage in toxic behaviours or build a pattern of coercive control, it's a matter of having the right combination of emotional problems, toxic beliefs (such as ones about entitlement, gender roles or what behaviours are acceptable when one is angry) and lack of willingness to do the work required to change when it's clear they are doing harm. Don't look for evidence of an evil master plan in order to decide whether someone is being abusive. It probably won't be there, but your experience is still real.

This is another reason why the "is this abuse?" question isn't necessarily the right one to ask. With toxic behaviour, you may decide it's *not* abuse—and if your internal flowchart leads to "then I should stay and work through this," that might keep you in a relationship that is not loving and not nourishing you. And we think people should be in relationships that are loving and nourishing.

This is a good place to return to our foundational question: "Is this relationship loving?" If your answer is "no," then you may decide that it's time to end the relationship regardless of whether, for you, it crosses the line into abuse, and regardless of whether you're ready to label someone as an abuser.

Missing stairs and other bad actors

Many domestic violence researchers refer to *situational* and *characterological* violence. Daniel Joseph Friend et al. explain that situational violence is "mutual, low-level violence (i.e., pushing or grabbing) perpetrated by both partners as a means of conflict management," whereas characterological violence is when a person uses violence to induce fear in their victim in order to manipulate and control them. The researchers specify that the psychological abuse in situational violence is "similar to the psychological abuse seen in characterological violence, but it occurs less frequently and is absent of controlling and dominating behaviors." (This concept maps onto the distinction we've drawn between coercive control and toxic behaviour.)

As discussed in the article, many couples resort to situational violence during conflict, and these couples tend to respond well to interventions such as therapy—but it's important to first ensure coercive control is not present, because characterologically violent people might retaliate against their victims, for example if the victim says something the perpetrator doesn't like during a therapy session.

The word "characterological" refers to a problem with a person's character, meaning personality. In the psychological literature, this idea describes a person's long-term, often lifelong, pattern of thinking and behaviour: a tendency to see themselves as the victim, to believe that violence is often legitimate, to feel entitled to certain kinds of deference, and so on. For our purposes, the idea here is not to make a connection between characterological violence and personality per se, and we're not here to diagnose people with disorders (or suggest that you try to, either). The important idea is the notion of a repeated pattern over time—in this case, a pattern of doing harm to partners and otherwise being "bad actors," meaning people who consistently return to the same problematic and harmful behaviours across numerous situations and partnerships.

We contend that characterologically violent people include many of the folks we call missing stairs. The blogger Cliff Pervocracy coined the term *a missing stair* to describe a dangerous person within a community whom everybody has just gotten used to working around or warning each other about—like a missing stair in a staircase—instead of setting clear boundaries or enacting direct consequences for the person's bad behaviour. If you're part of a nonmonogamous, kink or sex-positive community, you may have encountered this phenomenon, or maybe even "tripped on a missing stair" yourself. This scenario isn't inherent to nonmonogamy itself, but it may become relevant if you get involved in community groups. It's not in any way exclusive to sex- and relationship-related communities, either—you might know a missing stair in your workplace, at your gym or in any number of other settings. But it is particularly challenging within communities focused on sex and relationships, whose norms might be really different than the ones you'd find in a workplace, for example.

In addition, sometimes a missing stair is in fact a community leader of some kind, or otherwise in a powerful position, with the ability to ostracize or otherwise punish anyone who speaks out. The #MeToo movement exposed a long list of such people in the entertainment industry and well beyond. Unlike major Hollywood executives, not everyone can employ fixers, go-betweens or pricey PR agencies to try to shape the public's perception of events, or force people to sign nondisclosure agreements after they're subjected to harm. But in smaller communities and subcultures, small acts of exclusion and retribution can do a great deal of damage, and such acts—or the threat of them—may effectively serve as tools to silence people.

Arguably, this kind of situation might exceed the usual definition of a missing stair. Sometimes, successful exclusion means that most people in a community don't know the stair is missing at all, as opposed to knowing and not warning people about it. Sometimes survivors actively try to warn others but don't have the reach, credibility or power to do so effectively. And sometimes, powerful institutions intervene to cover up harm with the goal of preserving their own reputation, whether that's a brand image or a flock of faithful worshipers.

There is one common principle here, though: In social or group settings, whether a person's repeated harm is widely known but not discussed, or a secret kept through coercion or threat, any newcomer to the situation is not getting the information they need to make an enlightened decision about how to interact with the person, and they may end up at greater risk as a result.

Another abuse technique that can wreak havoc in communities is known as DARVO. DARVO, which stands for "deny, attack, and reverse victim and offender" is a tactic described by psychology researcher Jennifer J. Freyd at the University of Oregon in the late 1990s. As Freyd writes: "The perpetrator or offender may Deny the behavior, Attack the individual doing the confronting, and Reverse the roles of Victim and Offender such that the perpetrator assumes the victim role and turns the true victim—or the whistle blower—into an alleged offender."

DARVO committed by characterological abusers can be devastatingly effective because many of these folks are exceptionally good manipulators. If they suspect someone might report on their bad behaviour, they may try to "get ahead of the story" by telling their own story of victimization first. Or they may genuinely believe themselves to be the victim, possibly because of their own sense of aggrieved entitlement, or possibly because of their partner's own reactive toxic behaviours, which they may then use as an excuse for their own. In his landmark book *Why Does He Do That?* domestic violence expert Lundy Bancroft writes at length about abusers' own sense of victimization.

Whole books have been written—and more need to be written—on the subject of dealing with abuse in community contexts. We've listed a few in the resources. This isn't one of those books, so we'll leave it there. For now, we just want to name that these patterns exist, and prepare you in some small way to recognize them when and if they do.

Warning signs of abuse

The following are some signs of a potentially abusive relationship or polycule, especially if they happen persistently over time:

- Your partner controls who you talk with or see and where you go.

- Your partner controls your access to money.
- Your partner destroys your property.
- Your partner threatens you with violence or behaves in a physically intimidating way.
- You feel afraid of your partner.
- You feel frequently demeaned or humiliated by a partner or metamour.
- You feel pressured or forced to engage in sex or kink that you don't want.
- You feel that acceptance by your polycule depends on your participation in group sex.
- A partner or metamour reads your messages, emails, journals or other private information without your permission, or wants to make a rule that these must be shared.
- A partner or metamour threatens to harm you, your children or pets, or themselves if you leave them.
- You find yourself doubting your own grip on reality, especially as it pertains to a relationship.
- You feel like a partner or metamour is "two different people," or like you never know whether they will hurt you or support you in any given moment.
- You feel discouraged from communicating with your metamours.
- You feel you are expected to keep secrets from or about your metamours.
- You're made to feel that you are "not really nonmonogamous" if you express a concern, ask for a limit or communicate your feelings.
- You feel shamed for seeking out social supports outside your relationship or polycule.
- A partner or metamour invalidates your feelings or internal experience.
- A partner or metamour claims to be a gatekeeper, or the only or best source of reliable information about nonmonogamy.
- You feel that no one else will want to be with you or "put up with you" if you leave.
- You feel like the sole problem in a relationship or polycule.

The best resource for people in nonmonogamous relationships that might be harming them is The Network/La Red, or TNLR (tnlr.org). It's a survivor-led organization in the United States that specifically addresses partner abuse among queer, kinky and nonmonogamous people, so you can ask for help without having to go through the whole "why the nonmonogamy isn't the problem here" routine. TNLR has a hotline and informational resources. Unfortunately, we're not aware of a similar organization in Canada, but many local domestic violence and survivor support organizations are increasingly inclusive of the full spectrum of gender, sexuality and relationship diversity, and many 2SLGBTQI+ organizations offer support for people experiencing relationship abuse.

Abuse in nonmonogamy

While nonmonogamy can be challenging, especially as you experience the early growing pains of figuring it all out for the first time, it's not supposed to be all about suffering. Nonmonogamy is not about tolerating behaviours and actions that harm you. It's also not about letting yourself be pushed into relationships, agreements or sex that you don't fully want.

Plenty of abuse in nonmonogamy looks exactly like it does in monogamous situations. Often, there's nothing special or distinct about it. But a few manifestations are facilitated by nonmonogamy itself, so let's take a moment to look at some of them.

MANIPULATION OF NONMONOGAMOUS VALUES

Sometimes, a person may manipulate the discourse and values of nonmonogamy to bludgeon their partner into keeping quiet about their objections or agreeing to things they don't feel ready for or don't want at all.

This is similar to how members of any values-based or politicized community or subculture can weaponize the values of the group or system against other members. Examples abound. For instance, in the realm of spirituality and wellness, Andrea once heard of a reiki practitioner who was diagnosed with cancer; her colleagues blamed her for her illness, saying that if she'd been practising energy work properly on herself, she would never have gotten sick. And of course, cults are well-known for exploiting their members by convincing them it's for their own self-improvement or spiritual gain, twisting people's genuine desire for enlightenment into a way to extract profit or maintain control. One recent and well-known example is NXIVM, but the list is long and ever-growing.

In the realm of social justice, Kai Cheng Thom notes that certain communities take the idea of bodily autonomy so far that some members think it's wrong to intervene when someone is suicidal, which means, as a result, that more trans women end up dying by suicide. Social justice spaces in general are vulnerable to this kind of misuse of their principles, such as when an abusive person manipulates their victim's compassion, awareness of their privilege or desire to do the right thing to make them believe they should tolerate physical or emotional abuse, or even that they are themselves an abuser. One social media meme encapsulates this twisty thinking: "Oh, sorry, I didn't know you had trauma. You can continue being mean to me now." It might not be easy to set boundaries with people when you're trying to live out your political principles, but absorbing abuse and harm from your comrades is not supposed to be the price you pay for making the world better.

In sex-positive communities, people can find themselves pressured to be so "positive" that they engage in sexual practices that cross their boundaries, such as having group sex when they don't want to just so they don't "spoil the fun" for everyone else. If you're involved in a kink community, you may have come across dominants who use rhetoric such as "if you were a *real* submissive, you would do as I say," or conversely (but just as troubling), "if you were a *real* dominant, you'd behave the way I think you should." Sometimes, people are led to believe that submissives' consent isn't really necessary because they implicitly consent to being treated in certain ways simply by identifying themselves as submissive. People are also led to believe that dominants are never at risk for having their own consent violated, and that if they were truly dominant, such a thing would be impossible anyway because they'd just use their domly domliness to shut down whatever was happening that they didn't like. All these scenarios obscure the humanity of the individuals involved and objectify them within their preferred roles.

These are all different contexts, but the common ground is that they involve a person or a group of people twisting shared values in such a way as to shut down an individual's human needs, fears, concerns or objections. They are profoundly unloving ways of employing philosophical principles, practices or values to do harm. As Kai Cheng Thom writes, "Any ideology, no matter how liberatory in theory, can be corrupted for the purpose of domination under real world conditions."

A sort of inversion can also happen: Mononormative values can be used to shame you so that you believe, at some level, that you are causing harm simply by being nonmonogamous, and you need to compensate somehow for your very presence in a partner's life. Or you must agree to systems of control to prevent others from feeling afraid or insecure.

This means you need to watch out for people who treat the principles of nonmonogamy as more important than the real-life feelings of the people they're involved with. This takes us back to our axiom: The people in the relationship are more important than the relationship. They're also more important than the abstract ideals of nonmonogamy.

MANIPULATION OF POLYCULES AND OTHER PARTNERSHIP STRUCTURES

It can be easy to use the structures of nonmonogamy to enact harm. For example, in a triad, if two people agree on something and the third person doesn't, those two people need to take great care to avoid ganging up on the outlier and pressuring them to agree to something they don't want just because they're outnumbered. The same applies to larger networks, too. Also, a hinge or pivot partner in a vee or larger structure can blame everything that's going wrong on the partner who's not in the room at the time, and thus avoid taking responsibility for their own choices (see pages 131–133 and 342–343).

Situations like this aren't inherently abusive; sometimes, they're just about messy communication or lack of skill, and those things can be fixed. But someone who wants to do harm, or simply doesn't care whether they're doing harm, can use the slippages and messiness that often crop up in nonmonogamous structures to hurt others on purpose—or to maintain a sense of control and manipulate people into doing what the abuser wants them to do.

When a whole polycule gets involved, though, things can get particularly bad. This is where some cult theory can be useful. In cults, resources are funnelled inward from rank-and-file members toward a central figure, the cult leader. The leader keeps a close cadre of intimates around them, but instills a sense of instability among the members of this inner circle to keep them off-balance, and thus trying to please. They may move up or down in rank, or fall in or out of favour. All of this instability keeps the leader in control. In a polycule, this kind of manipulation can manifest as "good partner/bad partner" dynamics—with bonus points if everyone thinks they are the good partner and someone else is the bad partner! This tracks with the dynamic that Lundy Bancroft discusses in *Why Does He Do That?* in which an abuser's new partner becomes their biggest ally against the previous, abused partner—only here, it's translated into concurrent relationships.

It's also worth noting that, just as cult leaders are usually (but not always) cisgender men who primarily keep women in their circle of intimates, this form of abusive polycule dynamic is most common when there's a cisgender man at the centre of it. There are a variety of reasons for this, tied to the same reasons why new partners of abusive men tend to become allies in abuse of past partners: internalized misogyny that teaches women to compete with and turn on one another; the phenomenon Kate Manne calls "himpathy," in which people of all genders are socialized to privilege men's feelings; and a relative willingness to excuse men's bad behaviour while holding that of other genders up to closer scrutiny.

Essayist Barucha Peller has described the patriarchal phenomenon of "polyamory as a reserve army of care labour," where men engage in emotional "hedging" in which "men can 'hedge,' or invest, in various women, to the degree that they want to, and benefit from the returns until the investment is no longer worthwhile." On the way this affects the relationships among women involved with the same man, Peller remarks, "in polyamorous relationships where men have more than one partner it is a common occurrence that women end up competing with each other for the little bit of attention or return on their care labor."

We discuss triangulation more generally in chapters 6 and 19, but when a whole polycule becomes invested in the dynamic, particularly when one person is scapegoated, and particularly if the dynamic is isolating in some other way—such as an enmeshed, live-in polycule where group members spend most of their time together—it can easily become abusive.

Nonmonogamy offers many wonderful opportunities to expand your networks of support and care beyond a nuclear-family dyad. But there can be a dark side to it if your intimate networks become your sole source of support. If your polycule is your family, the threat of exclusion and ostracism can create powerful pressures to conform and comply. We're not saying by any means that these structures are inherently abusive, only that they present opportunities for a very specific kind of abuse. In monogamous relationships, an abuser's family can often become complicit in the abuse—but people don't tend to share emotional (or even physical) intimacy with their in-laws the way they might with members of their polycules.

RULES-LAWYERING, "DEBATE" AND OTHER TROLLING-STYLE TACTICS

These tactics can take any number of forms, but the essence is that if you're taking a rules-based approach to nonmonogamy, you may end up in situations where you're arguing about the technicalities and minutiae of an agreement rather than about the feelings, emotions and concrete harms that may have emerged from it. It's possible to follow a rule to the letter and still do harm. "You said you wanted me to check in before having sex with someone new. I did check in, five years ago when I first met them, and you said it would probably be fine if ever it happened. How was I supposed to know I needed to check again before suddenly having sex with them last night right before our date?"

An abusive person might turn any discussion of unacceptable behaviour into a philosophical debate about values or try to prove that you're objectively wrong to be upset—instead of addressing your feelings. Or they might make it so onerous to have a conversation about your needs and boundaries that it becomes too emotionally costly to bring it up at all. When the focus is on being "right" and not on addressing a problem in good faith, this can be an aspect of abuse.

Someone who truly wants to do harm might even engage in what's called malicious compliance, which means doing something on purpose that's well within the rules but that they know will wreak havoc or cause hurt. Imagine a scenario where a person wants to buy a second-hand car and the seller insists on being paid in cash; the buyer is annoyed by this requirement and decides to pay using dozens of buckets of loose change. Now imagine this attitude applied to nonmonogamous relationships. Not cool. For example, if two partners agree to tell each other if they're attracted to someone else, a maliciously compliant partner could choose to share that news either when they know there's no space to have a meaningful conversation about it, or at a time when it's calculated to be maximally disruptive. Or, if two partners agree to do some renovations in their shared home, a maliciously compliant partner might strategically knock out a wall and leave debris everywhere right before the other partner brings someone new home for the first time.

Protective factors of nonmonogamy

While it offers unique niches for abusive behaviour, nonmonogamy can also offer some protection from abuse.

For example, if you're involved with several people and one of them becomes abusive, it can be harder for them to manipulate you or induce self-doubt if you have other loving relationships that don't follow that pattern and reflect a more accurate understanding of who you are. The classic abuser statement that "nobody will ever love you better than me" doesn't work as well when others are actively loving you better! Also, if others in the polycule have healthy approaches to relationships, it can be harder for one person to isolate and control another person when everyone involved is part of a network of lovers, the members of which spend time with each other and notice each other's emotional and physical states. There might be opportunities to find support and understanding that might be much harder to achieve in a monogamous framework. The same applies, of course, if you have a strong and supportive network of friends who aren't part of your polycule.

If you're a member of a nonmonogamous scene that includes a "missing stair," while this is far from ideal, the whisper network in that scene may warn you about who to avoid—a benefit you won't get from, say, a random bar hookup or online dating. It's also fair to ask a person's other partners—or exes—for references, much as people often do in BDSM circles.

If you have been abused, you may also have access to validation and support from others within the community that can be hard to find in monogamous culture. This is especially true if the abuser has been involved with others within the same community. It certainly doesn't make the abuse itself any more acceptable, but that sense of mutual support can provide a kind of closure and warmth that's really valuable.

We're not bringing this up to provide false assurances; abuse very much still happens in nonmonogamy. But it is worth noting these kinds of examples because they provide an argument for cultivating nonmonogamous community and connections both within and outside your personal network of nonmonogamous relationships. There are lots of good reasons to do this beyond abuse situations, but these kinds of connections can really help if they're already in place should things go in the wrong direction within one of your relationships. Plus, at some point you may yourself be the supportive person who makes the difference in another person's life.

A note about kink

This book isn't an in-depth exploration of kink and BDSM dynamics, but we do want to say a couple of things about them here, both in general and because of the well-known overlap between kink and nonmonogamy.

Some people think that kink and BDSM are automatically abusive. If you're one of those people, we'd strongly encourage you to learn more about the many ways kink and BDSM can be positive, powerful, life-enriching practices. We're not going to get into an elaborate defence here, but we'd suggest reading some of the resources listed at the end of this book.

Let's assume, for our purposes right now, that you're generally kink-friendly. Maybe you're of the mindset that it's not for you, but you have no problem with people's sexual quirks. Maybe you've played around a bit at the edges of BDSM and enjoy it on occasion. Or maybe you're heavily involved in BDSM, Leather, fetish or kink communities and relationships. Regardless, you may have seen or experienced things that pushed up against the edges of what you consider safe or consensual—stuff that made you uncomfortable and left you wondering, "Was that abusive, or am I just not open-minded enough?" Or you may have witnessed or heard about unambiguous instances of abuse or coercion in your local BDSM community despite all the talk about consent. You may also have experienced abuse yourself within a kinky encounter or relationship.

Honestly, someone should write a whole book about this topic, because abuse and nonconsent can play out in kink in some pretty specific ways that are worthy of scrutiny. For our purposes here, we'd just like to make a few basic points.

Most importantly: Nothing about kink makes nonconsensual or coercive behaviour okay. We complicate that in kink with ideas such as "consensual nonconsent" and certain frameworks for D/s and M/s relationships, particularly the full-time kind. Kinky love might look really different from vanilla love in some ways: We might bestow or treasure a bruise the way a non-kinky person gives or receives a bouquet of flowers, and we might hear or use a nasty name as a term of endearment. And certain acts of control, dominance or possessiveness might in fact be agreed-upon expressions of love. But in all these contexts, consent is still necessary, true coercion is unacceptable, and the principle of "is this relationship loving?" still applies. No matter how hardcore your kinks, playing with them—and even living them 24/7—should lift up all participants, not break them down.

BDSM players of all kinds, remember that part of the "job" of being kinky is that no matter how wild you get, some part of you must always remain alert to the possibility of harm and injury—your own or someone else's—and keep watch accordingly. Part of that involves planning, negotiating, and learning about (and practising!) safety measures and techniques appropriate to the kind of play you want to do. Part of it involves remaining grounded and aware while you play, and keeping the lines of communication open, whether you use safewords, agreed-upon nonverbal signals or just regular old talking. And part of it involves proper aftercare, which should also be discussed ahead of time and adjusted as needed. (Should *everyone* think this way about *all* kinds of physical and sexual encounters? Why, yes! But that's a manifesto for another day.)

Role-players, your characters and personas must never become excuses to behave in ways that are nonconsensual or that enact real harm on others.

Fetishists, remember that the bearer of your fetish is still a human being. (Other people are real in kink, too!) Make sure that any consensual objectification you engage in still leaves the other person feeling desired, appreciated and respected, not reduced and erased.

Submissives, no matter how fully you give your submission to someone, it remains yours to give—and yours to withdraw if it's not held in a way that respects your consent and your inherent worth as a person. You need to own your power before you can legitimately offer it to someone else. And, when submitting, you must also always understand your dominant as a full and real human being whose consent matters as much as yours. Beware of objectifying the people you kneel to. And always remember that submission is not powerlessness: You, too, have the power to harm within your chosen role.

Dominants, no matter how fully you consensually dominate, possess or objectify someone, they must remain a full human being with dignity and worth in your eyes, and their well-being and safety must matter to you above the satisfaction of your desires. Self-restraint is strength. If you're not in charge of yourself, you're not fit to dominate anyone else. And, when dominating, you must remember that you are allowed to have feelings, needs and limits because you, too, are a full human being and not simply a need-fulfillment machine. Your humanity, and the vulnerability it comes with, is a dimension of your power. Get comfortable with that, and don't hide behind your dominance.

Finally, in nonmonogamy it's important to remember that everyone's consent is important if your play crosses into others' space. For example, don't suddenly turn what started as a playful, vanilla threesome into a nonconsent role-play or humiliation scene between two people unless it's been negotiated with the third person, too. And if you're in a 24/7 relationship that has rules about reporting back on communications or sexual activity with others, make sure the other people consent to the kinds of information being shared.

Kinky people of all varieties can sometimes get deeply involved in their explorations and communities, in ways that can become totally absorbing or feel like a full-time lifestyle. There's nothing wrong with this, per se, but try to maintain a life that still includes the rest of the world, your important non-kink relationships (friends, family, colleagues), the non-kinky aspects of yourself (professional pursuits, creative practices, spirituality, family ties, physical health), and a general sense of balance and perspective. Kink is not a cult, but folks who get so wrapped up in kink that they lose their ties to other important aspects of their lives and identities can end up more vulnerable to the predators and boundary-pushers who inevitably show up in all communities—and these people can use the language, equipment and practices of kink as tools to enact serious harm. It's wise to go slow, try things carefully and stay grounded as you fly!

Making the call

Sometimes it's hard to decide when to end things. Often a relationship slides from "good" into "harmful" slowly over time, so you're hooked into it—emotionally, practically, maybe even legally—when things start to go really awry. But remember, relationships are not supposed to hurt all the time. They're not supposed to bring you more pain than joy, or even come close to the 50-50 mark. They're supposed to help you be bigger, not smaller. They're supposed to be good to you and good for you! And you don't have to wait until there's zero good stuff left before you break up.

If you have a pattern of running from your intimate relationships at the very first sign of difficulty, you might want to do some introspective work to figure out why, and whether that's ultimately in your own best interests. But even then, as we've said, it is still entirely your right to walk away at any time you decide you're done.

Even if a relationship never crosses the line into what you would consider abuse, you are still within your rights to end it for any reason you see fit. Let's be really clear on this: You don't need anyone's permission to end your relationship. Your reasons don't have to be "good enough" or "valid" by anyone's measure other than your own. You don't even need to be able to explain your choice (though there are lots of reasons you might want to). This is the essence of consent.

Of course, ideally, you're able to engage in a conversation about what's working and what's not, and negotiate something that gets everyone's needs met. And if that doesn't work, ideally, a breakup should be kind, gentle and amicable, with enough goodwill and common ground that you can retain a friendship, or at least a respectful and warm, if distant, acquaintanceship. But not every relationship can end in an ideal way, and ultimately, your no is enough. In fact, the rest of those more pleasant options are only possible if you accept, at baseline, that each person has the right to say no at any time, without explanation. It's okay to give up. You're allowed to throw in the towel. It doesn't make you a bad person.

If you're having a hard time deciding, you might want to check out the book *Should I Stay or Should I Go?* by Lundy Bancroft, or work through the 36 questions presented by the book *Too Good to Leave, Too Bad to Stay* by Mira Kirshenbaum.

If you've been abused, now what?

If you are experiencing coercive control, the situation is overwhelmingly unlikely to change, no matter what promises your partner or polycule makes (apologies are part of the cycle of abuse). If you want the abuse to stop, we're sorry to say that eventually you are going to have to leave. This might require an elaborate plan to get out safely if your physical safety is being threatened. It might be as simple as sending a text message. Or pretty much anything in between, depending on your situation. In any case, get your support lined up as best you can so you're not in this alone—practical stuff if necessary, such as help with packing, plus emotional support from friends and loved ones and, if you are able, by finding a therapist.

Leaving might take a long time as you slowly heal and rally your energy and support systems to make the jump. Many people whose lives are entwined with those of their abusers also try to bide their time while they put legal, logistical and financial plans into place. The TNLR website includes a section on safety planning, and the folks at the TNLR hotline can help walk you through your options. Leaving might take you a few tries—that's not uncommon. Or it might be a fast and firm exit. It's beyond the scope of this book to give you advice on your specific situation. What's important is that you get out of the harmful situation as soon as you possibly can, without placing yourself at additional risk.

Then you'll need to deal with the immediate aftermath, which may include protecting yourself from stalking, harassment or further attempts at violence. Many abusers engage in smear campaigns after their partners leave them, or rally friend groups and communities to ostracize or monitor the victim (or both), sometimes even leveraging a community's abuse and consent reporting mechanisms to do so. As we've mentioned, people are also often at the greatest risk of violence right after leaving an abusive relationship. If you're feeling scared, you likely have reason to be. Take whatever precautions you deem necessary. Your safety is the most important thing here.

In the less immediate term, you will need to heal. That may look very different depending on your particular experience, your needs and the support you have available. Friends, family and a good therapist can be invaluable; you may also turn to a spiritual practice, make art, write, exercise, make a career change, get a totally new hairstyle, move to a new city, leave a community or reconnect with one, or find any number of other ways to reclaim yourself and rebuild. Reading stories from other survivors can be very healing, as can—in the case of serial abusers—connecting with others who've been harmed by the same person. Don't despair. You are not alone.

You may also need to make various practical decisions. For instance, you may need to pursue legal measures such as filing for divorce and navigating child custody, or engage in processes such as selling a home or breaking a lease. You may need to make decisions about disclosure: Do you want to disclose the abuse publicly, to select people, or only confidentially? Also, do you want to pursue legal recourse of any kind, undertake community justice or restorative justice measures, or simply move on? Make sure that whatever you choose to do is based on your own needs and goals, and not on pressure from others to take the measures they think are appropriate. You know you best.

Every situation is unique. There is no one right way to do any of these things, no perfect prescription, and no required timeline.

Just as experiencing an abusive monogamous relationship can change your relationships going forward, experiencing abusive nonmonogamy can change the way you engage in nonmonogamous relationships. You might decide you don't want to be nonmonogamous at all anymore, or that you want to take a break from it (many people take a pause from relationships entirely after an abusive one—it's up to you). You might also find that you have new challenges that you didn't have before. For example, maybe you had never experienced jealousy, but exposure to abusive triangulation now makes you hypervigilant about your partners' other relationships. Or you may have once been inclined toward kitchen table polyamory (see chapter 19), but now you can only engage in strictly parallel relationships. You may get triggered by anything that feels like a lack of transparency, or on the flip side, like your privacy has been violated. You might panic at the idea of conflict, even if you were once someone who communicated with ease and confidence.

It might take time to figure out how you've been affected and to heal, and things may never be the same as they once were. As you engage in new relationships and your intimacy and investment deepens, you may keep discovering new wounds you didn't realize were there. We're not going to try to put a positive spin on this: It sucks, and no one had the right to do this to you. Try to be gentle and patient with yourself. And if you're in a relationship with an abuse survivor, please remember that what happened to them wasn't their fault—and any effects their trauma has on your relationship are very much not about you. Be kind, and learn what you can about abuse so that you can be a supportive partner.

How did this happen?

If you've been in an abusive relationship, it can be tempting to blame yourself for "letting it" happen, for making poor partner choices, for not exercising good judgment, and so on. Sometimes, self-blame can help you regain a sense of control—if you did this wrong, then all you have to do is get it right next time and you won't be abused again. Strangely, self-blame can make you feel safer.

It's true that you can learn to look for warning signs, get better at setting boundaries, and so on. This is the kind of thing you can work on in therapy or other kinds of self-work. Introspection is not a bad thing, and neither is honing your judgment or your self-esteem. But don't go down the rabbit hole of self-blame. Nobody would date abusive people if they had "abuser" tattooed on their foreheads; abusers are often charming, warm and sweet at first, and they sometimes engage in what's called love-bombing, which mimics the way NRE works in a lot of non-abusive relationships. Some abusers are really strategic about approaching potential partners when they're vulnerable and meeting all their needs at first. Many have lots of friends who have never seen them with their charming mask off, and many have high standing in their communities. In nonmonogamous situations, they may even have a partner or two who they're not abusive with (or whom they haven't abused yet) who may act as cover (or even bait) initially, but who may later take part in group gaslighting or abusive "good partner/bad partner" dynamics.

Also, nobody would end up in abusive relationships if those dynamics were enacted right from the start. Abuse generally escalates slowly over time. It often starts with boundary-testing, where an abuser does subtle things at first to see what they can get away with. Of course, this often happens while you're in the throes of NRE and willing to give plenty of benefit of the doubt as you get to know them. The escalation of abusive behaviour often occurs only when you're already invested in the relationship and really want to make it work.

It's not your fault. Do not take the blame for another person's harmful behaviour. Recognize that you made the best decisions you could at each step, even if you would do things differently if you'd known then what you know now.

As well, abusive people often target very specific traits in others, and these are not bad traits. In her book *Stop Signs: Recognizing, Avoiding, and Escaping Abusive Relationships*, author Lynn Fairweather writes about "super traits." The language she uses is based on a cishet (cisgender and heterosexual) model of abusive relationships, but the concept applies regardless of the genders and sexual orientations of the people involved.

> In her book *Women Who Love Psychopaths*, psychologist Sandra L. Brown, founder of The Institute for Relational Harm Reduction and Public Psychopathy Education, writes about "super traits" in women who become involved with dangerous men. Most of the characteristics are seemingly positive, but when presented to an abusive mind, they become weaknesses ripe for exploitation. While all abusers are not psychopaths, their characteristics often match up, as does the mental and physical damage they inflict on intimate partners. Sandra's discoveries are important because they warn about traits we may unconsciously possess that enhance our vulnerability to a batterer's victim-tuned radar. The super-traits include:
>
> - Hyper-empathy
> - Extreme altruism
> - High relationship investment and high attachment
> - Hyper-focus on the sentimental aspects of the relationship
> - Low impulsiveness
> - High resourcefulness
>
> In my extensive work with abused women, I have found that women who become involved with pathological and nonpathological abusers alike share similar traits. Women who are "savers"—those scoring high in empathy, altruism, tolerance, and sentimentality—will almost always be drawn to a relationship where they think they can help or reform a "diamond in the rough" partner. Highly invested, nonimpulsive, and attached women will often try to stick it out and fix a bad situation.

Those who are highly resourceful frequently try to handle risky scenarios all on their own without seeking the necessary assistance of others.

If you were targeted for abuse, it is likely that you possess these "super traits," and that is nothing at all to be ashamed of. It takes a special kind of evil to turn these wonderful, valuable human traits into weapons. This is especially devastating since there seems to be a cultural idea that people who've experienced abuse are somehow weaker, more unstable or more manipulable than people who haven't—and abusive people will turn this idea against you in the process of abusing you, making you believe you are weak and unstable. There's also a related idea that people with strong partners cannot be abusive; nothing could be further from the truth.

If abuse has happened to you, it wasn't your fault. Avoiding future abuse doesn't mean snuffing out these qualities, but learning to recognize dangerous and exploitative people early on and swiftly removing them from your life.

If you think you might be abusing someone

When you read the descriptions of coercive control and toxic behaviour earlier, or the lists of red flags, did you recognize any of your own behaviour?

Maybe you learned how to be abusive because you were raised in an abusive environment. Maybe you're terrified of being powerless or out of control, and so you control your partners or try to maintain the upper hand as a way of managing this fear. Maybe you have a hard time being emotionally vulnerable, so you shield yourself from that by lashing out or treating others with contempt. Maybe you lack empathy and just don't really care whether you harm others—which may or may not be part of a personality disorder or a mental illness. Maybe you're dealing with addiction, and when you're drunk or high you have a hard time controlling violent or angry impulses. Maybe you're highly sensitive to criticism or are shame-bound, and you gaslight your partners because it hurts too much to be held accountable when you cause harm.

We hope you want to stop, and if you do, we hope you take action. To get there, you need to stop rationalizing and excusing your behaviour, or blaming it on others. Depending on how bad things have gotten, you might need to remove yourself from the situation so that you stop posing a danger to the people around you—which might mean leaving a relationship temporarily or permanently. If you're struggling with addiction, you need to get sober. And you need to get professional help to find your way out of this situation, heal your own wounds, manage your emotions (especially anger and fear), learn better communication, handle any mental illness or substance problems you're dealing with, and become a better person. This might mean a recovery program, therapy, medication, support groups, anger management classes, or any number of other strategies depending on your situation.

Recognize, too, that on top of harming people close to you, your abusive actions may have terrible consequences *for you*, up to and including life-altering legal repercussions. You can stop this behaviour before external forces do it for you in ways that might be pretty awful.

It is possible to change. The responsibility is yours. You can stop, but you need to decide to, and you need to make concrete changes. Start now.

On the use and misuse of advice

Remember how we mentioned earlier that any system or tool can be twisted and misused to cause harm? That's true for relationship advice in general, and for this chapter in particular. It's not hard to picture a scenario where someone reads this book or this chapter and twists up our words to do harm. "Remember that time you got angry at me? That's abuse! You're an abuser and I'm going to tell everyone if you don't do what I want!"

We can't stop this from happening (which, honestly, is pretty distressing), but we can say a couple of things in the hope of mitigating it.

First, this book is intended for you to use to better understand yourself and think through what you want, need and value in the realm of nonmonogamy and relationships, and to help you make decisions that bring you toward integrity, kindness and, ideally, joy. It's not meant as a set of standards with which to shame or bludgeon others, or for others to use this way against you.

Second, pay attention to how you react to feeling hurt or harmed within your relationships. If, when you feel hurt or distressed, you find yourself reacting by trying to control your partners' actions or force them to do what you want, punishing them for their failures, taking revenge, making fresh rules, or feeling better and safer when they're off-balance or under your thumb in some way, that may be an indication that you are becoming abusive. A healthy relationship is not adversarial, with someone winning and someone losing. If you feel good when someone else feels bad, that means you have an emotional incentive to harm people—and that's a problem.

In contrast, if your hurt or distress pushes you to try and fix or solve things, examine and correct your own behaviour, set clearer boundaries, ask for what you need, empathize with the other person's point of view and listen to their side of the story, collaborate, and ultimately seek harmony and peace, chances are that you're not an abuser—emotional chaos is not rewarding to you. However, your general goodwill may make you vulnerable to others' manipulation or poor behaviour. And you might be generally acting in good faith, but sometimes tip into toxic behaviours, either as a result of old patterns re-emerging or in response to toxic treatment by a partner or polycule.

To the extent that you're willing and able, we hope you use this book and this chapter as a tool for self-reflection to help you think through your own situation, but not as a tool to try and prove that you're right, push someone else to change, or make them feel bad about themselves. If you believe you are being abused, your best bet is almost always going to be to leave, get support and take care of yourself, not to fix or control someone else.

From this point onward, everything in this book is written from the assumption that abuse is not present in the relationships, unless otherwise mentioned.

QUESTIONS TO ASK YOURSELF

This chapter is already filled with questions and checklists, so we'll keep this section short. Here are a few final questions to reflect on:

- Are my partners or my polycule my sole sources of support? What other resources do I have available to me?
- Are there patterns of behaviour I have witnessed or experienced, in my intimate relationships or my family of origin, that I want to learn to leave behind? Do I need to seek help for this work, and if so, where can I seek it?
- What does accountability look like to me, for myself and for other people? Does my approach ultimately lead to healthier and more resilient relationships?
- To whom would I turn for support if I were being harmed in my relationships or polycule? To whom would I turn for support if someone told me I had done harm?

Part 2

A Nonmonogamy Toolkit

For those so inclined, nonmonogamy can be pretty awesome. But as you get deeper into this book and read about all the challenges ahead, you might wonder why anyone would walk down this road. You might be tempted to throw up your hands and say, "Nonmonogamy sounds too hard!"

We don't agree—at least not for the reasons people say. It's true that for some people, the costs of nonmonogamy will outweigh the benefits, and they might decide to return to exclusivity. But developing the skills to be successful in nonmonogamous relationships? That *is* hard work for many people. Learning to understand and express your needs, to take responsibility for your emotions, to hear and understand others, and to seek collaborative solutions can all be challenging. However, once you've developed those skills, nonmonogamous relationships aren't inherently any harder than other relationships. The skills we're talking about aren't unique to nonmonogamy; they'll benefit any relationship. So even if you decide later that nonmonogamy's not for you, the journey you took won't be a loss. But nonmonogamy in particular will be really, really challenging without those skills. They have to be learned. And, alas, they aren't often taught.

Think of it like adding compost before planting a garden, so that things will more easily grow. You're learning a way of approaching relationships that helps them run smoothly.

What skills are we talking about? Self-knowledge. Security, integrity, honesty and compassion. Communication. Understanding jealousy. These skills are not easy to master, but once you get a handle on them, all your relationships, including your intimate ones, become much easier. They're life skills, and they'll help when you're parenting your kids, negotiating chores with your roommates, or trying to navigate five generations at a family wedding.

Developing these traits is work, sure, but it's not relationship work—it's work you do on yourself. In fact, it's beneficial even if you have no relationships at all!

We discuss some big concepts in this part of the book: things like integrity, courage, worthiness and compassion. Don't get scared off. These are not states you need to attain, and there's no magic bar you need to reach before you'll be "ready" to be nonmonogamous. These principles are meant as guides, stars to navigate by. They are not innate character traits, but practices you can cultivate, skills you can learn.

Of course, a few chapters in one book can barely scratch the surface of the self-work that's involved in adjusting to nonmonogamy. What we're presenting is not a set of instructions, but a collection of principles that we believe are most important in building kind, honest open relationships. These principles are only a jumping-off point; you will need additional resources, which we've listed at the back of this book.

And if the things we discuss are linked for you to mental health issues, such as serious anxiety, depression or low self-worth, always consider getting professional help to work through those issues. We make this recommendation as people who have spent plenty of our own time in the therapist's office and have seen the transformative power of really good psychological help. Some problems can't be solved with self-help books. When you confront one of them, we urge you to get the help you need without shame or self-judgment.

It is a fault to wish to be understood before we have made ourselves clear to ourselves.
SIMONE WEIL

4 Tending Your Self

The first key element in a nonmonogamous relationship—well, really any relationship—is your relationship with your self. Of course, tending to your self is important in most areas of life, but being in multiple relationships with others can really accentuate the importance of self-care and shine a bright light on the places where you may need to make changes. This chapter focuses on some concepts that can come in handy for this purpose.

Nosce te ipsum

"Know thyself." No one will ever know themselves perfectly. But working on self-knowledge helps you figure out what you need and want, which is a solid step toward getting it, as well as your limits around what you will accept. It also helps you know what you have to offer, which helps you understand and communicate what commitments you can make to others. And if you find yourself behaving in ways you'd rather not, you need self-knowledge to figure out why you're doing it and how to change.

A willingness to question yourself, challenge yourself and explore without fear the hidden parts of you are the best tools to gain self-knowledge. Of course, people all change over time, so self-knowledge is not a one-and-done kind of job. It's important to retain a practice of introspection and self-analysis over the course of your life so that you can adapt your decisions as you learn yourself better and track the way you've shifted. But while self-knowledge can be a moving target, it is ultimately your own responsibility. When people choose not to try to know themselves, they're much more likely to end up in the relationships other people think they should have, not the relationships they want.

Part of having integrity in any relationship is taking responsibility for the emotional work you need to do. It's not easy. Most people are very good at hiding the truth about themselves from themselves. Some are very good at making everything seem like someone else's problem. Others are *too* good at taking on other people's problems as their own. No one's self-awareness is perfect. But it starts with the simple act of looking inward, of asking yourself, "What am I contributing to the problem? What are others' contributions to it?" As one of our readers once commented, "You can come with baggage, but you're responsible for knowing what's in the suitcases." This is often described as "owning your own shit." Self-awareness starts with awareness, period.

So what do you need to know? First, your needs. Most people are never taught how to figure out what they need, let alone communicate it effectively. Even for those who are really good at feeling their feelings (plenty of people aren't, for various reasons), it's normal to react to the *feeling* rather than the actual need. For example, it's common to think that when you feel angry, it's because someone else did something bad to you. So you react to that person, tell them how much they hurt you, and perhaps demand they stop. Sometimes anger really is about the thing you think it's about—anger is often an important warning sign about how you're being treated. But sometimes the anger is about a need that's not being acknowledged or expressed, or one you didn't even realize you have.

Getting in touch with those needs can be really hard. So working to understand the needs driving strong emotions is a valuable practice. Then there's understanding your needs as they pertain to relationships. Do you *need* to be nonmonogamous? Do you need to be monogamous? Do you need at least the possibility of eventually moving in with a partner—or are you entirely closed to the idea of living with someone? Is sex an indispensable part of an intimate relationship for you? Are you open to nonsexual intimate connections? Are you willing to be involved in hierarchical relationships, where you are a secondary partner or subject to a veto? Or do you need to have a larger say in the course your relationship takes?

Relationship needs are absolutely real. Particularly in attachment-based relationships, your partners' actions affect you deeply, up to and including your physical and emotional health, and there's no way around this, even if you might sometimes wish you could be less "needy" (which is a misogynistic trope anyway). There's a dangerous side to focusing on needs, though, which we mentioned in chapter 1: the risk of treating people as need-fulfillment machines. For example, it's not uncommon to see people create detailed descriptions of what their future partners will have to look like, be like and want: what role they should play.

One way to think about (and seek) the kind of relationships you want without objectifying others is to think about what you have to offer (or not). Examples might be: I can offer life-partnering relationships. I can offer intimate relationships that don't include sex. I am interested in financially supporting a family. I am interested in caring for a family. I am not willing to move out of my home for a partner. I have only two nights a week available for partners. And so on.

This exercise can be useful in setting boundaries and helping clarify the kinds of relationships you're looking for and can sustain. It also plays an important role in partner selection, something we'll talk about later. It's not going to be very satisfying, for example, for you to end up in a closed triad if what you really need is an open network with the potential to date other people. If you are looking for life partners, people who are looking for other types of relationships might not be the best fit.

Minding the gap

Lots of nonmonogamous people are idealists, particularly if they come to nonmonogamy because of political or ethical convictions. These convictions are often rooted in very real and valid observations about how harmful mononormativity can be. We agree with many of those convictions! But they're not always in keeping with a person's current emotional skill sets. You may have lofty goals for your relationships and how you want to conduct yourself within them. But becoming the kind of person who can live those ideals is a never-ending process. Doing the work is important, but understanding and accepting where you are *right now* is just as important. That includes understanding whether you are ready to be with a partner who has other partners, or to have multiple partners yourself. The problem with being an idealist about nonmonogamy is that if you aren't also a realist, you risk putting yourself into situations you're not ready for. If you do that, you risk hurting other people.

Although self-awareness is important, so is self-compassion. You don't look inward so that you can pass judgment on all your flaws. You do it so you can be aware of how your behaviour is aligning with your values, what effect you're having on other people, and how you may be sabotaging yourself and your relationships. Understand where you are, yes, but also understand that it's okay to be there, at least for now.

In her book *Daring Greatly*, shame researcher Brené Brown introduces the idea of "minding the gap." She's talking about the values gap: the space between who you are now and who you want to be. Minding the gap is part of walking toward the horizon we talked about in chapter 2. There will always be times when you are imperfect, when you fall short of the best possible version of yourself. Minding the gap is being *aware* of where you are now and striving to move in the direction you want to go. That's part of living with integrity. No one is perfect. People's lives are filled with struggles and mistakes. The effort to be perfect only drives people away from one another and damages their self-worth.

The reason you need to understand where you are right now is so that you can understand your limitations. Your relationships will benefit if you can examine your sensitive spots, both so that you can be aware of what is going on when you feel upset, and so you can communicate with others about what's going on and how to support you. Knowing where you stand now will help you figure out what tools you need to employ if you feel jealousy, resentment or other difficult emotions.

When you hurt others or make mistakes, it's handy to refer back to your values and your ethical system. This can help you to think in terms of what you're striving for and how you want to live, rather than in terms of your attributes: for instance, "I am someone who values integrity" rather than "I am a super-together person." That way, you can more easily realign your actions with your values if things go wrong. For example, if you think of yourself as a person who values kindness, you can respond constructively when someone points out that you have been mean to them. You can ask yourself questions like "What's making me respond to this situation in a way that doesn't reflect my values?" "What kind of support do I need to help me respond differently?" "What actions do I need to take?" Minding the gap is about being able to see these things.

Think of it as an opportunity to make a plan. If you need to travel from point A to point B, standing at point A and being mad at yourself for not having already reached point B isn't going to get you very far. Instead, do a little route planning, get your bike tuned up, check the tires, pack a backpack, get water and make some sandwiches, check the weather and hit the road. You will need resources to make this journey across the gap—shame, guilt and unrealistic expectations are not fuel, food and functional wheels. What do the metaphors of fuel, food, a well-packed backpack and bike repairs look like in real life? Depends on your situation. Maybe what you need is therapy to help reframe things, reassurance from your partner, support from friends, introspection time, exercise so you feel more balanced and able to be your best self, time to read a book and practise some new communication tools. Maybe you're dealing with a crisis and everything else has to wait while you get it sorted out. The point is, holding yourself to an ideal when you don't have the resources to meet that ideal is a recipe for failure. So focus on getting the resources lined up rather than dwelling on your own inadequacy.

Very few people make it to adulthood without getting a little broken on the way. No one can see other people's wounds; no one can really know what other people's struggles look like from the inside. But one thing's for sure: everyone has them. Nonmonogamy can push on your broken bits in ways few other things do. You may be able to build walls around deep-rooted fears, insecurities and sensitive spots in monogamous relationships—walls that nonmonogamous relationships will often raze to the ground. And because so many more people are involved, more people stand to suffer. *Everyone* has things they need to work on and gaps they want to bridge between their actions and their values.

We recommend *The Polysecure Workbook*, by Jessica Fern, for a series of in-depth exercises to help you understand yourself and how you function in relationships, and to cultivate secure attachment with yourself and others, as well as the exercises in her book *Polywise*, written with David Cooley.

Worthiness

Nonmonogamy will challenge your emotional resilience. Instead of building walls around painful feelings like fear and jealousy, you'll need to find a way through them. You may experience more loss; more relationships mean more possibilities for heartbreak. And you may encounter judgment: slut-shaming, trivialization of your relationships, and claims that you're treating your partners badly or neglecting your kids are some of the most common forms. We discuss these more in the rest of this book, but what's important here is developing a sense of self-worth that protects you from *internalizing* these corrosive messages.

Worthiness connects to your sense of belonging, which you get when you allow yourself to be vulnerable and are accepted as you are, within relationships where you know you are not disposable. But being able to allow that vulnerability, as well as to exercise discernment about who it's safe to be vulnerable with, requires—gotcha!—a sense of worthiness. To connect with others, you must take a leap of faith and believe you are worthy of connection. That kind of belief is something that tends to get instilled in people—or not—in their families of origin when they are very young. It's reinforced as they grow, in the interactions they have with the world around them and in the other relationships (intimate and otherwise) they have. Those who experience various forms of marginalization, especially, experience constant external attacks on their self-worth, which is a major reason that, for example, suicide rates are so high among queer and trans youth. In turn, not knowing what real belonging feels like can lead people to seek out or stay in relationships where they aren't treated well, which reinforces the cycle.

So if someone didn't have the privilege of having a strong sense of self-worth instilled in them from a young age—maybe if they've never experienced it at all—how do they even begin to believe they are worthy? What if the concept of "worthiness" is so far outside your realm of personal experience that you, perhaps, can't even imagine it?

Unfortunately, there's no one thing that works for everyone. We do know that you need to work at it. It sounds cliché, but it really is about cultivating a loving relationship with yourself—learning to offer yourself the love and acceptance you never received from others. A trusted therapist can offer you mirroring and acceptance within a safe container, and with time, you can practise sharing more of yourself with trusted friends. We also know some folks for whom working with psychedelics such as psilocybin and ayahuasca has been transformative for healing their relationships with themselves. As this process goes on, you may also begin to feel guilt, regret or shame for how you have talked to or treated yourself in the past, and then it's important to practise love and compassion for the past self who was mean to you as well as the past self who you were being mean to. If feeling worthy does not come naturally to you, you may need to work at it, to a greater or lesser degree, your whole life. If you slip back into a miasma of fear and self-doubt, just remember to start practising again, and slowly work your way back out.

The good news is that once you know what worthiness feels like, you know that you *can* experience it—even if you aren't experiencing it right now. A sense of worth is critical to counteracting a scarcity model (see pages 105–107) in both love and life. If you do not believe in your worth, you become disempowered, unable to advocate for your needs. You may turn to self-abuse, which in turn can lead you into other relationships that are abusive, whether you are the abuser or the abused. You may not see or embrace the love that is actually around you in your life. It becomes harder to treat your partners well, because you do not see what you bring to their lives. And if you don't understand your value to them, you are more likely to feed your jealousy and fear of loss.

Notice that institutions built on disconnection—too many workplaces, too many families—*always* inculcate a sense of low self-worth. Under capitalism, low self-worth is valuable to those who want to profit from your labour, to say nothing of profiting from you as a consumer of products and services to endlessly improve yourself. And in relationships firmly anchored in unquestioned traditional binary gender roles, low self-worth can keep everyone trying to achieve impossible ideals, as well as exploiting women for unpaid domestic labour. Since most people are raised in or heavily exposed to such systems, it's no surprise that low self-worth is a struggle for so many.

Worthiness is not the same as validation. A sense of self-worth comes from within, not from someone else. It can be tempting to look to the outside for validation—to look to your partner and say, "They love me, therefore I am worthy." That situation creates fear rather than reducing it, because when you rely on outside things in order to feel worthy, you fear losing them all the more. The same problem arises when you source your self-worth in your career, your body, the amount of money in your bank account, or any other measurable criteria. (Which is not to say that mistreatment or shaming in any of these areas of life won't erode your self-worth, or that you should be immune to it. We don't believe the cliché that "no one can make you feel anything you don't want to feel." But your self-worth is what helps you believe that you deserve better, stick up for yourself where you can, or find people who treat you better.)

Self-worth isn't about your accomplishments or about being good at things, or a good person, or sufficiently gorgeous or sexy. It's not about belonging to social categories that are seen as better than others or that hold more privilege, or trying to resemble people in those categories. *Self-worth is not based on measurable criteria.* It needs to be anchored in a belief that all human (or depending on your belief system, living) beings are worthy, and because you are human (or alive), that applies to you, too. Self-worth is also not about developing a big ego; it's not about thinking you're better than others. In fact, a big ego often indicates that a person is trying to compensate for or conceal low self-worth.

For some, it can help to think of self-worth as a universal right, like water and air and bodily autonomy. These aren't things you have to earn; they're your birthright, something you are entitled to by the simple fact of being human. For others, it can help to consider self-worth as a spiritual concept: If your deity created you, that presumes they believe you're worthy; who are you to contradict them? Still others might find it useful to think of self-worth as a building block of political activism or other core projects—the principle of "put on your own oxygen mask before assisting others" is highly relevant here. In some ways, self-worth is fundamentally based in a kind of profound humility: If you believe that every human is worthy, and acknowledge that you are neither superhuman nor subhuman, then you, too, must be worthy.

Self-efficacy

Let's say you've set out on your bicycle trip, and you make a wrong turn. A little while later, you're out in the middle of a tangle of remote logging roads with no cell signal, and the sun is going down. Do you know a few wild plants you can collect to feed yourself? Do you know how to find water? How to make a shelter and stay warm? If not, how confident are you in your ability to figure these things out? Will you begin to panic? Will you think, "Oh, my God, I'm going to die!" Or will you take a deep breath and say, "Well, I've never done this before, but here I am, and I'd better get on with it. Let's see, it's getting dark. I guess the first thing is to look for some shelter and figure out if there's something I can eat."

There's a kind of calm that comes from believing you can handle a situation, even one you haven't faced before, and that calm increases your competence. This effect is called self-efficacy. Trying new things—like writing a book, or exploring nonmonogamy—involves learning new skills, and research on academic performance repeatedly shows that *believing* you can learn has a big impact on *how much* you learn. Self-efficacy in nonmonogamous relationships is the feeling that you can make it through your partner's first date with someone else. That you'll figure out a way to manage your jealousy, even if you don't know how yet. That if you have to sleep alone some nights, even if it's been years and you don't remember what it feels like, you'll get through it and be okay.

This may seem to have a flavour of New Age, power-of-intention pop psychology, but the study of self-efficacy goes back five decades, and there's solid evidence supporting it. Whether or not someone believes they can do something has important effects on whether they can. This has been demonstrated for everything from learning new skills to quitting smoking.

As to developing this calming competence, research has identified several strategies for improving self-efficacy. Here are two simple ones:

Small successes. Step outside your comfort zone. Find something you can succeed at: something that seems hard to you, but not so hard it will result in you quivering under the covers in tears. Stay home while your partner is on a date instead of distracting yourself by hanging out with friends. Talk to your partner about your insecurity or jealousy instead of bottling up your fears. Each small step will build on the last, giving you a stronger sense of your ability to tackle the next challenge. Those challenges won't necessarily become easier. But the key is to develop your belief that *you can do this.*

The flip side of this strategy is to address how you cope with "failure," if it turns out you weren't quite as strong (yet) as you'd hoped. People with high self-efficacy tend to be resilient in the face of failure; they know that often you have to fail many times before you succeed.

Role models. An important factor contributing to a person's idea of whether they can do something is whether they see other people doing it. We can't stress enough the usefulness of having nonmonogamous role models, ideally people in your social network who you can talk to and get feedback from. Find your local nonmonogamy discussion and support group, or start one. As nonmonogamous people, we are surrounded by a culture that tells us, "You can't do this," "That's not possible," or even "That's morally wrong." It can be hard to maintain a belief in yourself and your abilities in the face of this social censure, especially when things get hard. That's why it's critical to establish a nonmonogamy-friendly support system and find people you consider to be good examples.

Building self-efficacy in other areas of your life also builds success in nonmonogamous relationships. It takes the bite out of two scary monsters: failure and being alone. For many people, for example, the first breakup is the scariest, because it's their first taste of the failure of the romantic fantasy. Will you find love again? What if the person you just broke up with was The One? Believing that you can be alone and thrive, that you can survive the end of something and rebuild, are important elements of self-efficacy.

Courage

In relationships, you need everyday, ordinary, non-heroic courage. The courage it takes to confess a crush. The courage it takes to say, "Yes, I am going to open my heart to this person, even though I don't know what the outcome will be." The courage to love a partner who loves another person even though you do not have the trappings of security that monogamy promises. The courage to sleep alone. The courage to begin a relationship with someone who's already partnered, trusting that person to carve out the space for you that you're going to need. The courage to apologize, and the courage to forgive.

This kind of moral courage comes from a willingness to be vulnerable, and to accept that you will be okay even though you don't know what will happen. And you know what? Courage is required because sometimes what you're trying doesn't work. Your vulnerability is rejected, or worse, betrayed.

That's the whole thing about courage. It can't promise a happy outcome. We can't say, "Just be brave and vulnerable and you will obtain love and master nonmonogamous relationships ever after." It wouldn't be courage if there were guarantees.

You may feel like saying, "Well, I'm just not that brave." But we're not talking about something you are or are not. Everyone has times when they act with courage and times when they don't. Courage is a choice: It's not something you *have,* it's something you *do.* You practise a bit every day. And if you fall down, if your courage fails you, you always get another chance. Courage happens in increments.

You'll need courage because nonmonogamous relationships can be scary. Loving other people without a script is scary. Allowing the people you love to make their own choices without controlling them is scary. The kind of courage we're talking about involves being willing to let go of guarantees—and love and trust your partners anyway.

So how do you learn to have courage, to develop this practice? By taking a deep breath, steadying yourself, and then choosing the difficult, scary path over the easy way out. As the theologian Mary Daly said, you "learn courage by couraging." The path of greatest courage also seems like the hardest: It takes you right past the places where your fears live. But just as you cannot put off learning to swim until the day you magically know the butterfly stroke, you cannot put off learning courage until the day you magically become courageous. This is work you must do, now, to create fertile ground within your relationships that allows you to move with integrity and compassion.

Discernment

The counterbalance to courage is discernment.

What does that mean? Well, let's give an example. Both of us do yoga, and it presents us with a great metaphor. Yoga often encourages us to push ourselves through difficult movements—to summon our courage and do things with our bodies that we might not have thought we could do. And sometimes that's exactly the right approach. Never tried a headstand before? With proper instruction, an explanation of the body mechanics involved, and a careful, step-by-step approach, you might well be able to do it. And that moment of going from "oh no I can't, this is terrifying" to "holy crap I'm actually doing it!" can be exhilarating. At the same time, yoga also generally encourages us to pay careful attention to our bodies and what they need; to breathe deep and assess whether we can bend a little further, but not to grit our teeth and ignore pain as we push ourselves to achieve a pose.

So how are you supposed to know which one to do? Push yourself past a limitation so that you can accomplish new things and discover things you didn't yet know about yourself? Or stop because you're about to injure yourself? Good question. Figuring out when to push and when to pause or pull back can be challenging. It means cultivating the ability to tell the difference between different kinds of pain. In the context of nonmonogamy, that means discerning between the psychic equivalent of a nice, deep stretch, and the pop of a tendon tearing or shoulder dislocating. You need to get grounded, listen deep and hard to your inner voice, reflect, consider. You need to look at how a situation is or isn't lining up with your value system, whether it's crossing your boundaries or respecting them, whether it's meeting your needs or falling short, whether you have more to offer or are tapped out, whether it's hurting you in an unacceptable and ongoing way or causing the kind of temporary pain you can work through with a little care and skill. Discernment is about cultivating your ability to listen to your inner voice—*and* your ability to tell your demons to take a hike.

This can be difficult work, and there's no one right path. It's a process of deepening your self-knowledge. Sometimes you do that on your own, by reading and reflecting, by journaling and taking time for introspection. Sometimes you do it through your body—yoga is one way, but there are lots of others. Sometimes you do it with the help of other people, like trusted friends, family, therapists or communities, or with the help of a spiritual system or ethical code to give you something to check against. For most people, it's a combination of tactics.

One thing that doesn't help is when someone else is pushing you hard in a direction that would work really well for *them*, or that lines up with *their* value system. For example, Andrea once did a hot yoga class with an instructor who barked instructions like a drill sergeant and came down hard on students who didn't keep up. Feeling under pressure, Andrea chose to push through what felt like impossible demands on their body—and ended up in pain for a week with a badly pulled muscle. Never again! On the flip side, they've also spent years doing a regular class with a beloved instructor whose routine is very predictable. It's wonderful, relaxing and affirming, but it's not super challenging, so if they want to grow and develop, they need to explore other instructors and styles as well.

If someone is pushing you (or perhaps you're pushing yourself) to be courageous around something where all you want to do is scream "no!"—or, perhaps more ambiguously, where you really aren't sure you want to say "yes"—be kind to yourself. Take more time. Think more deeply. Trust your instincts. Read, reflect, talk it over with people you trust. Listen to your feelings until you come to a place where you're feeling truly ready to move forward—or a place where you feel clearer that you're just not into it. Your authentic "yes" is important, your authentic "no" must be respected, and your authentic "I don't know (yet)" should be met with compassion—other people's and your own. Don't succumb to pressure or let anyone hurry you along. There is no rush. Nonmonogamy is not a deadline project. And it might not be a project for you at all. That choice is yours, and yours alone.

Yoga is an apt metaphor here for a number of reasons, not least of which is that in recent years the yoga world has been rocked by various scandals involving leaders who became highly respected, and even revered—but who exploited and abused their students emotionally, financially, physically and even sexually. Does that mean all yoga is bad? Certainly not. It does, however, mean that a context in which you're pushed to do and be "better" by someone you trust, particularly someone who others around you also trust, can end up being quite harmful. This is why it's important to maintain some kind of balanced perspective, retain your own independent sense of what is and isn't okay with you, and listen carefully to your inner voice.

In the context of nonmonogamy, that might mean a number of things. You might learn that if you take a deep breath, summon your courage and use your skills, you can get through some really difficult moments and come out happier and stronger both in yourself and in your relationships. You might realize that nonmonogamy itself is fine, but it's showing you things about your current relationships or your current agreements that aren't healthy for you, so you need to either fix those things or exit the relationships. You might realize that even if nonmonogamy is ethically okay with you, it's too difficult, too damaging and ultimately not bringing you joy or feeling right to you, so you need to stop, whether temporarily or permanently. Or you might even realize that nonmonogamy doesn't line up with your values or emotional makeup at all. For nonmonogamy to be truly consensual, all these options need to be on the table.

Heidi Priebe, mentioned on page 24, has talked about the idea of growing pain, which is the discomfort that ultimately makes you and your life bigger, versus shrinking pain, where you and your world are becoming smaller. In a YouTube video comparing these concepts, she lists five ways to discern whether you're feeling shrinking pain:

1. Does it get worse the more you engage with the painful situation?
2. How much do you have to work to make what is happening make sense?
3. Do you feel a sense of scarcity around joy, like you have to hold onto it at all costs, or do you feel like the life you're living is going to naturally produce it?
4. Are you focused on what you "should" be doing, thinking, feeling—or are you in touch with what you actually want?
5. Do you feel like you are going endlessly in circles, or do you feel like you are expanding?

We think these questions are useful tools, and if you're struggling with discernment in a painful situation, we recommend watching the whole video (listed in the notes).

To pick up an earlier metaphor for a moment: It takes courage to be a whistleblower. It takes discernment to figure out whether your actions will actually be able to help anyone, or whether you'll put vulnerable people in even more danger. Courage is not the only tool you need when facing difficult situations.

We can't tell you how to exercise your discernment. Every situation is unique and there's no one right answer. Also, you will make mistakes along the way; don't beat yourself up about them. Everyone learns and changes over time. Making a mistake doesn't invalidate your self-knowledge; it adds to it. Just remember that your decisions are your own to make, and the more you can cultivate trust in yourself, the clearer your discernment will become.

Fear of loss

Fear of loss presents another area where the stories you tell about your relationships affect the emotional experiences you have within them. Hopefully, you are with your partners because they bring love and meaning to your life and share intimacy with you. And opening yourself up to that love, meaning and intimacy makes you vulnerable, because life is uncertain. Many people try to protect themselves from that fear by never allowing themselves to fully open up, trying to prepare themselves for anything by imagining worst-case scenarios, or numbing themselves through distancing and deactivating strategies. Others protect themselves by trying to control the people or environment around them, to keep the possibility of loss at bay.

Your distress may be compounded by an amatonormative script that says if you aren't torn apart by the thought of losing a partner, it means you don't really love them. In reality, commitment and fear of loss are only indirectly related. Often the fear of loss is more closely linked to a fear of being alone than of commitment to a partner; in monogamous relationships where even platonic intimacy outside the couple is frowned upon, losing a partner *means* being alone. And, paradoxically, if you want something too badly, the fear of losing it can become greater than what you gain by having it. When that happens, you hold onto things not because they make your life better, but because the thought of losing them makes you suffer. Both having them and not having them become sources of pain.

The truth is that you *will* lose everything. Every one of your partners, friends, family members, everything that brings you joy and meaning will one day leave your life—either through life's normal uncertainty and change, or through the inevitability of death. So you have two choices: embrace and love what you have and feel as deeply and fully as you can, and eventually lose everything—or shield yourself, keep others at a distance...and eventually lose everything. Living in fear won't stop you from losing what you love; it will only stop you from enjoying it.

A practice of gratitude can't make that fear go away, but it can help you build resilience to it. Welcome the people who care for you and the experiences you have together; practise cherishing each moment for what it is, without attaching yourself to a particular outcome (shout-out from Eve to fellow anxious babes: I know this can be harder than it sounds). If the idea of gratitude doesn't resonate for you (perhaps you've heard a little too much "you should be grateful" in your life as a way of browbeating you into accepting things that actually aren't okay!), an alternative way to look at it is through the lens of joy. While we agree with Carrie Jenkins's critique of the notion of happiness as a goal of life, joy is a bit of a different beast. It's about allowing yourself to see and deeply appreciate moments of delight, connection and sweetness without holding back or second-guessing the experience. What's going really well right now? What brings you that feeling of warmth, laughter, pleasure or rightness? Focus on those moments and experiences, and really let yourself feel them. Even though they are fleeting, they are real, and taking the time to recognize them as they happen can make you more likely to notice and feel them over time.

The inevitability of change

We know our readers are approaching nonmonogamy from a lot of different places. Some of you have never had a monogamous relationship. Others are exploring nonmonogamy after decades of monogamy. Some of you will be venturing into nonmonogamy single, while others will be opening a previously monogamous partnership. Some of you may have a long history of healthy, secure relationships, including romantic ones, while others may never have experienced love that feels safe.

Security and some basic predictability: These are fundamental human needs. At the same time, autonomy, independence and self-reliance are also fundamental values for many people, including both of us. We've seen how a focus on these latter values alone can lead to some pretty poor treatment of partners. It's important to build relationships in such a way that the people within them *can* feel secure, feel a sense of belonging, and have some basic expectations they can rely on. But it's also essential that people have agency in their relationships, that relationships be built on a foundation of choice and free will. These are not mutually exclusive goals.

Here's an uncomfortable truth: If you decide to open your heart and your life to loving more than one person and letting your partners love others too, your life will change. You will change. If you started this journey with a partner, your partner will change. *Every* new person you let into your heart will disrupt your life—sometimes in small ways, sometimes in big ones.

Disruption is a fact of life. And that's okay. After all, almost everything else you do in life risks disruption to your relationships. Taking a new job, losing a job. Having a baby. Moving to another city. Getting sick or injured. Having problems in your family of origin. Taking up new hobbies. Experiencing a death in the family. Hell, every time you walk outside your door or step into a car, you're risking serious injury or death, and that'll disrupt a relationship real quick!

When they're offered a new job or decide to have a child, most people accept at some level that these choices will change their lives. Nonmonogamy is similar: You accept that changes in your intimate life will affect your relationships, you resolve to act with integrity and honesty to cherish your partners to the best of your ability, and you trust that your partners will do the same for you.

Many problems encountered in nonmonogamy, particularly in a relationship that was previously monogamous, come from attempts to explore new relationships without having anything change. Sometimes those changes involve coming face-to-face with one's deepest fears: abandonment, fear of loss, fear of being replaced, fear of no longer being special. Relationship change is scary. Sometimes it comes on in jarring ways.

Embracing nonmonogamy involves not only examining the expectation that your partners will never change, but also examining expectations about how and when they change. People don't always change in the ways or on the timetable you want them to. New partners bring new experiences, and these experiences will change your relationships. Good relationships always change you—it's one of the best things about them!

One of the standard tropes of mononormativity is that you can prevent infidelity by limiting your partner's access to other potential partners. Opportunity creates infidelity, or so you're told, so you limit opportunity. This approach is a lot more common in heterosexual relationships with rules against the amount of closeness permitted with members of one binary gender or another; it's a lot harder to do this in queer communities where groups don't always split easily down gender lines and people's friend circles are often also their dating pools. But even in queer monogamous relationships, sometimes partners limit each others' friendships and social lives by this same logic. In nonmonogamous relationships, this trope can manifest in more subtle ways, such as by trying to limit the depth of a connection or the time a partner spends with another partner. As we discuss in chapter 11, it's common for people in a relationship to seek to use their power to constrict, limit or regulate a partner's other relationships, in the hopes that this will make those other relationships less disruptive or threatening. People try all kinds of structures to do this: enforced power hierarchies, limitations on how much emotional or sexual intimacy a partner may experience with others, rules that an established couple will only have sex with a third person if both are there for it (often on the assumption that this will prevent jealousy), and so on.

Of course, not everyone will have such feelings. If the idea of controlling your partner's other intimate connections to protect your relationship seems strange to you, you probably won't run into the problems we describe in that chapter. An important skill in creating functional nonmonogamous relationships involves learning to see other partners, particularly a partner's other partners, as people who make life better for both of you rather than a hazard to be managed.

If such a perspective does not come naturally to you, though, it can be learned. Doing so requires investing in communication, overcoming fear and rejecting some of the harmful things you may have been taught about love and intimacy. It means accepting that you and your partners *will* grow and change, and the secret to maintaining relationships in the face of change is to be resilient, flexible and loving. It also means cultivating a strong sense of security, accepting that you'll all make mistakes, and building relationships robust enough to weather them.

Scarcity and abundance

People who are privileged enough to grow up with securely attached, attuned early relationships are more likely to experience love and connection as abundant. Those with insecure attachment styles, or who experienced certain kinds of neglect or abuse in either early life or adulthood, are more likely to have a sense of scarcity around relationships. The latter can also be true of people who are marginalized in various ways, such as being fat, disabled, racialized in ways that the dominant beauty model deems unattractive, or mentally ill in ways that are societally coded as "crazy" rather than just quirky or intriguingly troubled. These experiences, and the patterns they leave in people's bodies, in turn get carried forward as expectations of their future relationship lives. These mental models of relationship can be loosely grouped, to varying degrees, as abundance and scarcity models.

In scarcity models, opportunities for love and intimacy are rare. People with this mental model believe potential partners are thin on the ground, and finding them is difficult. Because most people you meet expect monogamy, finding nonmonogamous people to connect with is particularly difficult. Every additional expectation you have shrinks the pool still more. Since genuine connection is so rare and precious, you'd better seize whatever opportunity comes by and hang on with both hands—after all, who knows when another chance will come along?

In abundance models, opportunities for connection are all around. Sure, only a small percentage of the population might meet your criteria, but in a world of more than eight billion people, opportunities abound. Even if you exclude everyone who isn't open to nonmonogamy, and everyone who doesn't match up with your sexual orientation, and everyone who doesn't have whatever other traits you want, you're still left with tens of thousands of potential partners, which is surely enough to keep even the most ambitious person busy.

People learn their models through their lived experiences, but the models in turn tend to become self-fulfilling. If you have a starvation model of relationships, you may dwell on the times you've been rejected, which may lower your self-esteem, which decreases your confidence...and that makes it harder to find partners. You may start feeling desperate to find a relationship, which further decreases your likelihood of finding a new one or incentivizes you to settle for a bad one. So you end up with less success, which reinforces the idea that relationships are scarce.

When you hold an abundance model of relationships, it's easier to just go do the things that give your life meaning, without worrying about searching for a partner. When you do that, you're likely to meet other people who are doing the same. Cool! The ease with which you find people to connect with, even when you aren't looking for them, reinforces the idea that opportunities for love are abundant, which makes it easier for you to go about doing what you love, without worrying overmuch about finding a partner...and 'round it goes. Your perceptions are shaped by reality, but the reality you experience is also often shaped by your perceptions, as we discussed on page 96.

To be very clear, we're not talking about some pop-spirituality, law-of-attraction nonsense. First, your expectations really do shape your experiences: Cognitive scientists talk about confirmation bias—the tendency to notice things that confirm your ideas, and to discount, discredit or not notice things that don't. Even when good things are happening to you, a belief that good things *don't* happen to you can keep you from noticing them or giving them weight in your assessment of your life. Second, if you believe relationships are rare and difficult to find, you can be more likely to stay in a relationship even when it's damaging you. Because of the effects on your self-esteem, energy and emotional availability, being in one bad relationship can make it harder to find other good ones—in turn further reinforcing your experience of scarcity.

Naturally, there's a fly in the ointment. Sometimes the things you're looking for or the way you look for them creates artificial scarcity. This might be because you're doing something that puts other people off, or because you're looking for something unrealistic. If you're looking for a Nobel Prize–winning Canadian supermodel with a net worth of $20 million, you might find potential partners few and far between. Similarly, if you give people the impression that you've created a slot for them to fit into that they won't be able to grow out of, opportunities for long-term relationships might not be abundant.

We're also not trying to say that you can just decide to view love and connection as abundant, at which point healthy, fulfilling relationships will suddenly manifest. But there are a couple of ways we know of to begin to deconstruct a scarcity model in your life.

Heidi Priebe addresses this notion in a video about intimacy scarcity. In her definition, intimacy scarcity isn't the same kind of scarcity we've been talking about; it's the assumption that someone can and must get all their intimacy needs met in only one relationship. This idea is embedded in amatonormativity, for sure, but it's also experienced by people with relational wounds that make it very hard to open up with others and let them in. Once you find those one or two people you feel deeply seen by, the thought of losing them becomes unbearable, because it means losing your only mirrors and thus, in some way, your self. In her video, Priebe isn't advocating for nonmonogamy, per se, but for expanding your idea of how you can meet your connection needs—an opportunity that is admittedly greatly enhanced by breaking down mononormative assumptions about intimacy! Basically, you start by cultivating closer connections all around you, not just the ones that meet your definition of partnership. Priebe advises that you begin to break down intimacy scarcity by practising, incrementally, sharing yourself vulnerably with other people in your life, gradually building intimacy in your other trusted relationships until you no longer feel like an intimate partner is the only person by whom you can feel seen and known.

The second antidote to scarcity is, perhaps counterintuitively, learning how to be alone—a subject big enough it requires its own section.

Being alone

Some people are introverts or otherwise find solitude easy and pleasant; some people enjoy being single or single-ish, or prefer a solo poly approach to nonmonogamy in which they live alone and function as a free agent while still enjoying partnerships. If you fall into one or more of these categories, you might not experience a lot of fear of being alone in your day-to-day life—though you might still feel lonely if you lack intimacy, and you might not be immune to the more existential, long-term fear of aging and dying alone. But many people find being alone challenging to varying degrees. People are wired to connect; fear of being alone is part of being human.

But if you're so afraid of being alone that you think losing a partner will destroy you, it can have consequences on the health of your relationships. You can't as easily set good boundaries or make healthy choices. And if you don't feel like you've fully consented to a relationship, but instead are in it because being alone is worse, that's not a strong foundation for healthy intimacy.

In nonmonogamy, it becomes especially vital to come to terms with the fear of being alone, first because you *are* likely to be alone from time to time, even if you have several partners, and second because more than one relationship may be on the line. One of the core ingredients of successful nonmonogamous relationships is the ability to treat all the folks involved, including not only your partners but their partners as well, with compassion and empathy. It can be hard to do that when all you feel is fear.

Fortunately, it is possible to cultivate and grow your ability to be alone—to tolerate it, find value in it, enjoy it, and even eventually seek it out for the nourishment it provides. You can follow a structured program to work on this, such as the one suggested by Sara Maitland in her book *How to Be Alone*. If you're working with a therapist, you can bring it up as an issue you'd like to work on, and ask for suggestions and support on how to tackle it. Or you might want to wing it by simply doing things alone that you would normally have done with a partner, such as taking yourself out for dinner or a movie, going away for the weekend, or keeping yourself amused at home. You can also do activities where you aren't technically alone, such as having a meal with friends or family, but for which you'd normally have your partner at your side. Consider journalling about or otherwise putting some thought into how these experiences make you feel, what fears or other feelings they bring up, and what resources you marshalled to get through them.

You may find, over time, that you change in two areas. First, you'll find new strengths in yourself, new tools and resources, and new pleasures. You might discover pastimes that you didn't make space for before; you may learn new things, triumph over adversities, discover deeper inner strength, and feel more yourself. All these things, and many more, may lie on the other side of your journey into solitude. Second, these self-changes will likely have an impact on your current relationships, as well as any future ones. When solitude is no longer something you dread, it takes that particular pressure off your relationship decisions, so you can reach out to your partners more authentically. It can help you access your capacity for compassion and generosity, and it leaves you more emotional and cognitive space to come up with creative solutions for getting your needs met and meeting others' needs. If fear of being alone has kept you in a troubled relationship, your adventures in solitude can even help you realize that the relationship needs to change or end—and can teach you that you have the resilience to get through any related upheavals.

Solitude can be a source of great strength, power and joy if you're willing to invest the time and effort, and muster the courage, to stop seeing it as an adversary and make it your ally.

QUESTIONS TO ASK YOURSELF

To become more self-aware and identify your personal strengths, weaknesses and fears—especially as they relate to relationships—here are some questions to consider. Some of these are questions you may want to reflect on over and over through time, and in different relationships.

- What is my relationship to worthiness? Growing up, was worthiness nurtured in me, or undermined, or both? Can I think of a time when I felt worthy?
- What can I offer myself to help me feel cherished, loved and secure?
- What arouses fear for me in relationships, and where in my past does this fear originate?
- In what ways do I protect myself from being hurt? How do these strategies impact me, my partners and the connections between us?

- What signals has my body given me when I have been in an unsafe or unhealthy situation? Do I need to work on listening to these signals?
- Do I have a history of overriding my own intuition when making the decision to forge ahead, take a pause or pull back? If so, where did I learn this strategy, and how has it served me?
- What measures can I take to get more in tune with the part of me that's looking out for my well-being?
- What would summoning my courage to continue look like and feel like? What would summoning my courage to call things to a halt or set a boundary look like and feel like?

The longer I live, the more deeply I learn that love—whether we call it friendship or family or romance—is the work of mirroring and magnifying each other's light.

MARIA POPOVA

5 Nurturing Your Relationships

The first part of laying the groundwork for nonmonogamy concerns yourself: developing things like security, self-confidence and flexibility. The second involves creating fertile soil for growth in your existing relationship, if you have one.

The tools for doing these two different types of preparation are very similar. This chapter is therefore relevant to people who are currently single or single-ish, as well as partnered folks, because no matter what your current relationship situation looks like, your past relationship experience and the assumptions you carry with you can still surprise you in unexpected and unpleasant ways.

There are a zillion fantastic books out there meant to teach good relationship skills—some of our favourites are listed at the back of this book—and this section isn't meant to replace any of them. We're just going to touch on a few areas that, in our experience, are often tender in nonmonogamous relationships in particular.

Cultivating security

The word *security* can mean a few things. There's personal security of the kind we discussed in the previous chapter. And then there's relationship security—which itself can be used a couple of different ways: it can mean secure attachment (mentioned on pages 25–26), or it can just mean that there is no sense of the relationship being under threat.

As we mentioned on page 21, nonmonogamous relationships are inherently insecure in an attachment sense—meaning you have to put extra work into building attachment security (if a securely attached relationship is what you're going for). In *Polysecure*, Jessica Fern uses the acronym HEARTS to describe the actions required to cultivate secure attachment: being here (present), expressing delight and appreciation, attunement, rituals and routines, turning toward one another after conflict, and secure attachment with oneself. Because of the deep investment and commitment required to nurture a securely attached relationship, it is useful to try to be clear about when you are doing this so that you can be mindful about meeting the commitment it entails. But remember: When you are intimate with someone, attachment often forms even when you don't intend for it to, and believing you can control this process is the source of a lot of heartache in nonmonogamy.

We mentioned that security can mean that there's no sense that a relationship (attachment-based or otherwise) is under threat. A person can be in a relationship that's secure in that sense, meaning it's safe and they're not in near-term danger of losing their partner, but they can *feel* insecure for a variety of reasons, including low self-esteem and a mindset informed by mononormative stories. Or they can be in a relationship that is *insecure* in an attachment sense, meaning that one or both people in it has one of the three insecure attachment styles (avoidant, anxious and fearful-avoidant), or they are just not functioning in the relationship in a securely attached way. But there's another way that it's useful to talk about security in relationships, which is when the relationship is *not secure*.

Not-security means that yeah, actually, your partner does have one foot out the door, and your gut is telling you so. Maybe they are using nonmonogamy as a way to "trade up"; maybe they like to make themselves feel powerful by pitting their partners against each other; maybe they're addicted to NRE or novelty and are always chasing the newer, shinier partner, neglecting their more established partners to the point of abandonment. This kind of thing happens more often in nonmonogamous relationships than we'd like to admit, and unfortunately much nonmonogamy-related literature focuses on self-work as the solution to all feelings of insecurity in a relationship, which can be easily used to gaslight people who are in fact experiencing not-security.

Discernment is once again a valuable tool here. But that doesn't mean you should be doing all the work of discerning alone! Look at your values and ask yourself whether the current situation aligns with them, and if not, what would need to change for it to align. Do you need to do something differently? Do you need to ask your partner to do something differently? Revisit your agreements to ascertain whether your partner is respecting them. Post anonymously online asking for advice from nonmonogamous folks. Read a relevant self-help book or watch a video. Go someplace or do something that always helps you feel grounded, and consider the situation from that place. Speak with a trusted friend or two, or a therapist, to get some insight from others who care about you *and* are good at giving you honest reality checks. Sometimes you need to hear a perspective outside your own head, whether that's "Your partner did what? That's awful! I hate watching them treat you that way! They've done it five times now and I think that's over the line," or "Honey, I know you're upset and that's totally real and I'm going to treat you to an ice cream, but from what you're telling me, it sounds like they just made an honest mistake. Let's strategize on how you can bring it up with them." Put together whatever insights you come up with through all these strategies and check it against your inner voice. Does it resonate? Talk with your partner. How do they respond to your emotional distress?

We would love to be able to give you all the answers—some surefire ways to know what's yours, what's your partner's and when it doesn't even matter anymore because the situation is too untenable to go on. But we both know from experience that sometimes hindsight is 20/20. Sometimes dynamics only become fully clear months or even years later, whether you've stayed together or parted ways. Ultimately, cultivating security—the feeling and the reality—is a process, and the steps of that process will be different for each person and each relationship.

Building trust

Throughout this book, we position *trust* as crucial in nonmonogamous relationships. That means, first of all, trusting yourself—your knowledge of what does and doesn't feel right to you, your ethical system and values, your ability to discern the nuances of a situation, your sense of self and personal boundaries. It also means extending at least some trust to others as a starting point, knowing that you have the resilience to recover if trust is broken and needs to be repaired, or if it just turns out you've extended trust to someone untrustworthy. This isn't about trusting uncritically, or not listening to your inner felt sense of what's okay. It just means that trust is a basic ingredient in healthy relationships of all kinds, and that's all the more true in nonmonogamy, which involves building trust among more than two people.

Trust is built and maintained in small moments over time. All of the secure attachment behaviours in HEARTS (page 112) contribute to building trust, and so does consistency, when your words line up with your actions over and over again. Perhaps counterintuitively, one of the most crucial ways of building trust is through conflict: when people build a history together of generative conflict, where they are kind to one another, find solutions together, and reconnect afterward. (See the section on restorative relationship conversations in *Polywise* for one way to have generative conflict.)

Trust can be broken much more easily than it can be built, through lies and major betrayals, but it can also be eroded over time: through neglect, inconsistency, lack of transparency, unkept promises, minimization and denial of another's needs and feelings, and contempt. Broken trust isn't necessarily the end of a relationship; many times, with effort on all sides, trust can be repaired. Brené Brown compares trust to a jar full of marbles: each small trust-building act adds a marble to the jar, and each small betrayal knocks a marble out.

Of course, to build trust, you have to offer a jar for someone to put marbles into. We like a distinction between *trust* and *faith* offered by an anonymous blogger who goes by the name "the loving avoidant": "Trust is built over time, and it is evidence based." (That's the marbles.) Faith, on the other hand, is a quality that you have in yourself, the way you give others the benefit of the doubt and hold their humanity. It is a potential that exists with everyone you meet—depending on your histories, values and particular wounds, you may have more or less innate faith—and it is far more resilient than trust, though also far harder to restore once lost. If you combine this idea with the marble-jar metaphor, you can imagine faith as the jar, the container that trust is built within. There are some betrayals so deep, so irrevocable, that they break the jar, but as long as that hasn't happened, damaged trust can be rebuilt, though it may take time.

Fundamental to building trust is living with integrity. You build trust when you keep your promises—when you "walk your talk." Trust decays when you break agreements, violate boundaries and act in ways that are not in accordance with your professed values. Living with integrity can hold you together when nothing else can. When you have no easy choices, and the effects of those choices on people you care about are impossible to predict, what serves as your guide? When you fail, or make mistakes, are you able to look back and say, "I upheld the values that are most important to me"?

Sometimes in nonmonogamous relationships—as in many other situations in life—there are no good choices, and it seems like, at least in the short term, you can't win, and no one else can either. Maybe it's a question of where everyone is going to spend an important holiday. Maybe it's where the kids go after a breakup. Maybe it's what to do when two partners whom you cherish with all your heart can't stand being in the same room together. You can talk about negotiation and compromise and finding win-win solutions, but sometimes the happy medium doesn't exist. The more people you put in the mix, the more likely conflicts are to arise, and sometimes there are no easy solutions.

Sometimes you are stuck minimizing losses rather than maximizing gains, and no matter how you reason your way through a situation, it feels like crap to make choices that you know are going to hurt people. And sometimes you genuinely can't tell what will be best. Sometimes you're faced with choices that feel lousy in the short term and whose long-term effects can't be predicted. So when that happens—when you can't make a move without hurting yourself or someone else—how do you make your choices?

Integrity is a big part of navigating these difficult situations. But even that can be slippery. What does it mean to act with integrity? Some people define integrity as essentially the same thing as honesty. Others see it as consistency of action, or consistency of action with belief. But the root of the word integrity means "whole." Focusing on integrity, for us, means intense examination of the present moment: What am I doing right now, and is it in alignment with my values? If I look back at myself in ten years, would I like the person I see?

Practising compassion

The word *compassion* is all over the place these days. But what does it mean? It's easy to throw it out as a glib admonishment, and ironically, it can sometimes include a shaming undertone. As in, "I am a compassionate person and you are not," or "I am putting up with you because I am so compassionate." If your social set intersects at all with New Age circles, you probably know someone who likes to play the "more compassionate than thou" Olympics. (In fact, many of the ideas in this book can be used that way. Please don't do that.)

Compassion is—again—not something you *are,* not something you *feel,* but something you *practise.* It's putting yourself in another's shoes. You can sit with a person in whatever they are feeling and bear witness to their pain while still loving who they are. Sometimes that person is yourself.

Compassion is not politeness, and isn't even the same as kindness. It's definitely not doing good deeds for someone while quietly judging them! Compassion engages your whole person, and it requires vulnerability, which is part of what makes it so hard. You have to be able to allow yourself to be present as an equal with another person, recognize the darkness in them and accept it—and that forces you to embrace, as well, the darkness within yourself.

A lack of boundaries is not the same thing as compassion, nor is letting someone walk all over you, or overlooking poor behaviour or mistreatment of others. Real compassion requires strong boundaries, because if you are letting someone take advantage of you, it becomes very hard to be authentically vulnerable to them. Compassion requires a willingness to hold other people accountable for the things they *do,* while accepting them for who they *are.*

Compassion means coming from a place of understanding that others have needs of their own, which might be different than yours, and extending to them the same understanding, the same willingness to appreciate their own struggles, that you would want them to extend to you. Even when someone is causing harm or acting with ill intent, you can have compassion for them (while holding appropriate boundaries).

You practise compassion every time you feel that surge of annoyance when someone does something you don't like, and then check yourself and try to see the reason for their behaviour from their perspective. You practise it every time you are gentle with others instead of being reactive or retaliatory with them, even if you feel angry. And you practise it when you apply that same gentleness to yourself, every time you accept that you are flawed and imperfect but are worthy despite that. You practise it in every recognition of your own and each other's frailty and error.

As a nonmonogamous person, you face particularly pressing needs to cultivate compassion for your partners, their partners and other nonmonogamous people with whom you might share community connections. But perhaps most important of all is compassion for yourself. You are learning a new way of doing things. You're developing new skills that no one's taught you before and challenging yourself in ways that many people never do. You're trying to learn how to treat not just one partner well, but potentially a larger network of people whose well-being depends, to some extent or another, on what you do. And that's hard.

It's easy to beat yourself up for not being a perfect nonmonogamous person, especially with nonmonogamous activists putting their best faces forward publicly in order to gain mainstream acceptance. Whether you're feeling jealous and insecure, or you're having trouble with appropriate expressions of anger, or you can't figure out how to clearly communicate your needs...these are common challenges. You don't need to be a nonmonogamy perfectionist. You're not the first person to have felt these things, not by a long shot. Try to treat yourself the same way you would treat someone you cared about who is having the same problem: with compassion and acceptance.

Managing your expectations

We all have expectations. Most of the time, our expectations are reasonable and mundane. We expect that when we turn on the tap, water will come out. On a more basic level, we expect that the laws that govern our interactions with the world are stable and immutable. We expect water to be wet, fire to be hot, gravity to make things fall. Our expectations form part of the basis for our perception of the world. They provide a sense of stability and predictability; if we had no expectations at all, living would become nearly impossible.

Things get more slippery when it comes to expectations regarding other people. People are self-determining, with their own motivations and priorities. You can expect some things of other people. For example, you can expect that your friends won't set fire to the house or steal the cat when they come to visit—but your expectations are always going to be hampered by the fact that you can't really tell what's happening inside another person's head. Sometimes people do set fire to houses or steal cats. And lots of expectations aren't all that mundane, and may not even be that reasonable, but they're such an inherent part of your worldview that you don't even realize they're there. You might have expectations around how often someone will text, what they'll tell you about a new relationship, who will pay for dates, or a million other things that you may not even realize you need to communicate.

Expectations differ from related feelings like hopes, fantasies, wishes or desires. If you have any of those and they don't come true, you may feel disappointment or even grief, but that doesn't mean it's bad to have them. Expectations, on the other hand, imply a responsibility on the part of another person (or even an entity, like God or Fate or "the universe"). Expectations can extend to a sense of entitlement. So when they are not fulfilled, in addition to whatever disappointment you might feel, you also feel anger, resentment or blame. Expectations lead to disappointment when they aren't met, and fear of that disappointment can cause people to hide or deny their expectations—sometimes even from themselves.

Let's talk about "reasonable" and "unreasonable" expectations.

While there are clear and obvious extremes, such as that a friend won't steal your cat or that gravity should make things fall, between these obvious endpoints lie the waters filled with dangerous reefs, ready to shipwreck the unwary. Your expectations can run aground at just about any point in a relationship. Throughout history, different social contracts have prescribed, with more or less specificity, what reasonable expectations look like in a variety of relationships. These social contracts, though, are locally and culturally specific, and in today's diverse, globalized society, you're likely to end up forming a variety of relationships throughout your life with people who have been raised with at least some default expectations that differ from yours. Further, in nonmonogamy, you're intentionally rejecting large parts of the default social contract surrounding relationships that exists in most dominant societies today, so it can be really hard at the outset to know if you even have a mutual understanding with someone about what you're rejecting and what takes its place.

On the one hand, people do not, by and large, have the right to expect things of other people without their consent. A desire on your part does not constitute an obligation on someone else's part. And you can never reasonably be upset at someone for failing to live up to your expectations if you haven't talked about your expectations in the first place. That said, everyone—*everyone*—has some baseline expectations in relationships, and some of them can reasonably be expected as the baseline in a subculture that prizes consent, autonomy, equity and care. A manipulative person can use the idea of reasonable and unreasonable expectations, or the notion of all expectations needing to be negotiated and agreed upon, as a shield to deflect responsibility for being a jerk to their partners. Nonmonogamous blogger Ginny Brown describes this dynamic well:

> In a healthy conflict, needs are discussed against other needs, feelings against other feelings. You say "I want this thing because I feel X, Y and Z" and your partner says "I want the opposite of that because I feel Q, R, and S," and then you work together to see how you can best accommodate both sets of feelings.
>
> If instead you say "I want this thing because I feel X, Y and Z" and your partner says "Let's have a rational discussion of whether X, Y and

Z are good things to feel, or whether the thing you want will actually get you them, or whether Q, R and S are objectively more important than X, Y and Z"— that is a power play. Whether they admit it or not (they almost certainly won't), the principles they're injecting are in defense of the thing they want, but rather than meeting you on equal ground, direct personal want against direct personal want, they're going to jump to the higher ground of ideals and values. And you can't jump to the same level, even if you're able to think fast enough to dredge up whatever ideals and values would support your position, because you've already admitted you have a personal want on the line.

Here, we think a principle from restorative justice is useful. The colonial, prison-based justice system is focused on what rules were broken, who needs to be punished and what that punishment should be. In restorative justice, the focus is on who was harmed and what they need to repair the harm. In an intimate relationship, if someone is hurt because an expectation they had wasn't met, it's not really important whether the expectation was reasonable or unreasonable. What matters is that they're hurt, and what is needed now to tend to the hurt and restore the relationship. Their expectations, spoken or unspoken, can come into play in the aftermath, as the people involved sort out what needs were not met and how to meet them. It is also, of course, highly relevant whether an expectation exists because of an explicit commitment that has been broken.

However, like with anything else, if you take this notion too far in the other direction, you end up in another troubling place: a place where someone holds unvoiced expectations, gets upset when they're not met, and then wants their feelings centred and soothed, and their lashing-out ignored or forgiven, while never taking responsibility for saying what they want up front. When that becomes a repeated pattern, intentionally or otherwise, it puts the other person in the position of walking on eggshells and never knowing when there will be an emotional outburst about a thing they didn't know they were expected to do (or not do), and might or might not have agreed to if they had known. It's the "read my mind or I'll be mad at you" pattern, and it's one of the more toxic forms of indirect communication. This pattern can be super harmful to the person on the receiving end, as well as a deflection of responsibility—and it's rarely effective in helping anyone get their needs met.

So where does the balance lie between putting all the responsibility on one person to state every little expectation out loud versus putting all the responsibility on the other person to know every little thing that isn't being said? When is someone weaselling out of their responsibility to be a basically kind and considerate person, and when is someone weaselling out of their responsibility to own, acknowledge and share their feelings and needs? Like so many other areas, this is a place where discernment is in order. It's a lot easier to discern in the extreme instances. No, you should not have to tell your partner that you expect them not to set the house on fire; you should be able to safely assume they will not harm your home. No, you should not have to guess that your partner has a deadly allergy to strawberries; you should be able to trust that they'll inform you about life-and-death matters you can't possibly know about from any visible evidence. It's harder to discern responsibility in the murky middle.

If you feel like you're frequently struggling over unclear expectations in your relationships, whichever side of the situation you're on, it is probably most useful to look at how each person is approaching the matter, especially patterns over time. If you're repeatedly clashing over expectations, there's probably a deeper issue at play. Is someone sincerely looking to communicate to have their needs met? Or are they just looking for someone to blame? Do unspoken expectations repeatedly feel like they're coming up as a gotcha, or do they seem to be coming from real misunderstandings? Is everyone genuinely trying to listen and meet each other's needs as they understand them, or does it feel like someone repeatedly disregards the effects of their actions on others? Does it consistently feel like you're on the same team?

QUESTIONS TO ASK YOURSELF

Here are some questions it might be useful to ask yourself (and talk over with your partners or metamours, if you're in relationships) about how you care for your connections:

- In what ways do I exhibit attachment-secure behaviours in my intimate relationships (as well as in other relationships, such as with family and friends)?
- How do or can I communicate or demonstrate to my loved ones that they are secure in their relationships with me?
- Can I think of a relationship where I was secure but felt insecure? What was behind the feeling of insecurity?

- Can I think of a relationship I have had where I was not secure? What signs showed me I was not secure that are not present in my secure relationships?
- In what ways am I consistent or inconsistent in my relationships? Do my words and actions align? If not, can I improve this alignment?
- Am I comfortable with conflict? If not, what steps can I take to improve my conflict skills, and how can others support me in this?
- Am I a safe person to have conflict with? What can I do to make my conflicts safer for others engaging with me?
- What are some baseline expectations I have in relationships that others may not naturally assume? When and how do I think it is appropriate to communicate these?

We are not obliged to be perfect once and for all, but only to rise again and again beyond the level of the self.

RABBI ABRAHAM JOSHUA HESCHEL

6 Communication Pitfalls

If you've heard anything about nonmonogamy, you may have heard this: "The first rule of nonmonogamy is communicate, communicate, communicate." But what does that mean, exactly?

Communication is trickier than it sounds. It covers a lot more than saying what's on your mind and heart, and even saying what's on your mind and heart can be surprisingly tough. And that's before you get to the listening part. Good communication is reciprocal, it's a process, and it's essential to building trust, demonstrating respect and understanding the needs of the people you're close to.

When people talk about communication in nonmonogamy, they're actually talking about a very specific *type* of communication: speaking the truth about themselves, their feelings, their needs and their boundaries with honesty and precision, and listening with grace when their partners speak of themselves, their feelings, their needs and their boundaries. This kind of communication isn't really about words. It's about vulnerability, self-knowledge, integrity, empathy, compassion and a whole lot of other things we've discussed in previous chapters.

Communication is such a complex subject that we've divided it into two chapters. This first chapter addresses ways communication can run off a cliff, including when one or more people communicate in ways that are dishonest, indirect, coercive or otherwise ineffective. The next chapter discusses strategies to help you succeed.

When you don't want to communicate

Everything we talk about in this chapter and the next assumes that the people involved are trying to communicate with each other. But sometimes, people don't actually want to communicate. Even for those who grasp intellectually the value of communication, turning that understanding into reality can be really hard.

Communication is scary. People often fear open communication because they fear the vulnerability that comes with it. Open communication means exposing yourself to rejection, judgment or betrayal. It may mean finding out that you are wrong about what you assumed your partner thinks and feels. It presents the possibility of hearing "no" to your deepest wishes, and if the relationship is unhealthy, it may mean having your needs or desires turned against you. There is no communication—at least not meaningful communication—without vulnerability.

Communication can also be hard when it leads to embarrassment or shame. If you were brought up to believe that there are certain things (like sex) that you just don't talk about, shame can interfere with communication. You might end up wondering, for example, "Why is my sex life so unsatisfying?" and being afraid to hear the answer.

Another barrier to communication is the notion that people in a relationship "should" be certain ways or do certain things, so there's no need to talk about it. Many of these ideas come from the relationship escalator, and many of them are specific to given cultures and even families (we discussed this a bit in chapter 5). Yet another barrier is the common trap of thinking in generalities and allowing them to take precedence over the specific details of the people in the relationship—including what you expect others to enjoy in bed ("Everyone loves receiving oral sex!"), how you expect them to feel about certain activities ("Everyone hates doing the laundry!") and what you expect others to find upsetting ("Doesn't everyone get mad if you show up fifteen minutes late?"). But if you don't talk about it, you might never find out that your partner is ho-hum about receiving oral sex and really prefers to be bent over a table, enjoys doing the laundry because it's meditative and relaxing, and would much prefer that you show up fifteen minutes late than fifteen minutes early, because they always need a few extra minutes to perfect their hair before a date anyway.

If a relationship involves some element of consensual domination and submission, people may fail to communicate because they believe submissives should simply accept whatever the dominant partner wants.

Or they may believe submissives shouldn't have a say in their relationship, because submissives like to do whatever they are told and never, ever voice their own needs. Some people take this to such an extreme that they even believe submissive partners in D/s relationships shouldn't *have* needs of their own. Don't follow the example of people like this! This is not how healthy D/s actually works!

Communication is almost always most difficult precisely when it's most important. As relationship coach Marcia Baczynski has put it, "If you're afraid to say it, that means you need to say it." When you are feeling most raw, most vulnerable, most scared of opening up, those are the times you most need to open up. You can't expect others to respect your boundaries and limits if you don't talk about them or, worse, pretend they don't exist. You can't build trust with others if you don't share yourself enough for them to show you whether it's safe to do so.

Some people think that talking about everything takes some of the mystery out of a relationship. But think of it this way: People are all complicated, dynamic and always changing, and relationship dynamics are filled with mystery as it is. There's no need to invent more! There is easily enough mystery between any two people to fill many lifetimes, even when they're both paying very close attention and are as honest and transparent with one another as it is possible to be.

Relationships based on honesty and transparency, in which people pay close attention to each other and work to see and understand each other, are more subtle and profoundly complex than relationships that avoid this kind of honesty and knowledge. The more you get to know a person, the more you find there is to know. And people are all moving targets; they change every day. There will always be new things to learn, no matter how much you communicate.

Dishonesty

Honesty is widely considered one of the defining factors that separate nonmonogamous relationships from cheating. It's also, not surprisingly, one of the defining elements of good communication. However, it can be harder than it sounds. Even though most people probably agree that honesty is important in a relationship, it's surprising how often people still choose not to be honest, in both big and small ways. Otherwise well-intentioned people who generally act in good faith can end up making that choice, for any number of reasons.

The most common reason is emotional vulnerability: fear of rejection, fear of being ridiculed, fear of being wrong, of hearing no, of being found less desirable by their partners, even fear of being abandoned if they don't think their boundaries will be received well. And even as many people claim to want honesty, they may subtly discourage their partners from being honest with them because they don't feel prepared to hear truths that might be painful, or because they react poorly when partners share vulnerable truths.

Some people who are dishonest with their partners are trying to shape a partner's behaviour in a desired direction. They may lie outright, or they may be more indirect; they might selectively disclose information, conceal things or choose not to say what's on their minds, pretend to be okay when they're not, or pretend to want things they don't or to not want things they do. This isn't always conscious or malicious—in fact, most of the time, it's probably neither. Many people had to learn from a very young age to manage the emotions and behaviours of the people around them in order to receive the care and love they needed, or even to avoid being hurt, and the patterns they learned back then have been carried forward into the way they engage with their intimates as adults. But regardless of the reason, dishonesty is corrosive to intimacy and trust.

Another reason people can be dishonest is that they fear upsetting or offending their partners. This can happen in a lot of areas, but an especially touchy one is around sex: what they enjoy, what they don't enjoy, what they'd like to try, and so on. Being fully honest about sex can be terrifying! But it's also really worth it. Yes, awkwardness and discomfort might be part of the deal, at least at first—but these kinds of conversations can be life-changing and lead to connection and pleasure you might never have dreamed of. This is a place where mustering your courage can really pay off.

Perhaps the most common justification for dishonesty in a relationship is the notion that the truth will hurt worse than a lie. At the most extreme end, a person who cheats on a partner may think, "If I tell the truth, I will hurt my partner, but if I don't, my partner won't need to experience that pain." This reasoning says more about the person making the argument than it does about the person they are "protecting," because consent is not valid if it is not informed. By hiding the truth, this person is denying their partner the opportunity to consent to continuing a relationship with them. Even less extreme cases, such as concealing your true feelings about one partner in order to protect another partner's feelings, can harm both your partner and the trust between the two of you, because people tend to be able to sense when their loved ones aren't being honest. Controlling information to try to keep a partner (or to get a partner to do what you want) is one way to treat people as though they aren't real. If this behaviour is repeated and sustained, it can also become gaslighting.

And remember, honesty begins inside. A person who is dishonest with *themselves* can't be honest with anyone else. People can be dishonest with themselves for many reasons, including having ideas about who they should be. If they think desiring multiple partners is shameful, they may convince themselves that they don't, even if they do. Likewise, if someone wants only one partner, they may convince themselves otherwise because they believe nonmonogamy is more "enlightened."

People can lie to themselves for more subtle reasons as well. Above all, this happens when the truth is hard. When it would require them to change; when it would cause them to feel bad about themselves or hopeless about a situation; when it would challenge their self-concept or the choices they've invested in throughout their life. Here, too, you need to summon your courage. The truth is not always easy, and it does sometimes require you to change. You might need to make amends, or demand justice, or both; you might need to heal in some way, shift a relationship, choose a new path, forge a new identity, reassess a practice or your membership in a group, or revisit past decisions and make new ones.

Self-honesty can even put your survival at risk. As just one example: If you accept to yourself that you're queer or trans, facing that truth might lead you to have to consider some pretty major implications about what you do next in your life, what relationships you maintain, what family ties you risk losing, whether you will remain welcome in a faith community or social group, and even where it's safe for you to live, work and travel.

Not every truth has such potentially dire consequences (and certainly, not every queer or trans person faces all of these potential consequences in a severe way!). But it's understandable that sometimes, being truthful with yourself can take some time and effort.

And: for your own good, and for the good of the people you love, it's still worth it.

Indirect communication

Indirect communication refers to, among other things, communicating through subtext, avoiding direct statements and looking for hidden meanings. Indirect communicators may use techniques such as asking questions or making vague, indirect statements in place of stating needs, preferences or boundaries. Directly asking for what you want creates vulnerability, and indirect communication often comes from a desire to avoid this vulnerability. In many cultures, indirect communication is considered kinder or more polite than direct communication, and these expectations are often gendered. Indirect communication also offers plausible deniability; if you state a desire for something indirectly and you don't get it, it's easy to claim you didn't really want it. Stating your needs means standing up for them and taking the risk that others may not agree to meet them. It may also feel disempowering once you have a need on the line, especially if it turns out that the other person doesn't have a similar vulnerability.

One way people communicate indirectly is by couching desires as questions: "Would you like to go out for Thai food tonight?" (Or worse, "Don't you think it's been a long time since we went out for dinner?") To an indirect communicator, such a statement can be a coded way to say, "I would like to go out for Thai food tonight." The problem is, a direct communicator might naturally hear only what was said and give a direct answer: "No, I don't really feel like going out tonight." This can leave the indirect communicator feeling disregarded; they might end up thinking, "My partner never pays attention to my needs!" For the direct communicator, this approach can be confusing, because they didn't understand that it was a request. If they untangle the indirectness and figure out their partner wanted Thai food for dinner—especially if it's much too late to do anything about it—the direct communicator might end up thinking, "My partner never asks for what they want. They expect me to read their mind! If they wanted to go out, they could have said so."

Conversely, a direct communicator may ask, "Would you like to go out for Thai food tonight?" as a form of care, because they know their partner loves Thai. But an indirect communicator might hear the offer as a request that they feel obligated to comply with, even if they don't really want to go out. Either way, even a seemingly simple question can become a source of hurt and resentment if the people on either end of it don't have a similar frame of reference.

When you're talking about dinner, indirect communication might not matter too much (though don't underestimate the impact of little exchanges like these over time). When you're talking about things that are even more fraught, like emotional boundaries or relationship expectations, indirect communication can lead to crises of misunderstanding.

People who use indirect communication were often taught to do so in their families of origin. For example, in a lot of WASP (white Anglo-Saxon

Protestant) families, stating your needs or wants is considered selfish and rude. This cultural background is common enough in settler Canada that it's contributed to the whole country's reputation for "niceness," but that sometimes just means indirectness—and the way it plays out in practice can be anything but kind. Let's say you want the last cookie on the plate. Simply taking it, or saying "I'd love to take the last cookie," would be rude. Instead, you're supposed to ask if anyone else wants it, because that *implies* that you do. Everyone else is then supposed to insist that you should take it. If they take it, then *they're* being rude, because you, as the asker, had the implicit prior claim. Not only that, but if they decide to be direct—"Can you clarify, are you saying that you want the cookie? If so, you should totally take it, I don't need any more!"—*that* can be coded as even more horribly rude!

Every now and then some pop-psych article will surface that compares indirect with direct communication and says that neither is inherently better, and all you need to do is learn which style someone is using and adapt to it.

In nonmonogamous relationships, though, indirect communication is a disaster waiting to happen. It's true that some cultures do use very subtle, nuanced indirect communication, and there's nothing wrong with that in its own cultural context. However, in those cultures where indirect communication is the norm, the paratext—the subtle verbal and nonverbal cues that tell you the hidden meaning—are shared and understood. (Although even within a given culture, plenty of people still find the byzantine rules of indirect communication to be stifling, toxic, incomprehensible and inefficient. They can also be extremely difficult for some neurodivergent folks to navigate.) We wrote this book for readers in a North American context, where it's almost certain that you, your partners and their partners will have grown up with family and cultural backgrounds that are at least somewhat different from one another, and thus taught different assumptions about what cues convey what unspoken meanings. Looking for hidden meanings in such situations leads to a very high chance that you'll be quite simply wrong.

And while indirect communication can work in somewhat predictable and conventional social situations among people who share a vocabulary based in indirectness, it's often far from ideal when it comes to matters of the heart. It's one thing to drop a hint to your sibling knowing they'll catch on to the unspoken meaning. It's quite another to downplay, conceal or otherwise misrepresent what you're feeling, or avoid plainly saying what you want or need, when the stakes are higher. Indirectness is not a useless skill, but it needs to be used only when appropriate.

How can you tell what's appropriate and what's not? Let the results show you. The easiest way to know whether indirect communication has worked is to use the direct kind to check in about it. You may be shocked to find out how little someone has truly caught on—and how much they'd really like to give you what you want, if only you would tell them what that is! You may also be surprised to discover how much you were reading into a situation when the other person didn't have any of the intentions, desires or feelings you had assumed.

In its worst forms, when indirect communication includes implied threats or demands, it can tip over into manipulation. This can happen in many ways, such as by concealing your real motivations by couching them in pleasant-sounding but leading language: "I'm sure you would *never* suggest we skip Christmas with my parents because you *know* how upset that would make me." Or by waiting for a partner to misinterpret your coded language and then springing something like "You never listen to me!"

Whether someone is accustomed to direct or indirect communication, if they haven't taken time to unpack their own communication style, they're likely to see all communication through their own lens—they can't switch between direct and indirect communication. No matter how direct you are, an indirect communicator may remain certain there's a hidden message, an unstated request or a secret criticism buried somewhere deep in your words. Sometimes, indirect communicators come up with interpretations that can seem plain bizarre, even paranoid, to a direct communicator. But these interpretations come from their expectations of how much meaning other people hide in their words. Similarly, direct communicators (as well as plenty of neurodivergent folks) may be entirely unaware of the possibility that there's an additional meaning coded into someone's communication. Both types of communicators may walk away from exchanges with each other with very different notions of what was actually said.

If you've cultivated the habit of looking for hidden meanings, it can be jarring to realize that sometimes they aren't there—a person might actually just mean what they said, and nothing more or less. In nonmonogamy, it's worth doing the work to set aside any cultural conditioning you may have toward indirectness. It might feel uncomfortable or rude at first, but you can save yourself an enormous amount of frustration and angst by speaking directly and believing that others are doing the same.

If you are a direct communicator and someone misinterprets something you've said, or extracts a meaning you didn't intend, be patient and forthright. State your intended meaning plainly. Reassure them that your words carry no hidden intent. Make it clear that you genuinely want to understand. Respond to vague statements with clear, direct questions. Ask for clarification when they say something ambiguous. And above all, keep at it. Indirect communication can take a long time to unlearn.

Remember, though, that you can't change others, particularly when it comes to deeply embedded mindsets. If someone is really committed to an indirect communication style, or so unaware of it that they can't discern when it's happening, using these strategies might make no difference. It's up to you to decide how much you want to—and can—invest in adapting to other communication styles.

Storytelling

Humans are storytellers. We tell stories to ourselves, dozens of times a day, without even being aware of it. We use these stories to make sense of the world and to understand the actions of the people around us. Many of these stories relate to other people's motives. We know that people's actions aren't random. We build models in our heads that help us understand others, and these models are often flawed because they're made up of observation, guesswork, projection and empathy.

Unfortunately, it's natural to act as though these models are more real than the people they represent. People don't usually say to themselves, "I'm convinced to about 65 percent accuracy that my metamour is trying to replace me in my lover's affections, but there's considerable room for error." Rather, they say, "That jerk is trying to get rid of me!" The motives people ascribe to other people's behaviour are coloured by their own fears and past experiences.

Worse, most people are predisposed to view other people's motives less charitably than their own. Research has shown that people tend to explain their own behaviour as a reaction to the situation they're in, while they believe the behaviour of others is a direct indication of their character (this is known as the "fundamental attribution error"). When asked why they cut someone else off in traffic, a driver might say, "I was looking the other way and didn't see them," but when asked why someone else cut them off in traffic, they are more likely to say, "They're obviously a reckless driver who doesn't care about anyone else on the road."

In nonmonogamous relationships, as you might imagine, this behaviour can get pretty ugly. When you tell yourself stories about other people, you tend to run with those stories, rather than what the other people say about the matter. "Of course they *say* they aren't trying to separate me from my partner; that's exactly what they want me to believe!"

The cognitive behavioural therapy method for dealing with this kind of problem, known as examining evidence, can come in handy here. If you look around online, you can even find worksheets to help you out with this process. They'll ask you to write out your hypothesis about what's going on in a given situation, and then list your evidence for and against it. Doing this exercise can help you build a more realistic picture of what's happening. Maybe you really do have evidence that your metamour is trying to separate you from your partner in some way. If so, you need to deal with that situation! But maybe when you write it out, you realize that there's no compelling evidence for this hypothesis. In that case, the thing that needs work might in fact be your fear of losing your partner, or mutually insecure behaviours within the relationship. These, too, need to be dealt with—but probably not in the same way. Either way, examining the evidence can help you figure out what work you need to do, where you're missing relevant information, and what requests you might want to make of others.

Triangulation

One key principle of good communication (as we explain in the next chapter) is that it ideally involves the people directly affected. This sounds simple, but it can be surprisingly hard to implement. Triangulation starts from an early age. Most people who grew up around other kids—siblings, cousins or other kin, or just neighbours on the playground—can remember at least one time when someone said, "Mom, Danny's poking me!" or "Hey, Dad, Miranda won't stay on her side of the seat!" And thus the seeds were sown for some of the most tenacious communication problems you will ever face.

Triangulation happens when one person has a problem, concern or question for another person, but instead of bringing it up directly with that person, they go to someone else or bring someone else in to try to bolster their side. It happens when a child has a problem with their sibling's behaviour and petitions a parent to settle it. It happens online when one person has a problem with somebody else and goes to the faceless masses of the internet to seek validation. It happens when someone at a company has a problem with another person's performance and approaches a coworker about it. It happens when one member of a couple tries to get a relationship counsellor to take a side. And in nonmonogamous relationships, it's the easiest thing in the world.

One of the most common ways that triangulation occurs in nonmonogamy is when one person wants to control the flow of information among their partners. Most people don't like conflict, and keeping people from finding out things that might upset them can seem like a good way to avoid or reduce conflict. It can sometimes be a means of minimizing tensions or disagreements; if two of your partners aren't getting along with one another, you may be tempted to try to interpret one person's words for the other, in a way that shows the message in its most favourable light. It can also happen when you don't trust what your partners might say to each other, if you're in the kind of relationship arrangement in which everyone has met and has the ability to speak to one another independently of you, but you are uncomfortable with them talking alone.

Triangulation can also be used to diffuse responsibility. It becomes easy to tell one partner, "I can't do what you want me to do because Sage might not like it," rather than "I am choosing not to do what you want me to, because I think Sage might not like it." (Veto is arguably an extreme example of this diffusion of responsibility. For more on this, see chapter 12.) Another version of triangulation happens when someone blames one person (such as a metamour) for the hurtful actions of another (such as a partner).

It's much easier to blame a third party, casting you and your partner as helpless victims, than to be honest when you are making a choice that hurts someone. Similarly, it can be easier to direct your anger and frustration at a third party than toward the person who is actually hurting you when the latter is someone you are intimately involved with. And for a hinge, it's a lot harder to do the gritty work of negotiating solutions among competing needs and deciding how to share your time and resources than it is to stand back and pretend that those solutions are something your partners need to work out between themselves. (We discuss this a lot more in chapter 19.)

A final, and especially poisonous, form of triangulation happens when two or more people in a polycule gang up on one or more others, perhaps to shame or control them, or perhaps to gain status at their expense. The worst cases can easily become a form of emotional abuse. It's easy to triangulate using social media, too, such as by vagueposting about metamours or posting even veiled details of others' relationship struggles in forums where such details might be recognized. It's also easy to make an example of one partner in a polycule—or even an ex-partner—as a sort of object lesson to warn other partners: They're so controlling, but you're not like that. They get angry so easily, but you're so kind. They're so needy, but you understand my limits. Someone especially skilled at this strategy can even do it with all their partners at once!

The solution to triangulation is simple in theory—don't do it—but difficult in practice, because it's easier to talk about things that bother you with anyone but the person whose behaviour is at issue. And because when you feel wronged, it's natural to seek allies. In practical terms, you can't make other people communicate directly with each other. The best you can do is to limit your own participation in triangulation. Just back out and tell the other people they need to talk to each other. Refuse to let your partners vent to you about your metamours, or seek out your metamours' side of the story (this can be especially important for women who are involved with men, because of the ways patriarchy has trained women to turn on one another—and trained men to leverage this tendency). And *you* should address anything that bothers you directly with the person involved. If you need allyship or support, that's totally fine and reasonable, but seek it from someone you trust who's not part of the problematic situation, such as a perceptive friend or a therapist who can help you work through a problem.

Try not to be drawn into the role of rescuer when someone in your relationship network comes to you complaining about that terrible thing someone else in the network just did. Reserve judgment of other people in your relationship network, and encourage the parties at odds to talk directly to each other rather than through you, without allowing yourself to become a go-between.

One good resource on negotiating triangulation when there isn't outright abuse involved is Harriet Lerner's *The Dance of Intimacy*, listed in the resources.

Coercive communication

Coercion doesn't always involve physical violence or direct threats. It's actually quite easy for relationships to become coercive when the stakes are high—and when you are deeply attached or committed to another person, they are high. Coercion happens any time you make the consequences of saying no so great that you've removed reasonable choice. If your partner says no, and you start preparing for a fight instead of accepting their choice, you're probably being coercive.

If your partner sets a boundary or says no to a request, they probably have a good reason. That reason might not even be about you. It's important to respect a no even when you don't understand it. Show appreciation for your partner's self-advocacy and self-knowledge, be grateful for the intimacy they *have* shown you, and make it clear that you respect their autonomy and ability to make choices—even if you don't understand what's happening or why.

We're talking about boundaries your partner sets on themselves, which as we discuss in chapters 9 and 10, are quite different from rules they apply to you. It is always appropriate to negotiate restrictions another person tries to place on you, though it sometimes takes careful attention to recognize the difference.

It's also possible that in setting boundaries a partner is being manipulative, using boundary-setting as a way to coerce you. Withdrawal and silence, classic techniques of emotional blackmail—also known as stonewalling—can initially be difficult to distinguish from healthy boundary-setting. Stonewalling is the fourth and most deadly of relationship expert John Gottman's "four horsemen" that signal an imminent relationship apocalypse. A person could be withdrawing just to punish you, intentionally or unintentionally—but that doesn't change what you should do. The solution is never to try to force someone into emotional intimacy. Respect their choice, and do what you need to do to take care of yourself.

Of course, it's okay to want to know and understand someone's reasons for setting a boundary. Unexplained decisions aren't conducive to intimacy, and they have the effect of creating distance or, at minimum, missing an opportunity to build closeness. It's also okay to ask about the person's reasons—as long as you're coming from a place of wanting to understand rather than to change their mind or argue them out of a choice. If you're hurting because of a boundary your partner has set, knowing how to practise active listening can be especially useful. (We discuss this in the next chapter.) It is especially critical in these moments to be careful not to twist your questions into accusations or statements of intent. "Why would you want to hurt me this way?" is a manipulative, coercive question that will not lead to genuine communication. The important thing is to recognize that you don't have to understand or like a partner's decision to respect it.

Even without disproportionate power, people manipulate one another in relationships in many subtle ways. People might seek acquiescence by shifting blame, appealing to a sense of fairness, or implying that the other person is negotiating in bad faith. Appealing to social norms can be another way to try to coerce "agreement" in nonmonogamy. This includes making statements shaming someone for being nonmonogamous, or for failing to adhere to escalator expectations, or for being an "interloper" in an established couple. This kind of shame is powerful, and can easily get someone who cares to walk back their needs or agree to compromises that don't align with their values.

Still another technique for manipulating agreement involves preying on fear of abandonment. Statements that reflect sentiments like "What would you do without me?" or "I don't know why I even stay here and let you do this to me"—though they are rarely that overt—can be attempts to use emotional blackmail to compel agreement.

If you find yourself using coercive communication techniques, consider whether this strategy matches up with your values. If you've read this far, we're going to assume it probably doesn't—in which case, you may need to do some deep introspection, build some skills, or seek out support to find other, less harmful ways of getting your needs met.

If one of your partners is using coercive communication techniques, you may need to have a serious heart-to-heart, set some firm boundaries, and possibly seek out support to get your communication back on track. In the long run, no relationship that involves coercion can be truly good for the people in it.

QUESTIONS TO ASK YOURSELF

Communication in relationships, and nonmonogamous relationships in particular, can be like a proverbial minefield. As you attempt to negotiate this potentially dangerous territory, here are some questions to guide you:

- If I have a problem with someone's behaviour, do I discuss the problem with that person? If not, what are my communication habits instead? What work do I need to do in order to shift toward more directness?
- If my partners have a problem with someone else's behaviour, do I encourage them to bring it up with that person? Or do I fall into the trap of being a go-between? If I'm a go-between, what can I do to shift out of that role?

- Do I ever try to bring in someone else, such as another partner or a therapist, or repeat things I remember them saying, to help me gain the upper hand in a situation?
- Do I communicate indirectly or directly? Where did I learn my communication patterns? How can I work toward a communication style that's effective with everyone involved?
- How can I, or do I, manage the vulnerability that comes with authentic, direct communication?
- Is coercive communication happening in any of my relationships? If so, how does it need to be dealt with? What do I need to learn or do differently? What boundaries might I need to set with others?

Those who do not have power over the story that dominates their lives, power to retell it, rethink it, deconstruct it, joke about it, and change it as times change, truly are powerless, because they cannot think new thoughts.

SALMAN RUSHDIE

7 Communication Strategies

Communication is the lifeblood of a relationship. Every single thing that you can't or won't talk about, openly and without fear or shame, can be a crack in a relationship's foundation.

Strategies for successful communication are some of the most important tools in any relationship toolkit, but nonmonogamy often challenges people to communicate to a degree that other relationship models don't. If one member of a monogamous couple, for instance, is attracted to a third person, they're usually expected to pretend they're not. But you can't really have nonmonogamous relationships without acknowledging your attractions to others! It's always best to find ways to communicate what you're feeling with your partners, no matter whether you're monogamous or nonmonogamous. But if you want to build multiple sustainable relationships, you need to put a lot of topics on the table for discussion that monogamy might have let you avoid.

Communication basics

Learning good communication skills is a lifelong project, not a one-and-done thing. Even if you have a ton of skills, there's always more to learn—and most people don't start out with a ton of skills. We can't possibly cover the topic thoroughly in this book, so we'll cover only those communication issues we think are most directly applicable to nonmonogamy. We recommend that you make a commitment to improving your communication skills on an ongoing basis, particularly if you're serious about wanting to pursue nonmonogamous relationships—but it's worth it even if you decide you prefer monogamy.

Certain communication techniques should be in everyone's toolbox for *any* relationship. Each of the strategies we'll discuss has many books dedicated to it, so we'll just briefly touch on each one. You'll find great resources for developing these skills at the end of this book. Two of these essential communication tools are active listening and direct communication.

ACTIVE LISTENING

When people think about communication, their focus is often on getting across what they want to say. But communication breaks down just as often—if not more often—in the listening as in the speaking. Active listening is a great technique not just for effective communication, but for connecting with your partner: making sure they *feel* heard. As the listener, this is your chance to show that you are truly interested in and curious about your partner's experiences, feelings and thoughts, and that you really want to know them deeply. As the speaker, this is your opportunity to show that you trust your partner enough to speak freely with them, to express what you think and feel honestly and without reservation, and that you believe you'll be heard and received with kindness. It's an act of care and generosity for both partners. Active listening is often taught in conflict resolution courses and couples counselling.

As tough as it can be to practise, the mechanics of active listening are pretty simple. You listen intently to what the other person is saying, rather than using that time to think about the next thing *you* want to say. While you listen, think about trying to fully grasp what they're saying; to encourage them to express themselves fully, you can use your body language or expressions called minimal provokers, such as "mm-hmm?" or "yeah" or "tell me more." Then you repeat back to the other person what they have just said to you—in your own words, so that they know you understood. Part of active listening can involve linking facts and feelings, such as saying "So when we made those plans without checking in with you, you felt left out." Check to make sure you understood them correctly by asking a question, such as, "Did I get that right?" This is an opportunity for the other person to say yes, or to say no and explain further if, in fact, you've missed or misunderstood something.

You can then trade roles if needed, though this isn't necessary in every type of conversation. Once one or both people feel understood, you can move on to figuring out solutions together. Because a need to be heard and understood is at the root of many interpersonal conflicts, active listening can go a long way toward defusing intense situations, even when a solution is not yet apparent. Active listening can be challenging, because while you're the listener, it can be tempting to interrupt with your own perception of events, to defend your actions or to explain a misunderstanding. It can help to think of the process as a deliberate, temporary imbalance: You're setting aside your own ego and asking your needs to be patient for a little while so that you can fully focus on the other person. Creating this kind of space makes the other person feel safer, more heard, and ultimately softer and more receptive to hearing you in turn. As long as you're both willing and able to engage in this process equally, the listener's generosity of spirit benefits both of you in the end, as does the speaker's willingness to open up and be vulnerable.

DIRECT COMMUNICATION

Direct communication involves both being direct in what you say—without subtext, hidden meanings, coded language or tacit expectations—and assuming directness in what you hear, without looking for hidden meanings or buried messages. We discussed its counterpoint, indirect communication, at some length in the previous chapter, along with some of the challenges that arise when people are using different communication styles. Here, we want to dig deeper into what direct communication actually looks like. It's a skill that does not come naturally to everyone, but it's one everyone can learn—and one that we think every nonmonogamous person *must* learn if they want to communicate effectively within their intimate networks.

Many excellent resources exist for learning direct communication. Many universities and continuing studies departments offer workshops in direct communication (sometimes called "assertiveness training"). The books by Harriet Lerner listed in the resources section offer good strategies for direct but compassionate communication. We urge you to explore this topic more if it is new to you, but we will touch briefly here on what direct communication is and why it's so important for nonmonogamous relationships.

Let's dispel a couple of myths about direct communication from the outset. Direct communication is not the same thing as being inconsiderate or mean-spirited. It is totally possible to say what you mean without being rude or unkind. As the saying goes, "honesty without compassion is cruelty." So, for example, you can express that you didn't like the meal your partner cooked by saying "Normally I love your cooking, but tonight's dish just didn't work for me. Too much onion, I think? You're really good at modifying recipes, so maybe we could try a different version next week!" rather than by saying "Ugh, that dinner was disgusting." Remember that everyone makes missteps sometimes; if you say something directly in a way that's unintentionally hurtful, you can apologize and rephrase. It's important to find the balance between speaking too plainly and being too careful. But the only way you'll get there is by practising and honing your skills over time, not by holding back and self-censoring.

Direct communication also does not mean partners aren't responsible for taking in the more subtle cues, both verbal and nonverbal, that are a normal part of human communication. For example, if your partner is crying, don't assume they're fine just because they don't say "I am feeling sad!" Part of loving someone is paying attention to their overall affect, demeanour, body language, facial expressions, tone of voice and more, and learning the unique ways they express themselves. That doesn't mean you should try to read their mind; when you notice something, simply check in: "You seem upset! Do you want to talk about it? What do you need right now?" Over time, in most relationships, people build a shared understanding of each other's nonverbal cues such that they may not need to ask each time. But at first, and as needed over time, direct communication is a way to establish what those cues are and what they mean. It's part of getting to know someone. The more you build that shared vocabulary, the more shorthand you can create together, and that can feel really intimate. But don't start out by assuming your own shorthand is obvious to everyone else and easy to understand, and don't bend yourself into a pretzel trying to read someone else's cues with no further information to go on. Conversely, if your partner misses or misunderstands a cue, give them the benefit of the doubt; you can just tell them what it means. For example, "If you notice me pulling away like that, it's not because I'm upset with you, I'm just feeling overstimulated and need to take a step back," or "I tend to laugh a lot when I'm nervous, but please know I'm not laughing at you." In other words, nonverbal communication can be a valuable part of direct communication, but—especially in the early stages of a relationship—it's often most effective when supported by the verbal kind.

The single most effective way to start communicating directly is to use declarative statements rather than leading questions. For example, say "I would like to go out tonight," rather than "Would you like to go out tonight?" Statements that begin with "I want," "I feel" and "I need" are all markers of direct communication. They do not require a decoder ring to interpret correctly.

Plain language is another hallmark of direct communication. Make statements in active rather than passive voice ("I broke the vase," rather than "The vase got broken by my broom handle"). Use simple declarations rather than complex sentences ("I need you to take out the garbage," rather than "Taking care of this problem with the garbage was supposed to be your responsibility").

Use specific, concrete examples to illustrate what you're saying. Instead of saying "You don't pay attention to my needs," list examples of times when you feel your needs weren't met. Take responsibility for your desires, thoughts and feelings. If you're asked to do something you'd rather not do, don't make excuses for not doing it. Rather, take ownership of it: "I don't want to do that." Remember that even when they're a reasonable response to other people's actions, your feelings belong to you. Saying something like "I feel angry" creates more of an opening for empathy and connection than "You make me so angry." Give your partner the space to talk about their feelings as well.

Avoid hyperbole and absolutes ("You always leave your socks on the coffee table," "You never close the garage door") and inferences of motivation ("You're only doing that because you want to get rid of me," "You clearly don't respect me"). But you can certainly still point out when someone's words or behaviour leave you feeling unwanted, neglected, abandoned or humiliated, or when someone uses disrespectful or demeaning language. In the first case, you're making assumptions about the other person's motivations, whereas in the second, you're making a statement about your own feelings and experience. Sometimes people act in hurtful or disrespectful ways without realizing it, but if you bring it up several times and they deflect, deny or minimize, there is a bigger problem to deal with.

Direct communication and active listening are complementary. Active listening means paying attention to what your partner is saying, rather than interrupting them or thinking of ways to refute what they're saying. Direct communication is saying clearly what you want someone to pay attention to.

There is one other element of direct communication: the ability to say yes and, especially, no, without reservation. We've mentioned this before, but it's worth repeating: The ability to say no is vital to consent. When one or more partners don't have a meaningful ability to say no, the relationship becomes coercive.

Being able to say no also has another advantage. When you are accustomed to using indirect communication, or unable to set boundaries, or when you feel you don't have the ability to say no to something, it's very hard for your partner to have confidence in your yes. If you say yes to everything, then your yes might or might not be sincere, and your partner ends up having to guess whether you mean it or not. If you don't want to do something, you may become resentful when you do it, even if you said yes to it. Conversely, when you are able to say no and your partner knows it, they know your yes is genuine.

ASK FOR WHAT YOU NEED

Asking for what you need is hard for most people. And it's hard to learn to make requests in ways that are really requests, rather than demands, and are heard as such. But being able to ask for what you need, and in fact being *good* at asking, is pretty key to nonmonogamous relationships—or (as we keep saying) any relationships.

For one thing, there's the obvious (yet somehow commonly overlooked) fact that if you ask for what you need, you are more likely to get it. And then there's the fact that people who are getting their needs met tend to be more satisfied and content, and thus better able to be generous as partners. People sometimes think (or others may try to convince them) that they're being "too needy" when they ask for things, but everybody wins when someone's needs are being met, not just that person.

The simple act of formulating a request and deciding whom to ask, and how, forces you to get clear on what exactly you need—what's at the bottom of the emotions you're experiencing—and from whom, and why. But perhaps most importantly: Consistently asking for what you need means people can trust you to ask. They don't have to second-guess themselves, read between the lines or worry about you. They can simply enjoy being with you and discovering you, and they can trust that they will know when you need something, because you will tell them. When you ask for what you need, you give a gift to the people you love.

But few people are taught how to ask for what they need. Often people are socialized *not* to ask for things, because they're told that advocating for their needs is selfish. Sometimes people downplay their needs to conform to what they think is available. If you really want three cookies, you may think, "Well, three is a lot, and other people might want cookies too...I better ask for only one." When someone else comes along and asks for three, you end up thinking, "Wait a minute! How come they're getting so many cookies and I'm not?"

Asking for what you need, rather than what you think might be available, is kind to your partners because it communicates what you want authentically—as long as you are ready to hear a no. Asking for what you need isn't the same thing as pressuring someone, as long as the other person can say no and you can accept it. These techniques can help you ask for what you need:

- Ask for things in terms of "I need this thing" rather than "I need more of this thing than any of your other partners get." When you state your needs as they stand, and not with respect to what you believe other people want or have, your partners will find it easier to meet them.
- Be as explicit as you can while leaving flexibility for the other person. "I need consistency" followed by several examples of what consistency looks like for you, or ways that your partner has shown you consistency in the past, opens the door for you and your partner to find a solution that works for both of you. "I need you to text me at 9 a.m. every day" is a rigid approach that may leave your partner feeling micromanaged.
- Remember that a need is not the same as a feeling. "I need to know you'll spend time to help me feel valued when I feel threatened" (direct communication of a need) is different from "I need to not feel threatened, so I need you to never date someone who makes me feel that way" (coercive communication).
- Also remember that a need is not the same as a strategy. "I need a certain amount of one-on-one time with you each week to feel connected" is a need. "I want a date night every Friday" is a strategy—but it's not the only strategy that might meet the need.
- Let your partners know when your needs *are* being met, just as you tell them when they aren't. When your partners know they're doing right, it reinforces the right thing. It's better still when you can provide examples of how your partners are meeting your needs. This is also an important part of practising gratitude, discussed in chapter 4.

If you've been socialized to not ask for your needs to be met, what tools can you use to learn how to ask?

- Practise communicating directly. When you ask for something, make sure you're actually saying what you need! There is a difference between "I want to go to bed now," "Do you want to go to bed now?" "Are you coming to bed?" "I would like you to come to bed now" and "I would like your attention now." Be precise. Communicating directly may feel awkward at first, and you might not be good at it. That's okay. These are skills, and skills take practice.

- Talk about what you actually want, not what you think you *should* want or what you think might be available.
- Check your assumptions. If you think you hear implied criticism that was not stated directly, ask if that was what was intended. If not, you may be listening for indirect communication. This is especially true when someone says something like "I don't want that" or "I don't need that." A person habituated to indirect communication may hear "and therefore you shouldn't want or need that either," or some other message, when the speaker was actually just talking about themselves.
- Assume good intent. Your partners are with you because they love you and want to be with you. Even when problems arise, needs aren't being met or communication goes awry, this is still true. If you start with the assumption that your partners are acting out of malice, communication is never going to function properly.
- When a partner has done the work of asking clearly for what they need, take it seriously. Even small requests can be very hard to make, and they can lie at the tip of some very big emotions. If you can't meet the request, at least acknowledge it by saying no, and preferably explain why. If you can't do what your partner is asking, inquire about the underlying need; is there another way to meet it? "No, I can't be with you next Thursday, but is there another time when I can help support you?" is better than just no.

TALK ABOUT THE REASONS

As scary as it can be to advocate for your needs, it can be even scarier to talk about *why* you want or need the things you want or need. Talking about the reasons leaves you naked; it opens you up to having your reasons, or even your motives, questioned. It also requires that you look inside yourself and think about why you want what you want.

This can be difficult. "Because I just don't want that" is not good communication. If you ask for something, you need to talk about the "why" as well as the "what." This more effectively advocates for your needs, and it opens the door for a genuine dialogue about how to have them met.

Sometimes things that upset people are hidden inside the statement "I just don't want that." For example, some people, usually cisgender heterosexual men, approach nonmonogamy with the idea that it's okay if their partners have women as lovers, but feel threatened by the idea of their partners having other men as lovers. It's certainly easier to say "I just don't want my partner to have sex with another man" than to admit to feelings of vulnerability around sex, perhaps because they're afraid that if another man does what they do, they might be replaced. But talking about tender spots is necessary if you are to understand why you feel the way you do, and understanding your feelings is the only way to grow.

The purpose of talking about the things that upset you is not to make your partners avoid them, but to better understand them. When you can make sense of your emotional responses, you can more easily take responsibility for them, rather than making your partners (or, worse yet, your partners' partners) responsible for them. If, to continue with the previous example, you're a hetero man who feels threatened by the idea of your lover having sex with another man, talking about why, and owning that feeling, can help you become more secure in your relationship. Discussing how you feel gives your partner an opportunity to explain what value they see in you, and why another man doesn't have to be threatening to you.

"I just don't want that" tends to end rather than continue conversations. But continuing discussions about what you want—and, more importantly, why—is crucial to staying connected and intimate with your partners.

COMPROMISE AS COLLABORATION

In this book, we use the term *compromise* to discuss the process of coming to workable agreements when people's needs are in some degree of disharmony. However, in common parlance this word refers to a situation where two parties reach agreement by each making concessions—in other words, by each giving up something they want. And while that might need to happen sometimes, it's a pretty adversarial way to frame a process that can instead be collaborative, creative and generative. Rather than sitting down across a negotiating table with your intimate partners and figuring out who will sacrifice what, it can help to sit next to each other and analyze a problem or challenge together. Brainstorm as a team instead of haggling. Co-create instead of bargaining. "How can we creatively solve this in a way that we both get what we want?" is a much more productive question than "How can we negotiate this so that we both have to give something up?" What is the actual need or want at hand? What's important about it? What parts feel flexible to you? What opportunities and ideas can you come up with to get the need met? What resources do you each bring to the table? Can you recruit others to help, consider approaches that are outside your usual habits, offer an even better way than the original one for a need to be met, or otherwise come up with options by pooling your skills and resources?

If you think more expansively and with more curiosity, you may be surprised at what solutions you can come up with together. In addition, the exercise itself can be a real trust-builder, where each person feels they have an ally in finding ways to get what they want rather than an enemy trying to get between them and their desires.

When someone raises an issue, it's crucial to try to stay on the same team. As the blogger Shea Emma Fett writes, "If the goal of the conversation is to exchange power, and not to exchange understanding, you will never ever ever win." Eve likes to use the analogy of an escape room: You and your partner (or partners, or metamours, as the case may be) need to solve a puzzle in order to open the door and move on to the next room. It's a team effort, and everyone has to try to explore and look for solutions. It's all of you against the problem—not the person who raised the problem against everyone else.

MANAGING EMOTIONS

Being nonmonogamous doesn't confer immunity to negative feelings. Nonmonogamous folks experience jealousy, insecurity, doubt and the full range of other human emotions. If you wait for immunity to uncomfortable emotions before travelling this road, you'll never budge. What's necessary is simply to understand that you don't have to put your emotions in the driver's seat. You feel what you feel; the secret is to understand that you still have power even in the face of your feelings. You can still choose to act with courage, compassion and grace, even when you're terrified, uncertain and insecure.

This notion that you can control your actions despite your emotions seems radical to many people. The first part of making it happen is just realizing it's possible. Once you've turned that corner—and given all the social messages saying people are helpless in the face of their emotions, that's a tough thing to do—the rest is practice.

These guidelines can help prevent you from turning the wheel over to your emotions:

- Avoid making decisions, especially irrevocable, life-altering decisions, when in the grip of strong emotions.

- Try not to validate or hang onto your emotions, or to suppress or deny them. Don't deliberately try to keep yourself activated, and also don't tell yourself you "shouldn't" feel the emotions at hand. Just feel them, to start.
- Recognize an emotion, first and foremost, as an experience you are having in your body. Try to name and describe the physical sensations you are feeling: "My face feels hot and prickly, my chest feels tight and my heart is pounding." This strategy helps you remember that the emotion, no matter how unpleasant, is not an emergency and is temporary. It also helps you separate what you are feeling from the story you have about it.
- Understand that feelings are real and valid, but the stories you tell yourself based on those feelings do not necessarily reflect the facts of a situation. It's possible to feel threatened when there is no threat, for example, or to feel powerless when you aren't. That said, feelings are always information. They can tell you something real about what is happening in the world, or something real about what is happening inside you—or both.
- Once you have tended to the emotion and re-regulated, use your discernment before you decide what action to take. Do your feelings indicate that a boundary has been crossed, and if so, how do you need to handle that? Do they show you that you need more support in some area, or some reassurance, and can you ask for that? Do you think there's been a misunderstanding that needs to be fixed or sorted out? Are you being triggered into emotions that are based on past situations, or are your feelings all about the present—and either way, what kind of support do you need, from others or from within your own resources? Are you afraid of something, and if so, can you seek to alleviate that fear, on your own or with help? And so on.
- Learn how you best process your emotions, and then advocate for doing that. Some people process their emotions by talking about them immediately; others need to withdraw for awhile. Both approaches work for different people. If you need to say "I don't want to go to bed angry. I would really like to talk about this now," say so. (Though note that it's not okay to keep a partner up into the wee hours, preventing them from getting a good night's sleep.) If you need to say "Look, I can't talk about this right now. Let's come back to it in the morning," do that—but do try, if you can, to stay connected with your partner in some other, low-key way that's

not processing the conflict, like cuddling or watching a show, so they don't feel like you're stonewalling or abandoning them.

Emotions are data. They should never be ignored or dismissed; they tell you valuable things about what's going on inside yourself. However, they do often require some decoding. (Unfortunately, even if you can strive to be a direct communicator with others, your feelings have no such obligation to you.) For instance, if you're angry, that anger is real and there is always a reason for it. But is that reason "my partner was a jerk to me," or "my partner inadvertently said something that reminded me of some criticism an abusive ex used to harangue me with"? Or is it "I skipped lunch today and I feel like crap" or "I just got bad news at work and really needed a soft landing when I got home, but my partner had a stressful day too"? Figuring out what your emotions are telling you can help you reach the next step of taking action. In this case, the action might be anything from setting a firm boundary with your partner to having a meal and a glass of water.

BE CURIOUS

Many conflicts arise because one person has made judgments without full knowledge of the thoughts or feelings behind another person's actions. If the two (or more) sides in a conflict work from their own assumptions without checking whether they are true, no one feels understood, all become even more hurt and angry, and the conflict escalates.

Conflict-resolution professionals stress the value of curiosity, accompanied by active listening. Many conflicts can be avoided or de-escalated if someone is willing to set aside their prejudgments—and the intense feelings connected to them—and ask a question. And then be curious about the actual answer.

Not just any question, though. The question should be genuine and open-ended, a serious request for more information about another person's feelings, intentions or motivations. It should not be a choice between predefined alternatives, or an accusation followed by a demand for a response. It should be, as much as possible, unburdened from what you *think* will be the answer. That means being curious about what the answer really is.

Consider the following questions, arising from the same scenario:

- "When we went to that dinner party, you didn't sit next to me. Obviously you're ashamed to be seen with me. Why are you even involved with me if you don't want people to know we're together?"
- "When we went to that dinner party, you didn't sit next to me. I felt sad and hurt because social recognition of our relationship is important to me, and I have a fear that you don't want to be seen with me. Could we talk about why you chose that particular seat at the party, and ways you could be more visible as my partner?"

They both end with a question mark, but they are very different kinds of questions. One is a barely veiled accusation and expression of hurt; the other is a genuine request for information and an offer of collaboration. The answer could turn out to be anything from "I wanted to talk to Bill over there about his project" to "Honestly, I'm worried that if my boss sees me with you, he'll think I'm cheating on my other partner, whom I brought to the last party." Once the questioner understands where their partner is coming from, they will be able to respond to the situation using accurate information, not just their own stories. And the questioner will stand a better chance of being able to express their own feelings about the situation to their partner without putting words in their partner's mouth or putting them on the defensive, because the partner will know that the questioner now understands where they're coming from.

Moving away from defensiveness, assumptions and judgments and toward curiosity requires us to step outside ourselves. And that involves recognizing that the world may not be exactly as we think it is—we may have been wrong about our assessment of other people. It can be hard to restrain our emotional responses for long enough to express curiosity and try to understand the feelings of the very person we believe is responsible for our pain. But this strategy can defuse a lot of conflicts before they start.

DON'T LET THE DISHES GET CRUSTY

Good communication is not just reactive, but proactive. That means regular checking in, just to see how things are going—and not just with your partners, but with yourself. Talk about things that bother you while they're still small. Express what you want early and often. Don't sit on things, hoping they'll go away. Don't wait to talk until someone raises a specific problem; develop the habit of letting your partners know where you're at emotionally on an ongoing basis.

The purpose of checking in is simply to keep the lines of communication open, so problems can be spotted when they're still ripples rather than tsunamis. Noël Lynne Figart, author of the blog *The Polyamorous Misanthrope*, calls this "not letting the dishes get crusty." When everyone makes it a habit to wash the dishes as they use them rather than letting them pile up, no one has to confront the icky task of washing an entire sink full of crusty, three-day-old dishes.

It can be helpful to schedule check-ins with some kind of agreed-upon frequency to avoid the dreaded "we need to talk." The *Multiamory* podcast offers a good template for regular relationship check-ins at multiamory.com/radar.

MAKING COMMUNICATION SAFE

There's one more prerequisite for communication to succeed: It has to be safe for another person to communicate with you. Everyone wants their partners to be honest with them. At the same time, nobody likes to hear bad news. From ancient empires to modern boardrooms, bearers of bad tidings have paid the price for delivering messages distasteful to the recipients' ears.

It's easy to forget how many ways you can make it very expensive for people to be honest with you. When you love someone, it's hard even under the best of circumstances to say something that you know will make them unhappy. It requires a lot of vulnerability and courage to do that. But you expose yourself emotionally because your partners' feelings affect yours. When that vulnerability is met with defensiveness, annoyance, passive-aggressiveness, silence, anger, resentment or even punishment, honesty becomes damn near impossible.

If you want your partners to be honest with you, you need to accept what you hear without anger, recriminations or blame, even when you're surprised or you hear something you really don't want to. You must be willing to take a deep breath, switch gears and say "Thank you for sharing that with me."

This doesn't mean you aren't allowed to have feelings and reactions. It just means that it's beneficial to everyone if you can find a space between stimulus (whatever you've just heard) and reaction (whatever response you want to give). In that space, take the time to feel, assess evidence, find your curiosity and compassion, and allow big emotions to pass. Sometimes this is a three-second process; sometimes you might need to say "I need a half-hour break to think about that, can we pick up this conversation in a bit?" Some people need longer: Eve has learned that she needs at least two days between receiving upsetting information and being able to process it with the person it concerns. Take the time you need, and then you can approach the ensuing discussion with kindness for your partner and yourself.

Of course, there are also times when an immediate reaction is exactly correct. If a partner calls you names or threatens you, for example, you don't need to make them feel safe doing so. It's totally reasonable to say "Hey, that is not cool and you need to leave," or "You just crossed a line, and I'm outta here." Similarly, if the bad news is "the dog just died," it's okay to just burst into tears! Having the skill to deal with surprising or difficult news is great, but that doesn't mean you should use it in every situation. You're not a robot, and you're not invulnerable. Developing good discernment can help you figure out when to employ all your carefully honed emotional management skills, and when it makes sense to just respond.

Some people think that managing your reactions means you're being fake. But using these skills doesn't mean you're inauthentic; it's just a question of what kind of response will move you toward resolution versus toward conflict. You don't need to downplay your feelings or pretend. Honesty and clarity are still key here, and it's okay to say so if you're hurt, angry or sad. In a healthy intimate relationship, people should be able to express big feelings and support each other in them. The idea here is just not to be volatile or lash out, which tends to shut down communication and make it hard for someone to bring up difficult topics in the future.

The world through your own lens

Communication extends beyond words. Even when everyone agrees on the meanings of words, things can go wrong when people have different conceptual frameworks—different ideas about the way the world works. After all, everyone sees the world through the lens of their own experiences and ideologies. When you communicate, you filter the things another person says through your own frameworks. If someone holds what to you seems like an alien idea or a worldview you don't understand, or speaks from experiences very different from yours, communication can be lost.

You can't help but see the world through your own lens, and it's not always obvious where your perceptions of the world diverge from other people's. A big part of being able to communicate with someone who seems to hold a different worldview, or who has different experiences, is to listen and ask clarifying questions. It's tempting to impose your own understanding on other people—"You're just saying my jealousy is all in my head!"—and if you don't pay attention, you can end up doing this without even being aware of it. Effective communication succeeds more often when you ask questions than when you tell other people what they're saying (or, worse, tell them what they're thinking or feeling). In practice: "It sounds to me like you're saying I have to get over my jealousy by myself. Is that really what you're saying?"

It's also important to acknowledge that two people can have wildly different experiences of the same events—especially if emotions are high—to the point where they may remember various details differently. There may be times when it's important to determine whose recollection best reflects what actually happened—what would have been caught on camera—but this happens less often than people might think. It's common to attach more emotional weight to being "right" and to get others to agree with your version of events than you do to understanding others or having your perspective understood. That said, if someone is regularly challenging your perceptions and memories, and insisting you adopt theirs, that's a sign of possible gaslighting—particularly if they regularly deny having said or done things you experience as harmful. Again, it goes back to the purpose of a conversation: to exchange understanding, or to exchange power.

Sometimes, sadly, multiple worldviews or sets of perceptions cannot be reconciled or aligned. If two or more people's values are opposed, even if the people can agree on the facts of a situation, it can be impossible to resolve their differing feelings about it in a way that allows the relationship to continue in a healthy way. And if two people can't agree on the facts of a situation that's of some emotional significance, it can be hard to even get to the point of discussing their differing emotions or repairing any harm done. Avoiding such effort is one reason why some people engage in gaslighting—as Kate Abramson discusses in *On Gaslighting*, a gaslighter often cannot tolerate disagreement on certain key points, as it causes them unbearable anxiety, so much so that they find it preferable to both undermine and question the sanity of the person disagreeing with them.

When you love someone, it's often worth putting in the effort to find ways to bridge the gaps between your respective perceptions and understandings. But here's where your discernment comes into play: You also need to decide, at a certain point, whether it's possible to bridge that kind of gap, and what you want to do if it isn't.

Handling mistakes

Things will go wrong. You and your partners will make mistakes. People will get hurt. What happens afterward depends on how capable you are of forgiving one another for your errors, handling the consequences with grace and dignity, and learning from your mistakes. The way you handle mistakes is part of the process of building trust that we discussed in chapter 5.

Mistakes happen because someone is trying to solve a problem or meet a need. It's easy, in the emotional aftermath, to see a mistake as a consequence of selfishness or some other moral failing. But recovery from a mistake depends on being able to see your partners as human beings doing their best to solve a problem rather than as caricatures or monsters.

Compassion—self-compassion—is also needed when you're the one who makes a mistake. Sometimes it's easier to treat others with gentleness or compassion than it is to do the same for yourself; some people recognize the fallibility of those around them more readily than their own. You will make mistakes. It's the cost of being human. When you do, look to them as opportunities to learn, and remember that compassion begins at home.

Conversely, sometimes compassion can be weaponized. A partner who is behaving badly toward you might be taking advantage of your tendency to be compassionate so they don't have to do the work of changing their own behaviour. Or you, yourself, might be saying you practise self-compassion when in truth you're avoiding the work of looking at and fixing the places where you keep making mistakes. This is one more place where discernment is key.

QUESTIONS TO ASK YOURSELF

Strategies for better communication include, for starters, active listening and direct communication. As you practise these skills on a daily basis in your relationships, here are some questions to consider:

- How often, and how directly, do I ask for what I want and need?
- How do I handle hearing no? Do others find it hard to say no to me? Why or why not?
- Do I perceive criticism in my partner's statements even if they aren't directly critical, or hear hidden meanings in their questions?

If so, how do I remind myself to ask for clarification rather than making assumptions?

- What do I do to check in with my partners?
- How well do I listen to others? Do others communicate to me that they feel heard?
- What do I do to make sure it's safe for others to communicate with me, and to let them know it's safe?
- In my communication, how do I show that I'm taking responsibility for my actions?
- In what ways do I actively listen to my partners? In what ways do they actively listen to me? Where can we each improve in our active listening skills?

a monster is a part of ourselves that we don't want to find in the mirror. a part of ourselves that we try to cut out and split off and put inside other people so that they can carry it for us: our fear. our shame.

KAI CHENG THOM

8 Befriending the Green-Eyed Monster

Jealousy is often the first thing people bring up when learning about nonmonogamy, and many consider it the most important issue to address. Perhaps ironically, it's the subject of the shortest chapter in this book.

In part that's because there's so much material available on it already, and we want to focus on what we can add to the conversation. In part it's because we believe that in many cases there's an over-focus on jealousy, to the detriment of dealing with the many other very important issues in nonmonogamy.

You'll hear a wide variety of opinions about jealousy among nonmonogamous folks. Some believe it's possible to banish it forever by working on personal security. Some try to structure their relationships so they never have to feel it. Some feel it reflects attitudes of entitlement that need to be deconstructed. Overwhelmingly, people view it as something negative—the green-eyed monster, an unwelcome interloper to be controlled, vanquished or banished.

Each of these views has a piece of the picture; none is complete. Jealousy isn't just one thing, and so there's no one solution. We think of jealousy as more like twenty different emotions in a trench coat. In fact, it's pretty common for nonmonogamous folks to label any unfamiliar, negative feeling attached to their partners' other relationships as jealousy, which confuses the issue further. A big part of responding to jealousy is discerning the real mix of emotions that you're feeling, and what they're trying to tell you.

Further, for all the bad rap that jealousy gets among nonmonogamous folks, it's important to remember that jealousy is just a part of you—maybe a part that's scared, or angry, or hurt, or trying to protect you, or even prone to tantrums, but not an enemy (or a monster). Instead of fighting with or running from it, we would like to offer the possibility that you could instead try to welcome it, give it a hug, offer it a cup of hot cocoa and then, when you've both calmed down enough, listen to what it has to say. (At the risk of mixing our metaphors, you might find that once the trench coat is unbuttoned, what you really have is a pile of wet, hungry and cold kittens all requiring care. Just please don't give kittens cocoa.)

Jealousy isn't unique to nonmonogamy. In fact, many now-nonmonogamous people say their worst experiences of jealousy (their own or a partner's) occurred in the context of monogamous relationships. For some, this is a major motivation for wanting to be nonmonogamous—a combination of the greater likelihood of connecting with partners who've worked on their jealousy or have progressive ideas about what it means and how to manage it, and the relative safety of spending time in less mononormative social contexts, where jealousy is not seen as a valid reason for all manner of harmful behaviours. Mononormativity teaches that jealousy is a sign of love, and only in the most extreme cases are monogamous folks expected to actually work through their jealousy rather than cater to it; the relationship escalator model is designed in many ways to protect you from experiencing jealousy at all. A major difference in the nonmonogamous experience of jealousy is both the social expectation—and the relational necessity—that you don't let it dominate your life.

Soothing jealousy

Jealousy can make us feel threatened at a very deep, survival level, setting off panicked responses in some of the most ancient parts of our brains. Until those feelings have subsided, it can be hard to do the cognitive work that's needed to deal with jealousy for the long term. Even if you're someone who likes to process verbally during intense emotional experiences, beware of making any major decisions quickly.

Working through jealous feelings starts with accepting them. You can't deal with jealousy by wishing it away. Our emotions are what they are, and telling yourself, "I shouldn't feel this!" won't work. The feelings might be overwhelming for a while—even if you're experienced at nonmonogamy. Accept that there's nothing wrong with you for feeling this way. You are completely normal.

While we're here: It's important for your support people to accept your feelings, too. It's unfortunately all too common for nonmonogamous people to subtly or overtly shame each other for feeling jealous. You're not less evolved or less spiritual, you're not (necessarily) clinging to a scarcity or ownership paradigm, and you're not "not really nonmonogamous." You're a person who's having totally normal feelings.

The next step is to regulate and ask for support. Jealousy can present in a lot of ways: Sometimes it's just a fluttery feeling of uncertainty or insecurity. Other times it can be dramatic, manifesting as nausea, headaches, dizziness, dissociation, nightmares or even full-blown anxiety attacks. Do whatever self-care you need to soothe yourself and ride out the feelings. Take a bath, ask someone for cuddles, pet your dog—whatever you do to take care of yourself, do it now. Check out the tips for emotional processing on pages 146–148. Try, for now, to separate the feeling you're experiencing from whatever story you have about it. Don't make any big decisions. Don't break up with anyone! Know that this will pass. What you are feeling right now is not all you are.

If your jealousy is manifesting as anger, you might need to release that by screaming underwater or into a pillow, working out, or writing all those awful thoughts in a journal you never share or a letter you never send. Remember that no matter how awful you're feeling, you're accountable for your words and your actions. Things said can never be unsaid. Try not to lash out, and don't try to actually process the feelings until you feel calm enough to do so with kindness. And if you're supporting someone who's experiencing jealousy, don't push them to try to talk about it while they're still in an activated state.

Listening to jealousy

Once the emotional experience has passed and the triggering situation has ended—ideally after at least a night or two of sleep—it's time to start figuring out what your jealousy is trying to tell you. This can take some time. Jessica Fern offers a useful framework for discerning the varieties of experiences that we call jealousy: Is it "me, we or society?"

When jealousy is about "me," that means it's rooted in some kind of inner wound: unworthiness, fear, trauma, an insecure attachment style and so on. A lot of the nonmonogamy literature focuses on this kind of jealousy. Inner wounds are a common source of jealousy, to be sure. But a danger arises here because it can be so easy—both for you and others in your polycule—to assume by default that an inner wound is the source of all feelings coded as jealousy, and thus the solution is always to work on yourself. At best this perspective can keep you stuck, unable to address the source of the problem; at worst, it can lead to gaslighting, as every attempt to resolve a nonmonogamy-related issue in your relationships or polycule gets flipped back around as something you need to work on by yourself. Whether your jealousy is communicating a need for self-work is for you to decide for yourself, after careful reflection and discernment, and perhaps after conversations with a trusted therapist or friends.

Another "me" jealousy scenario is an experience that, according to Fern, is often labelled as jealousy but actually belongs in a different category altogether. This is "primal panic," which many people experience when they go through a rupture in an attachment bond, or have an experience that creates an acute fear of a rupture. Primal panic can be a debilitating physical experience that can feel like you're dying. Fern writes in *Polysecure*:

> Many of my clients report being highly anxious and off their emotional axis for hours, sometimes even days, before their partner goes on a date with someone else. Others seriously spiral out while the date is happening. Cognitively, they know that their partner is still alive, not abandoning them or doing anything wrong, but their body and emotions are in primal panic. In such cases, jealousy is not a sufficient or accurate description of what is happening for the partner in distress. When primal attachment panic gets mislabeled as jealousy, the partner experiencing it can be left thinking that there is something wrong with them, that this is their issue to figure out on their own and that they should be better at doing [nonmonogamy]. ... This can also escalate into panic attacks, meltdowns or an emotional crisis that can pit partners against each other or become extremely difficult for everyone involved to manage.

If you experience primal panic, it can be difficult to understand why other people seem to have a comparatively easier time managing their jealousy. Primal panic is a fundamentally different experience from any of the other kinds of jealousy in that it is profoundly embodied and can be much more severe and overwhelming than the other things people tend to call jealousy. Its implications and the tools to manage it are therefore distinct. (More on tools in a minute.)

When jealousy is about the "we," it means that it's pointing to a real problem in your relationship that's being illuminated by another relationship or situation. Fern says this kind of jealousy "can arise from experiences such as partners breaking agreements, saying one thing but doing another, downplaying or concealing the extent of their connections with others, or withholding important information." One common example is what Fern and her co-author David Cooley describe in *Polywise* as "justice jealousy," which is what occurs when you see a partner offering something to another partner that you'd long been needing in your own relationship but had been told would never be available, or even that your partner was incapable of providing. It could refer to a specific activity or type of care you've been craving, like weekend getaways together, or more generally to investment in and care of the relationship. It could be something that arises in a context where you were content with the role you had in a partner's life, but realize you aren't once you see them investing in another partner in a different way (see pages 250–252 on grapes and cucumbers). It could happen if your relationship was already in trouble, and a new relationship brought the fault lines into sharp relief (see page 301). Or your partner could be investing so much time and energy into another relationship that their relationship with you is withering from neglect.

The "society" variety of jealousy has to do with the stories you have about your relationships and what it means when your partners love others, what Fern refers to as "the societal narratives and discourses we've inherited about love, gender, possessiveness, status and perceived entitlements within romantic relationships—narratives rooted in influences like capitalism, colonialism and sexism." We discussed these narratives a great deal in the first part of this book, and "society" jealousy offers an opportunity to unpack them at a personal level. What narratives go through your head when you're feeling the things you call jealousy? Do you believe that a partner's attention to someone else means they care less for you? Do you fear your social status would be lessened if others found out? Do you believe that feeling jealous is proof of love? Do you want them to be only yours? Do you, at some level, believe that people can really only love one person, so a partner loving someone else means they don't really love you?

When she was researching her book *What Love Is*, Carrie Jenkins noticed an important difference in how people thought about jealousy in nonmonogamous relationships versus how they thought about it in monogamous relationships, or even other kinds of relationships such as those between siblings. Only in nonmonogamy was jealousy brought up as a possible reason to not have certain kinds of relationships at all, whereas in more normative relationships, it was accepted as part of the landscape. She suggests that this privileging of jealousy only in the context of nonmonogamy is connected to "the history of ideas of women as possessions, control of women's bodies... [risk to the] core connection, feeling under threat," as well as threats to identity and self-conception that could produce, as she calls it, "existential terror." This template of men's jealousy used as a reason to control women's actions within intimate relationships is transposed into mononormativity as a whole, at which point it transcends the idea of gender and gets applied across all gender pairings operating under a mononormative worldview—though note that its origins still map onto gender-based differences in rates of coercive control and intimate partner violence. This is one particularly unsavoury aspect of the mononormative fairy tale that many people need to unpack when they decide to start having nonmonogamous relationships, and it may require some emotional unlearning and relearning. While you can't usually change your emotional state entirely, you do have influence over the narrative you ascribe to that state, and the power of these narratives in turn can have effects over time on your somatic experiences of jealousy.

Integrating jealousy

It can be helpful to think of jealousy as a messenger. Once you've decoded what it's trying to convey, you can start thinking about what to do with the information.

While it's common to use battle-related metaphors to describe getting rid of jealousy, we prefer to think of it as relieving it of duty and letting it go into well-deserved retirement. Thank it for its service and let it go back to hanging out with your other emotions, satisfied that it has served its purpose for you.

If you're experiencing "me" jealousy related to self-worth or insecurity, the information in chapter 4 and the associated resources are likely to be most helpful for you in resolving your jealousy over the long term. The "parts" exercises in *Polywise* might also be helpful to you. If you're actually experiencing primal panic, you may need to spend more time working on emotional self-regulation. Fern says it also helps for partners to make a plan together. What kind of connection, reassurance and support do you need before and after a likely triggering event such as a partner's date with someone else—and in the relationship generally—to feel safe? When you are alone, what do you need to feel safe in yourself? Some folks need to plan to be with others during a triggering situation, especially at first, and especially other people they can co-regulate with. Fern advises having a plan, perhaps even a written one, for what you'll do if you'll become dysregulated, and a plan for reconnecting with your partner later. In a long-distance relationship, reassurance can be provided through an exchange of objects, or what she calls "letters of importance": messages you can read or listen to during times of distress that reassure you of your partner's love and care. Over time, you can work on attachment healing and addressing whatever core traumas are causing the issue. Because primal panic is such a somatic experience, it may help to incorporate physical practices into your other therapeutic and reflective work in order to relieve stress; for example, you might try exercise or breathing practices, self-massage or other sensation-based work, or things like taking a hot shower or going for a brisk walk in fresh air.

Fern says that for most people, the experience improves over time. But for some, it doesn't, no matter how much effort they put in. In these cases, it's possible that nonmonogamy just isn't a good idea for your nervous system, even if it's something you want. Only you can ultimately know how much work you want to do before deciding nonmonogamy is not for you.

If jealousy is communicating a problem in the relationship, bring it to your partner. You don't have to have the solution right away; it's okay just to know there's a problem. Tell them what you're feeling and why, and ask them to collaborate with you on a solution. Try to focus on your own relationship with them, not their relationship with anyone else. If you're making comparisons, use them as a source of information about your own needs. What do you need from the relationship that you're not getting? The tools in chapters 5 and 7 can help you in this process.

In some rare cases, unfortunately, you could be dealing with someone who simply enjoys triangulating partners in order to gain a sense of power, or who is "hedging" in order to get their needs met without investing much themselves (see pages 73–74). Such a person may also be more inclined to engage in the kind of gaslighting we mentioned on page 158. If you think there's a problem in the relationship and a partner or metamour is saying you're just insecure, take a step back and ask yourself: Are agreements being followed? Commitments being met? Assurances offered? Is our behaviour consistent? Are we nurturing secure attachment? Are my partners listening to me, taking my concerns seriously and trying to work with me to resolve the issue? Or are they just trying to get me to adjust my feelings to be okay with broken agreements, lack of transparency, unreliability or some other important relational issue? You don't need to convince anyone else of anything—you know your own truth—but if you don't feel like you and your partner are on the same team in addressing the issue, you likely have a "we" problem on your hands (and if you feel like you're being left to solve it on your own, that's further data about exactly what kind of "we" problem is present).

At the same time, someone who is experiencing a "me" variety of jealousy might try to blame the relationship and get their partner to agree to all kinds of accommodations so they can avoid feeling insecure. Extreme jealousy is in fact a common element of coercive control, discussed on pages 63–64. If you fear this may be happening, check out chapter 3 and some of the checklists therein. You don't need to try to convince your partner that their jealousy is their problem. You just need to get clear on what kind of treatment you expect from a loving partner, and what kinds of investments you are willing to make to help them feel secure with you.

If your jealousy is rooted in your stories—the "society" variety of jealousy—you can work on getting to the bottom of the stories you have and whether you agree with them anymore. You can try to tease apart which of your stories are rooted in fact, and which are rooted in culture, family, mononormative and amatonormative societal values, and so on. This can be a fun exercise to do with your partners, friends or members of your polycule, as long as you don't feel like you're being pressured to take a stance just because it's in someone else's best interest. If you like, you can try engaging in what Jenkins calls "re-storifying" your experience, which is just what it sounds like: developing a new story that can give you more control over the ways you're getting triggered into jealousy and the intensity of the experience when it happens. You probably can't just make up any story you want; you'll need to find something that feels powerful enough to you to be able to meaningfully integrate it into your worldview. It could come from your own history, the experiences of others, from fiction or mythology, or from a culture you are connected to—anywhere you find meaningful narratives.

If you don't feel (much) jealousy

Because jealousy is such a hot topic for discussion anytime nonmonogamy comes up, if you're someone who doesn't experience a lot of jealousy, you may be met with disbelief. People—monogamous and otherwise—may think you're deluded, out of touch with your feelings, or simply lying about them. You may be accused of not really loving or caring about your partners, or being dissociated or avoidant. You may be seen as bragging about being more enlightened than others. These misunderstandings might come from friends or acquaintances, or from your partners themselves.

Try to meet these reactions with compassion and kindness. If you happen to have an easy enough time with jealousy, or if it's not a big issue for you, don't act like a jerk about it when you're talking to people who struggle with it. It's rude and unhelpful, and it contributes to the perception that nonmonogamous people are condescending and believe themselves to be more enlightened than others. It's never fun to be misunderstood, but that's not an excuse for bad behaviour.

Some people don't naturally feel a lot of jealousy, whether that's because they somehow managed to miss a lot of the mononormative and amatonormative conditioning most people grow up with (or encountered other belief systems early on), or they have a general baseline sense of personal security, a secure attachment style, a particular set of personality traits (such as certain kinds of introversion), a great deal of trust in a given relationship, or even a set of spiritual beliefs that really work for them, such as Buddhist non-attachment. Other people have simply done a lot of emotional work to better manage their jealousy, and that work was successful! Regardless of your path, we want to emphasize that just as it's normal to feel jealousy, it's also fine if you don't. It doesn't make you a weirdo or a liar any more than it makes you a more spiritually enlightened being. It just means you either got lucky or did hard work in this area, or some of both.

QUESTIONS TO ASK YOURSELF

These questions can help prepare you before you experience jealousy, as well as in understanding your experience afterward.

- How can I take care of myself when I feel overwhelmed by my emotions?
- What reassuring things can I ask my partner to do for me when I'm experiencing intense jealous feelings?
- If the specific partner I'm jealous about is unavailable to me when I start feeling jealous, to whom can I turn for reassurance, empathy, companionship or positive touch?

- Am I uncertain about the value my partner sees in me? Am I not sure why they want to be with me? If this is how I'm feeling, what can I do to find confidence in myself, or what can I ask my partner to do to help me see what they value and desire in me?
- Are my needs being met in my relationship? Is there something I need to ask my partner to work on with me?
- Is my partner showing up in another relationship in a way I wish they would show up with me? Are they open to doing that for me? Why or why not? Am I okay with that?
- Am I worried that if someone "better" comes along, my partner will realize I'm not good enough and want to replace me? Do I think that if my partner falls in love with another person, my partner will leave me for that person? Do I think my partner doesn't really love me? If this is how I'm feeling, what can I do to change that way of thinking, and what role could my partner have in helping change that way of thinking?
- Do I believe that if I am not jealous, I don't really love my partner? Does my partner believe this?
- What other stories do I have about what it means when my partner experiences intimacy with others? How do these stories affect my emotional experience of jealousy?
- What sources can I draw on to formulate stories that can help me change my narratives around jealousy and my partners' other relationships?

Part 3

Nonmonogamous Frameworks

When you create intimate relationships, you invite other people deep into your heart. You allow them access to your mind, your body, your emotions. This intimacy is one of the most wonderful, most profoundly transformative things life has to offer. It changes who you are. It tells you that in all the vastness of the universe, you do not have to be alone. But it comes at a price. When you allow others into your heart, and they allow you into theirs, you become exquisitely vulnerable to each other. The people you choose to let in have the power to bring you incredible joy, and to hurt you deeply. If you are to respect the gifts of intimacy you are offered, you have an ethical obligation to treat one another with care.

In practice, this can be hard. Even when you allow only one person at a time to affect you so deeply, you must strike a balance between allowing your partner to be who they are and creating a framework where you feel safe. When more than one person has access to your heart, this balancing act becomes much more complicated—and scary.

In Part 3, we suggest frameworks you can use to create safety and security while still respecting the humanity and autonomy of the people you love. Just as Part 2 began with a chapter about your self, so does Part 3, because secure nonmonogamous frameworks begin with your self and your boundaries. The next three chapters discuss rules, hierarchies and various kinds of relationship agreements, and we provide some experience-based critique of some of the common and often unsuccessful ways people try to maintain safety in their relationships. Finally, we provide some ideas about empowered relationships and practical, realistic nonmonogamy agreements.

The differences between and relative merits of boundaries, agreements, rules and hierarchies are subjects of heated contention in nonmonogamous communities. Over the last fifteen to twenty years or so, the balance of opinion in mainstream polyamory, in particular, has shifted from rules and hierarchies as the accepted default to a broad rejection of both in favour of agreements, boundaries and non-hierarchical relationships. And yet the distinctions among these frameworks are nuanced and highly context-specific, and it's easy for conversations to get derailed over definitions. From the outside, the effects of a boundary, agreement and rule might look the same. Likewise, a relationship network with differing levels of priority and commitment might superficially resemble a hierarchical arrangement. Yet the underlying mechanisms at play are very different, partly because they are defined by where power lies—and doesn't.

When it comes to distinctions among boundaries, agreements and rules, it's common to see a simplified framing of "rules bad; agreements and boundaries good." In fact, you'll see this framing from both people who agree with it and people who don't. Not only is reality not that simple, but this framing often leads to people trying to disguise rules as boundaries to avoid falling afoul of this, er, rule.

We propose that, in the context of intimate relationships, boundaries and rules tend to come up most frequently when people are having difficulty making agreements, when one or more people don't trust the others involved, or when someone breaks or comes close to breaking the agreements that were made. Agreements are collaborative, and in intimate relationships, they are always preferable. Both boundaries and rules assert control: boundaries over oneself, rules over others. In this sense, boundaries are a better tool than rules, both because it's much easier to control oneself, and because they acknowledge the agency of other people, and thus treat others as real (axiom 1). Of course, people always have boundaries, and knowing them, as well as knowing how to hold them firmly but gently, is always important. But we believe that in a healthy, established relationship, most of the time you won't have to defend your boundaries too often, because most of the time you won't be running up too close to them.

Daring to set boundaries is about having the courage to love ourselves, even when we risk disappointing others.
BRENÉ BROWN

9 Boundaries

Many people use the terms *rules, agreements* and *boundaries* interchangeably. But these terms have subtly different meanings, and being unclear about those distinctions can create Gordian knots in relationships.

Any discussion of these three words has to start with boundaries, because boundaries are about you and your self. Understanding boundaries is essential to understanding what kinds of agreements might maximize your satisfaction, empowerment and sense of well-being. Strong boundaries are vital to building healthy relationships, while having poor personal boundaries can be damaging to your self. The well-known quote by therapist, educator and organizer Prentis Hemphill sums up this importance succinctly: "Boundaries are the distance at which I can love you and me at the same time." Boundaries are also essential to consent, and adult relationships are healthy only when they are consensual. This chapter is all about boundaries. We get into rules and agreements in the next chapter.

Defining boundaries

Boundaries concern your self: what is yours alone, which others may access only with your permission. Because boundaries are personal, people often don't realize where they are until they are crossed. You can divide personal boundaries into two rough categories: physical (your body, your sexuality) and emotional (your intimacy, your emotions, your affection). These categories of course overlap to some extent.

Your physical boundaries begin where you feel physically affected by another person. For most people, they begin a little outside your physical edges, in your personal space. (As with so many things we've discussed, what different people consider personal space is heavily shaped by their culture and family.) When you set physical boundaries, you are exercising your right to decide if, how and when you want someone in your personal space or touching you. Capitalism, and modern life generally, in many ways erodes people's ability to set boundaries and exercise consent on a daily basis, from the workplace to the medical system to public transportation. (See Kitty Stryker's anthology *Ask: Building Consent Culture* for in-depth exploration of the many facets of consent.)

In intimate relationships, you often negotiate shared physical space, especially when you live with a partner. So you may need to negotiate some space for yourself. For some people, this may be a room of their own. For some, it might be as simple as asking for quiet time on the couch. Or it might be saying, "I need to decompress by myself for a bit before I'm ready to cuddle." A relationship is only healthy if you have the ability to negotiate for individual space when you need it. You may always set boundaries about your physical space and your body. If someone ever tells you it's not okay to assert a physical boundary—especially regarding who you will have sex with or who is allowed to touch you—look out! There's a problem.

Your mind is your mental and emotional experience of the world, your memories, your reality and your values. When you engage with others, you let them into this mental space to a greater or lesser degree. Finding the edges of your mind is trickier than finding your physical edges. Humans are social animals, and even the most superficial interactions engage our mental faculties and our emotions.

When you engage in intimate relationships, you open up your emotional boundaries. You let a chosen few affect you deeply, allowing them in much further than you do a random stranger or a work colleague. This is beautiful and amazing, and one of the things that make life worth living. But your mind and your emotions always belong to you, and you alone. Your intimate partners, your family, your boss and the clerk at the grocery store only ever get access to those on loan, and if that intimacy is damaging you, you have the right to refuse that access. Always.

That means people all have a fundamental, inalienable right not to extend themselves emotionally to anyone they don't choose to. Every person has the absolute right to choose whom they will or will not be intimate with, for any reason or no reason.

Setting emotional boundaries is different from setting physical boundaries. When you set a physical boundary, you are exerting clear control over what you do with your body. "Don't touch me there," for example. "Don't move closer to me." "Leave my home." With emotional boundaries, you have to take care to not make others responsible for your mental state. That means you need to make it clear what you're asking for; it's the difference between "Never say anything that might upset me" and "It's not acceptable for you to make fun of my hobbies. Even if you're just joking, it really hurts my feelings."

It's important, here, to point out that responsibility for emotions is tricky. On the extreme ends of the scale, it can be fairly clear: If you say a cheerful "How's it going, sweetheart?" on an average day and your partner responds "Why would you say such a thing to me?!" and storms off, chances are high that you're not responsible for making them feel upset. Something else is going on, and that reaction isn't fair or kind to you. However, if you say the same thing in that same tone in the middle of a funeral, they might be more justifiably upset. The idea that nobody else can make you feel anything may be technically true, but the aim of a loving relationship is not to get away with being a jerk on technical grounds. People do have effects on one another's emotions. Your words, tone and attitude do have the power to hurt. And that means that in loving relationships, you do need to take some responsibility for how your partners feel based on the way you speak to them and act toward them. Likewise, it is reasonable to ask that your partners take some responsibility for how they affect your emotions, without having to give them a detailed list of what words or facial expressions are and aren't permitted. On some level, you have to assume positive intent, but you are also each responsible for being kind, and sometimes you fall short. The space between the extremes of behaviour—between obvious meanness and obvious kindness—is where you need to approach yourself and your partners with a balance of boundaries and compassion. The specifics are going to be different for every relationship.

Healthy boundaries in an intimate relationship aren't the same as boundaries at work or at a sex party. As author Nora Samaran writes:

> Someone with healthy boundaries is confident enough in their own ability to say yes and no that they can act *interdependent* and responsive to others *without losing themselves*, either in the moment or in the long term. If it takes you a month to know that you did a thing you didn't want to do, your boundaries may be overly porous and you may need work on doing deep inner listening in the moment to be able to know your own body's cues. If you erect walls that are so rigid you cannot hear or see when someone you love needs you, your boundaries may

> be overly hard and you may need to develop responsiveness and receptivity...Ideally, someone with healthy boundaries can trust in live time their own capacity to listen to their body, needs, and feelings, and not need external permission to do so, while they also have the resilience and self-awareness that *lets them empathize with and respond in the moment to those they care about without losing their own internal cues.* Healthy boundaries let you assess your *own* needs *and* the needs of others, in a moment-by-moment way. They let you act responsive to others *and* responsive to yourself.

When we talk about setting boundaries, we're not talking about restrictions on another person's behaviour, except as their behaviour concerns access to *you.* Of course, whether you choose to grant that access may in fact depend on how they are behaving in other circumstances. Examples of boundaries include:

- I will not be involved with someone who is not open and honest with all their other partners about dating me.
- I will not have unbarriered sex with partners whose sexual behaviour does not fall within my level of acceptable sexual health risk.
- I will not become involved with someone who is not already committed to nonmonogamy.
- I will not remain in a relationship with a partner who threatens me or uses violence.
- I will choose the level of closeness I want with my partners' other partners, subject to their consent.
- I will not be in a relationship with a partner who expects me to remain closeted.

The difference between "boundaries you set for yourself" and "rules you place on someone else" might just seem like one of semantics, but it is profound. *Rules* tend to come from the idea that it's acceptable, or even desirable, for you to control someone else's behaviour, or for someone else to control yours. *Boundaries* derive from the idea that the only person you really control is yourself.

Sacrificing your self

One way to damage a relationship is to believe that your sense of self or self-worth comes from your partner, or from being in a relationship. If you constantly seek reinforcement of your worth from your partner, your partner becomes your source of worth, rather than your equal. This kind of dependency is exhausting for your partner and destructive for you.

This is especially likely to happen if you have trouble setting boundaries. Fuzzy boundaries can lead to a loss of self-identity and an inability to tell where your self (and your responsibility to set your own boundaries) ends and your partner begins. Losing your self-identity opens you up to being manipulated or losing your ethical integrity. And you must be true to yourself if you are to be true to those you love. When you feel that you "need" a relationship, you may become afraid to raise your voice and assert the other things you need. It's hard to set boundaries in a relationship you feel you can't live without, because setting boundaries means admitting there are things that might end your relationship.

Many cultures worldwide are filled with stories of self-sacrifice, often framed as noble, dutiful or romantic. In Victor Hugo's *Les Misérables*, the romantic heroine Éponine dies after taking a bullet for the man she loves. In Oscar Wilde's short story "The Nightingale and the Rose," a nightingale gives her life to help a boy woo the object of his adoration—who rejects him anyway. The children's book *The Giving Tree*, by Shel Silverstein, is notorious for its portrayal of a tree that sacrifices everything, including her life, for a boy (and later man) who takes it all for granted. It's been so heavily criticized in recent years that another writer, Topher Payne, created an entire alternate ending for the story and called it *The Tree Who Set Healthy Boundaries*. These stories mean something about our culture—among other things, notice how often characters coded as women or feminine do the sacrificing.

If you've absorbed the idea that this kind of self-sacrifice is good and noble, it's not your fault! But as an adult, you may need to learn a new concept on a deep emotional level: that relationships are actually supposed to be fulfilling for you, too, and that laying your needs (or your personality) at the feet of a partner is not actually a noble or desirable thing. Loving someone, or giving to someone, is not supposed to hurt and drain you all the time. And if it does, something is wrong. But drawing that line can be very hard. And on those occasions when you must do so, you might experience guilt and self-judgment. Self-sacrifice is conditioning that can go very, very deep. And it is still powerfully reinforced by the culture around us, and sometimes even by our partners—even when they have good intentions.

Sometimes your boundaries will cause your partners pain. And when you see someone you love in pain, you may feel an immediate urge to help them. This is a normal and healthy impulse in all relationships—you cannot have healthy relationships without empathy. But this impulse is also exploitable by those who may not share that empathy, or who consistently see their own desires as more important than the boundaries, emotional health or even safety of their partners (as we discussed on pages 82–84). Empathy must exist hand in hand with boundaries.

One form of sacrificing the self is embedded in many versions of the fairy tales many people know well. Mononormativity and amatonormativity teach many toxic myths about love, but perhaps the worst is that "love conquers all." This myth hurts people in all kinds of ways—such as the untold zillions of hours spent and tears wasted by people trying to heal, reform or otherwise change a partner. Especially pernicious is the idea that you're supposed to "give until it hurts"—in fact, for some people, that the measure of their worth is their ability to give, right down to the last drop of themselves. That is wrong. Love isn't supposed to damage you, and you should not and do not need to sacrifice your self for good relationships.

Boundaries vs. rules

For a person accustomed to indirect communication (see chapter 6), the difference between a boundary and a rule may not be clear. An indirect communicator may impose restrictions on a partner by stating the restriction as a boundary, using "I will" boundary language when they are actually applying "you will" restrictions. The difference is in what happens if the other person doesn't behave as desired.

For example, consider a situation in which you set this reasonable boundary: "You are free to do what you like with your body with other people. I am free to decide my level of acceptable risk to my sexual health. If you engage in behaviour that exceeds my level of risk, I reserve the right to use barriers with you, or perhaps not have sex with you at all." If the other person has sex with other people that exceeds your level of risk, you can assess the situation and take appropriate action. You might, for instance, say "Since you are not choosing to use barriers with this other partner, I will use barriers with you," and then do so.

On the other hand, if this is actually a rule being stated in the language of boundaries, you may feel the other person did something they shouldn't have, or that you were *entitled* to make them always use safer-sex barriers with others. If you express recrimination or anger, or attempt punishment in response to your partner's choices, then you were instituting a *rule*, regardless of the wording. Genuine boundaries recognize that others make their own choices, and you do not have the right (or ability) to control those choices. Rather, you have the right and ability to determine for yourself what intimacy you choose to be involved in.

Speaking of punishment, however: Another grey area crops up here, because withdrawal of intimacy (physical and otherwise) *can* be used as a form of punishment, and this can be devastating for relationships (remember what we said on page 134 about stonewalling). You always have a right to whatever boundaries you need, but it's reasonable to expect that some boundaries will have consequences for your relationships, especially if they dramatically change the level of intimacy you have with a partner over time. And if you are feeling particularly hurt, it might be worth taking some time to consider—later, when you've had a chance to process your emotions—whether your boundaries are indeed only self-protective, or whether there is a little part of you that does want to hurt your partner in return. Every person will be different, and what you do with this knowledge is up to you. But regardless, the solution is never ever ever for someone to push on or cross your boundaries—even if those boundaries feel like punishment to them.

Compromise and self-abandonment

No two people have the same needs. Whenever you tie your life to others, especially in intimate relationships, there will be times when you can't have everything you want. The ability to negotiate in good faith and to seek compromise when your needs and those of others conflict is a vital relationship skill. But when you deeply value a relationship (or fear losing it), it can be easy to give up too much of yourself in order to make the relationship work. When this happens, you are abandoning your self in favour of the relationship—crossing your own boundaries. Remember, the people in the relationship are more important than the relationship, and that includes you. To understand where you can make compromises and where you can't, you must first know how to feel your own boundaries. Not all boundaries can be known in advance, but you can learn to recognize when they're being approached or crossed.

The best compromises are those that allow everyone to have their needs met in ethical, compassionate ways. For example, say you want to go on a date, but your partner wants you to spend more time with your kids. A compromise might be to schedule the date for late in the evening, after you've had time to help your children with their homework and they've gone to bed. Both objectives can be met.

On the other hand, agreeing to a compromise such as not having any other relationships until the kids have left home might violate your boundaries. If nonmonogamy is important to your life satisfaction and part of your identity, this compromise would require you to give up a part of who you are. With such a compromise, it's reasonable to question whether "spending time with the kids" is being used as a proxy for "I want a monogamous relationship, so I'm using concerns about the children as a pretext."

When you are asked to compromise in ways that require you to give up your agency or your ability to advocate for your needs, these compromises also threaten to violate your boundaries. Many parts of your life are available for negotiation, but compromising away your agency or bodily integrity (for example, by agreeing to have sex with someone you might not want to, or agreeing to limits on what you are allowed to do with your body) means giving up control of your boundaries. See also our discussion of compromise as a collaborative rather than adversarial process on pages 145–146.

Boundaries and single or solo poly people

People who value autonomy highly and take a solo poly or free-agent approach to nonmonogamy face some special considerations around boundaries. Relationships that don't ride the escalator are often perceived as less important, serious or legitimate than traditional relationships. So, unsurprisingly, these relationships are sometimes not treated seriously, even in the world of nonmonogamy.

For these reasons, free agents must state their boundaries and advocate for their needs very early on. "I'm never likely to live with you, but I still consider this relationship significant, and I still want to feel free to express what I need and have you consider my needs" represents a reasonable boundary. As a single or solo person, you also need to be clear on the value your existing relationships have to you and what your commitment is to them, or they may be trivialized in the minds of potential partners or metamours who don't understand what commitment looks like to you.

A common complaint from solo poly folks is that many people assume they're only looking for casual sex. Because society so tightly conflates sex, relationships and life interconnection, this can be an easy mistake to make. But not wanting to move in does not necessarily mean you only want casual sex. Negotiating boundaries around sex, particularly the expectations attached to it, is important to help you navigate the tangled thicket of assumptions that might pop up.

Because solo poly people place a high emphasis on personal autonomy, things such as veto arrangements, hierarchies and rules that constrain how the relationship is allowed to grow tend to be especially problematic for them. Most solo polyamorists will not agree to such arrangements. Ironically, people who do seek prescriptive hierarchies and look for "secondary" partners will often gravitate toward solo poly people, erroneously believing that if solo poly people don't want the trappings of a conventional relationship, they don't become seriously invested in their relationships. This misperception often leads to pain.

The free-agent model can also have a dark side. Just as people who try to prescribe a specific relationship structure can misuse boundary language to control others, people who prefer a free-agent model can use boundaries around their personal decision-making as a way to avoid responsibility for the consequences of what they do. The choices you make belong to you, but so do their consequences. If you emphasize personal autonomy to the exclusion of listening to your partners' needs, you're not asserting boundaries, you're being a jerk.

Setting new boundaries

Early in your relationships, when everything is going well, you may be inclined to overlook faults and annoyances. Your hormones are telling you that you want to become one with your partners: share everything with them, love them forever. This is when setting boundaries is most important in order to lay a good long-term foundation—and also when you're least likely to set them. Patterns laid down now can entrench over the years, your personalities can polarize in overfunctioning/underfunctioning dynamics (where one partner "takes care" of the other, removing their agency) or other unhealthy patterns, and the boundaries around your sense of self can blur. If you get stuck in a dysfunctional dynamic and want to reclaim your self and re-establish a healthy relationship balance, you need to learn how to set new boundaries in old relationships.

Even in perfectly healthy relationships, people can change. What was okay last year may not be okay today. When relationships are good, they make you better, they make your life bigger, and it's easy to forget about your boundaries, because there is no reason to enforce them. Yet when communication erodes, when trust comes into question, when you feel out of control or deeply unhappy and *then* you try to set a boundary, the experience can be terrifying.

Setting a new boundary is a change, and change is rarely comfortable. To your partner, the change can feel nonconsensual. The key with boundaries is that you always set them around those things that are *yours*: your body, your mind, your emotions, your time, intimacy with you. You *always* have a right to regulate access to what is yours. But by the time the boundaries of your self have become blurred with those of your partner, setting boundaries and defining your self may feel like taking something away from your partner that they had come to regard as theirs.

Harriet Lerner's *Dance of Intimacy* (listed in the resources) is an excellent tool for anyone needing help with setting relationship boundaries. Lerner describes the "change back" responses that are common when a new boundary is set. When you establish a new way of doing things, your partner may work to re-establish the old, comfortable pattern. Countermoves take numerous forms, from outright denial to criticism to threats to end the relationship. The trick with countermoves is to not try to stop them, but to allow them to happen while holding firm in the change you have made.

If your partner is setting a new boundary, remember that they have a right to do so, even if it means they're revoking consent to things they agreed to before. The change may hurt, but the solution is not to violate the boundaries or try to talk your partner out of them. No one should ever be punished for setting personal boundaries, or for withholding or revoking consent. Among other things, do not ever threaten the relationship if you are not prepared to follow through, including veiled or nonspecific threats. If there is any degree of attachment in play, bringing up the possibility of breaking up, whether directly or indirectly, is almost guaranteed to cause distress and fear of loss. If you really mean it, then of course it's important to talk about, preferably from a place of honesty and vulnerability. If you're using the threat because of its power to rattle and destabilize your partner and thus make them more likely to agree with whatever you're asking for, that is a form of emotional blackmail and is devastating to trust and security. It's like taking a wrecking ball to the foundations of the relationship you are, in theory, trying to preserve.

The way you can tell whether you're holding to your own boundary or trying to emotionally blackmail the other person is to figure out whether you're actually willing to walk away. "I won't stay with you if you change career paths" is manipulative if the expected outcome is that your partner will stop pursuing their dreams; it's genuine if you really don't feel okay with their next steps and are willing to let them go if they want to pursue them. It's the difference between "I want you to keep earning a six-figure salary even if you're miserable because I like our lifestyle" and "I know you need to step out of your six-figure job for your own well-being, but your new plan to earn a living by selling bootleg booze that you make in the bathroom is illegal, and I'm not willing to be complicit in that, so I will leave if you intend to follow through on it." If you find yourself repeatedly making threats that you don't follow through on, or going hot and cold with a partner depending on how pleased or displeased you are with the partner's behaviour (provided that behaviour isn't abusive), there's a good chance you're using boundaries as a form of emotional blackmail.

That being said—if your partner sets a boundary that's within their rights, but that feels unacceptable to you, then you are within your rights to opt out of the relationship. It's never okay to coerce someone to do things the way you want. But it is always okay to say "I'm no longer going to participate under the current circumstances."

Pushing back gently

People rarely cross your boundaries intentionally, unless you're in an abusive situation. However, people sometimes cross them accidentally. Because of this, healthy boundaries need flexibility. They can't be so brittle that the slightest touch threatens to end a relationship. You need to be able to accept a certain amount of push and reassert your boundaries by pushing back gently. You need to be able to say "Hey, I would prefer you not do this thing," rather than "You monster! How dare you!" (A great resource for thinking about and communicating your boundaries is therapist Sander T. Jones's book *Cultivating Connection*.)

This is a tricky balancing act, because abusive people are skilled at probing boundaries. One of the tools of a predator is to ignore a no in small ways, testing how people respond, finding weaknesses, and choosing people who won't reassert a no. Alternatively, some people can make all the right sounds and say all the right things when you assert a boundary—including compassionate listening, apologies and promises to change—but simply not change their behaviour. This may be because it's not easy or convenient, or because on some level, they simply don't see a problem with it. Or it could be because they are being intentionally manipulative. Or they just may not have the skills to shift their behaviour in a way that better respects your boundaries.

To an extent, it's worth considering the reasons for repeated boundary violations. Your sense of what's going on behind the problem might make a difference as to how you want to handle it. Have you been totally clear about what your boundary is and what the consequence will be for continuing to violate it? How many violations or what kind of violations are you willing to tolerate? For how long, and under what conditions? For instance, maybe you can extend some patience if your partner is actively working on their communication skills with a therapist, but are less inclined to do so if they've quit therapy and insist everything is fine. But bear in mind that just because someone doesn't have evil intentions, they don't get a free pass indefinitely to cross the lines you set. There comes a point where intention isn't the important thing: effect matters more. Plus, some skilled boundary violators will string you along, playing on your compassion to convince you to stay while they continue to behave in ways that harm you. Can you tell the difference? And more importantly, what is the point at which that potential difference doesn't matter, because you've reached the end of your tolerance?

You need to use your discernment to make decisions about how to handle boundary violations. This might mean doing introspective work, like journalling, meditation or movement that helps you connect with your inner sense of clarity. It might mean reaching out to resources such as a trusted friend, a therapist or a self-help book to try and get a sense of where "please stop" should become "I'm breaking up with you." However you reach clarity on this, the line will be different for each person and in each situation. The key is to allow some flexibility for unintended boundary violations, but also to be willing to reassert your boundaries—or end a relationship—in the face of repeated infringement.

Boundaries and mental health

One place where boundaries in any intimate relationship can become especially difficult to navigate is around issues of mental health. The focus in many nonmonogamous communities and in literature on self-work and independence often leads to perspectives that in practice are quite ableist, where everyone is expected to go it alone with regard to mental health, and mental health issues are only welcome as long you can manage to keep them from becoming anyone else's problem. This expectation encourages people struggling with mental illness to mask, and can lead to them feeling disposable if they can't keep their shit together all the time. In recent years, the popularization of words like "narcissist," "borderline" and "sociopath"—words derived from clinical diagnoses but used pejoratively by laypeople without any real precision—has increased stigma around certain mental health diagnoses or symptoms related to them.

And yet, each person has the right to set whatever boundaries they want, and these include boundaries concerning whether they can be with or how they can support partners with certain mental health issues. A person who grew up with an alcoholic parent might be sensitive around dealing with substance abuse, for example, and might set a boundary that they will not start a relationship with someone who drinks or uses drugs. Someone who has trauma from a relationship with a family member or former partner who had a certain diagnosis might not be able to share intimacy with someone else with the same diagnosis—not because the new person is likely to harm them, but because some behaviours may remind them too much of someone who did. That's a choice each person is allowed to make. You can decline to enter into a relationship for any reason, and that extends to mental health. Plus, if you know you're not prepared to show up compassionately and supportively for someone, the kindest thing to do is not enter a relationship with them to begin with.

Fully disclosing your known mental health issues is an important part of maintaining honest relationships too, both because withholding information from anyone about things that affect them erodes informed consent, and also because honest disclosure helps your partners support you. Early disclosure will also help you discern whether someone has the capacity to support you without shaming, pathologizing or blaming you. If you have a mental health issue that affects your ability to engage in relationships, it's also important to take whatever steps you can to take care of yourself. This might mean things like therapy, treatment, and trying to get enough exercise and sleep. But it's also important to have partners who are willing and able to support you and work with you on accommodations you might need in the relationship. For example, someone with anxiety may need to hear from a partner every day. That's a reasonable request, but not one that everyone can meet. If someone can't offer that, neither of you is wrong, but you're not compatible in that way.

That said, nobody can guarantee to a partner that they'll never develop a mental health issue in the future. It's just not realistic to expect that even the happiest, most secure person in the world won't someday experience new trauma or severe life stressors, or even ordinary life phases, such as pregnancy, menopause or old age, that induce changes to physical and mental health. When this happens within an established relationship, it is certainly reasonable to ask your partner for help and support.

Unfortunately, the stigma attached to mental health problems can discourage full disclosure. It's your responsibility to treat these disclosures with understanding and compassion, and to make it safe for your partners or potential partners to talk to you. And it's important to challenge the preconceived notions you may have about mental health and mental illness. There is no sharp dividing line between "mentally healthy" and "mentally unwell"; our understandings of what mental health is shift over time and based on the prevailing winds in our culture. Western colonial concepts of mental illness tend to be very medicalized and often overlap with efforts to police marginalized social groups, such as 2SLGBTQI+ people, poor people, BIPOC* people, young people and more. In contrast, many Indigenous and non-Western cultures make space for phenomena within their social structures and spiritual systems that Western medicine might label as "illness," and provide approaches for support and treatment that are rooted in traditional medicines, spiritual practices, ancestral knowledge and kinship networks.

On a positive note, even Western medicine, in the last number of decades, has seen major shifts in diagnostic categories away from pathologizing people's identities and sexualities: For instance, 2SLGBTQI+ people are no longer considered intrinsically mentally ill, and society has a much better understanding of the social determinants of mental (and physical) health overall, such as poverty, sexism, homophobia and racism. There have also been shifts in the way addictions are treated, for example through harm reduction approaches, and various prescription drugs have been refined and improved greatly over time. People are beginning to better understand the vast range of neurodiversity—how common it really is, and how often it is simply benign human variation. (Check out Alyssa Gonzalez's book, *Nonmonogamy and Neurodiversity*, for some insights!) Researchers have increasingly studied and learned about the effects of adverse childhood experiences on people's future

* Black, Indigenous and people of colour

mental and physical health, about brain plasticity and our capacity to heal, and about the widespread nature of trauma as well as novel ways to treat its symptoms. (Gabor Maté's accessible masterwork, *The Myth of Normal*, summarizes several decades of trauma study, if you're curious.) And some great resources are available to teach you how to support the people you know and love who have mental illnesses, such as JoEllen Notte's books about sex, depression and interpersonal support, listed in the notes and resources.

However, there has also been a steady expansion of diagnostic categories, and increasing criticism of the arbitrary and unscientific process by which these are established. Contemporary neoliberal approaches to health care often emphasize a reliance on pharmaceuticals, self-management and short-term therapeutic intervention, while de-emphasizing the importance of community support, culturally appropriate social services and long-term relational therapy. Holistic approaches are increasingly popular, and can be very helpful for some, but aren't always well regulated or appropriate; homeopathy is snake oil, for example, and sometimes "go meditate" or "try mindfulness" can be just one more way for a doctor to dismiss a person's symptoms—and depending on the type of mental illness in question, these techniques aren't always beneficial anyway. Many people can't afford or access the most appropriate kinds of treatment for their problems, so may turn to addictive substances as self-medication; meanwhile, the formal study of cannabis, psychedelics and various Indigenous traditional medicines for mental illness treatment is in its infancy and often bumps up against anti-drug policies.

What does all this add up to? It's a complicated picture, and any one individual's mental health situation might benefit from various advances or be compromised by the systems' various failings—or some of both. So before simply saying "I won't date a person with X mental health diagnosis," or whatever else, it's worth taking some time to get educated about all these topics, as well as learning about a given person's specific situation and how they manage it.

One further important point is that a person's behaviour is not necessarily determined by their mental health status. Plenty of people with mental illnesses are kind, compassionate and generous, with deep self-knowledge and great communication skills. And plenty of people who violate boundaries, act inappropriately or inconsiderately, speak unkindly or haven't developed great communication skills do not have diagnosable mental illnesses. It's worth considering whether you want to set boundaries around mental illness itself, or whether your boundaries around how you're willing to be treated would be sufficient to cover whatever arises, regardless of someone's mental health status. Whatever your boundaries may be, it is your responsibility to express them, preferably after getting some education, and before you have put someone else's heart on the line. With this or any other kind of boundary, you cannot expect another person to guess. And if you hear a boundary that you know applies to you, it is also your responsibility to respect it, even when it's difficult.

Often mental health issues are surrounded by walls of shame and guilt; they are not easy to talk about. But again, people cannot consent to be in relationships with you if that consent is not informed. If a prospective partner has expressed a boundary, and you don't feel safe sharing your history of mental health issues or substance use, that's okay, but it's still ethically necessary to tell that partner, "I don't think we're compatible."

Having, and being able to assert, good personal boundaries is a vital prerequisite for the next part of creating frameworks for successful nonmonogamous relationships and negotiating agreements and (maybe) rules. Only by clearly understanding your own boundaries can you hope to work out relationship agreements that meet your needs while still honouring the needs of everyone else involved.

QUESTIONS TO ASK YOURSELF

If you aren't sure whether a problem is just a normal bump or instead points to a boundary violation, ask yourself these questions.

- What are some boundaries I know I have in intimate relationships? How good am I at setting and holding them gently, compassionately and firmly?
- Are there areas where I tend to feel resentment in my relationships? Could these point to any boundaries I have that I am not honouring?
- Are my boundaries rigid or porous, or firm and flexible? Do I feel I have learning to do so I can better show care for myself and others at the same time?

- Do I tend to be a "giver" in relationships? Do I find myself frequently agreeing to cross what I thought was a bottom line? If so, how can I recognize when this is happening, and what other choices could I make that honour my own boundaries?
- Do I ever try to use boundary language to control the behaviour of others? Do I ever use boundaries as a form of punishment? If so, what non-manipulative strategies could I employ to get my needs met?
- Do others feel safe saying no to me? Am I able to hear when I have overstepped someone's boundaries? Do I make it safe for people to disclose this to me? If not, what can I do differently to shift this?
- Do the people in my life seem to regularly respect my boundaries? If not, how do I communicate with them about this, or how can I start communicating with them better about it?

The lifeblood of a relationship is people feeling they can influence each other, particularly about really important things.
MIRA KIRSHENBAUM

10 Rules and Agreements

Many people have strong feelings about rules in nonmonogamous relationships. Rules that work, rules that don't, alternatives to rules, distinctions between rules and agreements—these are issues we carefully examine in the next few chapters.

For most people, monogamy comes with a set of expectations and rules bundled in. What exactly those are can differ widely from one person to the next, which is a source of much conflict in some monogamous relationships. Does flirting count as cheating? Noticing someone else? Going to a strip club or watching porn? Masturbating? Having certain kinds of friends? Being affectionate with someone? Each of these situations can be handled any number of ways. However, while any two people's expectations of monogamy are likely a bit different, most monogamous people at least think they know what those expectations are and, in theory, try to live by the rules. If that's the framework you're coming from, it's tempting, then, to ask, "Okay, so what rules do I use for nonmonogamy?"

This approach works for some people, but there are dangers in thinking about relationships in terms of rules. For instance, we both often hear people say, "Any rules are okay if you both agree to them." The use of "both" here underscores how stubbornly the assumptions of monogamy and couplehood can cling, even in communities that ostensibly practise nonmonogamy. It assumes there are *only two* people, that those two will be negotiating with each other (but not with others), that their needs are of prime importance, that they will call the shots, and that they can make decisions for anyone else who becomes involved with either one of them about the best way to build relationships. What matters is what *they both* agree to, not what *everyone* agrees to.

But we encourage an approach to relationships that gives a voice to *all* the people in those relationships.

Many people starting nonmonogamous relationships also want to know: "How can I keep things from changing? And what guarantees do I have that things won't go wrong?" Rules are often an attempt to answer these questions. The answers we offer are: You can't, and you don't have any. And that's okay.

Before we go into that, it's helpful to clarify the difference between a rule and an agreement. Rules, agreements and boundaries are all, at their core, mechanisms for changing behaviour. The differences are in how these different mechanisms go about doing it, what assumptions they make, how they are created and to whom they apply.

Agreements involve all parties

As we use the word, *agreements* are negotiated codes of conduct established among people who are in relationship with each other. An agreement is a covenant negotiated by *all* the parties it affects. Something negotiated between one set of people—a couple, for example—and then presented as a take-it-or-leave-it proposition to others is not an agreement as we define it. We call that a *rule.* If Edouard says "I never want you to spend the night with anyone else," and Maria says "Okay," this is not an agreement—because it affects Maria's other partner Josef, who wasn't consulted. If Josef's voice is absent from the negotiations, Edouard and Maria have instituted a rule.

Agreements also allow for renegotiation by any of the people they affect. An agreement that does not permit renegotiation is more like a rule. An agreement that is binding on people who did not negotiate it *is* a rule. Here are some examples of agreements:

- If one of us wants to spend the night with someone else, we will let the others know in advance so we can discuss it.
- If one of us wants to have sex with someone else without barriers, we will all first discuss sexual history, risk and testing before we reach a decision.
- We will immediately talk about a situation that makes us feel threatened, rather than sitting on it.

- We will not start new relationships while there are problems in our existing relationships.
- We will negotiate safer-sex boundaries with each of our new partners.
- We will make our sexual health information available to new partners who want it.

Even when the negotiations include all parties, you must still take care to make the negotiations equitable for everyone. Power in relationships is almost never distributed equally. When a new person starts a relationship with one or more people who are already together, if the established relationship is strong, the newcomer will probably have less power than the pre-existing partners do. If, on the other hand, the established relationship is under stress, the newcomer might be in a relatively empowered position if they represent the possibility of an uncomplicated relationship without a lot of baggage. In a fair negotiation, any person with a disproportionate amount of power must negotiate compassionately, rather than using that power to browbeat others to "consensus."

It's not possible to totally negate or equalize power differences, but that doesn't mean you can't navigate them. Sometimes power differences come from the relative position of each person in the nonmonogamous arrangement, such as long-term vs. newer partnerships, same-city vs. long-distance, and out vs. closeted, among others. Sometimes they're about socially enforced power structures, such as differentials based on gender, race, class, age and ability/disability, among others. Sometimes they're about personality type and skill sets, such as the difference between someone who's confident and at ease expressing themselves and someone who's shy or has difficulty talking about their feelings. Often it's about who is more invested in a relationship. Also, more than one power differential can be present at the same time—and not always in the same direction!

It's beyond the scope of this book to try to sort out all the possible nuances here and what to do about them. But we believe that a minimum first step is for each person to make a point of trying to notice these differences, acknowledge them out loud if possible and figure out, in a collaborative way, how best to make decisions in a way that compensates for them. This process can be tricky. It's not always easy to see and accept the places where you're more powerful than others, or to stand up for yourself in places where you're less so. This is ongoing work for pretty much everyone and, needless to say, it extends well past the boundaries of nonmonogamous relationships.

We discuss practical approaches to creating workable agreements in chapter 14. But we know rules can still be tempting—so read on to learn about some common types of rules, their rationales, where they may cause trouble and how they can still sometimes be useful.

Rules place restrictions without negotiation

As we use the term in this book, *rules* are binding limitations placed on someone's behaviour that are not up for negotiation. Even when a rule is agreed to, it's a mandate that can only be obeyed or broken. Breaking a rule is assumed to have consequences, such as loss of the relationship.

Why be skeptical of rules? Monogamous society teaches you that to keep your partner faithful and yourself secure, you should limit their opportunity, keeping them away from desirable people. If that mindset carries over into nonmonogamy, it leads to trying to keep yourself secure by limiting who your partners are allowed to have relationships with, or how much time they can be together, or what they do.

Sometimes people try to use rules to address things they are shy about discussing. It feels scary to talk about your vulnerabilities and insecurities. Often talking about rules becomes a way to try to do that by proxy. It doesn't work, because if you can't talk about the reason for the rule, your partners won't understand the rule's intent, and that leads to trouble, mischief and rules-lawyering: insisting on the letter of the rule without being clear on the intent.

Not all rules are intrinsically bad (see, for instance, "Limited-duration rules" on page 198). However, rules always have the potential to become straitjackets, constraining relationships and not allowing them to grow. Sometimes this is intentional—and such rules can be very damaging indeed. If your partner tells you, "I don't want you ever to grow any new relationship beyond this point," and eventually a relationship comes along that you want to see flourish, your original relationship may end—not in spite of the rule, but *because* of it.

Rules that seek to dictate the structure of a relationship that has yet to exist (for example, "We will only be in a quad") are attempts to map a country you have not yet seen. These types of rules are most often created by people with little experience in nonmonogamous relationships. Often they attempt to impose order on something that seems mysterious and dangerous. Psychologists have observed that people are remarkably poor at predicting how they will respond to novel situations. Most people want certainty; they don't want to get too far from familiar land. But you cannot explore the ocean if you're unwilling to lose sight of the shore. Trying to retain the (seeming) certainty and order of monogamy against the apparent scary disorder of nonmonogamy usually ends up failing.

Some rules indicate fears or discomforts that someone doesn't want to face. Someone might say, "We want to have other partners, but the thought of my partner prioritizing anyone else when I want attention brings up my fears of abandonment. So we will pass a rule saying I can always interrupt my partner's other dates, or I must approve my partner's scheduled time with other people." When two (or more) people have discomforts they're trying to avoid, they may play the mutual-assured-destruction game: I will let you control me to avoid your discomforts, if you let me control you to avoid my discomforts. Avoiding discomfort isn't really the same thing as creating joy; real joy is often on the other side of your comfort zone.

The defining element of a rule is a restriction placed on someone without their input or negotiation. Some examples of rules around nonmonogamy that people sometimes try to use are:

- We will never spend the night at another lover's house; we will always come home at night.
- We will always use barriers when one of us has sex with another lover.
- We will not refer to any other partner by the same pet names we use with each other.
- We can have sex with other people, but we won't love another person as much as or more than we love each other.
- We will not bring any other lover to our favourite restaurant.
- If one of us wants the other to break up with another partner, we will do it. (This is called a "veto" and is discussed in chapter 12).
- We will not have sex with other partners in certain sexual positions, or if the other is not there.
- We will only start relationships with people who are willing to be in a relationship with both (or all) of us.
- We will only start relationships with people who are willing to be exclusive to both (or all) of us.

These rules may superficially sound a lot like the agreements listed in the previous section. They all start with "we." The difference is that all of the rules listed here materially affect a third person who did not have a role in negotiating them, and that person must accept them in perpetuity—often before fully understanding their emotional effect—or leave the relationship.

Safeguards against COVID-19 offer a useful framework for discussing the distinctions between rules, agreements and boundaries, because it is a serious, life- and health-threatening illness that people have strong opinions about, and disagreements over how to handle it have led to the fracture of many relationships (and polycules). It also offers a good example of how the distinctions can become very confusing. For example, while many people have stopped paying attention to the virus, many others still refuse to spend time around unvaccinated people, mask in crowded public spaces and prefer to eat outdoors. These are boundaries, because they describe what the person making the decision is or isn't willing to do. If your friend will only eat outdoors and you want to have dinner with them, you'll have to agree to eat outdoors if you want to see them—but no one is making you see them. People who spend time together, whether short-term such as at a dinner party or long-term such as roommates or nesting partners, need to try to reach agreements about their behaviour before and during the time they're together. "No unvaccinated folks allowed" or "everyone must take a rapid test within two hours of the event" might feel like a rule (for the people attending), a boundary (for the people hosting), or an agreement (if everyone is of like mind and came up with the protocols together).

One key thing here is that even if it's a rule, that doesn't make it inherently bad: We happen to think it's perfectly fine to make and enforce rules to protect yourself and others from disablement and death, for example. But it *is* an indication of who is wielding the most power in a situation. If an agreement cannot be reached, people will default to rules and boundaries; rules are set by people with power, and boundaries can only be enforced by those who have enough power to do so. Take one more example, of a person renting out a room in someone else's home. The homeowner may have the power to unilaterally impose rules about COVID-19 protections (or lack thereof), but the renter has no such power—they can only try to convince their landlord (and therefore reach agreement), or they can move out, which may be more or less feasible depending on the rental market and the renter's resources. So here, even setting boundaries might be difficult. The same holds true for workplaces.

Under capitalism, people are forced to accept that they have to obey some rules, and that setting boundaries may sometimes be impossible. In intimate relationships, we should not have to make such concessions. The absence or presence of empowerment by all parties is therefore a litmus test for whether something is a rule or an agreement in a relationship. Are all the people affected empowered to make their objections heard? Will the others consider the objections seriously, or will some people's objections always be overruled? What happens if someone wants a structure that doesn't work for someone else? Are negotiation and compromise possible, or is leaving the only alternative? Agreements empower people, whereas rules enforce power imbalances.

People don't generally make up rules by rolling dice or drawing words out of a hat. A rule is made to solve a problem or meet a need. Leading with the need ("How can we help make sure I understand how I am valued by you?"), rather than the action, opens the door to finding collaborative ways to solve the problem without disempowering others with rules.

Rules as an antidote to fear

To some people, the sense of control offered by rule-making feels like an antidote to fear. In cases like this, it's useful to approach the situation in a compassionate way. If you're a person who wants to make rules, think about whether there are other ways to manage your concerns (more on that in a minute). If you're a person who's chafing under another person's attempt to make rules, see if you can try to understand where their fear lies, and then see if you can work together to address it. Creativity, communication, kindness and trust are of the essence here.

It's not possible to ever feel completely secure in a relationship whose structures are built on fear. Even if you follow all the rules, or the rules are easy for you, on some level you will always be aware that another person's potential fears are a driving force in the relationship.

In extreme cases, rules can become tools of emotional blackmail. They constitute a contract that specifies acts of betrayal, and a person who breaks a rule is cast in the role of the villain. Rules-based systems judge people's character on the basis of adherence to the rules. When rules are used as a tool with which to attack someone's character—especially if the attacks are based on creative interpretations of the rules—they can become a nearly invisible but extremely corrosive form of emotional abuse.

How agreements become rules

It's not surprising that agreements become rules when they are grounded in fear. It often goes like this: People in a relationship—often a couple—sit down and negotiate a set of relationship agreements. At this point there aren't any other partners, so the people negotiating the agreements rarely consider the effect these agreements will have on others. Then a new person comes along. The partners present the new person with the agreements, with the expectation that the new person will sign on. The new person has little investment in the relationship at this point—and may be inexperienced with nonmonogamy and unfamiliar with any other models of it—so they agree.

After a time, one or more of the original two partners experience some sort of insecurity or feel threatened. The newer person is blamed for violating the agreements—or sometimes a subtle, creative interpretation of them. The original partners either end the relationship with the newer person over this infraction, or use the infraction to justify imposing greater restrictions. The new partner agreed to it, right? What gives them the right to complain now?

When things go wrong—when an agreement is hurting someone or isn't having the intended effect and needs to be renegotiated—saying "But you agreed to this!" is just twisting the knife (and never helps solve the problem). At the beginning of a relationship, you are not yet emotionally invested in it, and you don't know how it will progress. So it can be easy to accept rules or agreements that later, as you become more vulnerable and more emotionally invested, become quite painful.

Rules that new partners are expected to sign on to, but over which they have little or no say, rarely provide space for new relationships to grow. Sometimes these rules are deliberately designed to keep new relationships away from sunlight and water, forcing them to remain stunted or to wither away altogether.

When you didn't write the rules

In nonmonogamy, you will likely find yourself starting relationships with people who already have partners. And that may mean going into relationships that have rules already in place. Accepting someone else's nonnegotiable rules at the beginning of a relationship sets a precedent: It says that you're on board with relationships that are built around other people's needs without considering your own.

Anyone who goes into a rules-based relationship, knowing the rules up front, is agreeing voluntarily to be bound by them, right? Well, maybe. All kinds of things might cause someone to enter a relationship that isn't a good fit—a scarcity model of intimacy, for example.

It's absolutely true that if you enter a rules-based relationship, you are, implicitly and explicitly, agreeing to those rules. And yet, "You knew the rules when you signed on!" is often the parting shot amid a relationship's wreckage. Consider why. Most of the time, when you start a relationship, you expect your partners to meet you in the middle, to negotiate with you, to consider your needs. Those seem like reasonable expectations. So it can be quite a shock when your partner suddenly slams the door on something and says it's nonnegotiable. That's all the more true the longer a "new" relationship lasts. The rules that initially seemed like no big deal might start to grate a little as the relationship deepens over time.

It is okay to assume that flexibility and agency in your relationships are part of the social contract. It probably wouldn't occur to you to even *have* to say "By the way, if we're getting into a meaningful relationship, I expect you to be willing to consider my needs." So in that sense, "You knew the rules when you signed on" is not actually true. People cannot be expected to grasp that flexibility and negotiation are permanently forbidden, or what that will feel like after they have emotionally invested and developed some degree of attachment.

At the beginning of a relationship, you can't predict what feelings you will have, or how deeply you will attach to someone, because *you aren't there yet*. Therefore, it's easy to say yes to rules that treat you as disposable, or don't give you a voice in advocating for your needs, because you don't have the needs yet.

In addition, rules-based systems tend to represent, or lead to, a rigid mentality that's focused on obedience and reward versus disobedience and punishment. In such a framework, a person's moral character is judged based on whether they're obeying the rules. Misunderstandings, failures and changes of heart are coded as acts of betrayal, in which the "betrayer" is necessarily the bad guy and the "betrayed" automatically the good. This framework places a high price—being a moral failure—on any person who finds the rules too confining, forgets one, makes an error in judgment or otherwise doesn't follow the system. Such a system doesn't lend itself well to compassion, kindness or open communication about what is and isn't working.

Rules that cause problems

Certain relationship rules among nonmonogamous people are fraught with problems and require great care if you attempt them. To the people who make them, they may feel like agreements. But here, we focus on their effects as rules for the people who did not have a hand in creating them.

"Don't ask, don't tell" (DADT). In these arrangements, a person says, "You can have other lovers, but I don't want to know about them." DADT relationships affect everyone who becomes involved with the people who have them. They often include restrictions on calling a partner at home, and they almost always preclude visiting a partner at home or spending time in public with them where others could see and mention it to the other partner. These arrangements certainly don't make room for someone to meet their metamour to check on how this setup is sitting with them, making it easy for someone to claim they're doing DADT when they're actually just cheating. We'll have more to say about DADT on pages 266–267.

Rules that require a person to love or be sexually involved with another. When you make love, sex or intimacy with one person the price of sex or intimacy with another, you plant the seeds of coercion. Love and attraction cannot be decreed. You either feel them or you don't. So making either a requirement is almost guaranteed to fail—or generate dishonesty as someone tries to fit the requirement. Besides, how can you feel truly desired if someone's having sex with you just because you set yourself up as a barrier they have to get past if they want to sleep with your partner? Ick.

Rules that fetishize or objectify people. Some people treat a partner's other lovers as fetish objects, demanding detailed, blow-by-blow accounts of every sexual encounter for their own gratification. Your partner's significant others are not your sex aids. Unless they consent to having the details of their sexual encounters shared with a third person for the purpose of arousal, they have a reasonable expectation of privacy.

"One-penis policies." Also known as OPPs, one-penis policies usually crop up among cisgender, heterosexual couples. Under such arrangements, both partners are allowed to date people with vulvas, but not with penises, hence the name "one-penis policy." These agreements are

usually articulated as "we both only date women" (the possibility of dating trans or nonbinary folks doesn't usually appear to occur to many folks who suggest OPPs).

OPPs are usually in place to assuage a man's insecurity and ostensibly to prevent jealousy, and they expose a number of troubling assumptions. The first is the heteronormative assumption that intimate relationships between women are somehow less serious or "real," and therefore less threatening to men. This is often combined with the fetishization of sexual relationships between women, and the idea that a straight man could use his partner's relationships with other women as a form of titillation. It's rare for women to initiate OPPs, but if that happens, it's equally problematic, because it places restrictions on men's bisexuality or renders it taboo. A version of this happens in some areas of swinging culture, which discourage men from being sexual with each other directly, or assume men are never bisexual in the first place, but encourage women to be sexual with each other—often to entertain men.

A couple of cisnormative assumptions are also at play, primarily the aforementioned assumption that everyone with a penis is a man (or the failure to consider gender diversity entirely). (Content note for the rest of this paragraph for frank, and fairly explicit, discussions of transphobic thought processes.) Every now and then you may find a couple who are open to relationships with people who aren't cisgender, and who articulate their OPP explicitly in terms of anatomy. But in many ways this is even worse, as it conveys an explicit assumption that trans men without penises are less threatening because they aren't "really" men—and that even when they have penises, usually those don't "count"—and that trans women who have penises (and sometimes those without them) aren't "really" women. To be honest, the more we try to explain the distinctions that people with OPPs try to make among "categories" of people, the more clear the absurdity of trying to divide people this way becomes.

Finally, OPPs privilege men's feelings. They're based on an assumption that the women involved will just handle any insecurity or jealousy they feel about the man's relationships with other women—or perhaps, even an implicit patriarchal assumption that the man is entitled to other relationships with women in a way that women are not entitled to other relationships with men. Since men having affairs with women has long been normalized, a woman having a relationship with another man may be seen as more transgressive.

Rules that restrict certain things, places, activities or sex acts to one partner. These rules are often seen as ways to protect the "specialness" of one relationship. And it is fair to want to keep some things that are just between you and your partner. A pet name, a special little waterfall deep in the woods, a song. These rituals are part of how we create security. Such rules also court disaster, though, in two ways. The first is when the lists of limited activities become—as they may over the years—long and complicated, thus becoming difficult to remember and increasingly limiting for other relationships. The second is when the "special" activity is either fairly common, or one of among very limited options. If someone is used to calling all their partners "sweetie" or "my love," it might be difficult and unfair to try to restrict those terms to one person, but maybe not too disruptive to ask that you be the only one they call "cookie monster." Wanting to keep the bistro in New York City where you had your first date special to two people is different from wanting to keep the one nice Italian joint in your rural town of 10,000 people to yourselves.

Rules that specify what happens if one relationship runs into trouble. For example, there could be a rule that other relationships must be ended or scaled back. When a couple agrees "If we run into trouble, we'll drop any other relationships to work on the problem," they are treating their other partners as disposable. (However, see page 312 on "temporary vessels.")

Double standards. Rules that place different restrictions on different people are problematic in any situation, and nonmonogamy is no exception. Double standards can be blatant and obvious: For example, *Playboy* founder Hugh Hefner was famous for having sexual relationships with multiple women simultaneously, all of whom were expected to have no lovers but him. But double standards can also be more subtle and sneaky. A common example is when a couple has a rule stating that they can interrupt each other's dates with other partners if they need attention, but their other partners are not allowed to interrupt the couple's dates with each other.

Sometimes double standards are deliberately engineered to create different classes of partners. If members of a couple claim the right to veto relationships with other people, but other partners are not given veto power over the couple's relationship, a deliberate double standard exists. The couple may see this double standard as a way to prevent new partners from "causing" them to break up.

Whenever rules apply unevenly to different people, there is potential for trouble, resentment and jealousy. (Ironically, double standards are often instituted as a way to *prevent* jealousy, at least within an established relationship, but far more often they end up creating it.) Rules that codify a double standard are disempowering.

Rules as "training wheels"

Another common notion is rules as "training wheels," a way to learn the skills to navigate nonmonogamous relationships without feeling threatened. A person (or more often a couple) may start out with a list of rules, thinking they will learn trust by seeing other people obey the restrictions. Once that trust has been built, they think, the rules can slowly be relaxed.

This idea may have become popular from the observation that lots of happy nonmonogamous relationships seem to have grown this way. A couple or group will sometimes start out by drawing up a long, detailed relationship agreement with many pages of rules and specifications, and then, as it's renegotiated over time, it becomes ever simpler and more general, until perhaps a ten-page document has been condensed to something like "Use good judgment. Be thoughtful. Take responsibility. Don't be a jerk." The group's success makes this strategy look like a winner, and they proudly blog about it.

In fact, we believe the popularity of this idea confuses cause and effect. Because they were thoughtful people who take responsibility, they didn't need ten pages of rules in the first place. And if they hadn't been thoughtful people, the rules wouldn't have helped.

"Training wheels" rules are a seductive idea. They offer a justification for a tightly restrictive model of nonmonogamy, but also offer the promise that someday they won't be necessary. Some people even think that empowered nonmonogamous relationships are only an option for people who already have lots of experience in nonmonogamy or a secure attachment style. Everyone else starting out is supposed to need the comfort of rules to learn the trust that leads to nonmonogamous enlightenment.

The biggest problem with the "training wheels" metaphor is that it doesn't treat people as real. People who use it are essentially telling new partners, "I don't really trust you, and I don't have the skills to treat you well, so I'm going to use you as practice to learn how to treat future partners well."

But not everyone learns to ride a bike by using training wheels. Some people even believe that relying on training wheels teaches bad habits that must be unlearned when the training wheels come off. In nonmonogamous relationships, using rules to avoid dealing with thorny problems like jealousy and insecurity can cause you to learn some very bad relationship habits. Even under the best of circumstances, talking about your fears and insecurities is hard. When you talk about your frailties, you become exposed and vulnerable. Relying on rules to deal with these feelings teaches you that you don't have to talk about them directly, which prevents you from learning the skills you need to find lasting solutions.

The entire purpose of many relationship rules is risk avoidance. If you already have a relationship when you start exploring nonmonogamy, it's natural to say, "I would like to protect the relationship I already have, so I want to explore nonmonogamy without risk." If you come to nonmonogamy when you're single, it's natural to say, "I want to protect my heart, so when I have a partner, I will ask them not to do anything that makes me feel threatened."

Unfortunately, when you seek to reduce risk by imposing constraints on other people's behaviour, you transfer that risk onto others. By doing this, you say, "I want to explore nonmonogamy, but I don't want to take this risk, so I will transfer it onto any new partners, by asking them to be open and vulnerable while also limiting how much they are allowed to advocate for their own needs."

It can take a great deal of courage to start exploring nonmonogamy without relying on rules to feel safe. It does seem that the secret to healthy, dynamic relationships keeps coming back to courage. Forget training wheels. Forget trying to figure out the right rules that will keep you safe forever; there is no safe forever. Instead, go into the world seeking to treat others with compassion whenever you touch them. Try to leave people better than when you found them. Communicate your needs. Understand and advocate for your boundaries. And look for other people who will do the same. Trust them when they say they love you; where communication and compassion exist, you don't need rules to keep you safe, and where they don't exist, rules won't help you anyway. You don't learn how to be compassionate by disempowering other people; you learn how to be compassionate by practising compassion.

Limited-duration rules

All this being said...sometimes a rule can be useful, even necessary. The work it takes to become secure and confident can be *hard*. In some situations, rules that are specific, narrow in scope and, most importantly, limited in duration can be valuable tools for problem-solving. If you've found that something your partners are doing just absolutely drives you up the wall, asking them to temporarily stop doing it can give you the emotional space to process whatever's underneath.

Implementing time-limited rules can be helpful in specific situations, but there's also a risk in doing so: When you're comfortable, you tend to want to stay there. That's why we recommend a sunset clause in any rule: for example, "After three weeks (or some other period of time), we will revisit this issue." And it goes on the calendar. How much time? That depends on the circumstances and the people, but broadly, for most people a week is too short, and a year is too long.

A sunset clause doesn't mean you're under a deadline to fix the emotional issue. It's merely a promise to re-examine and renegotiate at that time. The person asking for the temporary rule is asking their partners to trust that they are willing to work on whatever the underlying problem is, and that they won't simply keep extending the rule every three weeks into infinity. The partners who are agreeing to the temporary rule are asking the rule-maker to trust that they genuinely want to help support the rule-maker in fixing the issue and that they are willing to give the rule-maker space to work on it.

Alternatives to rules

When we talk about relationships that are not rules-*based*, we're not talking about relationships with no rules whatsoever. Rather, we're talking about relationships that don't use rules as the first go-to problem-solving tactic, and that don't attempt to deal with emotional or security issues solely by creating frameworks of rules.

Many people say they need rules in their relationships, but when they are asked why, it quickly becomes obvious that what they need is actually something else. It is usually something like security or stability; a sense of empowerment, predictability or safety; or an ability to set boundaries or negotiate with their partners. Those are all reasonable needs—and it is possible to have those things without rules.

Conflating rules with needs is common, because many people live in societies that teach them that they need external structures and authority in order to treat other people well. These people internalize the idea that the only way they can rely on others to behave with kindness, responsibility, respect and compassion is to create rigid codes compelling them to. Many people are told that if they make choices from personal autonomy, then responsibilities will be neglected and kindness will fade.

In reality, relationships without rules are (usually) far from a free-for-all in which everyone does whatever they want without regard for anyone else. Instead, if you look at such relationships, many show high levels of communication, negotiation, compassion and understanding. Mononormativity teaches people that "rules" and "commitment" are almost interchangeable: You demonstrate commitment by agreeing to rules that limit your behaviour. From that position, it can be hard to imagine what a relationship without rules would even look like.

Relationships, especially cohabiting relationships, often involve many commitments and responsibilities. You might think, "How can I be sure the kid will be picked up from school if I don't have a rule telling my partner to be home by 3:30 on weekdays?" Or "If there's no rule against late-night dates, how do I know my partner will be able to get up in the morning to go to work?" And the answer is: You don't. But if a partner is willing to skip out on commitments and responsibilities, they're probably just as willing to break rules!

To understand relationships that are not rules-based, we need to go back to two of the themes we emphasize in this book: trust and boundaries. You have to trust that your partners *want* to take care of you—that given the freedom to do whatever they choose, they will make choices that respect your needs and honour their commitments.

As Andrea once wrote: "Rules have an inverse relationship to trust. They are intended to bind someone to someone else's preferences. They are aimed at constraint. I will limit you, and you will limit me, and then we'll both be safe." The problem with rules, though, is you can never actually force your partners to abide by them. A partner who can't be trusted to meet your needs can't be trusted to follow your rules. What you need is a trustworthy partner...and you need to be trustworthy yourself.

Sometimes rules try to compensate for poor boundaries. Some people might say they use rules to prevent drama or to protect themselves from someone who might want to split up their relationship. But nobody can make you and your partner split up, or engage you in messy dynamics, if you don't agree to it. If you can simply say "No, I won't participate in this dynamic," or "I choose to remain with my partner. I'm not interested in dissolving our relationship," then you don't need to rely on structures or rules to attempt to do that for you. These are just good boundaries in action.

In the end, whether you choose to rely on rules or agreements, or simply advocate for your needs and give your partners the opportunity to address them, no relationship will succeed if your partners don't want to invest in it. If they cannot be trusted to make the relationship work, it won't, rules be damned.

QUESTIONS TO ASK YOURSELF

When considering your needs for agreements or rules, or whether to sign on to someone else's, these questions can be useful:

- What needs am I trying to address with this agreement?
- Does the agreement offer a path to success?
- Does everyone affected by the agreement have the opportunity to be involved in setting its terms?
- How is the agreement negotiated, and under what circumstances can it be renegotiated?
- What happens if the agreement doesn't work for my partners or their partners?
- Do I feel like I need rules to feel safe? If so, will the rules actually keep me safe?
- Are my rules equally binding on everyone they affect, or do they create a double standard?

People like certainty more than they like hope.
JOSIE DUFFY RICE

11 Hierarchy and Primary/ Secondary Polyamory

We have talked about some of the ways people try to deal with the risks inherent to nonmonogamy, and the strategies we recommend. Before we go further, we want to examine some of the underlying forces that shape any relationship.

We're going to simplify—a lot—to construct a framework that lets us get our ideas across. The three main forces we will discuss here are *connection, commitment* and *power*.

How hierarchies emerge

Connection can mean a whole bunch of things, but here it represents what people see as the exciting bits of a relationship: intensity, passion, shared interests, sex, joy in each other's presence. It's the things that bring you together.

Commitment consists of what you build in a relationship over time. It includes expectations: perhaps of continuity, reliability, shared time and communication, activities that will be done together, or a certain public image. It also includes attachment in the sense discussed on page 25 (like we said, this is super simplified). Commitment often supports life responsibilities, such as shared finances, a home or children.

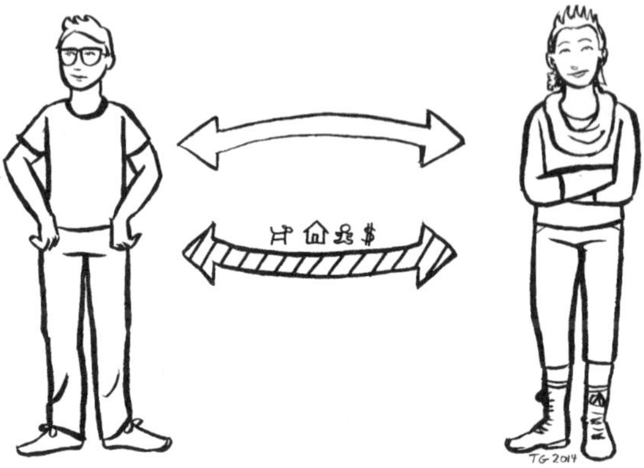

It's common for connection to start out very large and exciting and shrink as a relationship deepens and stabilizes, or sometimes to start out small, grow to a peak and then wane. Commitment tends to start small and grow. People in long-term, very committed relationships may still struggle to maintain connection.

Each of these flows—connection, commitment—gives people power in a relationship. Power tends to be proportional to the size of the other flows. The more you've committed to a relationship, and the more connection you feel with someone, the greater the power that person has—to affect not only yourself and your relationship with that person, but all your other relationships as well.

Ideally, the power flows within intimate relationships would always be equal. In practice, they often are not. Power imbalances tend to arise when the other flows are asymmetrical: when one person feels more connection or commitment than the other. That's normal. The person who feels less connection or commitment tends to hold more power. Other things influence power dynamics too, of course: things like economic or social status, physical dominance or persuasion skills.

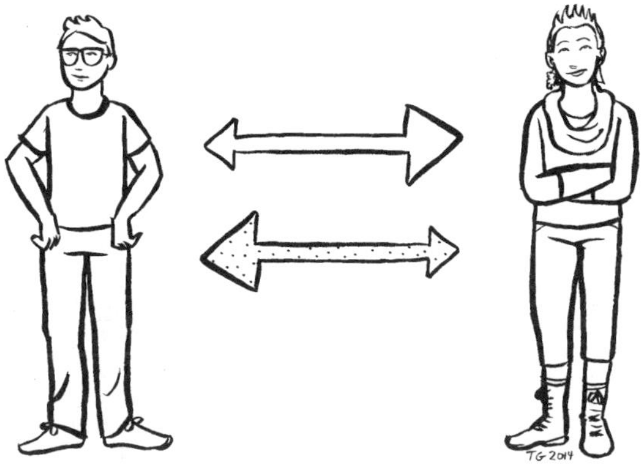

When someone is in a relationship with a large mutual commitment, especially when that commitment supports a lot of life responsibilities, it's common for one member of that relationship to feel threatened when their partner's new relationship has a really big connection—perhaps one that feels (and maybe is) bigger than the existing connection.

Often, it's just the *idea* of a big connection that's scary, even when the flow is new and small. And the idea of a partner creating significant commitments to a new partner may feel (and sometimes is) threatening to the commitments that already exist.

One way people deal with this fear is by using the power from within their own relationship to restrict the connection, commitment, or both in other relationships.

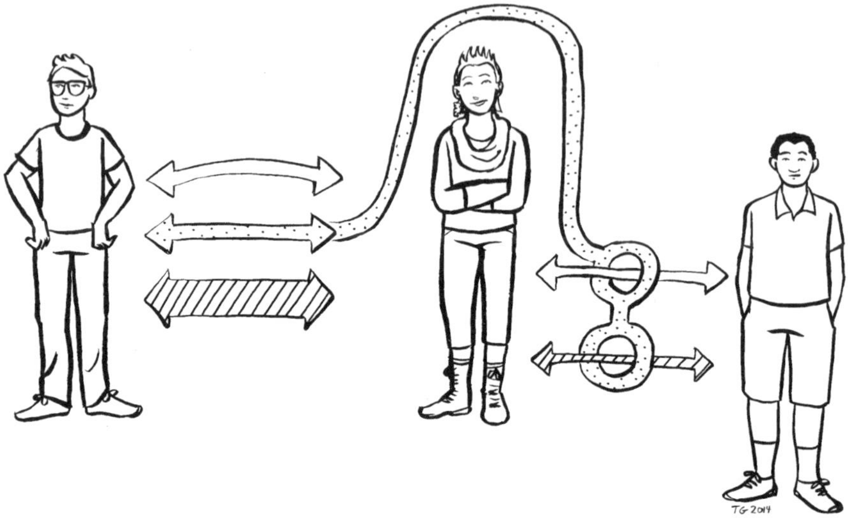

Such restrictions have a couple of defining features:

- *Authority.* A person or people in one relationship, which may be called a "primary" relationship, have the authority to restrict other relationships, which may be called "secondary."
- *Asymmetry.* The people within the secondary relationships do not have the same authority to limit the primary relationship.

When these two elements are present within a nonmonogamous relationship, that relationship is *hierarchical.*

What is hierarchy?

Some people use the word *hierarchy* whenever one relationship has more commitments or responsibilities than another—for instance, members of a long-married couple with a house and kids becoming involved with a friend-with-benefits. This is *not* how we are using the word in this book. When we talk here about a hierarchy, we mean a very specific power dynamic in which a relationship is subject to the control of someone outside that relationship. For instance, a hierarchy exists if a third party has the power to veto a relationship or limit the amount of time the people in it can spend together.

Hierarchical behaviour might take the form of rules such as "No other partner may ever live with us," for example, or those discussed on pages 188 and 193–196. Alternatively, it might manifest as restrictions on how serious another relationship is allowed to become, or on what a new person is allowed to do, where they are allowed to go, or what they are allowed to feel. Some common examples of prescriptions in hierarchical nonmonogamy are:

- The primary couple always comes first with regard to time or other resources.
- Each member of the primary couple can veto any secondary partner of the other. (We discuss vetoes in detail in the next chapter.)
- Members of the primary couple are not permitted to spend the night with a secondary partner.
- Members of the primary couple pledge to love each other most.
- If the members of the primary relationship run into trouble or feel threatened, they can put secondary relationships "on hold" while they work things out between them.

People often assume these prescriptions are okay because secondary relationships are "casual"—but often they are not. Some secondary relationships are emotionally serious, long-lasting and deeply committed. Nevertheless, secondary relationships are defined as relationships subordinate to a primary relationship—by rules determined by the primary partners.

Prioritization of pre-existing commitments does not necessarily imply hierarchy by our definition. For example, if you own property with a partner, the mortgage must be paid before you spend a lot on dates! And if you start dating a new partner, that new person doesn't immediately get a vote on whether you sell the house.

Other examples: You probably don't give the keys to your car to someone on the first date. And most parents, monogamous or otherwise, are rightly cautious about whom they introduce their young children to, and when. Exercising your personal judgment in these kinds of decisions, and expecting your partners to make good judgments, is not displaying a hierarchy toward the person affected. Nor is requiring a partner to get your consent for things that concern both of you (such as property or children).

But if you control when and how your partner can make relationship decisions with *others,* and this prescription is intended to overrule the choices of your partner and their other partner, that is hierarchy.

Children are often used to justify hierarchy. If you are co-parenting, hopefully you are co-parenting with someone whose judgment you trust, and whom you trust to protect your children's interests. Deciding what parenting values you both share and will honour, and setting mutually agreed-upon expectations for shared responsibilities and the structure you will provide for the children, is not imposing hierarchy per se, if you trust each other to make decisions within your other relationships that honour your commitments to one another and the kids.

The relationship structure becomes a hierarchy, though, when one partner expects to make decisions about how the other partner will conduct their other relationships, or what level those other relationships will be permitted to reach, to ensure that the commitments to the children are—in their opinion—met.

A critical perspective on the terms *primary* and *secondary*

The use of the words *primary* and *secondary* to refer to partners first became popular among early-generation white polyamorous people (some people even had tertiary partners). Often these adjectives got pressed into service as nouns, so people had "primaries" and "secondaries." In many places, these words remain popular, and it's still fairly common to hear people talk about primary relationships, but the word *secondary* is falling out of favour (although some people simply use "non-primary" instead).

This language can get confusing, because not everyone who uses the words *primary* and *secondary* is talking about a hierarchical relationship. The confusion arises because these words may be used in two different ways: prescriptively (as when a primary couple decides in advance what limitations any other relationship will be subject to) or descriptively (to describe whether a relationship has naturally grown to be more or less entangled than another). For example, some people use *primary* to refer to all live-in relationships and *secondary* for all relationships that aren't financially or domestically entwined. Hierarchical polyamorists often (though not always) expect that there can be only one primary relationship, whereas with descriptive "primary/secondary" relationships, someone may have more than one primary partner. Some people who practise non-hierarchical nonmonogamy may even say, "My primary is whichever partner I'm with at the time" (even if it's more than one partner).

In an ideal world, we'd like to see people stop using the terms *primary* and *secondary* in a descriptive way for a couple of reasons. First, and most importantly, because it's not accurate. A hierarchy isn't something that happens because you're close with someone or have built a long-term relationship with them. The word refers to a chosen and deliberately enacted power structure. For example, in a workplace, someone who has seniority isn't necessarily placed highly within the company hierarchy. They might have more experience in a certain area, or know the workplace culture better, or have had the time to build greater trust with their colleagues, or even have specialized expertise—but the newly hired CEO still outranks them within the hierarchy. So if you're not creating a relationship structure based on rank, why borrow its terminology?

On the flip side, if your relationship is effectively operating as a hierarchy, with someone outranking someone else as a matter of permanent status, then we think it's pretty important to say so very clearly so that everyone involved knows how things work. Bear in mind that many people find the word *secondary* hurtful, and that hierarchical relationships come with a number of built-in dangers and ethical challenges, as we discuss in this chapter and elsewhere in the book. But one of the first things you can do to manage those dangers and challenges is to be super honest about the model you're using. In other words, don't pretend your relationship isn't hierarchical if that's really what it is.

Third, use of these terms descriptively can lead to a sort of bait-and-switch, where people are in fact practising a power hierarchy while claiming it's just about priority. The descriptive use of these terms often provides cover for their more problematic prescriptive sense. We are personally wary when people become defensive of their choice of the words *primary* and *secondary* to describe differing priorities and commitments, as it very often points to the presence of a power hierarchy beneath. More on that in a bit.

In this book, we only use the terms *hierarchy*, *primary* and *secondary* when speaking of explicitly and prescriptive hierarchical relationships.

Couple focus

Hierarchy almost always focuses on a couple. The couple may explicitly choose a hierarchical model as a way to add other relationships "on the side," or they may not realize how hierarchical they will become in a pinch, but to them, the couple is always the relationship that matters. The emphasis on a "core couple" can permeate a relationship in ways that are both obvious and subtle. When this emphasis is taken to its extreme, a couple may see others as simply expendable, to be ditched without warning or explanation at any sign of trouble. A lot of nonmonogamous people who became involved with a couple who they thought loved and respected them have tales to tell about abrupt loss of all contact: phone calls and emails unanswered and no further communication.

People in hierarchical primary relationships may view a secondary partner's needs or expectations as a problem, or even imagine that future secondary partners should not have needs or expectations at all—if they even think that far. The well-being of the secondary partner may not even have occurred to them.

The members of a primary couple may have a belief—even a tacit, almost unconscious belief—that having more than one primary partner is not possible. Many newly nonmonogamous people believe you can have only one primary partner, as in the mononormative ideal: They believe when push comes to shove, you can only *really* love one person. This model might be called "nonmonogamy as modified monogamy," including the idea that you can only have one "soulmate" while still having multiple partners.

Unfortunately, because this model maintains the primacy of the couple and therefore, in theory, is not too threatening to the general social order, it's the one that a lot of mononormative culture is most comfortable with. That means that a lot of people new to nonmonogamy come across this model first, and they might not think to question it. It also leads to other problems. For instance, therapists who aren't conversant with nonmonogamy may instinctively support and promote hierarchical models when their clients ask for advice. Many hugely popular advice and pop science books promote understandings about what love really is and how secure attachment works that rule out the possibility of non-hierarchical nonmonogamy. This is why we love Jessica Fern's groundbreaking work *Polysecure*, on how to cultivate secure attachment within nonmonogamy! But the whole world hasn't read that book (yet!), so there is still a lot of general social support for the idea of hierarchy...even when it does a great deal of harm to both secondary partners and primary partners alike.

The power dynamics of hierarchy

In a hierarchical relationship by our definition, power is diverted from within one relationship to restrict another relationship, forming a sort of "gate" to limit commitment or connection. When the natural flow of connection or commitment is smaller than the width of that gate, everything is fine. This is usually what's going on where people point to hierarchical nonmonogamous groups in which prescribed roles are working well for everyone involved—basically, it's luck. Of course, if the natural connection and commitment are small enough to fit within the "gate," hierarchy probably isn't necessary; that relationship would remain where it is on its own.

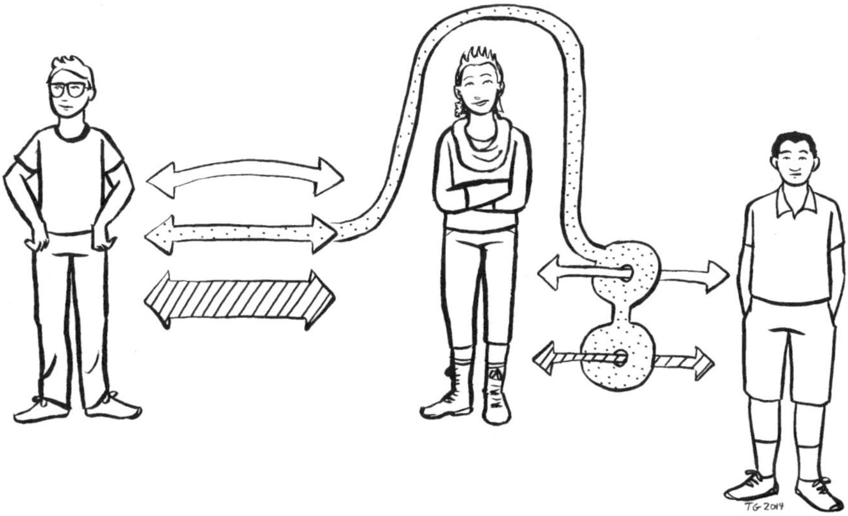

Problems arise when the natural flows are bigger than the gate. They won't shrink on their own, much as people might wish they would, so they continue to push back on the gate. The restriction might stifle or eventually kill the new relationship, suppressing its growth in the way a sunshine-loving plant growing under the shade of a big tree becomes stunted. But if the flows are too powerful, they will eventually crash through the gate, often causing great damage to the relationship from which the power originally emanated.

Mononormative conditioning goes very deep, and it's hard to root out all the ways it influences your thinking. It's hard work to consider the implications of your decisions on unknown future partners, and it's very tempting not to do that work. And it's particularly difficult to consider someone else's needs when you're scared. So it is often true that people in hierarchical relationships may behave in ways that are unnecessarily cruel to some partners—not out of malice, but merely out of thoughtlessness.

You could think of a relationship about to be opened up as a big tree with deep roots—maybe one that's been bearing fruit for many years, seen a few rough seasons and spread its branches. Then you plant another seed in your garden: a new relationship. You don't know what the seed will grow into, but if you're like many primary partners, there's a good chance you have some hope, spoken or unspoken, that it will be an annual, or stay small, or at least thrive in the shade of that big tree. Certainly it won't ever get as big or demand as much space, right?

People tend to think of secondary relationships as "new" relationships, without giving thought to the fact that they might endure for years. It's common to hear variations on this theme: "But you can't expect a new partner to have the same rights as a spouse!" True, but relationships don't stay new forever. There was a time when your spouse of fifteen years was your new partner, and a time could come when your relationship with your new partner will also be established. Sure, it's possible that you'll want the same kind of relationship in fifteen years that you wanted at six months, but it's unlikely.

Yet couples often seem to hope to keep secondary relationships frozen at that new-love size and shape forever. It doesn't work that way. If you plant an acorn in a flowerpot and the sapling manages to survive, you'll just end up with a broken flowerpot.

Often primary couples manage this structural flaw by simply jettisoning any relationship that threatens to grow bigger than the space they allotted to it. Many people often implicitly assume that a secondary relationship that becomes too well established may threaten the primary relationship—which is odd, considering the primary relationship has already had the time and energy to grow deep roots. Commonly, a secondary partner will sense that their happiness is not that big a concern to the primary couple, even if the secondary partner can't put their finger on why. They may be sensing that even though the couple have never actually been callous or unkind, the *structure* of the relationship itself may not respect the secondary partner's rights and feelings, or give their relationship space to grow.

Ironically, hierarchy can create precisely the situation the primary couple is trying to avoid: A person who feels relegated to a subordinate position may demand more decision-making power or more freedom to grow in the relationship. These demands may feel hostile to the primary couple. They may respond by tightening the restrictions or by reminding the secondary partner—"Hey, you agreed to all these rules when you signed on"—which only makes the secondary partner feel more disempowered. And the next thing you know, what could have been a positive and healthy relationship ends up eating itself in a big ball of suck.

Another danger unique to hierarchical relationships is that a secondary partner might start a new relationship with someone else, someone who does not subscribe to hierarchy, and that new relationship can feel threatening to the partner in the primary relationship—not because it's a threat to the couple, but because the new relationship offers things the hierarchical relationship doesn't. People in hierarchical relationships sometimes find that "letting" a secondary partner have other partners is scarier than "letting" their *primary* partner have others!

In contrast, some primary couples think that if a secondary partner wants more time and attention, the solution is exactly that: for them to go find a primary of their own. We've discussed before that people are not need-fulfillment machines, and that (except in certain limited instances) the "My needs aren't being met, let's find someone else" approach to problem-solving in nonmonogamy is fraught with peril.

If your car needs an alternator, you can go to an auto parts store and pick one off the shelf. But people are not car parts. Each person is unique, and it's the things that make them unique that matter. Swapping one person for another in the hopes that the new person will meet the needs unfilled by the old really doesn't work. Even if they do find a fulfilling primary relationship of their own, that doesn't mean they'll stop having needs particular to you.

Non-hierarchical terms for relationships

Many nonmonogamous people have made the choice not to use hierarchical terms, and they tend to find that words such as *partner, lover, sweetie, girlfriend, boyfriend, fiancé(e), husband, wife* and *spouse* convey more meaning than the words *primary* and *secondary*. Many people call the partners they live with *nesting partners*; some people also refer to *domestic partners*, *life partners*, *queerplatonic partners* or *life mates*. People who share parenting duties may call each other co-parents, but this may or may not indicate that they're romantically involved; some people use it in the context of partnership, but others use it to refer to a person with whom they're raising a child outside a romantic relationship, such as a gay man and a lesbian who decide to team up for the purpose of having kids, or amicably divorced people who share custody, or even two or more metamours who aren't romantically attached to each other within a polycule but have chosen to raise kids as a group (living together or otherwise). Many nonmonogamous people refer to all their partners as *sweeties* or *loves*. There are plenty of additional made-up terms and phrases too—you may have noticed that nonmonogamous people are good at making up words!

Service secondaries

At the time of the first edition of this book, it wasn't uncommon to hear of primary couples who approached potential secondary partners with the notion that they must provide the primary couple with some form of service as compensation for being in a relationship with one of them. For instance, the secondary partner may have to babysit. (One case was even published on a blog in the mid-aughts dealing with a secondary partner who was expected to present in public as a couple's nanny.) Or they were expected to perform other domestic duties. Sex is another service that secondary partners are often asked to provide, in cases where they are expected to be sexually involved with both members of a couple.

We refer to such arrangements as "service secondaries," and unless service is a specific kink that all people involved greatly enjoy and agree upon in a transparent way, you would be well advised to avoid them—no matter which role you would play in the structure. What's wrong with these arrangements? Isn't it fair to look for partners who will want to support you, help around the house and participate in your family life, if that's what matters to you? Well, sure. But starting out with the view that a new partner is *taking something away*, and therefore *needs to compensate* by doing work for the couple, is not a healthy foundation for a relationship. These arrangements tend to be nonreciprocal, objectifying and lopsided.

It's fortunately been a long time since either of us came across people with arrangements of this kind, but just because people aren't being this explicit about their arrangements doesn't mean they're not still happening. None of this is meant to disparage people with service kinks; if you think you might be one of them, you might enjoy reading some of the books written or edited by Raven Kaldera (see the resources section at the end of this book) and implementing service activities on purpose and with deep reflection on what they mean to each person involved. It's also fine if you're not a kinky service lover but you do voluntarily express love and care through acts of service, or enjoy receiving them. That's pretty common and totally nontoxic within a certain range! But remember that nonconsensual expectations of service as a condition of being in the relationship can very quickly become coercive or abusive, particularly in the context of a relationship hierarchy where the lower-ranked people may feel they have no choice. It can also be deeply degrading to your self-esteem to be in an intimate relationship where you are essentially expected to routinely apologize for simply loving your partner, as though you're doing something wrong by being there at all. And it's worth noting that these kinds of expectations are often directed at women or people coded as feminine—it's pretty rare to see cis men asked to babysit or perform household chores as a condition of dating someone.

Why it's hard to talk about hierarchy

Few things are the subject of more ongoing, heated debate among nonmonogamous folks than the topic of relational hierarchies. In many ways this debate, which has raged for decades now—with different sides emerging as temporary victors every decade or so—feels profoundly stuck, which is one reason we devote so much time to hierarchy in this book. A big reason for this impasse seems to be that people often can't even agree on what they're actually talking about. We think one of the reasons that this confusion is so hard to dispel (can't folks just decide which definition they're using for a given conversation and use that?) is because it actually serves a purpose.

Like the words *primary* and *secondary*, some folks argue that they are using the word *hierarchy* descriptively, claiming that it refers merely to any nonmonogamous situation in which one relationship gets more time, energy, priority, commitment, sex or other resources than another relationship. We find, though, that this definition isn't very helpful—at least if clarity of communication is your goal—because it applies to basically all relationships, intimate or not. The word does have a use, but it doesn't have to do with communicating an idea. It has to do with obscuring another one.

THE TOWER AND THE VILLAGE

About a decade ago, neuroethicist Nicholas Shackel described what he called the motte-and-bailey doctrine. The name refers to a kind of castle that was popular in Western Europe in the early medieval period. The motte is a hill topped by a fortified tower, often surrounded by a ditch or moat. The bailey is the surrounding land that contains the rest of the castle's buildings, which are outside the moat and also surrounded by a fence or wall. To make this a bit easier to follow, we're going to refer to the motte as the "tower" and the bailey as the "village."

The tower, being on a hill and fortified, is much easier to defend than the village. When the village is attacked and the walls are about to be breached, everyone can run to the tower, bar the doors, and dump boiling oil on top of the attackers (or whatever other horrific defence strategies were employed in the 12th century). But no one really wants to live in the tower very long—it's too small, cramped and stuffy, and they can't do everything they want to do in there. Ultimately, they need to go back to the village and live their everyday lives. So the tower is only defended until the attackers have been beaten back or have moved on, at which point everyone reoccupies the village.

The motte-and-bailey doctrine describes how this same tactic can be used in an argument. You have two positions: one (the tower) is easy to defend, but ultimately not the one you really care about. The other (the village) is a lot harder to defend, but it's also the thing that matters to you. So in an argument, you defend the village—until you can't, at which point you retreat to the tower, and defend *that*. Once the pressure has lifted, you can relax and head back out to your village.

When conversations about hierarchy in nonmonogamous communities get stymied over definitions, it's often because someone is using this argument strategy. Let's be clear from go that while some people are probably doing this in bad faith—knowing full well they're playing rhetorical tricks to wiggle out of being legitimately challenged on relationship approaches that can really hurt others, particularly non-primary partners—it's often a purely emotional course of action. People retreat behind their defences when they feel attacked, and often the anti-hierarchy school of thought can have that effect on people. If you're invested in a hierarchical mindset, it can be really scary to step outside of it, while it's also scary to feel like you're being accused of being a bad person for wanting hierarchy. So what do you do? Try to find a way to keep the hierarchy, but either hide it or defuse the arguments against it! The tower-and-village strategy is a way to do the latter.

The "tower" argument—easy to defend—goes like this: *hierarchy* is a descriptive term, and it just acknowledges the very real and logical differences between one relationship and the next, based on entwinement, commitment, attachment, longevity and so on. No two relationships—even those prescribed by rigid gender and social roles—are or can ever be exactly the same, and no reasonable person would argue that they should be. People defending this tower will say that "egalitarian" nonmonogamy entails an expectation that all the relationships be the same—which, of course, is not a reasonable notion, so it makes sense to shoot it down. (While we're on the subject of argumentative tactics, though, this one's a straw man, and straw men are notoriously easy to defeat.)

The tower argument takes the natural variation present between all human relationships and calls it hierarchy—not because it actually is, but because this exaggeration helps protect the village, which is the definition of hierarchy we just gave on pages 204–206: where certain partners expect to exert direct, asymmetrical control of their partners' other relationships. In a conversation, it tends to become clear that this is what's really going on because once someone has defended their tower—getting you to agree to the obvious statement that yes, all relationships need different resources and have different priorities—you can often see them tiptoeing back out into the village.

An example of this might be when someone starts talking about the idea of "respecting" a primary (or marital, or nesting, or parental, or whatever you call it) relationship. With the possible exception of some relationship anarchists, most people will accept at face value the idea that you should respect a partner's other relationships, in that it's a good idea to support your partner in keeping their commitments and doing things that support the health of their relationship life. Most people also readily acknowledge that long-established, entwined relationships tend to involve more time, energy and priority than newer or less entwined relationships. These acknowledgements are the tower.

But is that person also saying that "respect" means not voicing criticism of abusive or manipulative behaviour? Not advocating for your own needs in a relationship? Not expressing your own feelings of love or attachment? Never asking for your relationship to take *some* priority *some* of the time? Then that's a power hierarchy: the village.

Watch what happens when you challenge this argument. Does your interlocutor retreat to the tower? Do they say things like "Well, you wouldn't give someone the keys to your house on the first date!" "We've been together ten years, so we just have more sweat equity!" "You can't expect everyone to be equal." And the classic "We have to put our children first."

None of these statements are wrong. They're the tower—easy to defend. But these conversations aren't really about them. They're about the village: how much control someone has over what happens in another person's relationship.

Defining non-hierarchical nonmonogamy as "everyone gets the same" and hierarchical polyamory as "every relationship is different" makes non-hierarchical nonmonogamy seem easy to dismiss, and people who try to practise it, impractical idealists. This conversational trick can be devastatingly effective at shutting down discussions about the ethical implications of power dynamics in relationship networks.

Lest we be accused of being too hard on primary partners, let us point out that less-entwined partners can also employ rhetorical tricks that confuse discussions of power dynamics, just not the same ones, or for the same reasons. They're unlikely to use the tower-and-village strategy, because they're not trying to obscure a hierarchy—they're often trying to prove one exists. Instead, a common strategy is to look at *any* unequal distribution of resources and call it a hierarchy. Since the idea of hierarchical relationship networks has, over the last few years, become increasingly frowned upon in many nonmonogamous subcultures, if a partner accuses you of having a hierarchical relationship, it's often a criticism—and can really sting! Especially if you're actively working to avoid the power imbalances that we describe in this book! The accusation may be accurate—many dyads *do* operate in a hierarchical way without wanting to admit it (some folks call this "sneakyarchy"), hence how common the tower-and-village strategy is in the first place. But the accusation may also not be accurate, and may instead point to other problems, such as a partner wanting something and not getting it, or not feeling heard—which is legitimate, but can just as easily happen in a non-hierarchical situation.

Some folks seem to use these tactics out of sheer intellectual dishonesty, regardless of their position in a given relationship structure. But we think that very often, it's more innocent than that, and comes from a genuine confusion over what power within healthy relationships looks like. It can also be hard to tell, from outside a relationship, exactly what the power dynamic is within it. That's the next bit of confusion we want to address.

INFLUENCE AND CONTROL

Any healthy relationship involves a certain amount of influence. While it's not a good idea to rest your hopes for a relationship on your partner changing, or to make your partner into a project, good partnerships *do* change the people in them. You may learn new habits, new skills, new hobbies, new ways of communicating. But you also have to learn to prioritize another person's happiness as well as your own. That means allowing your partner to influence you: paying attention to what your partner's experience is, what their needs are, and working with them to help them get their needs met, along with yours. It means sometimes not doing something you want to do, and sometimes doing something you don't really want to do, in order to make the relationship work for both of you. It means give and take.

In healthy relationships, this give and take is negotiated and consensual. Boundaries are respected, bottom lines are recognized and not pushed. You may have to give up pizza on Friday because you've had it three date nights in a row and your partner's craving Thai, you may have to move to a city that's not your first choice (or even on your list), you might have to take a lower-paying job to make more time with the kids—you may have to make big sacrifices or small ones. But you won't have to give up friends, family, economic or emotional security, self-worth, self-expression, or any of the things that are important to making you *you*. And this influence is reciprocal: your partners listen to you and seek compromise just as much as you do. You *all* prioritize each other's happiness and well-being.

The other side of this coin is control. Control is what happens when the give and take stops being consensual and reciprocal, when you stop respecting a partner's boundaries, when you make your own happiness and meeting your own needs more important than valuing your partner's agency. We discussed control tactics at length in chapter 3, but as we mention there, toxic behaviours are often used in both monogamous and nonmonogamous relationships without becoming coercive control.

In a nonmonogamous relationship, intimate influence may affect the choices you make about how you interact with other people. It may mean that you don't date someone you want to date, or you limit the amount of time you can commit, or you put the brakes on a relationship that's growing too fast and big...because of the way it might affect your other partners, or because of concerns they have. It might even affect your decision whether to be nonmonogamous at all (see pages 312–314).

Or, you might make all those same choices because you have a partner who's exerting control over your other relationships—whether as part of a hierarchy that you agreed to, or as part of a pattern of coercive control. And it can be difficult to tell the difference between the two from outside a relationship—especially if you're someone, like another partner, who is directly affected by the choices being made.

Let's give an example. In her memoir *A World in Us*, author Louisa Leontiades describes her metamour, Elena, giving an ultimatum to Louisa's husband, Gilles, who was also Elena's boyfriend: "It's her or me." Elena made it clear that she could no longer remain in a relationship with Gilles as long as he was in a relationship with Louisa. Did Elena's actions constitute an attempt to veto Louisa (see the next chapter for more on vetoes) or a firm expression of a personal boundary? An outside observer would not be in a position to say, because the difference comes down to expectation and intent. Elena had every right to set boundaries concerning what kind of a relationship she was willing to be involved in—up to and including who she was willing to be metamours with. But in giving Gilles an ultimatum, was she prepared for the possibility that he might say no—thus leaving her in the position of having to make good on her promise to end her relationship with him? Or was she working from an expectation that he would say yes—thus making the ultimatum dangerous for only Louisa, and not for herself? Did she believe she had an agreement with Gilles that he would always defer to her over Louisa? What would her response be if Gilles said no? Would she use shame and guilt to try to get him to do what she wanted? Or would she accept his decision but carry out her promise to leave the relationship? (You'll have to read the book to find out what happened.)

An underlying element of all these questions is this: Did Elena feel *entitled* to have Gilles choose her? Healthy relationships are ones in which you can express your needs and desires, but it's when you feel entitled to have your partners do what you want that things go off the rails. Entitlement makes people feel like it's okay to overrule their partners' agency (and that of their partners' partners). If they're part of a socially sanctioned couple (in our example, Elena wasn't), this is especially dangerous, because they've got lots of mononormative messages feeding that sense of entitlement. And the most damaging parts of hierarchical setups tend to come about when people enshrine entitlement into their relationship agreements.

Back now to our tower and village. Let's say you've managed to get past the tower argument of "hierarchy means unequal distribution of resources" and you start discussing the real issues—specific kinds of rules, or arrangements such as vetoes. At this point, people invested in hierarchies often produce a *new* tower argument. This time it's around the question of influence: "I want to be able to ask for what I want, express my concerns about my metamours to my partners, tell my partners how their other relationships are affecting me," and so on. Once again, this is a relatively easy position to defend, because in healthy relationships, partners can influence each other.

Once the tower of intimate influence is defended, however, you may see the village once again reoccupied. The village now is things that a person feels entitled to control in their partner's relationship, or rules and structures that are put in place to ensure that one person's needs are always favoured in the case of resource conflict.

Tower: I want to be able to tell my partner how I feel about a potential new partner and have them consider my feelings in their decision.	**Village:** I expect my partner not to get involved with a person I'm not comfortable with them being with.
Tower: I want my partner to be available to me during emergencies or when I am struggling emotionally.	**Village:** I expect my partner to always be willing to cancel plans with other partners in order to be with me whenever I'm having a hard time, no matter the impact on the other partners.

Tower: I have a lifetime commitment with my partner, and I want to feel like they will make choices that honour that commitment.

Village: I don't want other partners to express desires for commitment from my partner, because I fear it will undermine their commitment to me.

A lot of people, when they say "I need hierarchy" (or "I need veto"), are really saying "I'm afraid I won't be able to influence my partner." It's not that they specifically want control; it's that they want influence, and they either haven't been taught healthy ways to gain or use it (especially in nonmonogamous situations), or they have only been in lousy relationships in the past where they *didn't* have influence—so they don't know what it really feels like.

Now, it is a fact that for most people, most of the time (but with many exceptions), longer-established, more committed or more entwined partners are likely to have more influence on a hinge than newer, less committed or less entwined partners. And that influence *is* going to affect what happens in other relationships. Sometimes, it may mean not starting a new relationship, or even ending an existing one—even when no pre-established structures are in place to ensure that certain partners are always favoured, even when there's no control.

If you refer back to the illustration on page 204, the arrow coming from the left and making the circles on the right is power from within the relationship on the left, and it's affecting the level of intensity and commitment in the relationship on the right. But what can trip you up in evaluating this situation is that the power arrow can come from influence or it can come from control. And if you are the person on the right, your experience of the hinge's decision may be very much the same regardless of this distinction.

As a result, in any situation in which there is an unequal distribution of resources—or influence—the person who has less may be inclined to look at the situation and say, "This is a hierarchy." But ultimately, what they are saying is really "I feel disempowered." And that matters—and is, more than the definition of a word, what you really need to pay attention to.

Is it loving?

Is it possible to practise hierarchical nonmonogamy in a caring way? Maybe, but it takes special attention to avoid hurting people. A secondary partner is in a uniquely vulnerable position and may feel they have limited recourse when problems arise. It is particularly vital to consider this factor whenever you make decisions that affect them directly. This doesn't mean that consideration for the secondary partner should override any and all needs within the primary relationship. Avoid either-or thinking: that if someone's needs *don't* come first, that must mean another's needs *do*. Instead, work together to give everyone space to voice their needs. There might be many ways to have certain needs met, and needs do not always have to be in conflict even when they seem to be.

Primary partners should be especially conscious of how their decisions will impact their secondary partners, and take care to treat the secondary partner's needs and feelings gently and with compassion. In particular, when things get stormy in a primary relationship, it's easy for the couple to become so concerned with their own issues that they forget to pay attention to the secondary, who may also be hurt.

In chapter 2, we introduced the Relationship Bill of Rights. It contains, we believe, standards by which to judge whether a hierarchical relationship is healthy. These rights apply to all relationships, but hierarchical relationships in particular risk infringing upon many of them. The following are examples of specific relationship rights that are at risk in hierarchical relationships and ways in which these rights are commonly overridden:

- *to choose the level of involvement and intimacy you want, and to revoke consent to any form of intimacy at any time.* Both the hinge or pivot partner (the person in the middle) and the secondary partner in a hierarchical vee structure can have this right violated if the primary partner restricts the intimacy they can choose with each other, or if the primary partner requires that the secondary partner be intimate with them too.
- *to revoke consent to any form of intimacy at any time.* This right can be violated if the primary couple keeps relevant information from the secondary partner.
- *to hold and express differing points of view.* It's common for primary couples to shut down complaints or concerns from the secondary partner if they contradict the primary couple's rules, or to forbid a secondary partner from attempting to renegotiate the rules.
- *to feel and communicate all your emotions and needs.* Both the pivot and secondary partners may be subject to rules restricting what they are allowed to feel. Generally speaking, rules against specific

emotions are really rules against communicating feelings, since people cannot control what they feel, only what they express. When a secondary partner does express "forbidden" emotions, they are often dismissed as less real or less important than those of the members of the primary couple.

- *to set boundaries concerning your privacy needs.* Some primary couples do not recognize the right to privacy of the members of a secondary relationship, or of each other with regard to the secondary relationship. There may, for example, be expectations that the hinge will tell their primary partner intimate details that the secondary partner considers private.
- *to seek balance between what you give to the relationship and what is given back to you.* It is common to see secondary partners expected to give things to the primary couple that are not reciprocated.
- *to know that your partner will work with you to resolve issues that arise.* Often secondary relationships are subject to rules that were put in place before the secondary partner came on the scene. If a rule is not working for the secondary relationship, will the members of the primary relationship renegotiate?
- *to make mistakes.* There may be an expectation that a secondary relationship will be ended the first time the secondary partner makes a mistake.
- *to decide how many partners you want, and to choose your own partners.* Hierarchy often includes a "screening veto," discussed in the next chapter, that restricts people from selecting their own partners.
- *to have an equal say with each of your partners in deciding the form your relationship with that partner will take.* In many hierarchies, the primary couple has more say than the secondary partner in deciding this.
- *to choose the level of time and investment you will offer to each partner.* The pivot partner's ability to choose the level of investment they want to give to each of their relationships may be limited by pre-existing rules set by the primary couple.
- *to understand clearly any rules that will apply to your relationship before entering into it.* Many secondary partners feel that they did not fully understand what they were getting into, and many primary couples feel free to unilaterally change the rules of a secondary relationship at any time.

- *to discuss with your partners decisions that affect you.* Many primary couples make decisions about the secondary relationship, then present them as a fait accompli.
- *to have time alone with each of your partners.* Some primary couples have rules prohibiting this.
- *to enjoy passion and special moments with each of your partners.* Hierarchical relationships often have rules restricting the amount of intimacy or "specialness" the secondary relationship can have.
- *to choose the level of involvement and intimacy you want with your partners' other partners.* The rules in hierarchical relationships often prescribe how metamour relationships will look, sometimes even requiring the secondary partner to be sexually or romantically involved with both members of a primary couple.
- *to seek compromise.* Often the primary couple expects to dictate terms.
- *to have relationships with people, not with relationships.* The primary couple may expect the secondary partner to interact with them as a unit, limiting the individual relationships that may develop.
- *to have plans made with your partner be respected; for instance, not changed at the last minute for trivial reasons.* Primary couples often assume they are free to change plans whenever they "have to," the criteria for which may not be fair to the secondary partner. The secondary partner usually has no such reciprocal rights.
- *to be treated as a peer of every other person, not as a subordinate, even when differing levels of commitment or responsibility exist.* Hierarchical relationships tend to be disempowering to at least the secondary partner, and often to the pivot partner in the core couple as well.

So, are hierarchical relationships inherently disempowering? Or can they be practised fairly and with respect for our ethical axioms, in a way that benefits everyone and does not violate the Relationship Bill of Rights? We are hesitant to give a categorical yes or no. Because of the continued popularity of hierarchical nonmonogamous relationships, we would like to be able to say yes. But the truth is, in our combined personal experience and in all the hundreds of stories people have shared with each of us, we have *never* seen a truly hierarchical relationship that worked well for everyone over the long term.

It's common to hear people say that a hierarchical relationship "works for us," if by "us" they mean the primary couple. But if you look at their relationship histories, you'll often find a string of past secondary partners who were either vetoed for trying to renegotiate the rules once they became too constricting, or who left the relationships because of poor treatment—or perhaps, who are still involved, but have suffered deep damage to their personal well-being and self-esteem.

Many people who have been a secondary partner in a hierarchy have sworn never to do it again. It's difficult to say that hierarchy is "working" when we include these people in our assessment. As well, couples often complain that they just can't seem to find secondary partners who will stick around in the kind of primary/secondary arrangement they're looking for—which often means people who won't want a say in the rules that govern them. When couples consistently can't find partners willing to participate in their flavour of hierarchy, it's difficult to say that hierarchy is working for *them,* either.

We *have* seen relationship networks where people have carefully worked to maximize well-being and respect the relationship rights of everyone involved, while upholding their commitments to their partners. But in our experience, by the time someone has managed to avoid the pitfalls above and remains focused on, say, a long-standing lifetime partnership while treating newer or less-entwined partners with integrity and compassion, the structure that is left tends to no longer resemble a hierarchy. Such relationships instead begin to look like empowered relationships, the subject of chapter 13. But before we talk about those, we need to talk about a particular kind of agreement that's a keystone of many hierarchical nonmonogamous relationships: the veto. That's the subject of the next chapter.

QUESTIONS TO ASK YOURSELF

You may encounter relationship hierarchy in one of two ways: by instituting it in one or more of your relationships, or by entering a relationship with someone who is already part of a hierarchical structure. The questions to ask yourself will differ depending on which situation you're in.

If you are considering implementing a relationship hierarchy:

- How do I view potential new partners, both for myself and for my existing partners? Do I see them as potential problems to be managed, as potential sources of joy to enrich my partners' lives, some of both, or something else entirely? How does my approach to hierarchy reflect that view?

- Are there specific assets, commitments or people (such as children) I am seeking to protect with a hierarchy? Can I imagine other avenues for achieving that protection?
- Am I open to secondary relationships someday becoming primary relationships, given enough time and investment?
- What will I do if a secondary partner becomes dissatisfied with the rules that apply to them? Am I willing or able to involve that partner in renegotiations of those rules?

If you are considering entering a hierarchy as a secondary partner:

- Do I clearly understand both the letter and the intent of the rules that will apply to my relationship? Am I comfortable maintaining a relationship within those rules? Am I comfortable with the reasons for the rules?
- Do I know whether the rules that apply to my relationship are subject to change? If so, who may change them, and how? What input will I have into those changes?
- Will the term *secondary* be applied to my relationship, and if so, do I understand how the primary couple is defining the word? Am I comfortable with the definition and with the use of that term?
- Will it be possible for the secondary nature of my relationship to evolve into primary, if my partner and I desire that? If not, how will I feel about my relationship remaining secondary long into the future—say, ten or fifteen years—or if I become deeply attached?

The trouble with human happiness is that it is constantly beset by fear. It is not the lack of possessing but the safety of possession that is at stake.
HANNAH ARENDT

12 Veto Arrangements

The word *veto* is Latin for "I forbid." It refers to one person's power to prevent something from happening. When we talk about veto in nonmonogamous relationships, we're talking about something very specific: an agreed-upon-in-advance right for one person to tell another "I want you to break up with your partner," and have the breakup happen.

Identifying a real veto situation can at times be tricky, because some people use the word *veto* to describe things that aren't a veto by this definition. For instance, you might run into people who say, "We have the right to talk to our partners if one of their other relationships becomes a problem, discuss the problems we see and ask for resolutions, which might include changes up to and including ending the relationship." We prefer to call this sort of arrangement good communication, not veto. If you have something you call veto that looks like this, we are not talking about you.

A veto, for the purpose of this discussion, is a one-sided decision to halt a relationship between two other people. It is not a negotiation or a request. The key elements of a veto are that it is unilateral (that is, only one person needs to think there's a problem) and it is binding (that is, the person exercising a veto has reason to believe the other will obey it). A veto moves the locus of control away from the people in a particular relationship and gives it to a third party.

Veto arrangements are one of the most common, and most zealously guarded, of all the rules in hierarchical relationships. In our experience, most hierarchies include a veto arrangement, even when they include few of the other rules we've talked about. Vetoes promise the ultimate fallback: If a partner's relationship becomes too difficult, or their other lover is too unlikeable, or jealousy becomes too unbearable, veto can make the problem just go away.

Stories about relationships ending by veto may vary in detail, but they all share a common thread: The person who is vetoed feels that the veto was unfair. (Often, the hinge who was in the position of enforcing the veto thought it was unfair, too.)

The subject of veto is likely to generate controversy in any discussion about nonmonogamy. Some people feel passionate about the value of veto. The word itself is powerful: It conjures up feelings of empowerment and control. Even people who don't have a veto according to our definition will often insist on using the word *veto* to describe what they do because the word itself creates such a compelling feeling of safety.

Veto of an existing relationship

For people who are subject to the possibility of a veto but do not hold that option themselves—for example, the new partner of a person whose pre-existing partner has a veto—the word *veto* is just as powerful, but often it is powerfully negative. It creates an environment where no matter what you do or what kind of investment you make, your relationship can be ripped away at a moment's notice, without discussion or appeal. It summons an image of the sword of Damocles, always hanging over the relationship, ready to fall at any misstep. This risk creates an environment where it's nearly impossible to feel safe in that relationship. Vetoes are like nuclear weapons: They may keep others in line, but their use tends to forever alter the landscape.

Many hierarchical relationships have a veto provision that can be exercised at any time, even after another relationship is well established. This kind of veto is popular because it seems to provide a safety switch for the members of an original couple to shut down another relationship that becomes too intense or threatening. But that sense of safety can carry a very high price. In practice, many couples who execute a veto break up shortly thereafter; the use of the veto is an emotionally violent power move that destabilizes everyone involved. Any time you choose to break our partner's heart, the damage to your own relationship may be permanent.

Now, when a partner of yours vetoes another partner, you actually do have a choice. You can either end the relationship that's being vetoed, or you can say "No, I refuse to accept this veto." But neither option is likely to lead anywhere constructive. If you say "No, I refuse to accept this," the partner who used the veto now has a choice to make: stay in the relationship and sulk? Leave? Whatever choices each person makes, bitterness is pretty much guaranteed. Even if your partner uses their veto and you enact it, responsibility for the breakup is still yours. If your relationship has been vetoed, it's easy to say "I am ending this relationship because my partner made me do it." In reality, the ethical responsibility belongs only to the person doing the breaking up.

Screening veto

Not all vetoes are intended as tools to shut down a relationship once it's already underway. Some people use what might be called a screening veto. This means a potential new relationship may be vetoed before it becomes established, but not after. A screening veto is safer than a veto exercised on a relationship that's actively happening, in that it is less likely to create a sense of violation. However, even this variety of veto can have damaging consequences.

Vetoes often come from a place of fear and threat. It can be intimidating to see a partner excited about a new relationship with someone else, especially when you feel insecure. All the demons start whispering in your ear: "What if I'm not good enough? What if this person is more exciting than I am?"

A screening veto has problems because, like all vetoes, it tends to end conversations rather than start them. It can be hard to say, "Wow, seeing you excited about a new person makes me feel insecure. Let's talk about what that means, and how we can work together to strengthen and support our relationship until what *we* have brings you this much joy." It's much easier to say, "I don't want you to see that person again."

While it's not as damaging to veto a person before a relationship begins, depriving a partner of a source of joy is still a dangerous thing to do. When you see a partner clearly excited about someone, and you try to take that person away from them, you risk undermining your partner's happiness, and that is likely to damage your relationship.

It might be tempting to look at the examples above and call them abuses of veto, rather than situations where veto is useful and appropriate. We disagree. The problem is that nobody with veto power ever believes they're using it capriciously. People tend to be the heroes of their own stories. The problem with veto is not that some use it inappropriately; the problem is that it tends to cause damage no matter *how* it is used.

And sometimes veto becomes a way to defend your own dysfunctions and entrench them.

In nonmonogamous circles, you may hear the idea that you should only add relationships that enhance your existing ones. Or that you should screen new partners to make sure their communication and relationship styles mesh with your existing relationships. That does seem like a good way to avoid conflict and promote stability. But just as often, it can lead to enabling behaviours. You can easily end up constructing an echo chamber where dysfunctional relationship patterns go unchallenged.

But what if you have reason to be concerned that the new person is disruptive, manipulative, a bad influence, emotionally unstable or dangerous to your partner? Isn't that a good reason to use a veto? After all, your beloved is all caught up in twitterpation, aglow with hormones and unable to think clearly. It's true, many people gloss over flaws in the flush of a new crush. Isn't it your job to see the things your partner might be missing? To notice warning signs and tell them?

Well, yes, but you can do that without a veto. In a strong and healthy relationship, one partner's opinions and feelings matter a great deal to the other. If you're really concerned that your partner has hooked up with an axe murderer, saying "Honey, I'm really concerned that your new partner is an axe murderer" should be enough to give them pause. And if it's not...wouldn't you want to know that? Using a veto to control your partner's course of action essentially means you'll never know what judgment call they would have made all on their own. So you don't get to watch them prove that they value your relationship, share your values and respect your feelings, because you cut off the situation in which that kind of demonstration would happen. You also don't get to watch them make a mistake and fix it, which is another kind of trust-building opportunity. And on the truly negative end of the spectrum, you also don't get to watch them show if in fact they don't value your relationship, share your values or respect your feelings—which means you may end up staying longer in a relationship that in fact really should have ended for your own well-being.

There's also no reason to imagine that the veto-wielding partner is any more objective than the twitterpated partner. After all, it's scary to watch your partner get distracted by the new shiny relationship. And when you're scared, you don't make wise decisions. Which isn't to say that the veto-wielding partner is always wrong and the infatuated partner is always right. There's just no particular reason to assume one is necessarily more "right" than the other. The only way through the swamp is to communicate openly about whatever concerns or misgivings you have, and then to let the person *in* the relationship be the one to make the decision. Because even if their choice of partner is a mistake, it is that person's mistake to make.

Screening veto agreements deprive people of their ability to make their own mistakes, and to learn and grow from them.

Ethical problems with veto

There's nothing wrong with trying to manage risk—you do it every time you put on a seatbelt. Managing risk through veto, though, raises serious ethical concerns. It violates both of our core ethical axioms: The people in the relationship are more important than the relationship, and other people are real.

How does a veto treat people as though they weren't real? A veto makes a person expendable. It does not give that person input into whether or not their own relationship is ended. While it's true that even in monogamous relationships the person being broken up with often doesn't get a say in the matter, the nonmonogamy veto situation is unique. Here, a third party *who is not actually in the relationship* is ending something that both of the people in it still want.

A veto arrangement also makes a relationship more important than the people in it, because it requires that a relationship be ended without consideration for whether it is healthy or beneficial to the people in it. Nor does it consider the harm that may be done to them by the veto.

It's true that when you have several relationships, some may cause pain in others. Despite raising the issues, despite ongoing negotiation, the hinge may choose to remain in a relationship that one of their partners thinks is harmful. If you are the partner who might want to issue a veto, consider stating boundaries for yourself instead. You could say, "This situation is degrading my happiness to the point where I can no longer imagine being happy if it continues. If you keep going down this course, I won't be able to remain in this relationship." Indeed, this is an important part of consent: You always have the right to withdraw consent, for any reason. You *never* have to remain in a situation that hurts you.

That being said, let's acknowledge how painful setting or enforcing such a boundary can be. Yes, you have every right to leave—but let's not pretend it's an easy thing to do, especially if you've built an entwined life with your partner or are still very much in love with them. There is a balance to be struck here: Our rights exist, but it can still suck to exercise them. On paper, it can look simple. In real life, when a relationship begins to fall apart in this way, it can be heartbreaking and come with a ton of practical challenges. Should you stay, even though the situation is hurting you, or should you leave, knowing that leaving will bring its own pain? We come back to discernment here. Ending a meaningful relationship is not a light choice to make, and rarely an easy one. Given this, using a veto can be really tempting, or maybe even seem like the lesser of two evils. But it remains a costly shortcut that rarely works out the way it's intended to. It's worth doing the deeper work of carefully considering what the right course of action is and taking each step with compassion for all involved.

Issues of power and risk also come up when you start thinking from the perspective of your values and ethical systems. If you have veto power and you say "I cannot stay with you if you remain in this relationship," you know ahead of time that you will "win" this particular play. Your partner has promised you in advance—probably when their other partner was still hypothetical and not yet a real person—that if this scenario ever arose, they would "choose" you.

Because you're pretty sure what the outcome will be, the risk for you in enacting a veto is lowered. You can deliver an ultimatum and still (in theory) not lose the relationship. You do not have to shoulder the risk and vulnerability of saying you are prepared to leave and really mean it. In other words, the consequences of your actions—and thus, the bar you need to reach before you issue an ultimatum—are lowered for you, giving you more power and less incentive to act in good faith.

At the same time, *all* of that risk is unloaded onto your metamour. This shifting of risk—telling another person to bear both the normal risk that comes with any relationship plus extra risk shifted from your relationship—is one of the things that makes vetoes unethical according to our axioms.

If, on the other hand, you do *not* have veto power, the outcome is not predetermined. There is a chance that your partner will not break up with their other partner. So you have to accept the vulnerability of telling your partner, "I can't take this anymore. I will have to leave if you continue that relationship." You have to be *sure.* It seems to us that if you're ready to take a step as serious as ending another person's intimate relationship, it's fair to ask that you put as much on the line as they have.

And then, without a veto, your partner has the opportunity to do what they believe will be best for them in the long run—rather than having to make a choice they may not want to make because it was agreed to long before another real human being was involved. *The people in the relationship remain more important than the relationship.* Including that third person, and including the hinge. When the outcome is predetermined through a veto arrangement, the third person has no room to negotiate or to defend themselves or their relationship. If the situation is so untenable that the hinge really does need to choose one or the other, maybe the newer partner even has a case for why they are a better partner for your partner than you are—and they should have the right to make that case, just as you do.

Even if you have a strictly hierarchical, primary/secondary relationship, the ethical considerations of veto deserve some attention. Any relationship can end, for any number of reasons. Not all relationships last; that's a fact of life. But even when the primary partner in a hierarchical relationship decides they need their partner's secondary relationship to end, the ethical thing to do, according to our axioms, is to involve the secondary partner in the discussion and allow them to respond to concerns.

Practical problems with veto

Aside from ethical concerns, and aside from the pain and bitterness a veto may cause, veto arrangements present other practical problems you may not have thought of. For example, a veto arrangement that's justified by a bad past experience holds a bad actor's actions against a new person who wasn't involved. Say your partner became involved with Sam last year, and Sam rained chaos all over. If that makes you ask for veto, then when Alex comes along, you're making Alex pay for the sins of Sam. *You* are perpetuating Sam's chaos.

Another problem is escalation. You can't, short of use of force, actually make a partner break up with someone else. When you use a veto, even a mutually agreed-upon veto, you are giving your partner a choice: Break up with your other partner, or else. The "or else" part is often left unspecified; few veto negotiations include provisions for what might happen if the veto is ignored. But a veto can, in fact, be ignored. Then what?

Veto creates a trust imbalance. The new person is often told, "Trust us. We won't use this veto inappropriately." But what does this say to the new person? "I want you to trust that I won't veto you inappropriately, but we have a veto arrangement because *we* don't trust *you*." Is it reasonable to ask someone you don't trust to trust you?

On an even more pragmatic note, people who have great skill sets for nonmonogamous relationships—people who have experience with nonmonogamy, have demonstrated good communication skills, and are compassionate problem-solvers with good conflict-resolution skills—usually avoid anyone who has veto. So by having a veto in place, you stack the deck *toward* relationship problems, because so many experienced nonmonogamous people with good skills will avoid you. Many people even use "Do you have a veto agreement?" as a screening question with potential partners. If the answer is yes, it can be a deal-breaker. People who value the ability to have a say in their own relationships are unlikely to agree to give someone else ultimate authority over whether their relationship lives or dies.

Alternatives to veto

People can become confused when talking about relationships without veto because they may have a mistaken notion that "no veto" means "no input." Some new partners can indeed be damaging or even dangerous, and it's important to be able to speak up when you see problems. Think about "right of consultation" as an alternative to "right of veto." You want conversation to open up, whereas a veto ends conversation. You need to be able to say "I got a bad feeling from the way they treated you there at the bus stop," or "I went online and found they have a restraining order against them"—and have that be perceived not as a threat, but as useful information. Your partner needs to know you will go on to say "So please be extra careful, and I'd like it if you could message me a few times to let me know you're okay."

The most common justification you'll hear for veto power is that it's necessary to prevent a new partner from trying to break up the existing relationship. There certainly are people who will try to do this (see pages 311–312 on cowpokes). Unfortunately, veto treats *all* new partners as bad actors simply because *some* might be. And your partner isn't a delicate Grecian urn, an object to be stolen away by an enterprising burglar. Your partner is a person, and people can't be stolen, at least not for relationship purposes. If some new shiny person tries to "steal" them, your partner has to consent to being stolen. Veto or no veto, if they want to stay with you, they will.

So the real question is not, how can you protect your relationship from people who want to steal your partner? The real question is, do you trust your partner to want to be with you, even if some cute new person asks them to leave you? If someone says "run away with me," what do you think your partner will say?

Trust isn't something most people are taught when growing up. The fairy tale tells you to find true love and you'll be happy ever after. It doesn't mention trusting your partners even when you're afraid. It doesn't tell you how to assert good boundaries when faced with potentially disrupting relationships. Committing yourself to trusting that your partner wants to be with you, and will choose to be with you even if someone else tries to tug them away, takes courage. Asserting good boundaries around your partner's other partners takes work. But in the end, your partner is going to make the choices they make no matter what rules you put in place, so what other options do you really have?

Solid boundary-setting is another important tool in managing veto-free relationships (see chapter 9). Your partner may choose a partner you don't particularly like to be around. They may choose a partner who encourages them to make choices that hurt you. At these times, you need to be able to set clear guidelines about what you will and won't accept *within your own relationship.* You do not need to spend time with someone you don't like. If you feel uncomfortable or unsafe with a certain person in your home or your bed (or around your children or pets), you have a right to (and should) set limits about who you will permit in your space.

Of course, your partner also has the right to choose a different living arrangement if your boundaries become unworkable for them.

If you expect certain standards of behaviour—to be told the truth, for example, or to have plans reliably kept—that the other relationship is interfering with, you can express these expectations to your partner without managing the other relationship. And of course, if you are in a relationship without veto, it is especially important to respect the boundaries your partner sets around their body, their mind, their choices and their space with regard to *your* other partners, even when they inconvenience you.

Chapter 4 talked about the idea of self-efficacy: your belief in your own ability to make yourself heard and to positively affect your own situation. Veto can seem like a form of self-efficacy, but true self-efficacy lies in believing that if your partner's new relationship starts to go horribly wrong, you can talk about it and make yourself heard. Veto is an indicator of low self-efficacy; it is a way of saying "I don't believe I can get my partner to listen to my concerns unless I have a kill switch."

We talk more about setting boundaries with your partners' other partners in chapter 19, and about negotiating directly with your own partners in chapters 6 and 7.

Line-item veto and emotional blackmail

Many people who don't have a formally negotiated veto arrangement come up with ways to veto their partners' relationships anyway. One of these is the line-item veto. That's when, on a case-by-case basis, you frequently restrict what your partner can do with their other partners and when. Eventually enough dates get cancelled or interrupted, enough activities curtailed, that the relationship withers and dies. You don't have to demand that your partner end a relationship in order to make it end; you just have to starve it of the resources it needs to thrive.

Another form of veto-by-another-name is emotional blackmail. In this context, it's a weapon you can use when you don't want your partner to do something—like go on a date, continue a relationship or engage in a certain activity—but you have not been able to negotiate up front what you want. Your partner, after considering your input, has decided to make another choice: go on the date, continue the relationship, do that thing. But instead of accepting your partner's choice, you make sure that it carries a price. You have an emotional meltdown an hour before that date, and your partner has to stay home with you. You send them anxious text messages every five minutes whenever they're with the partner you don't like. You keep making nonspecific threats of disaster—emotional or physical—when your partner does what you don't want.

As damaging as this behaviour is, many people often unintentionally reinforce it when it happens. They want to be there for their partners, they don't want to hurt them, and most people don't really like conflict. If your partner's objection to that thing you wanted to do is so important to them, you don't *really* need to do it, right? That one date really isn't so important; you can schedule another one.... The trouble is, people use this behaviour because it works: It gets them what they want.

If your partner exhibits this kind of behaviour often, if most of your decisions they don't like end up with you paying an emotional price, or if their blackmail continues more than a couple of months into a new relationship, then you have a problem—a potentially serious one, with no easy solution. The two of you will need to learn more appropriate negotiation techniques that do not involve emotional threats. Point out the behaviour to them and explain the effect it is having on you and your relationships (including the one with the partner exhibiting the behaviour). Consider reading the book *Emotional Blackmail* by Susan Forward together, and consider getting professional help from a nonmonogamy-friendly counsellor. If the behaviour does not stop, you may need to consider ending the relationship (see also the checklists in chapter 3).

If you're the person exhibiting this behaviour, approach yourself with compassion. Your feelings are always valid, and you always feel them for good reasons. But those emotions may not be based on a full set of facts, and even if they are, the meanings you attach to a given set of facts might not be an accurate match for others' realities or reasons for their choices. Your distress may be rooted in everything from unresolved childhood trauma to pure misunderstanding. Your attachment styles might not mesh well with those of your partners. There may be a sore spot or a lack within the relationship that needs tending and repair, and the current situation may be pressing painfully into that spot. In short, the feelings are real, but the reasons for them might be a lot more complex than that thing your partner is doing with their partner on Wednesday night.

Everyone is allowed the occasional meltdown or outburst. But if this is happening on a regular basis—and if your partners are giving in to your demands simply to avoid dealing with your behaviour—you may want to consider getting professional help to cope with your emotions. Also, remember that what you do about your feelings is a matter of choice. Just because you are feeling intense emotions doesn't mean you're entitled to cross lines of acceptable interpersonal behaviour. If you recognize yourself in this section, in addition to counselling on your own and potentially with your partners, you may want to reexamine whether nonmonogamy in general is really working for you. You may also want to revisit the idea of primal panic, discussed in chapter 8.

Pocket veto

Pocket veto is a legal term. It refers to when an elected official vetoes a bill indirectly by hanging onto it and neglecting to sign it until it's too late to deal with it during the legislative session. In nonmonogamy, a pocket veto is when you stop your partner from doing something you don't want them to do using indirect tactics such as delaying discussions or saying "Yes, but only after..."—in which the "after" never comes.

A pocket veto might be used when one partner wants a specific thing within a nonmonogamous relationship structure. "I am afraid of X. Please let's not do X until I stop being afraid." That "X" could be just about anything: meeting the metamour, okaying an overnight stay with a lover, going out in public as a triad or quad, or whatever else.

A pocket veto can also arise when it comes to the question of whether or not to do nonmonogamy at all. "Sure, I'd love to try nonmonogamy, but after I graduate, so I'm not so stressed out. Actually now that I've graduated, I'm super stressed about my new job. And now I'm stressed about this new project, and..."

Sometimes a nonmonogamously inclined person ends up in a relationship with a monogamously inclined partner who agrees to nonmonogamy, but only after they "feel secure in the relationship." That can turn out to be...never. Of course, if your reward for feeling secure is something you don't want, you don't have much incentive to ever feel secure. These relationships can last for years before ending, with the nonmonogamous partner forever hopeful that someday the monogamous partner will eventually "get there."

In the next chapter, we discuss being judicious about when you start new relationships: perhaps it's better not to bring in new partners when an existing relationship is in crisis, just after a major life upheaval, or when serious mental health issues are erupting, to name a few. (We also mention the idea of "temporary vessels" on page 312.) The trouble is that this idea of "readiness for nonmonogamy" can become a pocket veto if it does not include a clear time frame. If you need time to work through an issue, get used to a new partner or adjust to an idea, then agree to a time frame for it. If the time frame expires and you want to renew it, especially more than once, understand that you have crossed into pocket veto territory.

The main problem with a pocket veto is that it's an indirect and misleading way to say no to something. Saying no is not, itself, an issue. Maybe you don't actually want to be nonmonogamous. That's okay! Then say so, and have a frank conversation with your partner to figure out how to proceed in your relationship. Or maybe you're just never going to want to meet your metamour or go out in public as a quad. That could present some challenges depending on how everyone else concerned feels about the topic. But using a pocket veto to avoid dealing head-on with these challenges just prolongs the stress and tension, as the requesting partner tries to be patient and understanding while maybe also feeling sad or disappointed or frustrated, and the vetoing partner feels scared and pressured. In any case, you're not having the conversation you need to have in order to deal with the problem truthfully. And so it festers, and can eventually poison the whole relationship. If they figure out that they're being subjected to a pocket veto, the hinge may feel betrayed, lied to, manipulated or otherwise hurt, in which case the relationship may need a lot of repair work if it's to survive, or it may end on a much unhappier note than it otherwise could have. In short, pocket vetoes come with the same potential for harm as the straightforward kind of veto, only amplified by avoidance, indirect communication and dishonesty.

Sometimes you hit a point in a relationship where you realize that you won't ever see eye to eye with a given partner on a given issue. And sometimes, that issue is a deal-breaker. They want something crucial that you cannot give them, or you want something crucial they cannot give you. It's a painful place to arrive at, especially if you've invested a lot of time and energy in the relationship, shared lots of hopes and dreams, or entwined your lives. But it makes the whole thing worse when you avoid the topic or string someone along with promises that you'll eventually give them what they want when you have no intention of doing so. Work up the courage to be clear about your no instead of indulging in perpetual avoidance by means of a pocket veto.

QUESTIONS TO ASK YOURSELF

The questions around veto fall into three categories: those for people who want to have veto over their partners' relationships, those for people who are considering giving veto power to another, and those for people who are considering becoming involved with someone whose partner has a veto.

If you want your partner to give you veto power over their other relationships:

- Under what circumstances do I feel it's appropriate for me to use it?
- Who do I think should have the final say in deciding whether a relationship ends? Why?
- What do I believe will happen if I ask a partner to end another relationship, and they say no? Why will that thing happen?
- Do I trust my partner to consider my needs and well-being in their decisions about whether to stay in a relationship that is hurting me? Why or why not? If not, what can I do to improve that trust?
- Do I trust my partner to make good decisions about the people with whom they start relationships? Why or why not? What might the consequences be if they make a poor decision, and how might I deal with those consequences?

- Do I use the word *veto* to describe something *other* than an ability to unilaterally end a partner's relationship? If so, why, and what does the word *veto* mean to me that other terms do not?

If you are considering giving your partner(s) veto:

- Am I prepared to bring someone I care about (or will come to care about) into a situation where I must break up with them at someone else's will? What are my ethical obligations in such a situation?
- Can I think of ways to make a new partner feel safe in a relationship with me under these conditions?
- Do I understand the needs my partner is seeking to meet by requesting veto, and have we discussed alternative ways of meeting those needs?

If you are considering starting a relationship with someone whose partner has a veto:

- If I start a relationship with someone who is already partnered, what kind of input do I feel it's reasonable for their other partners to have in our relationship?
- What would I need in order to feel safe opening my heart to someone who has given the power to end our relationship to someone else? What kind of boundaries do I need to set, or what kind of requests do I need to make?

The most vital right is the right to love and be loved.
EMMA GOLDMAN

13 Empowered Relationships

People who are empowered in their intimate relationships can express needs and ask for them to be met. They can talk about problems. They can say what works for them and expect that their partners will try to accommodate their needs as much as they can.

Empowerment, like security, is a two-way street: It's not possible to *make* a person feel empowered, just as it's not possible to make a person feel secure. The best you can hope to do is to create an environment that welcomes participation and encourages empowerment. You can, however, *dis*empower people, and that can be very dangerous. People who are disempowered have little to lose by breaking the rules. Disempowerment breeds resentment, and eventually, losing the relationship might not seem so bad.

Some defining elements of empowerment in an intimate relationship are:

- engaging and participating in the decision-making process for decisions that affect you
- having a full range of options available when decisions are made, not a simple yes or no option (or, in extreme cases, the "accept it or leave" option)
- having agency over your own body, relationships and life
- being able to express needs, opinions, desires and boundaries
- having access to the information that materially affects your relationship, your body, and your safety or security
- being able to propose alternatives

- having the ability to object to, and having open negotiations about, the rules, agreements and structures of your relationships
- having the ability to give, withhold or withdraw consent

It's no coincidence that many of these characteristics resemble some of the relationship rights we listed in chapter 2.

When you use these criteria to define empowerment, it can become clear that an empowered relationship is not necessarily one in which everyone has equal power. Rather, it is one in which no one is actively *dis*empowered, intentionally or unintentionally, by the structure of the relationship or the behaviour of the people in it.

Empowerment is not equality

When you bring up the notion of nonmonogamous relationships without hierarchy, people often imagine you're talking about equal relationships, where *equal* means everyone has the same things. That might mean, for example, trying to create a relationship structure in which everyone has the same amount of time, the same status or the same resources. Perhaps it means everyone is having sex with everyone else, everyone lives under the same roof or everyone loves everyone else "equally."

This definition pops up as both a good-faith misunderstanding and as a straw man presented by advocates of hierarchy. It's not reasonable, these advocates will say, to give the long-distance comet you've known for a year the same influence over major life decisions as you give your spouse. And that's usually true. That's why we find it more useful, when thinking of alternatives to hierarchy, to speak of empowerment. Because different people want different things, empowerment is more useful than sameness as a relationship principle. What if one person naturally wants more time with a shared partner, and another less? Is it reasonable to tell them both they're only allowed to have the same amount of time? What if one relationship has existed for six years, another for six months? It doesn't make sense to expect the same level of commitment and entwinement from each.

A literal take on "equality" might be that everyone should have the same obligations to share a home and the same vote in how to handle the mortgage. A more rational take might mean that everyone has equal power to choose how they run their lives.

People who have long been together often have a vested "sweat equity" in the relationship. They've made sacrifices and incurred obligations together. Those obligations look like the big commitment arrows on the illustrations in chapter 11. In an empowered relationship, a new person is not told, "You have the same standing and the same voice in these existing obligations and responsibilities." Rather, that person is told, "As you invest in the relationship, you, too, will build sweat equity. You will not be denied the opportunity to do this."

In the context of nonmonogamy, an empowered relationship also means that no one *outside* a relationship has the authority to place restrictions on that relationship. The flows of connection, commitment and power within a relationship can be of any size, and can even be unequal within relationships. But the defining element of hierarchy—*power from within one relationship that controls or restricts another relationship*—is absent.

"Equality" is also not the ideal framework because it can end up meaning an equality of bad behaviour. For example, some people's logic goes like this: "I'm jealous, so I want you to break up with your other partner. But it's okay, I will break up with my other partner, too, so it's fair." This might sound like an extreme example, but the impulse often exists, when people are faced with unpleasant emotions, to treat others as expendable.

Owning your power

Nonmonogamous relationships clearly highlight the gap between your *perception* of your power and the *reality* of your power. It is often easier to see someone else's power and privilege than to see your own. Science fiction writer Samuel R. Delany compares our perception of power to "a fog over a meadow at evening":

> From any distance, it seemed to have a shape, a substance, a color, an edge. Yet, as you approached it, it seemed to recede before you. Finally, when common sense said you were at its very center, it still seemed just as far away; only by time it was on all sides, obscuring any vision of the world beyond it.

If your partner begins a new relationship, you might see how they invest in the new relationship and feel powerless—without recognizing how the established structures, history, commitments and shared life experiences in your own relationship give you a tremendous amount of power that the newer partner doesn't have. You're at the centre of the fog. The new partner, however, is often *keenly* aware of the power you have as the established partner, because they're just arriving at the meadow from outside the fog. It doesn't mean newer partners have no power—far from it. But they lack the already-built structure and history of a pre-established relationship, which is very real and substantial.

Not recognizing your power doesn't just affect metamours, by the way! If you don't understand that you have power in your relationships, it can lead you to do really hurtful things without realizing it. Things like unkind words, passive aggression, withdrawal and refusing to show vulnerability can be extremely painful for someone who cares deeply—but if you don't think you're worthy of that kind of care, and you don't understand how someone can feel that way about you, then you may not even realize when you're hurting someone by not showing up fully.

A key to practising empowered relationships is to recognize and understand the power you hold. For this, you need to return to the ideas about security and worthiness in chapter 4. Without a strong *internal* sense of security and worthiness, you will find it nearly impossible to be aware of your power in your romantic relationships. When you feel unworthy, you feel disconnected—even when your loved ones are craving connection with you. You feel isolated and alienated, even when you're surrounded by love and support.

While you're working on the project of your own worthiness, though, you can also seek to understand your own power—even if you don't yet feel it in your heart. You must look for evidence. If you are terrified of losing a ten-year relationship, step back and think about the fact that your partner has chosen to be in a relationship with you *for ten years.* This didn't happen by accident! It happened because for ten years, you have added value to your partner's life.

If you feel you need hierarchy to protect a co-parenting relationship, think about what it means that your partner has chosen to make the enormous commitment of having children with you, and look at evidence they give you daily in the form of care and investment in your children. Practise gratitude for all of the ways, large and small, your partner invests in your relationship. It will help you understand the value of the relationship to them.

At the same time, it's common for people to hoard power in relationships, or to consciously or unconsciously conceal the power their partners have. This might come from an actual desire to control others, but often it comes from their own fears—of vulnerability, of not being in control of their own lives—or from shame that shrouds their own needs. Being vulnerable, having and expressing needs, and being attached all give someone else power. If you've been hurt or traumatized, or have had that kind of power misused against you, then it can be incredibly scary to let others see that they have it. Concealing your needs and vulnerability, and thus limiting others' awareness of their importance to you, is a tendency in all the insecure attachment styles. Avoidant people deal with it by telling themselves they have no needs or vulnerability (and no one else should, either); anxious people deal with it by overfocusing on the needs of their partners (and usually feeling resentful about it); and fearful-avoidant people, who tend to be keenly aware of power dynamics, often directly try to manage them.

So as usual, it's not simple: Understanding your own power isn't just about building your own self-esteem and rationally examining your partners' investment in you. You're not a mind reader, and if someone is obscuring the power you hold in a relationship, you can't be expected to understand it without their collaboration. But given that about 50% of the population has insecure attachment styles, and that they tend to be drawn to one another, it makes sense that if you don't understand the power you have in a relationship, there are likely to be elements of both issues at play.

Empowered relationships and children

When starting a new relationship, it's important to be forthright and clear with the new person about your existing commitments. In fact, demonstrating that you keep your commitments to others is a good way to show a new partner that you are worthy of their trust and investment as well. Most nonmonogamous commitments should offer multiple paths to meeting those commitments while still making room for new partners. Flexibility also allows for the renegotiation of agreements, including the ways in which commitments are met when new relationships alter the playing field.

Children are the most important commitment many people will ever make. If you're a parent, your children are probably the most important people in your life. Children are dependent: They need people to take care of them, and their parents need to prioritize meeting those needs. Only slowly do they develop good judgment, free agency and decision-making power on their way to adulthood, so they need special consideration and protection for many years. These overriding needs can get in the way of adult partnerships, which is tough. If you have or want children, you likely (and hopefully) choose partners who understand this fact.

So surely, given the unique vulnerability of children, some hierarchy must be necessary for nonmonogamous families with kids? Are empowered nonmonogamous relationships even possible with children?

Well, as far as we know, parents, at the moment of their child's birth, don't suddenly become incapable of honouring commitments and responsibilities on their own. If you were a responsible adult before your kids were born, you will remain a responsible (if highly sleep-deprived) adult after.

Responsible adults do not secretly want to ignore their children's well-being so badly that, if not for hierarchy, that's what they'd do. If people can be trusted to make good decisions in other realms of life, such as friendships, employment or hobbies, they can be trusted in their intimate relationships and as parents. We have the optimistic view that if you are given the ability to make your own choices, you will honour your agreements, uphold your responsibilities and care for the people you love—partners and children.

Perhaps the best way for parents to work toward creating stable and loving homes is to seek partners who are other mature grown-ups and share their values and priorities, then work to build a strong foundation for all their relationships and demonstrate over time that they are reliable and trustworthy. And then trust each other to make decisions that will benefit their relationships and their families.

In empowered relationships, when a co-parent is about to make a choice that another parent doesn't feel is best for the family, the concerned parent can bring it up. The adults can talk about the issue and make their choices accordingly. If one person in the partnership begins consistently making choices that aren't best for the family, then it may be time to re-evaluate that partnership—just as happens in monogamous relationships. And just as happens in monogamous relationships, sometimes the best thing for everyone may be for the parental dyad to share parenting some other way—such as living apart or in a live-in, platonic co-parenting relationship. (This kind of arrangement is not uncommon among nonmonogamous people and queer people. It's even becoming trendy among some monogamous folks these days, and we think that's a great thing!)

If you don't like how someone is (or isn't) honouring their commitments to you, or you don't feel they can be trusted to honour their commitments and you can't talk it through with them, then they may not be a good choice as a co-parent. If an adult is willing to abandon their commitments, then hierarchy isn't going to force them to keep them!

So what happens if the original parental dyad does dissolve? Must this scenario be prevented at all costs if there are kids involved?

Relationships end. In a family with children, the end of a relationship will be sad and stressful for everyone. But the same thing happens in monogamous families, and there are ways to minimize the stress on the children. Often, in fact, a new relationship created with a more recent partner is more beneficial for a child than the parents' relationship was, if the parents' relationship was dysfunctional. This happens commonly with monogamous blended families, and the same is true for nonmonogamous families. Disruptions, discussed in the next chapter, happen to everyone, not just to nonmonogamous people. Sometimes children are affected.

Many of us still carry an idea, preserved from the mononormative fairy tale, that a parental dyad is critical, often above all other concerns, for a child's well-being. Many still imagine that keeping someone in a bad relationship "for the sake of the children" is better than allowing two parents to live apart. But the nuclear family is a modern invention, and it's by no means the only way to make a family or raise children, or necessarily the best. When people focus on this structure as the only valid one, it causes a few problems. It erases other family structures from the discussion—everything from the broad, multigenerational webs of care common in many Indigenous cultures, to single parents, to post-divorce blended families, to queer co-parenting networks. It also posits an ideal that is in fact nearly impossible for most parents to uphold, and that doesn't represent reality anyway. The vast majority of families with kids actually rely on a ton of non-parental help in raising them: babysitters, daycares, schoolteachers, grandparents, neighbours, friends, relatives and more. And that's not a sign of failure. Kids thrive when they have multiple trusted adults watching out for them, teaching them and contributing to their socialization, growth and development. Additionally, the emphasis on the nuclear family places the focus on the structure and not the content. Some nuclear families are happy, healthy, enriching environments for kids. Others are rife with abuse, addictions, neglect and stress. It's not the structure that determines the quality of a family life; it's the behaviour of the people within it. And the isolation that can result from a nuclear family structure can actually be really damaging to all concerned if what's happening inside that family is toxic.

For a child, having secure parents who are committed to that child (in whatever configuration those parents come, and even if that configuration changes), and who are living lives that fulfill them, is far superior to having two parents who are "together" dysfunctionally only because rules and a hierarchy keep them in line. And this situation is certainly better than having people in or adjacent to the household who are treated as secondary to other people. If children observe such behaviour in their families, they will take those ideas out into the world and treat other people the same way.

An empowered approach to nonmonogamous parenting might include agreements that look like this:

> I have chosen to parent with you because you share my values and hopes, and I trust you to honour your commitments to me and to make decisions in your relationships that are in the best interest of our family. If your decisions do not support us, I will tell you how and why, and I trust you to work with me—and your other partners, if necessary—to make it right. If you begin behaving in a way that is harmful to me, our relationship or our child, and you don't rectify it, we will need to renegotiate the terms of our relationship and our co-parenting arrangement.

It is absolutely true that guidelines and structure benefit *children*. They thrive on order, predictability and outside direction, and can be distressed when given freedom they can't yet handle. Parents can create structure and prioritize their children without making one adult partner subject to restrictions created by another partner. Guidelines and structure can be achieved without hierarchy, because adults can be trusted to build a family out of goodwill, free choice, and their love for their partner and their children.

Trust and flexibility

Empowered relationships rely on trust. Trust that your partners want to cherish and support you. Trust that if you make your needs known, your partners will *want* to meet your needs. This requires courage, care and good faith on all sides. Building relationships on a shared understanding of needs means having the courage to stand in the face of a negative emotion and ask, "What is this feeling telling me? Is there a need that is not being met? Is there something I can do to enlist my partner as my ally in dealing with this?"

If you're the person whose partner is experiencing emotional hardship, it can be tempting to read this chapter as a way of saying "You have the responsibility to deal with your own emotions, so I don't want you putting restrictions on me." That is partly true, in the sense that you can't solve someone else's problem for them, and if your partner places restrictions on your behaviour, those restrictions rarely resolve the underlying issue. But it's a mistake to put what Douglas Adams calls a Somebody Else's Problem field around a partner's distress. If you care, you will help. Behaving with compassion means working *together* to overcome relationship issues.

Another valuable technique in the toolkit of strategies for empowered, trusting relationships is to let go of attachment to the *form* that a partner's behaviour must take. For example, suppose you feel you aren't getting enough time with your partner. One way to address this is to insist, for example, that your partner be home by nine o'clock each night. This may or may not succeed. Your partner might start coming home by nine, but then spend the rest of the evening talking or texting with the person they just left, or go to bed early, or get some extra work done. You might have assumed that them being home at nine meant spending time together, but that wasn't what you actually asked for. What might work instead would be junking the nine o'clock rule in favour of a direct request: "I need some of your undivided attention every day."

Life is occasionally chaotic and unpredictable, from flat tires to late-night emergency-room visits. Sometimes, even when you make a good-faith effort to meet your partners' needs, life gets in the way. Flexibility is important. Resiliency in the face of adversity is a powerful tool for building good relationships.

Fairness

"That's not fair!" People below a certain age say this all the time. Past that age, their vision gets longer, and they learn that fairness operates best on a global, not a local, scale. If you did the dishes last night and it's your sister's turn tonight, but she isn't doing the dishes because she just got back from dental surgery, it may seem unfair to you from a purely selfish perspective...but really, would you want to trade places with her? And if you were the one who'd just been through the root canal, wouldn't you appreciate a pass on the dishes tonight? Sometimes compassion dictates that a rigid schedule should flex.

By the time they're adults, most people have pretty much figured this out. That, or they've just given in to exhaustion and stopped worrying so much about what's "fair" on such a granular level. Yet in relationships, and *especially* in nonmonogamous relationships, the little whisperings of your five-year-old self can poke through and say "That's not fair!" when things don't go the way you expect. Even when you don't talk about your expectations. Even when you suspect your expectations are unreasonable. Hell, sometimes even when what's happening is not only fair, but most excellent as well.

In dealing with human beings, issues of "fairness" sometimes need to go right out the window. People change and needs change, but often their notions about what is "fair" remain static, so deeply buried that they're not even aware of them. The fairness that is important in relationships isn't the tit-for-tat "I did the dishes last night, so it isn't fair that I have to do them tonight too!" variety. In fact, sometimes a tit-for-tat approach to fairness creates a situation that's decidedly *unfair*, such as if someone demands that their partner break up with a metamour but promises to break up with their own other partner as well, for the sake of fairness. Four broken hearts instead of one is a peculiar definition of the word *fair,* and it illustrates an important point: Symmetry is not the same thing as fairness.

The kind of fairness that really counts is the kind that begins with compassion. Doing the dishes two days in a row because your sister has just had a root canal is compassionate. On the other hand, saying "I'll dump my partner of many years just to get you to dump yours" is hardly compassionate. Fairness means saying things like "I realize that my insecurity belongs to me, so I will not use it as a blunt instrument on you, nor expect you to plot your life around it. I may, however, ask you to talk to and support me while I'm dealing with it."

This isn't the kind of fairness your inner five-year-old understands; that child is far more likely to be worried about someone else getting something that they don't have, or getting something for a lower "price" than they paid for it. At the end of the day, though, your mental five-year-old isn't likely to make your life better, no matter how much of a fuss they put up.

OF MONKEYS AND CUCUMBERS

You may have seen this experiment on YouTube or TED: Primatologist Frans de Waal experimented with primate reactions to inequality by placing two monkeys within sight of each other and rewarding them for doing a small task, such as handing a rock to a human lab aide. The reward was either a tasty piece of cucumber or an even tastier grape. When both monkeys got a cucumber, everything was fine—they'd happily complete the task dozens of times. But if one of them got a cucumber and one got a grape, watch out! The "lower paid" monkey completely lost it: throwing the cucumber back at the aide, pounding the floor, rattling the cage. Like any good scientist, De Waal repeated this experiment many times, with different species and variations. Same result.

We prefer to avoid the quagmire of evolutionary psychology; our intent with this example isn't to talk about how your feelings about fairness may be rooted deep in your brain. Instead, we want to talk about how you decide what are "cucumbers" and what are "grapes" in your relationships. By way of example, think of a fictional polycule we'll call Ali, Tatiana and Alexis. Ali lives with Tatiana and is also in a relationship with Alexis. Ali and Tatiana have two young children. Their relationship involves a lot of housework, diaper changes and arguing over the budget. Their downtime together consists of a lot of cuddling in front of *Doctor Who*, but not much sex and only the occasional night out.

Ali and Alexis only see each other a couple of times a month, so their time together is intense. They usually spend half of it having sex, the other half in deep conversation or doing exciting things—all focused on one another. Maybe once or twice a year they'll get away together for a long weekend at a bed and breakfast.

Most people in Tatiana's position would feel like she's getting all the cucumbers and Alexis is getting all the grapes. The things Ali and Alexis do are *fun*, right? They're *dates*—something long-established couples can have a tendency to forget about, or not have time for. And it *is* very important for live-in couples to take time to care for their relationship, so they don't take each other for granted. But it's also worth considering why you might think Tatiana is getting the cucumbers—and how, to Alexis, those cucumbers might actually look a lot like grapes.

Ali and Alexis might have a "vacation" relationship—they may have more fun together, and Ali and Tatiana more work. But Ali and Tatiana share some things that are arguably far more precious, and which Alexis may never have access to. Things like

- being able to wake up nearly every morning together
- having each other close enough to touch, almost all the time
- curling up on a rainy afternoon with each other, snuggling beneath warm covers
- building a private language from a shared history of experience
- standing by each other through the shared struggles of building a life
- being able to plan a future with each other
- working together to bring two small humans into the world.

After all, Ali and Tatiana *chose* the life they have together. If they had wanted, they could have had a relationship that looked instead like Ali and Alexis's. They did not have to move in together, mingle finances or have children. They *chose* to. They valued the things on this list. When people talk about taking a relationship—or a partner—for granted, it often means these sorts of things are being discounted. And these things, in a relationship, can be very sweet indeed, if you take time to appreciate them.

If you feel like you're getting all the cucumbers and someone else is getting all the grapes, then ask your partner for some grapes, for sure, but also remember that you and your partner chose to have the kind of relationship you have. Take time to notice and express gratitude for the benefits that come from it. If you have a live-in partner, those benefits might be the small touches, the opportunities to care for each other (even if it's grumbling as you pick up someone's dirty socks), the chance to sleep close to each other, the cuddles and shared meals, your small daily interactions, the future you're building together. If you live apart and see each other less frequently, when you find yourself longing for some of these more entwined behaviours (and you know they aren't available to you), it may help to notice the fact that your partner is carving out time from their busy and full life to focus exclusively on *you*.

This is another reason why fairness is not the same thing as symmetry. Tatiana and Alexis may envy each other for the things each has with Ali. They may need to work with Ali to reshape their relationships so that each gets more of what they need. But it's also possible that we primates all have a hard time seeing the value of what we have when we are busy looking at what someone else is getting. The monkeys in the experiment threw their cucumbers away—cucumbers that a few minutes before, they were eager to have. And it's also important to remember, if you're the hinge, that very few relationships can survive on only cucumbers or only grapes. Most relationships need a mix of work and play to grow strong over the long term.

QUESTIONS TO ASK YOURSELF

Empowerment in nonmonogamous relationships and structures can be difficult to define, but its presence or absence is usually clearly felt. Here are some questions that can help you and your partners think about the level of empowerment in your relationships:

- How do I encourage decision-making participation by all my partners? In what ways do I show my partners they are empowered?
- If I feel a desire to restrict relationships between my partners and their partners, what underlying need am I trying to meet?
- What are my existing commitments? How can I meet them while still making room for new relationships?
- What evidence do I have that my partners love and care for me? How do I show my partners I love and care for them?
- What specific things can I ask my partners to do for me to help me feel loved and cared for? How can I do better at showing my partners I love and care for them?
- In what ways am I empowered in my relationships? What things help me to feel empowered?
- Can I renegotiate the agreements in my relationships? Can my partners?

I've worked really hard to eliminate the words "have to" from my vocabulary. Because the reality is, I'm choosing to. I'm choosing to show up and meet my commitments.

LAUREN BACON

14 Practical Nonmonogamy Agreements

In the last few chapters, we talked about the distinctions between rules, boundaries and agreements, and we made a case for why rules-based structures can create problems in nonmonogamous relationships.

Preparing the ground for relationships to flourish means thinking carefully about not just how to meet your needs, but how to meet the needs of all the people involved. In this chapter, we discuss practical strategies for approaching relationship agreements with this careful analysis as your foundation. It starts with thinking about why people do what they do.

Here's a story that illustrates the issue. Andrea likes to go to the movies. They noticed, one year during a big film festival, that the trees lining the sidewalk near one popular cinema all bore little laminated signs that read "DO NOT LOCK BIKES TO THE TREES," with pictures of trees with little sad faces on them. It seemed like a fair rule, until they tried to find a bike rack and discovered that despite attracting thousands of moviegoers, the festival had set up only one rack with a half-dozen spots on it. All full, of course—and municipal racks were nowhere to be seen. Given the choice between going several blocks to find another bike rack and missing part of the movie, or locking their bike (carefully) to a tree that was exactly the right size and in the right place, they locked their bike to the tree, as several others had already done.

If you're an urban cyclist, you've likely noticed a ton of problems like this—instances where putting appropriate infrastructure in place would eliminate a problem, but rules are imposed instead, and then people break those rules because they impede the normal flow of everyday activity (or even put people at physical risk). It happens in a lot of other areas, too. In the case of the film festival, the people locking bikes to trees weren't trying to harm the trees or flout a rule for funsies. They just weren't left with any other reasonable options that would let them achieve their very reasonable aim: to get to their movie on time. The festival didn't add more bike racks of its own, liaise with the city to provide municipal racks, or provide information on where the closest additional racks were. They made a rule that didn't account for the need, and the need wasn't going to disappear, so people broke the rule.

Not every relationship situation is as obvious as the bike rack problem, but it does help a lot to figure out what people's needs are before getting upset about their choices or behaviours. People tend to do things for real reasons, not just to be jerks. (Though of course there will always be a few jerks.) Effective relationship strategies take work. They aim to meet people's needs. And meeting these needs involves asking why people are doing whatever you wish they wouldn't do. What need does their behaviour meet? What function does it serve? Could they do something else, something that might be less undesirable, to meet the same need? How invested is the person in doing that particular thing, and why?

Creating such strategies also involves looking at some scary things inside yourself. Why is it not okay with you if that person does that thing? Are the problems you see *really* problems? Is your desired strategy actually an attempt to shift responsibility for managing your emotions onto someone else? Does the person doing the thing reasonably have a right to do it? How much does it really affect others, and in what way? Are you just trying to avoid discomfort? If so, is your discomfort more important than someone else's choices? (Is the rule really about saving the trees, or is it about not wanting an "unsightly" crowd of bikes in front of a fancy movie theatre?)

From there, you can work on installing bike racks, or even setting up valet bike parking (as Eve's city has done). What might help everyone get their needs met? If something makes you uncomfortable but is part of exercising someone's reasonable autonomy, how can the person do it and still support you?

Creating effective relationship agreements

Agreements and boundaries will be part of any nonmonogamous relationship. The agreements that work most consistently are those that are rooted in compassion, encourage mutual respect and empowerment, leave it to your partners' judgment how to implement them, and have input from—and apply equally to—everyone affected by them. These include principles like the following: Treat all others with kindness. Don't try to force relationships to be something they are not, and don't try to prevent them from being what they are. Don't try to impose yourself on other people. Understand when things are Not About You. Own your own challenges, but ask for support (and support others). Favour trust and communication over rules.

Here are some other common characteristics of successful relationship agreements:

They are not games of Mao. Named for the Chinese Chairman Mao Zedong, whose rule was characterized by widespread persecution and constantly changing laws, Mao is a card game where at the start of the game none of the players except the dealer know the rules...and the players are penalized for breaking them. The players who figure out the rules the slowest lose. If you have relationship agreements, they must be clear and comprehensible. Everyone involved should know and understand them—and equally important, understand the intent behind them, the spirit as well as the letter.

They seek to place controls on one's self, not one's partners. You can't really control anyone but yourself. "You must," "You cannot...": Those kinds of statements work only if other people choose to let them. Note that multiple people can agree to bind themselves in a reciprocal agreement, however, such as "we will always check in with each other before we go on a date with a new person.

They are clear, specific and limited in scope. "You must care for me more than you care for them" is not clear or specific. It doesn't define what "care for me" means or what steps can be taken to get there. "We will not have unbarriered exchange of bodily fluids with others before discussing it with each other" is clear, specific and limited in scope.

They have a defined practical purpose. Successful agreements address needs directly, while considering feelings as important pieces of information that can help you figure out what to do. As we've mentioned, emotions are data. Don't ignore them! Just remember they're not the only data you need to factor into your decisions.

They do not seek to sweep problems under the rug. "I get jealous when I see you kiss someone, so don't kiss anyone in front of me" does not deal with the jealousy, it only addresses the trigger. The jealousy is still there, just waiting to emerge in some other way. It's okay to ask for some space to deal with both the jealousy and the trigger (see limited-duration rules on page 198), but it's not a long-term solution. That will come from within.

They have a sunset clause if they are meant to provide space to deal with a problem. A sunset clause (see also pages 198 and 312) means a restriction expires on a certain date. If there is no sunset clause, once the emotional trigger has been removed, it can be all too easy to say "I'll work on the problem tomorrow." And tomorrow becomes next week, then next month, and then we're back to pocket vetoes (see chapter 12).

They address the underlying needs. A clear agreement aims to address what's really going on ("I'm scared of losing you") rather than handling it by proxy ("Never travel without me"). That means you need to talk about what's really going on. (See also page 143 on needs vs. strategies.) Sometimes, an "illogical" attachment to a specific way of meeting a need is really no big deal (we all have our quirks!), as long as it's not onerous for everyone involved and doesn't become a flashpoint for resentments or the beginning of a pattern of creeping concessions.

They are renegotiable. Any agreement should be open to discussion at any time by anyone it affects. This includes anyone who enters a relationship after an agreement is made. Life is change, and you need to deal with it. Even if life never changed, you rarely build something exactly right the first time.

They do not disempower people. We've talked about this at length already. In relationships conducted according to our ethical axioms, every person has a voice.

They do not try to legislate feelings. People cannot provide or eliminate feelings on demand. Attempting to legislate feelings (for example, by saying "You must love both of us equally" or "You are not allowed to feel jealous") usually works about as well as trying to legislate the weather.

Negotiating in good faith

When you are negotiating agreements in your relationship, it can be hard to hear that your partners have different needs or sensitivities than you do. Truly understanding that other people are as real as you are is hard. If you want to negotiate in good faith, here are some things to keep in mind:

- *Focus on mutual benefit.* To succeed, an agreement must benefit everyone. Even when people have what seem to be contradictory goals, it may be possible to find a solution by looking for the need underneath a proposed agreement.
- *Treat the other people in the negotiation as collaborators, not problems.* It's easy to think, "If only you would do what I say, everything would be okay!" Remember that these people are not your adversaries; you all want happy relationships. Treat people with compassion. (And see page 145 on collaboration.)
- *Don't compromise on behalf of other people without their input and consent.* When you agree to limitations on your actions with other people, you are limiting them as well. They deserve a place at the negotiating table.

The best agreements are not ones that steer people away from bad things, but rather ones that point everyone involved toward good things. The best way to create security in a relationship is to prioritize kindness, mutuality and joy: The people in the relationship are more important than the relationship.

Writing it down?

There are many situations in which explicit, written agreements are just common sense. Business arrangements are a prime example. It's too easy even for honest people to remember a verbal agreement very differently from each other, or for one to genuinely forget they even made it.

Written relationship contracts are nothing new. A ketubah, for example, is a traditional Jewish marriage contract that outlines the groom's responsibilities to the bride. Ketubahs are used across various gender pairings today, and couples often draw theirs up as a beautifully illuminated document that holds pride of place on a wall in their home. Quaker marriage certificates are similar, and are signed by all guests present at the wedding, who agree to support the couple. Prenups and marriage documents are also forms of relationship contracts—legally binding ones! And if you've been at all involved in the kink/BDSM world, you're probably familiar with the idea of a D/s or M/s contract that specifies people's limits and commitments in the context of their kinky relationships. They're not all that common in practice, but for some people they can be deeply meaningful (even sexy), even though they're not at all legally enforceable. In recent years, some households have found it desirable to have written agreements covering COVID-19 protocols, to make sure everyone is on the same page.

Some people who give nonmonogamy advice will urge you to write down and even sign your agreements, particularly when they're addressing couples who are planning to open up. Some people like to create a "relationship contract" in such situations. But while written relationship contracts might seem like good communication, there is reason for caution. Communication is a dialogue. A contract—especially one that's presented to new people as a done deal—very often isn't. Communication and discussion are essential for the health of any relationship. This is why, as we have said before, we see agreements as far better and more functional than rules. It's also why we maintain a healthy skepticism about relationship contracts, while recognizing they can have benefit for some people.

Turning an agreement into paperwork can often become an expression of power, a way to shut down communication. Contracts are not universally bad, but they're by no means universally good, either. They also tend to freeze an agreement in a moment in time, which can impede or discourage open and ongoing dialogue about how an agreement should work in practical, everyday situations that no one written contract can possibly foresee. If you're having that kind of frequent, fluid communication, a contract might just not be very relevant. And if you're not communicating frequently, a contract isn't the most intuitive tool for getting started. You might be better off scheduling regular check-ins, taking communication workshops together, practising the exercises in a self-help book, or otherwise investing your time in developing that skill together.

In general, written agreements are more successful when they

- are short enough to remember without needing to reference them often—generally less than one or two pages long
- have a narrow focus

- are intended to solve a specific problem among a specific group of people
- concern only those people present in negotiating them: in other words, "I will do this for you," not "Others will or will not do this" or "I will or won't do this with others."
- include statements of goals or intentions, focus on shared principles rather than rules and specify the purpose of the agreement
- are flexible and open to review and renegotiation.

Written agreements tend to work poorly when they

- are lengthy and highly detailed
- attempt to define or regulate every aspect of a situation
- affect people who are not present in negotiating the agreement
- prescribe specific actions to implement a stated intention (that is, allowing only one way to get there)
- attempt to control things beyond the control of the negotiating partners, such as future intimacy (see page 284) or the behaviour of others
- allow no room for renegotiation or change.

Successful written agreements are documents that you hold *yourself* to, not something others hold you to, or to which you hold them. They are reminders to yourself of commitments you have made and tools for communicating those commitments to other partners. They should not be used as devices to shame, manipulate or punish. And remember our axiom: *The people in the relationship are more important than the relationship.* If you find yourselves haggling over clauses in an agreement and whether they have been violated, rather than discussing the hurt feelings, the needs behind a partner's actions and ways to make amends, you've probably reached a place where the people are serving the contract, and not the other way around.

Perhaps the most serious danger in written contracts is when they are inflexible. The longer and more complex they are, the more they are likely to be trying to script a relationship or treat people (at best) as a threat to be managed and (at worst) as a commodity, both of which violate axiom 1. If one partner is finding themselves unable to hold to a provision of the agreement, there's a good chance the agreement needs to be renegotiated to work for all partners—and not that the person is dishonest or doesn't care about the agreement.

People who keep long, complex written agreements often build relationships that are unable to change when their needs change. They often spend a lot of time rules-lawyering. Ultimately, this kind of contract often does not lead to greater relationship satisfaction, because real life is a lot more fluid and dynamic than a hyper-specific contract can account for. It's the wrong tool for the job.

The exception is a BDSM contract among people who share an erotic enjoyment of setting, enforcing and obeying rules. However, even this kind of contract can become difficult to manage unless, on the one hand, its scope is restricted to playtime, or on the other hand, the partners are committed to a truly all-encompassing lifestyle that's also realistically integrated with the non-kink aspects of their existence. Such contracts must be flexible enough to account for other life obligations, commitments and unpredictability. Nobody should ever be placed in a position where they can't reasonably attend to their physical, mental, financial or relationship health because of a BDSM, D/s or M/s contract. If you're considering a contract that would place this kind of restriction on you, this is not a sign of a healthy, functional dominant-submissive partnership.

Good written agreements are reminders of our own boundaries or commitments, expressed as principles. One very short contract Eve has seen contains elements such as "My partner is important," "Do your chores before going on a date," "Don't spend joint money on your own dates," and "Don't fuck it up." An agreement that's about what you will each do to care for each other is also a very different thing from an agreement that tells new partners how *they* are expected to behave.

We urge those of you considering written agreements to draw up short, specific lists of boundaries or intentions, rather than long, complex documents that tell others what they are and aren't allowed to do. Ultimately, remember that your relationship belongs to the living, feeling people involved in it, not a list of rules. Make sure that *people,* not paragraphs, are always at the centre of your relationships.

The permission model

A "permission model" of relationships is the idea that when you enter a relationship, you give up control over your actions to your partner. If you wish to do things like start another relationship or visit another partner, you must seek the permission of your established partner, who becomes a gatekeeper.

In our experience, relationships that provide everyone in them the most satisfaction follow a different model. It starts with this premise: "I can have the kind of relationship I want. I can make choices I want to. My best course of action is to learn to choose people who want something similar, to take responsibility for the consequences of my choices, and to pay attention to the effects my choices have on the people around me."

Checking in with your partners is a good thing. Communication builds trust. And for both emotional and practical reasons, it's best to keep up an ongoing dialogue with the people who are affected by your everyday decisions. But when you operate from a permission-based model, instead of treating your partners like supportive companions sharing a journey with you, you're setting them up as barriers between you and whatever you want. This can lead to resentment instead of collaboration and mutuality. It's the difference between "How would you feel if I were to…?" and "May I…?" These two types of questions can lead to very different conversations. The first might sound like "I'd be pretty grumpy if you had dinner with your crush on Sunday night because you already committed to dinner with me and my parents. Could you make it another night instead?" It opens up both practical negotiations and opportunities to talk about feelings, needs and creative solutions. The second is a classic yes-or-no question, which doesn't invite further discussion and can more easily lead to misunderstandings.

Disruptors

At a few moments in your life, you are likely to come to pivot points that profoundly alter the course of your life from that point forward. These may be decisions that you have time to think about and prepare for, such as choosing between a school close to home or one across the country, taking or refusing a major job offer, undertaking a gender transition, coming out as queer, converting to a different religion, or having children. They may be twists of fate, such as an accident (or a near miss), a loss, a lottery win, going viral online, an unexpected medical diagnosis, or a random encounter that profoundly changes your thinking or outlook on life. They may be sudden realizations you didn't see coming: "I hate accounting, and I want to be a massage therapist."

And of course, they may have to do with your relationships. A disruptor, in the realm of intimate relationships, is a relationship that causes you to rethink *all* your relationships, and maybe even your life, entirely. It may be a mind-blowing relationship with someone wonderful who shows you a whole new way that relationships can work and raises the bar on what you want and need from other relationships. But a disruptive relationship doesn't even have to be a *good* relationship. It can be one that's dysfunctional on such a deep level that it changes what you look for thereafter.

Disruptive relationships are scary. That's true regardless of what approach you take to relationships (single, solo poly, monogamous, swinging, polyamorous and many more) and what kind of relationship you're talking about. You might experience an encounter or short-term connection so meaningful (or so awful) that it alters the course of things from then on. Maybe you meet the person you suddenly realize you want to spend your whole life with—or you suddenly realize you must get away from the person you're with at all costs, despite a long-term commitment. Maybe you realize that you want to invest in a devoted friendship or platonic partnership as a bigger priority than anything romantic. Anytime you're coping with a major change, particularly a sudden one, it can be terrifying, exhilarating, or both at once, as well as bringing up many other emotions.

Many nonmonogamous people harbour a fear of a particular kind of disruptive relationship: the amazing new relationship that shows up in a partner's life and makes that partner realize they actually want to leave you, shack up with the new person, and possibly even become monogamous with them. People often put a lot of time and energy into trying to prevent this from happening while still enjoying all the benefits of nonmonogamy.

The desire not to lose what you have because your partner meets someone new is rational and reasonable. And it does happen! Thing is, it happens to people regardless of whether they're monogamous or nonmonogamous, whether they have lots of rules or none at all. It's an inherently unpredictable phenomenon. What is neither rational nor reasonable is attempting to build structures that allow your partner to have other relationships while guaranteeing that nothing will change for you. Relationships don't work that way. We live in a world with no guarantees. And, regardless of nonmonogamy, no promise of "forever" can stand up to the #39 bus with bad brakes that puts someone in a coma. These are the risks you take when you open your heart to someone else. Sometimes things really change.

Andrea sometimes talks about the difference between an ethic of care versus an ethic of protection. If your focus is on protecting one specific relationship, then you'll spend a great deal of time and effort on building walls around it—bulletproof rules, careful agreements, limits galore—so that you can enjoy the experience of connecting with other people as much as possible, *but not too much*. The premise sets up one established relationship as ideal and casts all others as threats. It invites a sense of competition for limited resources.

If you shift toward an ethic of care, then you don't need walls. Your focus becomes on cultivating. What is your relationship like? What does it need to thrive? How can you feed, nourish and care for it? When another relationship comes along, what does that one need to thrive, and how can you care for it too? Can you find ways to synergistically nourish both at once, or do they need really different things? How can each partnership support the others?

Once you're operating from an ethic of care, you begin to ask different questions and come up with more creative answers. You and your partnerships develop resilience as you try things, make mistakes, talk about them, course-correct and try other things. You're engaged in an ongoing process of co-creation with the people you're involved with.

Disruptors will show up in your life at unexpected moments no matter what. By their very nature, you can't protect yourself or your relationships from them. Or rather, put a different way, the care—not the walls—is what actually provides protection. When you put all your energy into avoiding or preventing challenging experiences, and they show up anyway (as they do), you end up having very little practice actually managing them together. But when you welcome change, and you build experience having tough conversations, facing and solving complex problems together, and rolling with the punches as you each grow and evolve over time, this strong and flexible foundation prepares you for the big disruptors you can't predict.

Disruptors provide a great opportunity to go back and review your values and your ethical system. They're not an excuse to throw it all out the window as you barrel into a new situation. In fact, if your values are only meaningful when things are going smoothly and easily, or if your ethical system only applies when your world is steady and predictable, we'd suggest they're not robust enough! Values take on their true meaning when they're tested; ethical systems are the very thing you need to hold onto when the world seems really chaotic. They're what help you make decisions in such a way that you can look back on them later and feel at ease with yourself. How can you best live up to your values and operate within your ethical system as you make decisions in the face of great change? Alternatively, has this disruptor caused you to reconsider your values or ethical system, or some element of either? If so, how, and what amendments do you need to make? Shifting your system isn't necessarily a bad thing, but it should be done with caution and care, and not just for the sake of expediency.

Re-evaluating agreements

It's incredibly easy to fall into prioritizing the agreements made within a relationship over the well-being of the people involved. Here it's important to remember again, *the people in the relationship are more important than the relationship.* Sacrificing the happiness of human beings in the service of agreements, rather than making agreements that serve the needs of the people, takes you further away from joyful, fulfilling lives, not closer to them.

Anyone should be able to reopen discussions about an agreement at any time. It helps to think of agreements as mutable, organic things that will be revisited and modified as people grow and relationships change. When you see these structures as static, they can make relationships less rather than more stable, because they will fail to adapt to change...sometimes spectacularly.

A good relationship is not something you *have,* it's something you *do.* The happiest relationships tend to be those whose members are constantly willing to renegotiate the groundwork beneath them so that they can grow and change with each other over time—as their lives and priorities evolve, as new situations arise, and as they get to know themselves and each other more deeply. In fact, some people set periodic dates in their calendar when they will review their relationship agreements with each other to make sure they're still working and see if anything needs to change.

When looking at the structures of your relationship, ask yourself regularly: Are they honest? Are they necessary? Are they kind? Are they respectful? Are they considerate of others? If you've made agreements with an existing partner that you expect new partners to abide by, ask yourself, "Would I have become involved with my current partner if I were bound by these agreements at the start?"

Creeping concessions

Flexibility and willingness to renegotiate agreements are vital parts of a growing, thriving nonmonogamous relationship. There's a potential danger lurking in this flexibility, though, which we call "creeping concessions."

Sometimes people can end up in relationships that cross boundaries without those people even noticing. For example, perhaps you have a partner who's having difficulty and asks you to give up something while they work through the issue. You naturally want to support your partner, so you agree. Later, that person may say, "Well, this still isn't working. Dreadfully sorry, but can you give up a little bit more? I'm really struggling with this."

Because your partner's happiness is important to you, you say yes. And perhaps time goes by and your partner says, "Look, um, I'm terribly sorry to bring this up, but I'm still having issues here. Can you perhaps find it in your heart to make this other small concession over here, just this one little thing that will really help me?" Bit by bit, inch by inch, you may find yourself negotiating away things that are important. If each individual step is small enough, you might give up a boundary without even seeing it.

At times you may be aware that you're conceding things you once thought inviolate, but you do it anyway because you've already invested so much. Economists have a name for this: the sunk cost fallacy. A sunk cost is an investment of time, energy, attention or something else that can't be recovered. If you spend a year in a relationship that isn't a good fit for you, you can't go back and get that year back again. The "fallacy" part involves making decisions for the future based on that past investment, rather than on whether the decisions are likely to benefit you in the future. Say, for example, you're at a movie, and you realize early on that you're not going to enjoy it. You already bought the tickets; you can't get your money back. Do you stay and watch the movie and have a miserable time, or do you walk out and browse the nearby bookstore, which is much more enjoyable? For some people, it's hard to walk away from the movie, although the cost of the tickets is gone either way.

When you're deciding whether to agree to a compromise or concession that gives you a sick feeling, knowing that the alternative might be to end the relationship, you might think "I've invested a year of my life in this relationship. I can't let it go!" rather than "This relationship is not working, and if I make this concession, it's going to work even less. It is better to choose whether to agree based on my future happiness, not on the year I've already spent."

Agreements about privacy and disclosure

We've talked a lot about how open, honest communication is absolutely essential to nonmonogamy. However, everyone has the right to set boundaries around access to their bodies and their emotions. One of those boundaries concerns privacy. The right to privacy is often considered a basic human right.

Balancing the responsibility for disclosure with a reasonable expectation of privacy is not always easy. There is no bright line where one stops and the other starts. Agreements about either disclosure or secrecy can make sense. For example, communication about sexual boundaries and sexual health is necessary to give informed consent, and a rule that text messages will be kept private protects the intimacy and trust of partners. But it can be easy to go to extremes and create agreements (or rules) that violate someone's right to privacy or consent.

For example, a nesting partner may want to see every single communication, such as texts and emails, between their partner and their metamour. Most people would probably agree this is a serious violation of the metamour's privacy; it is difficult for intimacy to grow under the eye of an outside observer. You need private spaces if you are to reveal to a lover the deepest parts of yourself, the furthest corners of your heart, and (especially!) the wounded and vulnerable places within yourself.

Compulsory sharing is always a bit suspect. When others demand that you reveal yourself, intimacy is undermined rather than strengthened, because something that is demanded cannot be shared freely as a gift. Intimacy is built by mutually consensual sharing, not by demands.

At the other extreme, some people insist on knowing absolutely nothing about a partner's other lovers. Not even how many, not even their names. These "Don't ask, don't tell" (DADT) relationships raise troubling questions about boundaries, consent and denial. If you know nothing about a partner's other activities, you will find it difficult to make informed choices about your relationship—particularly the sexual aspects.

Demanding to know everything undermines intimacy, but so does demanding to know nothing. When you demand to know nothing, you cut yourself off from a part of your partners' experience, and that must necessarily limit how intimate you can be. Anytime you interact intimately with another person—including "just sex"—you learn things about yourself, and you come out with a slightly different viewpoint on the world, even if it's a microscopic difference. If you're not free to share these developments with your partner, you're creating a situation in which you're virtually guaranteeing you'll begin to grow apart, even if it's just a little increment at a time.

DADT arrangements tend to get a lot of side-eye in nonmonogamous communities, and for good reason. In addition to the problems they can cause, they often point to unresolved insecurities or a partner who doesn't really want to be nonmonogamous. That said, in some cases DADT can form part of a strategy for dealing with specific situations. For example, if partners live apart and one of them is going through a significant life stressor, that partner may prefer to restrict conversations about other partners' relationships until they have more bandwidth. People in comet or strictly parallel long-distance relationships may not feel that being kept up to date on their partners' love life is how they want to spend limited time with their partners. Someone whose partner is experiencing a lot of relationship turnover, especially over a long period of time, may prefer just not to hear about it until things have settled down. Or if a hinge consistently struggles with maintaining boundaries, taking responsibility and avoiding triangulation (see pages 337–344), one or more of their partners may prefer to implement DADT and maintain a laser focus on their own dyad until the hinge can get their act together. Note that in many of these situations, though, DADT isn't a permanent solution, but a way of temporarily creating space or relieving pressure until the root issue can be resolved.

The issue always seems to circle back to these questions: How much do you trust your partners? How much do you trust your relationships? Do you trust your partners enough to allow intimacy, not limiting what you can hear? Do you trust your partners enough to leave them their private spaces, knowing that they will share things that are important and relevant to you so you can continue to make informed choices?

Broken agreements

Trust is a precious and fragile thing—far more so than many people realize. Recall our discussion of the marble-jar metaphor on page 114? When someone respects agreements consistently over time, it adds marbles to the jar. When someone breaks an agreement, it might remove marbles or, if it's a significant enough break or hits at a particularly weak spot, it might even shatter the jar, making repair impossible. A single massive betrayal might pour all the marbles out, but when someone breaks agreements consistently over time in small ways, the jar slowly empties. Either way, you may end up with little or no trust left. But that doesn't have to mean the end of the relationship (if you don't want it to). It may take time, but if both of you want it and are willing to make the effort, it's possible to slowly rebuild trust.

Sometimes a person breaks an agreement because they're a bad actor. They have malicious intent and are testing boundaries, trying to see how much they can get away with (see page 177). But that's not the case most of the time. You might not be on the same page about what the agreement really entailed, which led to differences in how you each interpreted it on the fly. You may have come up with an agreement together that's impractical or difficult to respect, or too complicated to remember in all its detail when making decisions in the moment. Or you may have agreed to something that, as it turns out, you really don't want after all, but you didn't figure that out until something unexpected happened—and you chose to go ahead anyway and hope for the best.

For a relationship to continue to be based on a foundation of honesty, you need to talk about it once any of those things have happened. The consequences may or may not be serious, but either way, a broken agreement requires a conversation to figure out how to repair things and how to move forward.

Be wary of moving on without doing the work of repair. Sometimes, simply committing to not repeating the mistake is enough to make things right, but often it takes a little more than that. A broken agreement does not have to spell the end of a relationship, but if you don't take proper care to repair things, it certainly can. (We discuss breakups a bit more in chapter 21.) Or it can be the start of a longer-term erosion of trust. What would be a meaningful form of repair for the person who's been hurt? Take the time to figure it out together, and then act on it. This work adds marbles back into the jar, which is a different job than simply not taking any more out. To use another metaphor, it's great to stop stepping on a person's foot, but if you broke a bone, simply removing your foot from theirs doesn't heal the break, which can set poorly if left untreated.

Separately from the repair question, now that you know something wasn't working about an agreement, what next? Do you need to renegotiate the agreement, scrap it entirely or recommit to it with a renewed understanding of how to respect it? Think back to our discussion about locking bikes to trees on pages 253–254. People do things for reasons. What was the reason the person broke the agreement? How can you set up better infrastructure to address that reason in a way that works for everyone involved? Remember the importance of co-creation and collaboration. Instead of casting one person as the bad guy who has to do better, look at the situation holistically. What needs to change to make it workable for everyone? It's certainly okay to hold firm on key boundaries here, but the more curiosity and creativity you can bring to the table, the more likely you'll be in coming up with a way forward that's likely to succeed.

If your partner has broken an agreement with you, you might also need outside support as you figure out how you're feeling about it and what to do next. You may want to work with a relationship therapist who's well versed in nonmonogamy, or maybe you need to work with your own therapist or confide in a trusted friend. Choose your support system wisely. In a monogamous relationship, when someone cheats, they're automatically the bad guy. It's a story people know well, with roles that play out endlessly in movie and TV plots, song lyrics and memes, and it elicits predictable sympathetic responses from the people around the "good guy." But when other kinds of agreements are broken, it can be harder to find support and sympathy from friends if they aren't also, themselves, nonmonogamous, or from therapists who are trained in working with nonmonogamous clients. Monogamous folks may not get why an agreement was important in the first place ("Wait, it's okay for your partner to have sex with someone else, but you're heartbroken because they watched the new *Star Wars* with someone else?"). Or they may say "I told you so" and blame nonmonogamy itself, or encourage you to leave what they see as an inherently unhealthy relationship when you want to repair it—thus invalidating your choices and values instead of being supportive, even if they mean well. So if you don't have a solid network made up of nonmonogamous or nonmonogamy-literate people, you may find yourself misunderstood and lacking support.

But rest assured, if someone breaks an agreement, your feelings of betrayal are valid. In nonmonogamy, you write your own relationship stories and create your own meanings, and they are just as powerful as the ones that mononormative society prescribes for you, even if they're not as widely shared.

QUESTIONS TO ASK YOURSELF

These questions can help guide you toward ethical agreements that work.

When considering an agreement:

- What is the purpose of this agreement?
- Does the agreement serve the purpose it is intended to serve?
- Is this agreement the only way to serve this purpose?
- What will happen if someone breaks the agreement? Do we have a path for re-establishing trust?
- Is everyone affected by the agreement included in negotiating it?
- Can the agreement be renegotiated?

When renegotiating an agreement:

- How have the needs now changed compared to when we agreed to this?
- Has anyone been harmed by this agreement? How can we rework it to make that unlikely in the future?
- Is this agreement serving the people involved, or are the people serving it?
- What have we all learned from this agreement and the experiences we've had while it was in place?
- What do we most need going forward, and how can we best express that in a simple, principle-based way that we can all agree to?

Part 4

The Nonmonogamous Reality

Despite what you may think after what you've read so far, most of the time nonmonogamous relationships are pretty much like monogamous relationships. There's coffee and movies and cuddling and sex and talking, meals and arguments and chores and balancing the house accounts. (Okay, maybe there's more talking.) Plenty of situations are unique to nonmonogamy, though, and many things that also crop up in monogamous relationships involve special considerations when more than two people are involved.

In Part 4, we go deep into the nuts and bolts of nonmonogamous relationships. First we examine how nonmonogamous relationships are different from the way people are often taught relationships should work. Then we look at special considerations for a few common nonmonogamous configurations. We then get into the common challenges with opening up a coupled relationship, followed by looking at the special issues that come up when a nonmonogamous person partners with a monogamous one. We cover how to find nonmonogamous partners, and then get into the finer details of managing relationships among multiple partners. After that we move on to considerations around sex and risk, which are important for any sexual relationship, but all the more so when more people are involved. We finish off with some thoughts on the special challenges that come with nonmonogamous breakups and relationship transitions.

We can change, evolve, and transform our own conditioning. We can choose to move like water rather than be molded like clay. Life spirals in and then spirals out on any given day. It does not have to be one way, one truth, one voice. Nor does love have to be all or nothing.

TERRY TEMPEST WILLIAMS

15 How Nonmonogamous Relationships Are Different

The variety of nonmonogamous relationships is, as we've mentioned, huge. We can't make assumptions about the shapes or paths of your relationships. However, most nonmonogamous relationships do pass through certain stages, like new relationship energy and the start of a new relationship while in an established one.

These stages present uniquely nonmonogamous challenges. Here are some places where nonmonogamous relationships diverge from monogamous relationships and the old templates no longer apply.

Finding community

As a nonmonogamous person, you might have a hard time explaining your relationships to your friends, getting advice and support for your problems, and finding like-minded people. It can help a great deal to find or create a circle of friends who share your ideas and values about relationships.

To find nonmonogamy-related discussion and support groups, Google, social media sites, Meetup.com and polygroups.com are your friends. Do a search for terms like *nonmonogamy*, *polyamory*, *solo polyamory* or *relationship anarchy* (depending on what interests you) and the name of the closest city or large town, and see what turns up.

If you can't find a nonmonogamy-related community where you are, create one! This can be as simple as starting a Facebook group or a meetup on a site like Meetup.com. Decide on a schedule and a venue (lots of nonmonogamy social meetups happen in restaurants or cafes), and commit to being there every month. You might get only one or two people showing up, or even nobody at all the first few times, but that's okay. Perseverance pays off. The women's discussion group that Eve helped organize for several years went more than a year with only two or three people showing up before it took off; after a while, meetings often filled to capacity within a few hours of being announced.

If you'd rather have a focused discussion, with topics and moderation, find online nonmonogamy communities (social media sites are valuable for this) and announce your intentions. Set a time and a place, maybe your home if you like (it's quieter and more sociable than a restaurant). Create a website or social media page if you can. Again, you may not get many people at first, but these things tend to gather steam over time. If your interests are more in building a social network, host nonmonogamy board game nights or have nonmonogamy outings to events such as open mics, book readings or shows.

There's a lot of overlap between nonmonogamous and kink communities. The organized BDSM world is older and more established than the organized nonmonogamous one, so towns that don't have a nonmonogamy-specific group will still often have gatherings of kinky people. Even if you're not that interested in kink, you can sometimes find nonmonogamous people by attending BDSM munches, which are social events where kinky folks get together in low-pressure public spaces to chat and socialize. You don't need to be kinky to attend a munch, though people will probably assume you are—so make sure you're comfortable with that possibility, and with frequently clarifying, before you go this route. If kink isn't your thing, fear not; once you've connected with a few nonmonogamous people, you'll find it easier to meet more.

Today, any relatively open-minded and progressive community probably has its fair share of nonmonogamous folks, too. That includes groups and gatherings focused on social justice activism, art (including Burner communities), technology, gaming, spirituality, various geeky interests and so on. The world has changed a lot in the last few decades, and nonmonogamy has increasingly moved into the mainstream, which means it's easier than ever to come across like-minded people without having to box yourself into a niche.

Coming out

The question of whether and how to come out as nonmonogamous has changed a lot. We're now living in a world where the term *throuple* has made it into mainstream discourse, the number of news articles dealing with nonmonogamy has skyrocketed, research on nonmonogamy has proliferated, and nonmonogamy is a not-infrequent plotline in movies and TV shows. There's also an increasing number of next-generation nonmonogamous folks out there—people whose parents were or are nonmonogamous and who grew up familiar with it. In short, concepts that were once rarified and shocking are now banal, and a disclosure that would have made people's jaws hit the floor in 1994 might elicit a yawn in 2024.

Does that mean coming out is totally risk-free, though? Not necessarily. Nonmonogamy is not a protected status. In some places, far-right thinking dominates, and people can pay a steep price for being visibly nonmonogamous—everything from being shunned in their communities to losing jobs to having their child custody threatened. As well, family members and friends may judge you harshly and treat you differently once you come out. If you're already out as a 2SLGBTQI+ person or as part of the BDSM/Leather/kink world, you may have established support systems—or from that experience, you may already know exactly how closed-minded the people around you are.

Assess the real and realistic risks before you come out, and make decisions with your partners (if you have any) about what to say, when, and to whom. It's easier to be authentic to yourself when you don't need to hide who you are. It's easier to act with integrity when you're authentic to yourself. Not expecting partners to be closeted, and being willing to acknowledge partners as partners, helps promote strong, secure relationships. Balance these truths with your knowledge of your own specific situation, and take it from there. For a much deeper dive into coming out, check out *It's Called Polyamory: Coming out About Your Nonmonogamous Relationships* by Tamara Pincus and Rebecca Szymborski.

The timing of new relationships

There's no perfect time for a new relationship to start, nor a set schedule for how quickly or slowly it should develop. Sometimes opportunity knocks at the most inopportune times. New relationships are wonderful, joyous and stressful. Attempting to script how and when they develop amid your existing ones is like trying to corral elephants; these things have a certain inertia of their own, and sometimes all you can do is learn to be nimble on your feet. This doesn't mean you should barrel ahead without consideration for the shape of your life, your commitments and the needs and feelings of the people around you. You aren't powerless in the grip of out-of-control new love. You are always at choice. You aren't always in control of your feelings and desires, but you are in control of what you do about them.

Some people prefer to start new relationships infrequently, and to impose a moratorium after a new one begins to allow it to grow roots before starting any others. Others choose not to start a new relationship if there are problems in any existing relationship, or during times of turbulence or stress. Still others prefer to remain open to new relationships whenever connections might occur. None of these strategies is always effective. Allowing relationships time to solidify before taking on new partners is not a guarantee that new partners won't be disruptive, and being open to new relationships all the time doesn't necessarily mean you'll end up with a lot of them (or even one).

To some extent, the approach you'll take will depend on your personal nonmonogamy style. People who favour a closely connected network of intimate relationships might be more likely to decline opportunities for new relationships shortly after getting a new partner, whereas people with a more solo or independent nonmonogamy style might be more open to relationships whenever and however they form.

New relationships can often feel threatening or, at the very least, destabilizing, and it's common for other partners to need time to process them—especially if the established relationships don't themselves feel fully secure. This is where many people adopt another strategy: moving at the pace of the slowest person. Making sure everyone has time to adapt to changes in a relationship, especially big changes, certainly has its advantages. The gotcha is that "Move at the pace of the slowest person" can turn into a pocket veto. "Not now, not yet" can, if unchecked, quietly become "Not ever." If one person is urging others to slow down, that conversation should ideally include a discussion about parameters: how slow, what's being done in that slowness to enable the new relationship to happen in the future, and how you'll check in about it along the way. If "no movement" is a person's intent, they should say so up front.

Rushing into a new relationship can lead to instability. But moving much more slowly than what's natural for a relationship can also damage it. Relationships, like living things, have a natural pacing and rhythm. Artificially limiting a relationship's growth for too long can leave people feeling hurt and frustrated. Counterintuitively, it could cause the relationship to be *more* disruptive.

In any relationship, it pays to check in often with yourself and your partner about the state of the union. Is it growing in ways that serve your needs? Is the pace of the relationship appropriate for your mutual desires? Does it cause unnecessary difficulties for your other partners, and can these be mitigated?

New relationship energy

New relationship energy, or NRE, as it's known, is that giddy, I-can't-stop-thinking-of-you, everything-about-you-is-marvellous feeling that people who experience romantic attraction often get at the start of a new relationship. It's a wonderful thing for the people experiencing it, and can also come with both joys and challenges for previously established partnerships.

The biochemistry of NRE is becoming fairly well understood. During the early stages of a romantic relationship, alloromantic brains produce several neurotransmitters, most notably dopamine, serotonin and norepinephrine, in greater quantities, generally causing emotional effects that are part attraction and devotion, part intense preoccupation, part mystical experience and part physical lust. You become infatuated and you feel twitterpated whenever the person is near. In this state, you're biochemically predisposed to overlook their flaws and faults, see the best in everything they do, convince yourself that you are meant to be with them, and crave their attention. When people make distinctions between "love" and "being in love," what they describe as "being in love" is generally something like NRE.

NRE isn't (necessarily) the same as limerence, though a lot of people confuse the two. Psychologist Dorothy Tennov coined the term *limerence* in 1979 to describe a state of romantic attraction characterized by intrusive thoughts of a person, overwhelming fear of rejection by that person, and a powerful, obsessive need for reciprocation. Limerence, in other words, may be what some people feel when they fall in love with someone, regardless of whether it's mutual; NRE isn't quite the same thing, because it involves an actual new relationship. In addition, not all new attractions involve the more negative features of limerence, or its intensity. In fact, some people say they associate limerence with unhealthy partner choices; they know they're choosing well when they're actually suffused with a sense of rightness, groundedness and calm around the new person in their lives and not that "floaty" sense of infatuation. Your mileage may vary!

NRE can be transcendent. It lets you start a relationship bathed in delight. There's a reason this biochemical response exists: The excitement and giddiness can help lay the emotional foundation for a rewarding, loving partnership. It bonds you to a new partner by filling you with a big hormonal *yes*. But to enjoy NRE while preserving your other relationships, you need to recognize it for what it is, remember to nurture your other partners when you feel it, and not decide that it will necessarily lead to abiding love.

For the partner of a person starting a new relationship, NRE can be scary stuff, particularly if they don't yet know whether their newly enamoured partner will continue to show up the way they did previously. Sometimes, NRE can cause the affected partner to make comparisons with their already established relationships, which might feel drab by contrast. Vocalizing these contrasts out loud to either the new or the established partners can be incredibly damaging. Worse, the tendency to idolize new partners can easily trick people into making too many commitments too quickly, which can create chaos in their existing relationships. For these reasons, a lot of policies in nonmonogamous relationships are designed to mitigate the effects of NRE, but they're often not terribly successful.

A more effective way to deal with a partner's NRE involves both communication and patience. Talk together about how to manage this new and exciting thing. How can you accommodate this addition to the picture and encourage them to enjoy the sweetness of it while also maintaining the relationship you have? How can you continue to co-create the relationship you're in given these new circumstances? What do you need in order to feel secure and loved, and what do they need in order to feel free to exercise their agency?

NRE creates a boots-on-the-ground opportunity to grow and reaffirm trust between you and your partner. Your actions, as the established partner, can show your ability to be flexible, to support your partner's growth and joy, to put into practice all the principles you value. As an anchor in an attached relationship, you can create the conditions in which your partner is able to go out there and explore and then return to you. Your trust that they will indeed return—after a date, a weekend away, or eventually in the context of an ongoing attachment to a new person—is key here. And your partner's actions, in turn, can demonstrate their commitment and really show that they value and cherish the relationship you have, no matter how much excitement they feel about someone else. How do you each convey this commitment to the other's authenticity in a way that's clear and meaningful? Do you need to maintain certain small gestures of affection, a weekly ritual of Friday night French fries and foot rubs, a habit of texting every day at lunchtime? How much do you want to know about the new person (within their boundaries, of course)? Do you want to meet them, or wait a bit? What would help strengthen your sense of security so that you can send your partner off to their date and feel good about it, or at least neutral? Talk about all of it.

When you're the one experiencing NRE, mindfulness is one strategy that tends to be successful. Be aware that your brain is swimming in a powerful chemical soup. Enjoy it, but don't make life-altering decisions right away. If you know you may be predisposed to neglect your established relationships, think about strategies to mitigate this—both on your own and in consultation with your partners—and then put those strategies into action. Be willing to do a reality check, both within your relationships and by talking with supportive friends.

In some ways, the way NRE plays out in nonmonogamy is the purest distillation of what makes nonmonogamy different from monogamy. It gives you the opportunity to learn and show each other that loving more than one person is really possible. Even in the throes of some of the most intense emotions a human being can feel, you can still make choices that honour and respect the people you love—precisely because you love them and want to be good to them always, no matter what else is going on. And even while being attached to someone, you can send them out the door to see someone else and genuinely want them to have a good time—again, precisely because you love them, and you want to see them reach all the heights of joy this world can offer them. (That's kind of always a group project, whether you're nonmonogamous or not.)

This is also the place where you can experience a range of emotions that's uncommon in other relationship styles: the feeling of being happy to spend time with one person while simultaneously missing another, for example, or the feeling of compersion, where you're truly thrilled to see the joy that your partner is experiencing with someone else. Is it always that easy? No, certainly not! But here is where you can figure out, together with all involved, how to make it possible—or whether, for you (at this time, or ever), it is not. And you only get there by communicating about it at every step of the process.

Long-term partners can also benefit from the surge of chemicals that a new partnership inspires. When one person is full of hormones from a new connection, it's not unusual for that to have a ripple effect on pre-existing connections too. It's wise to maintain good boundaries and remember that other people are real, not just convenient sources of chemical highs. But that doesn't mean you have to pretend you're not in the mood to get it on with your long-term lover if you really are! You're allowed to enjoy the state you're in.

NRE does present some other dangers, particularly if you find it challenging to separate the excitement from the practicalities. For example, when the hormonal cocktail begins to wear off, a person who doesn't understand what's happening may become convinced that the relationship is no longer interesting and was probably a mistake from the start. They may start casting around for a new relationship, which they pursue with zeal until that NRE too wears off. In monogamous culture, this takes the form of short-term serial relationships. In nonmonogamy, this pattern can present as a series of ongoing relationships that begin explosively and then wither from neglect. The person keeps pursuing the next new hit of the body's endogenous high, very much like they might experience addiction to an external substance. To avoid this problem, you need a good dose of self-awareness and discernment: Is this the chemicals talking? How will you know? What are your checks and balances—do you have a wise friend or two, a therapist, a less NRE-ful partner (or several), or other sources to help you stay grounded? How can you make sure your choices and actions best align with your values and fit with your ethical system? Make decisions cautiously while NRE is happening so that you don't effectively treat partners as sources of excitement rather than as full human beings. NRE is a great place to return to axiom 1: other people are real.

Living together

Being involved with multiple partners complicates the logistics of cohabitation. Commune-style living exists, but more often, we see households of two or three people, some or all of whom may have non-live-in relationships with other people. Some of those other people might have live-in relationships with their other partners.

As we've said, there's no standard model. Whether the people in a nonmonogamous relationship live together depends only on their own needs and choices. After all, just because you love Dorian and Taj, and you can see yourself living with either or both of them, that doesn't necessarily mean Dorian and Taj can (or want to) live with each other!

Not everyone wants to live with even one person. Some folks prefer having their own space. In fact, for people who practise a solo poly model of relationships, living alone may be vastly preferable to sharing a home, regardless of how committed a relationship is or how long it continues.

An entire class of problems can appear when you live with multiple partners. Living with anyone in itself can be a source of stress and discomfort, whether they're a partner, a family member, a roommate or even a guest. A lot of unnecessary suffering can be avoided with partners when you employ the same strategies as for non-romantic roommates—strategies like negotiation and clear expectations around dishes in the sink, household chores, basic courtesy, respect for other people's sleeping schedules, and willingness to clean up after yourselves.

It would be possible to write a whole book about nonmonogamous living arrangements: co-owning property, renting, managing small spaces, dealing with conflicting work or school schedules, handling the logistics of where long-distance partners stay when they visit, figuring out what "respect" means to all involved in sharing a space, dealing with money management styles and income differences, taking care of kids and pets, accommodating everyone's needs related to disability and other considerations, and so much more. In fact, there is at least one such book, *The Polyamorous Home* by Jess Mahler. Suffice to say, it's a huge topic for discussion and worth approaching with real care and consideration. Living arrangements can have a huge impact on our relationships, so don't take them lightly.

Commitments in nonmonogamous relationships

The huge variation in nonmonogamous relationships means there won't be a clear road map for what commitment looks like. Some folks argue this means nonmonogamous relationships can't be committed. Naturally we disagree, though we will say commitment in nonmonogamous relationships is often quite different from the monogamous template.

In mononormative culture, many commitments look like the relationship escalator. People who start dating each other and continue awhile often expect a commitment to stop dating other people. Most monogamous dating couples who don't break up will eventually live together. Most people living together who don't break up will eventually feel they need to commit to getting married, owning property and maybe having kids together. There is tremendous social pressure, particularly in heterosexual society, to do these things by a certain age. Sometimes this is justified by the idea that people with uteruses only have so many reproductive years if they want to give birth. A lot of it is wrapped up in toxic ideas, such as that a woman's attractiveness has an expiry date, and thus so does her ability to "catch" a man; that if you don't settle down by a certain point, there must be something wrong with you (guys, you might be gay! horrors!); and that the only real commitment is one in which you "put a ring on it." Given all these pressures, a lot of people get married at the "correct" time, but to a person who might not be their ideal match for a lifelong commitment. And then, predictably, they have a midlife crisis from all the pressure or as they get to know their own wants and needs better as they age, and they divorce and feel like they've failed—when in fact doing it all "correctly" might have been their real mistake. Or, put more kindly, a learning experience from which they might emerge with a clearer sense of self.

There are less-tangible commitments in monogamy as well, many of which translate quite well to nonmonogamy. Most monogamous couples would probably agree that they have a commitment to seeing the relationship continue as long as it can. Most monogamous couples have a commitment to one another's well-being, which might mean anything from bringing chicken soup to a partner who's sick to driving a partner to work if their car breaks down.

Part of the beauty of nonmonogamous relationships is they can look like almost anything the people involved want them to. The usual scripts don't need to apply, or at least not as a package deal. But that means nonmonogamous people are responsible for questioning the mononormative notions they were likely steeped in throughout their lives, and making conscious decisions about their relationships. It's essential to be crystal clear when making commitments, and to *never* assume a commitment unless it's been explicitly stated. Simply being in a relationship with someone is not a commitment to the traditional relationship escalator. A pattern is not a commitment—and an assumption that it is can lead to a feeling of entitlement, or at least unspoken expectations, on one side and confusion or pressure on the other. Nonmonogamy means creating relationships deliberately. If you want your partner to make a certain commitment to you, ask. If you are uncertain what commitments your partner thinks they have made, ask.

Also, be realistic about what commitments you can make. This means not just being realistic about your other commitments now, but about the flexibility you may require in the future when a new person enters your life. One challenge with nonmonogamous relationships is that they require a willingness to leave space for other people who have their own needs and desires. This means that some types of commitments are especially problematic in nonmonogamous relationships, and the need for flexibility on everybody's part is much greater.

For example, longer-term commitments are trickier than short-term ones. You can easily commit to a date with your partner next week, but to commit to a date with them the same night every week forever? That overlooks the fact that you may someday have someone new in your life, and that's the only night they can see you. Or maybe you'll someday want to go to Mexico for a week with the new partner, which will mean cancelling your date night with your original partner. Of course, a weekly scheduled date night is perfectly fine, as long as there's an understanding that someday it might need to be renegotiated.

Financial commitments in nonmonogamy need special attention, too. It's common for people in a monogamous relationship to combine their finances. In nonmonogamy (and frankly, in monogamy, too!), we believe it's important to have access to some money that's just yours, even if you have joint finances with another person. There are lots of reasons this is a good idea, but in nonmonogamy specifically, it helps prevent one source of resentment and conflict. When all money is joint money, and then one person spends some of it on dates with someone else, this can be cause for upset. When each person has some amount of money that is theirs to use as they wish, this helps eliminate the feeling that one person is subsidizing another's dating life.

Advocating for needs and navigating commitments can create a special challenge for solo folks. People are accustomed to judging a relationship's significance by how far it's gone up the escalator. So when they don't see the conventional markers of a "serious" relationship, they may underestimate its depth and how much investment has gone into it. People who take a solo approach often look for partners who value them and their needs even when the relationship doesn't follow a recognized trajectory. So it's often not their partners who misunderstand the importance of their relationships, but their metamours. A partner's other partner can easily trivialize a relationship that doesn't appear "committed" because it doesn't have the normal markers (such as moving in together) that society associates with commitment. Many solo poly people, when considering a relationship with a person who is already partnered, find it essential to talk about their expectations and ideas about commitment early on.

There's one last type of commitment that can trip you up that applies to *any* intimate relationship, nonmonogamous or otherwise, but we think it's important to mention here. That is commitment to future intimacy. Many of the commitments we make in relationships—things like legal and financial responsibilities, a shared home or children—are actually commitments to life-building, not to feelings. And not to never changing your boundaries. When you're head over heels in love (or feeling NRE), you may want to promise to love your partner forever. You may even want to promise to desire them forever—as much as you do now. But as much as you may want to build a life with someone, consent to intimacy exists only right now, right here, in this moment. Consent means that you will be able to choose at all times the intimacy you participate in.

Being in a consensual intimate relationship means you are never obligated to any future intimacy, meaning anything that enters your personal boundaries. This could be sleeping together, having sex, hugging and kissing, sharing emotions, living together, having certain shared experiences or making shared choices. You can state *intentions* for the future, but you cannot legitimately pre-consent, because no one knows what the future holds. Both people must recognize and respect personal boundaries in the present time, regardless of intentions stated in the past. This is important to understand, or else the relationship can easily become coercive.

Many people build structures against free exercise of consent in the future to protect themselves from their fears: "Never leave me." "Love me forever." Such statements are you or your partner asking for a guarantee of the other's future feelings and choices. But even if you have already made such promises, you can always withdraw consent, always draw new boundaries. If you truly can't, then it's not consent at all. The moment you ignore your partner's boundaries, desires or needs, or you feel your partner has no right to them because they made a prior commitment, your relationship has become coercive.

Long-distance relationships

When you look around at nonmonogamous people, you'll see a disproportionate number of long-distance relationships (LDRs). Often you'll see deeply committed, long-term LDRs—something that's comparatively rare among monogamous people.

Monogamy makes assumptions that are poorly suited to distance, and it can be difficult to maintain sexual exclusivity for long periods when your partner is far away. But because nonmonogamy doesn't necessarily include expectations that partners will live together, and because it doesn't restrict sex and intimacy to one person, long-distance nonmonogamous relationships are more feasible. Another reason you see so many LDRS is that many nonmonogamous folks meet online or at conferences and gatherings that bring people together from far and wide. Plus, because nonmonogamous people represent a relatively small portion of the population, the selection of local nonmonogamous partners can be limited.

LDRS exist in a constrained space. Time with a long-distance partner is scarce, meaning it's at a premium whenever the opportunity comes up. But there are many ways to nourish an LDR when you and your partners are apart, from frequent messaging to sending snail mail gifts to having date nights where you get on the phone and watch the same movie at the same time in two different places. LDRS are an opportunity to get really creative about how you express your attraction, thoughtfulness and care.

The time when long-distance partners are physically together, surprisingly, can create the most stress. When you have both local and long-distance partners, it can be easy to get so caught up in the normal, day-to-day relationship with a local partner that you forget to make space for the distant one. Sometimes literally. A long-distance partner can be a sort of "invisible" person, someone whose needs aren't necessarily obvious. For example, do you leave a place in your home for your long-distance partner to stay on visits? If you have a regular schedule with local partners—every Friday is date night, say—are you flexible enough for a long-distance visitor to interrupt that routine?

Local partners may resent visits that disrupt regular schedules. (We talk a lot more about scheduling and questions of "fairness" elsewhere, but some things are worth going over here as they pertain specifically to LDRS.) When your long-distance partner is in town, naturally you want to maximize the time you spend with them. From the perspective of a local partner, the visits can look like all grapes and no cucumbers (a distinction we explain on page 250). You may go out to eat more often, take trips, spend more time playing tourist, and do other fun things to make the most of the limited time you have together. Your local partner might end up saying, "Hey! When do I get to have that fun?" If your long-distance partner visits for a week and you want to spend every night with them, your local partner might say, "That's not fair! When do I get to spend the night with you?" (The answer, of course, might be "During the other fifty-one weeks in the year.") It's important to avoid one-to-one comparisons here, as the nature of each relationship is so different. At the same time, if you feel something is missing in any one of your relationships, by all means sit down together with your partners and figure out how to meet that need! Comparisons are odious, but that feeling of missing out on something can be a legitimate indicator that you should make a change.

LDRs concentrate the fun, flashy parts of a relationship, but at the cost of all the small things that build intimacy every day. Local partners might want that "vacation" feeling with their sweetheart, but if they stop and think about it, few would be willing to trade places with a long-distance partner and miss out on the day-to-day joys instead! LDRs also create special concerns around relations between metamours, because visits may not allow much time to build metamour friendships. The partners in the LDR may need to sacrifice some dyad time if they want to get to know their metamours. Metamours, for their part, need to be able to recognize the scarcity of time the long-distance partners have with each other, and realize that it's probably not personal if they don't get as much time as they'd like to get to know each other. Because distance makes time such a valuable commodity, flexibility from everyone is vital.

Nonmonogamy with children

Nonmonogamy can be a tremendously positive thing for children. It can potentially mean there are more loving adults in the family, and it can allow children to see more examples of healthy, positive, loving relationships. It exposes children to the idea that love is abundant and can take many forms. Also: more birthday presents!

Children of nonmonogamous parents grow up with adults in all kinds of configurations. Many nonmonogamous parents end up living with one or more non-parental partners, some of whom may have kids of their own. It's quite common to see live-in vees consisting of a couple with children plus another adult partner who often participates in child care and may have a close, stepparent-like relationship with the children. Bigger networks may live in a great big house with six or seven kids—it's all been done. Some non-parental partners are more like aunts or uncles, some more like friends of the family who don't have much involvement with their partners' kids. Some (but not many) nonmonogamous people hide their nonmonogamous relationships from their children, seeing partners outside the home or treating them as "friends."

There is no magic formula for nonmonogamous parenting, no configuration that will work best for every family or every kid. The strongest, healthiest homes for children are those with happy, emotionally healthy adults who model integrity and good communication. The children's needs must be cared for, and the parents absolutely need to be present for and committed to their children, but that does not mean sacrificing their own needs, happiness or interests to every want of the children. Most people seem ready to accept parents' complexities and trade-offs for other things, such as careers—not just when both parents work, but when a parent needs to uproot the family to move cross-country for a career or educational opportunity. It's really not so different for relationships.

If you have children or plan to have them, and you want to be nonmonogamous, it's worth taking some time to unpack your ideas about what it means to be a good parent. Our society has long idealized nuclear families, but there are all kinds of families, including plenty of children who grow up without "traditional" nuclear families. A lifelong, live-in romantic dyad is *not* the only healthy or acceptable way to raise children, and in fact the isolated nuclear family is a historically recent aberration. The expression "it takes a village to raise a child" isn't (always) a metaphor. It's an accurate reflection of how many Indigenous cultures across the world have approached child-rearing for millennia, and have an expansive and communal mentality about what counts as a family. Plenty of cultures today value multigenerational living arrangements, with three and even four generations under the same roof or on the same street. If you were raised to believe the nuclear family is the only kind that counts, it's worth seeking out and learning about these other models, which are by no means extinct. As a nonmonogamous person, you might end up creating a beautiful live-in quad or triad with dedicated co-parents, not unlike the way your great-grandparents grew up, surrounded by aunts and uncles. Or you might lose your romantic relationship with your co-parent and end up as a single parent, or in a platonic co-parenting arrangement with your former partner, or in something that resembles a monogamous blended family (separated parents living with stepparents).

Parental shaming is rampant in North American culture, and as you might imagine, nonmonogamous parents are frequently targets of this shame. Folks here are immersed in so many messages about what "good parenting" looks like that by the time you get around to having kids, it can be tough to shake off the guilt, *no matter what you do.* Mom working outside the home? How can you be so selfish? Not working? You'll never afford a safe town with good schools! Don't want to (or can't) breastfeed? You're ruining your child's chance at good health! There are a million ways for parents to "fail," and parents are measuring themselves and others against every one of them. If you don't get it right, your kids will grow up to be failures—and it's *all your fault.*

Your monogamous friends may tell you that when you have kids, you'll settle down and grow out of this whole nonmonogamy thing. Some of your nonmonogamous friends may tell you that empowered nonmonogamous relationships are impossible with children, because without a hierarchical structure, no one would look after the children's needs. Everyone will tell you that good parents always put their kids first—but what that means is very culturally specific. Everyone thinks they know what's best for kids, and damn near everyone is ready with judgment and blame when the parents they know (truthfully: usually mothers) fail to meet their expectations. Add the fact that nonmonogamous people are in a PR war in which we're putting our cheeriest, most stable and photogenic nonmonogamous families out in front, and that gives nonmonogamous parents just one more thing to measure up to.

Are you okay with the idea of raising your kids in a family that doesn't meet the mononormative and amatonormative script of a romantic dyad? Do you believe you can still do right by your kids if you end up raising them in a home with one or three or more parents or an extended network—something that looks different from what you expected? Or will you feel you have "failed" your children? If you are going to live in fear every time your partner is away with another partner because you believe that if you can't maintain a "primary" romantic dyad you'll somehow be harming your children, how can you interrogate those beliefs?

Children certainly do complicate time management. Young children especially require huge time commitments from parents. It's essential to be realistic about how much time you have available to invest in intimate relationships, including with your co-parents, and whether that time is enough to allow you to treat an additional partner well—especially if a relationship becomes serious. If you're in a co-parenting relationship with one person, and your co-parent is extremely fearful of the loss of time for young children that another relationship might represent, it is worth considering whether nonmonogamy is a good choice for you at this stage in life.

One final thing to consider is the situation of new parents. Many thoughtful people try to space out new relationships, allowing time for each to become secure and established and aiming to understand the impact it will have on their lives, before being open to another one. You may want to take a similar approach when a new baby arrives. And given the emotional upheaval, life changes and sleep deprivation that come with having a new baby, this is an especially good time to be cautious when deciding whether you are available for new connections. In fact, many established relationships, both monogamous and nonmonogamous, end due to the stress brought on by the birth of a child. Remember: Whatever your reasons, if the circumstances of your life do not allow you to treat multiple partners well, then it is not kind to seek them out.

COMING OUT AND CHILDREN

One question nearly every nonmonogamous parent has is when and how to explain things to children, and how much to disclose to them. The best guideline we know of, repeated to us over the years by dozens of nonmonogamous parents, is to be open, within age-appropriate boundaries. For you to answer questions honestly as they arise may be all many children need or want; you may never need to have a serious sit-down talk about your lifestyle (although your child may someday want to initiate one). The healthiest nonmonogamous homes we know of are the ones where the parents are open about their partners.

Trying to conceal relationships from children is unlikely to work and may lead them to feel that your relationships are somehow shameful or dirty. At the same time, there's rarely a need to disclose *anything* about your sex life to your kids.

The situation is a little different if you have older kids and decide to open your relationship. Your children won't have grown up accustomed to having other partners around. Then you probably will need to have The Talk. You will likely find it easier to come out to them once you actually have a new partner, or at least when someone's on the horizon. Again, you don't need to disclose more than is appropriate for your child's age. A younger child may just need to know that the new person is important; an older one should be told that they are a partner. You may or may not choose to go into the word *nonmonogamy*.

Your child will need many of the same reassurances as adults: that your being nonmonogamous doesn't mean their parents don't love each other anymore. That it doesn't mean you're going to have a string of strangers parading through the house. That you are committed to keeping them safe and happy, and that you want to know about any concerns they have about any partner of yours.

Be prepared for the possibility that your children, particularly preteens or teenagers, will reject your nonmonogamy outright. It may take them years to understand and accept. In fact, nonmonogamy may become part of the focus of their teenage rebellion. They may hurl toxic judgments at you, as happens to lots of parents with teenagers; you've just given them a special target. The fact that it's to be expected—and it's ultimately not about you—doesn't mean it won't hurt. Have faith that by the time they are adults, they are likely to come around.

Children also complicate whether to be out publicly. Depending on where you live, you and your kids may experience stigma, and you may even face legal threats. Particularly in some conservative areas of the United States, nonmonogamy can be and is used as a powerful weapon in custody battles. (In most parts of Canada, where nonmonogamy has been recognized by the courts as legal, evidence of nonmonogamy is very hard to admit into child custody or child protection cases.) Teachers and other parents may react badly to your lifestyle and end up taking it out on the kids. (If you do need to educate a teacher in your life about nonmonogamy, you can pick up the short guide *Nonmonogamy and Teaching* by Ashley Speed.) These are all considerations in the decision whether to be out.

Many nonmonogamous parents *are* out in their wider communities, and many find that—sometimes after a period of adjustment—it presents little difficulty. (Your mileage may vary, of course: This is *very* location-specific.) Even if you live in a fairly accepting community, you may find that your kids feel embarrassed about not having a "normal" family. It's a good idea to think about how to balance your own need to be out against your kids' needs or desires for privacy, especially as they get older.

What about marriage?

Nonmonogamous relationships may be live-in or separate, local or long-distance, sexual or nonsexual, entwined for life or autonomous, open or closed, shared or networked or entirely independent. Given that, some people ask, "Why would a nonmonogamous person even bother to get married?" But many people are nonmonogamous and married, for all sorts of reasons.

Plenty of nonmonogamous people choose to marry, though their marriages lack the pledge of sexual (and often emotional) exclusivity that is a hallmark of traditional marriages. They do so for the same reasons monogamous people get married: for someone to build a life with, to build wealth with, to raise children with, to grow old with. Nonmonogamy does offer a great deal more flexibility in how you structure a marriage and what elements you make a part of it. For example, it need not include sex or children, shared finances, or even living together. A marriage is a commitment between two—or in the case of nonmonogamy, sometimes more than two—people. What that commitment includes is up to them.

A marriage is also, often, a public celebration of the commitment. People who have been in a relationship for a long time and are making a serious commitment to each other often want to share their joy in that commitment and declare it to the world, which is another great reason why many nonmonogamous people do choose to marry. Depending on the situation, a ceremony between two nonmonogamous people might be indistinguishable from a wedding between monogamous partners, or it might be creatively reimagined to include additional partners in ways that recognize their roles in each other's lives. A nonmonogamous grouping might come up with a whole new kind of ceremony to celebrate their unique connection.

However, marriage is also a legal institution—the core legal institution developed to enforce compulsory monogamy and the nuclear family as an organizing unit of society. So the law in most places still does not account for nonmonogamy in a way that reflects the real-life marriage practices of nonmonogamous folks. For example, in Canada, it's not legal to have any kind of marriage ceremony with more than one person (unless you divorce one of them first). This comes from the country's anti-polygamy laws, which were upheld in a British Columbia Supreme Court ruling in 2011 in the context of an intensive investigation into an isolated Mormon polygamous sect operating in the town of Bountiful. The case was focused on religiously motivated coercive practices involving men with multiple wives, including child marriage, and advocates pointed out (accurately) that women were treated unequally and abuse abounded. All true, and terrible; and sadly, Bountiful is just one of many polygamous sects in North America with similar problems. But none of this is reflective of the average nonmonogamous adult relationship that's increasingly common in nonreligious and noncoercive contexts all over Canada.

In contrast, a Newfoundland court declared in 2018 that three adults who formed a polyamorous triad were all considered the legal parents of the child they were raising together. Where does that leave nonmonogamous people? Some say there needs to be a Supreme Court challenge to settle the question, but there doesn't seem to be one on the horizon. As a result, much like same-sex couples before same-sex marriage was decreed nationwide in 2005, nonmonogamous groupings in Canada who want to have some sort of recognition of their relationship—whether religious, legal or in any other formal way—are left to improvise and hope for the best.

Some more affluent people may hire lawyers to draw up custom contracts of various kinds, but those might not stand up in court if challenged, especially if they involve children. Others cobble together protections by strategically using the available options, such as marrying a long-distance partner as part of helping them enter the country while maintaining property ownership with a local partner. We're not lawyers and can't advise on what the right approach is. And in fact, until there is some kind of legal framework that recognizes the existence of fully consensual nonmonogamy, it's unlikely there will be a single "right" approach for nonmonogamous people. The systems that govern our world, in the Global North at least, are not built for us. We must navigate them with the same creativity we bring to our unconventional relationships in the first place.

QUESTIONS TO ASK YOURSELF

Building nonmonogamous relationships means carefully assessing how you define your commitments and expectations, how you think about partnership, and how you think about the paths your relationships should, or could, take. These kinds of relationships also require you to build your commitments with an eye toward making space available for future partners, if you are seeking them. Here are some questions that can help:

- What are my current commitments? How much time do they leave for new partners?
- When am I open to finding new partners?
- What assumptions do I make about what commitment means in my relationships?
- How do I define *commitment*? Do my definitions leave room for nontraditional commitments and nontraditional relationship trajectories?
- If I am open to new partners, how do I leave—or how can I make—space for them?

If you have children, or are thinking of having them, here are some additional questions worth considering:

- When I think about family structures that I think are healthy for children, what features do they all have in common?
- How can I and the other adults in my life contribute to an environment that is safe and nurturing for children?
- What does it look like for me, my partners, and other members of my intimate network to be supportive of our responsibilities to children within the network, including mine?

Life has taught us that love does not consist of gazing at each other, but in looking outward together in the same direction.
ANTOINE DE SAINT-EXUPÉRY

16 Opening from a Couple

It's still very common for people to come to nonmonogamy from an established monogamous couple. Monogamy is still the default for most relationships, and even people for whom nonmonogamy is the best fit often discover it only after starting monogamous relationships.

A lot of nonmonogamy advice assumes that everyone is starting out from being part of a couple, which is not the case—you might be a solo person who stumbles across a sexy couple you'd like to hook up with, or you might suddenly discover group chemistry with several other solo people, or find yourself dating a member of a triad, or any number of other scenarios. And it's increasingly common, especially among younger and queer folks, to see people who have always engaged in nonmonogamy in some form. But because the starting point of couplehood is so common, we do need to spend some time talking about this trajectory in particular. (For an even more in-depth look at this exact scenario, check out Jessica Fern's excellent book *Polywise*.)

People who want to transition their relationship from monogamous to nonmonogamous tend to ask a lot of questions like: "How can I protect the relationship I've already built?" "How can I ensure that I will continue to meet my existing obligations?" "What do I do if someone gets jealous?" "What happens if a new relationship threatens the existing one?" "What if my partner meets someone they love more?" "How can I still feel special?" "How do I find nonmonogamous people to date?" "How do I tell my partner I want this?" and "What if my partner is the one who brought up the idea, and I'm kinda shocked about it?"

The last two questions need to be dealt with first, so that's where we'll start. Note that, while it might not necessarily be obvious, once you've had this conversation, your relationship has changed. Even if you ultimately decide not to pursue nonmonogamy, just the fact that one of you has expressed interest means a part of your relationship is now different. We hope you can find a way to make that a positive thing—an example of your ability to have complicated conversations, be honest with each other and really listen to each other's concerns—regardless of whether you end up pursuing nonmonogamy together.

If your partner brought it up

Simply having the question of nonmonogamy raised is, for some people, a difficult thing to accept. If your partner has just started this conversation, you're probably having a lot of feelings about it—negative, positive, confused or mixed.

Remember, you are at choice at every step, though you might not like all the options in front of you. In fact, it might feel like there are only two: staying together and doing this nonmonogamy thing you didn't see coming and wouldn't have asked for, or splitting up because you really don't want to do nonmonogamy. That's a tough position to be in. We'd suggest not making any fast decisions. Take the time to learn, think about and digest this idea, and talk with your partner a lot. You might want to work with a relationship therapist who's knowledgeable about nonmonogamy. You're not obliged to try nonmonogamy, but even if you don't, it's worth exploring what this means to your partner, why they asked, how they'd envision it working, and so on. You might learn that you're fundamentally incompatible, but you also might learn that you can find ways to creatively meet each other's needs instead of splitting up, even if you never open up your relationship.

If you're reading this, you're probably at least a bit open to the idea of nonmonogamy, or at least willing to learn more before you run screaming. Or maybe you're quite open to the idea but not sure how to go about it, what you want, or how not to screw it up. Either way, glad you're here! Keep reading!

If you want to bring it up

If you're the person bringing up the idea of nonmonogamy with your partner, there is no "right" time or "right" way to do it. You're talking about negotiating a change in the most basic story of what your relationship is. This is not likely to be a conversation that happens in five minutes while you're chopping vegetables. The idea will probably take a while to sink in. It may be weeks or months—or longer!—before you're finished talking about it. Likely both of you will need some time to come to terms with this degree of change.

Start simply. Say to your partner, "I've been hearing about nonmonogamy. What do you think of it?" And then, listen to the answer. This is a dialogue, and dialogues are two-way; half of communication is listening. If you go into the conversation with the goal of persuading your partner to do what you want, they may end up feeling pressured or coerced. Talk to your partner about how you came to this idea. More importantly, talk about *why*. Talk about what interests you and what you find appealing about it. Be direct and honest, but also compassionate. If your partner has fears, listen to them. Talk about your own fears. And then listen some more. If a nonmonogamous relationship is to be healthy and successful, it has to work for everyone. That means your partner can't just do it for your sake; it has to work for them, too. When a person goes into nonmonogamy when it isn't a good fit for them just because their partner wants it, there's tension baked in from the start.

When you start discussing the idea of nonmonogamy, remember there's a very real chance your partner may *never* be on board with a nonmonogamous relationship. Some people, no matter how open-minded or secure, are just happiest in monogamy, and that's okay. If your partner is monogamous, that isn't a rejection of you, and it doesn't mean your partner is unevolved or unenlightened. It may, however, mean you have to face some tough questions: How important is nonmonogamy to you? Can you be happy if your partner wants you to remain monogamous for life? If not, you may be faced with ending the relationship to take a risk on the life you want.

If your partner accepts the idea of nonmonogamy, it's normal to sit down and try to negotiate agreements about how you will approach it. Be careful! Think about what effects any agreements you make will have on future people who get involved with you. Think about what assumptions your agreements are based on. It can be easy to forget that each of us has the right to build a life suited to our needs. Nonmonogamy isn't a privilege your partner extends to you. If you start from the premise that you don't actually have any right to be nonmonogamous, that your partner is doing you a favour by permitting you to "get away with" having other partners, you can end up believing that you should accept whatever conditions your partner may impose, even if they don't feel good to you or if they mean anyone you start a relationship with is likely to be hurt.

Giving it a try

If you're in a monogamous relationship and your partner suggests nonmonogamy, or if you're single and considering dating someone who's nonmonogamous, it's tempting to think, "Okay, sure, I can give this a go. If it doesn't work, we can go back to being exclusive." That makes sense at first blush, but as soon as another person is involved in the relationship, that person's heart is on the line. Their feelings matter, and they deserve to be treated like a full human being, not like a lab experiment.

You'll often hear nonmonogamous people talking about how scary it is to open a relationship. You don't hear this as much from people who are starting a relationship with a member of an established couple, even though it's just as scary. Couples are able to make all kinds of rules to transfer their risk onto new partners, without recognizing that a person starting a relationship with one or both of them is already assuming a lot of risk. When you fall in love, you are vulnerable; you put your heart in other people's hands, knowing it might be broken. Too often, the vulnerability and fear within an existing couple is given the highest priority, with little or no recognition of the vulnerability and fear of a new person starting a relationship with them. Everyone in the foxhole is at risk, but that doesn't make it okay to use anyone else as your human shield.

The other problem with the "just give it a try" approach is that it doesn't always fully account for your own feelings, either. Nonmonogamy isn't for everyone, and you can't predict what effect it will have on your life. We're not saying you can never close a relationship after opening it—but if you try to go back to your old monogamous relationship, you will find that it has changed. Everyone has the right to end a relationship that they don't want to be in anymore. But you can't put the toothpaste back in the tube. Once you've opened up, it's very unlikely that you'll be able to go back to exactly the same situation you were in before and have it be unchanged by the experience.

Seeking a closed triad

A very, very common chain of reasoning among couples made up of one man and one woman, usually where the woman is bisexual and the man isn't, goes something like this:

> We want to open our relationship to new people. But also, that's scary. How can we keep from feeling jealous and left out? Aha! Maybe we can date together! If we present ourselves as a package deal, nobody will be able to come between us. We need a bisexual woman, of course, so she can have sex with both of us—and the thought of another man in the mix is uncomfortable anyway. That woman can be with both of us, so she won't come between us or make one of us feel left out. And we'll make it an exclusive triad. She'll be just with us, so we won't feel threatened by her other partners. That way, we will both feel safe and comfortable.

Couples looking for this setup are so common that they're a cliché among nonmonogamous people, particularly in mainly cishet circles. (They're also a well-known joke in queer women's circles, since couples like this often target them in bars and on dating apps.) Very, very few such couples ever find their imagined third person. These couples often join organized nonmonogamy groups, but become frustrated and upset that their requirements are rebuffed. Many nonmonogamous women do identify as bisexual, and more than a few are open to having a man and a woman as partners, and plenty do like to play with couples, but experienced people almost always say no a closed triad whenever a hopeful couple approaches. The couple usually offers an unequal balance of power, even when they believe they're offering equality; after all, they're the ones setting the terms of the relationship.

The entire premise is also based on heterocentrism, homophobia and misogyny, whether the couple realizes it or not. It sets up the original heterosexual partnership as the "real" or "main" relationship, with the new same-sex partnership being a pleasant add-on that's expected to never rise above a certain limit of importance, because relationships between women aren't actually real. It also often sets up the two women as entertainment for the man. (Do queer couples sometimes seek closed triads? Yes, but not in sufficient numbers or with sufficiently gendered assumptions to have developed the specific kind of terrible reputation that straight couples have.)

So if you're part of the couple and those are your thoughts, know that you've chosen a difficult quest, and you will most likely never find such a person. Indeed, women willing to sign on to such a relationship are often called unicorns, because they're about as thin on the ground as mythical horned horses. As reasonable as this idea might sound from your perspective, it is very unreasonable from her perspective.

Think about what the offer would look like from the side of the potential third person: First, the couple says they want you to date both of them. Almost always, you will be expected to have sex with both of them, and you may also be told you can't have sex with one without the other there (because that might breed jealousy or resentment). And you will be expected to love both of them "equally."

From the start, you're put in a position where you have little voice. Your relationships have already been scripted. Alas, the human heart rarely follows scripts. It is rare for someone to be attracted to two other people in the same way at the same rate at the same time. So you're likely to be more attracted to and more connected with one member of the couple than the other, and that's likely to create tension. Often, if you express more attraction for one person than the other, you'll be kicked out immediately.

Plus, not everyone who's nonmonogamous is an exhibitionist or likes group sex. Asking someone to have sex only in a group and only with two people is likely to come across as controlling, even to someone who *does* like group sex. All healthy relationships need some one-on-one time.

But let's say you agree and start dating them both—and, somewhere down the road, some sort of problem or incompatibility arises with one of them. What happens then? You'll probably be told, "You *knew* we were a package deal. If you stop having sex with one of us or stop wanting a relationship with one of us, we will both break up with you." That puts you in the unenviable position of being told your only choices are 1) to continue having sex with or being romantically vulnerable to someone you don't feel close to; or 2) to have your heart broken. The relationship becomes coercive.

As for the polyfidelity requirement, under which you'd agree to date only this couple, most people come to nonmonogamy because they reject the idea that being in a relationship means they can't love anyone else. Yet that's what's being offered in this arrangement. People who identify as nonmonogamous generally won't be excited about entering such a restrictive relationship. Those who do so tend to emerge saying they would never do it again.

Add this all together and it's not hard to see why unicorn-hunting is a bad idea.

We're not saying polyfidelitous triads don't exist. The good ones we've seen, however, have formed when a member of a couple starts dating a new partner and then, some time later, that new partner develops an attraction for the other member of the original couple. The triad formed organically, rather than being scripted.

The truth is, structure can never solve the problem of jealousy. Having a polyfidelitous relationship can seem like a way to "ease into" nonmonogamy, but that's a bit like trying to ease into skydiving by saying, "I don't want to just jump out of the plane. That's too scary. So I'll climb out carefully, maybe sit on the wing for a while to get a feel for what it's like, and get comfortable trusting my parachute." Not only will this not work, it will put you and your fellow skydivers in jeopardy.

If you don't trust your parachute, skydiving probably isn't for you. By "trust your parachute," we mean building the tools of communication and jealousy management, trusting your partner, and believing that they want to take care of you even if other partners are involved in the mix...*before* you open up.

Couplehood and identity

One of the problems that can arise in opening from a couple to nonmonogamy is the competing expectations of mononormativity and nonmonogamous culture. In mononormativity, marriages are often portrayed as combining two lives into one. Society expects that couples do almost everything together. A spouse is often called "my other half." In extreme cases, each person becomes so dependent on the other that they're unable to express their needs as individuals or make decisions alone.

Yet when you're looking for a partner, very often it's who you are as an individual that makes you attractive. Couples who think of themselves as a unit aren't likely to be seen as attractive prospects, because it can seem as if there's no room for anyone else. If the two people think of themselves as one, where's the room for a new person to have and express individual, distinct relationships with each of them? And what happens if a conflict arises within the couple, or between the new person and one member?

Attempts to assert individuality can feel very threatening, especially to couples who have been together a long time. But as scary as it may be, asserting your individuality doesn't mean damaging your existing relationship. You were individuals when you met, and that worked out, didn't it? You can still be individuals while you maintain close, intimate bonds with your partner. Presenting yourself as a whole person who is closely connected with another and can become closely connected with new people too, rather than as half of a unit, makes finding new partners and developing new relationships much easier.

Maintaining a separate identity within an intimate relationship is known as differentiation. If you struggle with differentiation, the book *Polywise* has some great exercises you and your partners can work through.

Relationship broken?

There's a snarky saying among nonmonogamous folks, often delivered with an eye-roll: "Relationship broken? Add more people!" This expression is used to refer to people—often but not always monogamous couples—who seek new partners to try to fix issues in their own relationship. Perhaps they're feeling bored or stifled. Maybe the sexual spark is gone. Perhaps they're having difficulty talking about their needs. Regardless, the solution (or so it seems) is to open up to new, exciting relationships, in hopes of turbocharging what's already there or fixing the broken bits.

Nonmonogamy won't fix a broken relationship. We're not saying a relationship needs to be perfect before you open it to nonmonogamy, but nonmonogamy will put pressure on any weakness that exists. It is not a solution to relationship problems. Nonmonogamy may make it easy for one person to escape an issue temporarily by retreating into the new shiny relationship, but the issue will always come back—often worse than before. And once you have more partners, there are more people who can be hurt.

There may be certain narrow exceptions. For example, we've known people with specific sexual kinks not shared by their partners who have started relationships with others who share those kinks. And if monogamy itself is the problem with your relationship—if you are compatible partners but are chafing at trying to squeeze yourselves into a monogamous mould—then nonmonogamy might help. Generally speaking, though, nonmonogamy will work best when any and all of your existing relationships are in good shape. People are not duct tape, something you wrap around the leaky pipes of your current relationship. You need to get help with your plumbing (or DIY it!) first.

Swinging as a starting point

Swinging is a sexual subculture that's primarily made up of couples seeking sexual experiences with other couples, small groups or individuals. These couples are almost always made up of one man (historically straight, though this seems to be changing) and one woman (straight, bi-curious or bisexual). Some of it takes place at swingers' clubs, cruises and resorts. Much swinging is a private affair, where a small group of people, often close friends, will get together and have sex. Long-term personal friendships can and do develop out of this kind of swinging.

Often swingers are married couples who consider themselves emotionally faithful but sexually adventurous. Many even self-identify as monogamous. Quite a few swingers operate under the premise that they are free to explore *sex* outside their relationship, at least in controlled settings such as parties, but not love and emotional intimacy. This doesn't describe all swingers, of course, but it is a common theme among many.

There's overlap between swingers and people involved in polyamorous communities as well as other types of nonmonogamy, and many people come to nonmonogamy from the world of swinging. After all, sex and intimacy are closely linked, so although a swinging couple may start out seeking sex, they are still susceptible to getting attached to their sex partners. Sometimes things go the other way, too: A person may be nonmonogamous and also seek out casual sex within swingers' groups.

If you arrive at nonmonogamy from swinging, you'll likely find the transition a lot easier if your swinging didn't include the assumption of emotional fidelity. If it did start from that assumption, welcome! You'll probably find a lot in common with people in mono/poly relationships (relationships where one person is nonmonogamous and the other monogamous; see chapter 17). Some of the challenges of nonmonogamy will likely be fairly easy for you to handle. You've likely already resolved at least some of the sexual jealousy that people in a mono/poly relationship may face, though many swingers deal with this jealousy by only having sex with others while they're together, and this may not be sustainable in another kind of nonmonogamous relationship. Other challenges, like mourning and letting go of the desire for emotional monogamy, will probably be similar, and the same strategies apply to dealing with them.

If you're considering exploring swinging as a step into nonmonogamy, it's worth noting that the subculture is not for everyone. While things vary a lot across the countless smaller circles that make up the larger swingers' subculture, in general it's not the friendliest place for queers or trans people, and it can be very objectifying of both women and men. Some clubs and events require that people submit pictures of themselves, and grant membership only to people with certain looks and body types. Women are sometimes pressured into performing bisexuality for the titillation of men, while men are often actively discouraged from exploring their own bisexuality. Club and event prices are often based on a binary notion of gender and aim to discourage single cis men but encourage single cis women. Also, if you're accustomed to a consent culture approach that's based on the premise that you should always ask before touching someone, the "touch first and see how they respond" approach that can be the norm in swingers' spaces (regardless of written rules) can be very uncomfortable. Does all this apply to your local swingers' club? Maybe, maybe not! Consider this fair warning as you check out what's available in your area to see whether the vibe works for you.

Queer and BDSM subcultures as starting points

Queer subcultures often have a lot of room for sexual exploration. Gay men have bathhouses, sex parties and hookup apps (at the time of this writing, Grindr is one popular one, but there are many others), as well as a long history of park cruising. (Marcus McCann's book *Park Cruising* is a thoughtful and poetic exploration of the subculture and its politics—a real must-read.) Queer women also have their own lineages, dating back to the nonmonogamous lesbian communes of the 1970s and various lesbian and bisexual historical figures, as well as present-day bathhouses, sex parties and apps. Major festivals like Pride are often opportunities for queers of all stripes to find all manner of encounters. And queer and trans conferences and campus groups are a whole thing too. Because of these baked-in elements of queer subcultures, a lot of queer people are exposed to ideas about—and opportunities for—nonmonogamy just by virtue of showing up in community settings.

But just because this is true doesn't mean all queers are nonmonogamous, or that it's a simple and easy shift to nonmonogamy if you haven't lived that way thus far. In fact, sometimes the ubiquity of nonmonogamy in queer circles can come with its own problems, such as shaming of monogamous people. Some monogamously oriented queer people bemoan the lack of like-minded people to date!

Similarly, you'll encounter a ton of nonmonogamy within BDSM, kink and Leather circles and communities across all sexual orientations. These subcultures are highly focused on sexual exploration, so it makes sense that they're also places where people tend to enjoy a variety of partners. We can't do justice to the range of possible nonmonogamous configurations within BDSM-based and power-based relationships here. But it's worth noting that BDSM makes space for some kinds of nonmonogamous relationships that are uncommon elsewhere, such as the idea of play partners (people who do BDSM play together, with or without sexual contact, but aren't romantically involved), role-specific relationships (partnerships based on power roles that may not be sexual or romantic), Leather families (households of various configurations based around family-type structures translated through Leather roles) and many more.

You might start out by coming into queer or kinky communities and, through them, discover nonmonogamy. Or you might seek out these communities as part of your explorations in nonmonogamy. Depending on your trajectory and your desires, as a couple, you may encounter a range of different challenges. This chapter addresses a lot of them already, but it's worth noting that just because these communities expose you to nonmonogamy in ways that other social circles might not, that doesn't mean you should expect yourself to get on board quickly and easily. For example, if you're in an up-til-now-monogamous queer relationship, you might have the advantage of more cultural exposure to ideas around nonmonogamy as compared with the average heterosexual person, but that doesn't mean you magically have more skills or emotional comfort with the idea! And if you're a previously monogamous couple exploring kink, you might find yourself overwhelmed by how many people approach you for play, together or separately.

Take your time. Don't push yourself to be the coolest and most politically enlightened queer couple ever, defying societal norms at the Radical Sex Week workshop but having private meltdowns once you get home together. Don't feel like you and your sweetheart have to play with others just because you showed up at a play party and five people approached you for co-topping scenes before you even had time to adjust each other's cute new leather outfits. It's okay to go at your own pace and figure out what you want, not just what the people around you all seem to be doing.

Seek out support that makes room for all your identities as you undertake this transition—for example, you may want to make sure that your relationship therapist is not only knowledgeable about nonmonogamy, but also queer- and kink-friendly. Queer people, you may want to gear your nonmonogamy reading toward works by queer authors, of which there are many. Kinky folks might want to check out resources such as *Playing Well with Others* by Lee Harrington and Mollena Williams, or Raven Kaldera's collection *Power Circuits*, which is about polyamory in D/s and M/s relationships (full disclosure: Andrea has an essay in there). You may also want to seek out (or start!) discussion groups, support circles, and other local or online resources specific to your situation.

Navigating the complexities of queer or kink identities, practices and community involvement on top of figuring out a shift into nonmonogamy is no small feat, and for the sake of your own well-being and the health of your relationship, it's worth doing thoughtfully and with support.

Nonmonogamy after cheating

Many people begin looking for a path to nonmonogamy after an episode of cheating. Some nonmonogamous folks have a history of cheating in monogamous relationships, often because monogamy felt stifling but they didn't know that nonmonogamy was possible. When they find out about nonmonogamy, they set out to build nonmonogamous relationships. Other people cheat on a partner, then try to transition that relationship to nonmonogamy, perhaps after confessing or being caught. Making this journey is possible, but it's a long and rough road, and the success rate is not high.

Starting new relationships openly on a nonmonogamous footing is much easier than trying to rebuild a relationship damaged by cheating. That's because cheating represents a profound betrayal of trust. It's the trust, more than the sex, that creates a hard path to nonmonogamy. The cornerstones of nonmonogamy, as we've discussed, are consent and communication. Cheating undermines both, and it's nearly impossible to rebuild a relationship until trust and communication are restored.

There are many reasons why a person might cheat. Some people like the thrill of the forbidden, or the rush that comes with doing something they might be caught at. Some people cheat because they want to experience something new but don't know how to ask for it, or they believe it's not available to them. Some people want to experience multiple sex partners but don't want their partner to do the same thing—which, as you can imagine, is especially problematic from a nonmonogamous perspective. Others just fall in love (or limerence) with someone new but don't want to lose their partner or family, and they don't know that any other option exists.

The reasons a person chooses to cheat are important when looking for a path from cheating to honest nonmonogamy. And yes, it is a choice. Many folks who are caught cheating say "It was an accident!" as though they slipped on an icy sidewalk and fell into someone's bed. Cheating might not be planned, but "unplanned" is not the same thing as "accidental." Calling cheating an accident is a way of avoiding responsibility for making the decision.

Finding the path to nonmonogamy starts with acknowledging the affair—and, just as importantly, acknowledging that it was a choice, not an accident. It also requires assuming responsibility for the cheating. All too often, cheaters shift the blame: "If my partner were different, then I wouldn't have needed to cheat." The "different" might be "more sexually available" or "more adventurous" or "less reluctant to do what I want." In reality, the affair is a choice made by the cheating partner, and that's where the responsibility lies.

Rebuilding trust is hard. We talk on page 267 about how to repair after a broken agreement, but cheating tends to create such deep wounds that we advise talking to an experienced, nonmonogamy-friendly counsellor or therapist. Professional help will almost certainly be an important part of building the trust necessary for a healthy nonmonogamous relationship.

That trust will never be rebuilt unless you are willing to tell the truth about everything. Come 100 percent clean. No evasions, no holding back. The path from cheating to nonmonogamy isn't easy, and an absolute commitment to honesty is the only thing that makes it possible. Honest, open transparency is a learned skill, and mastering it takes time and effort. A relationship might have all sorts of patterns that make honesty hard. Again, this is something a qualified counsellor or therapist can help with.

In this case, it's also important to think about whether nonmonogamy is really what you want. Many people who try to move from cheating to nonmonogamy originally started their affairs because having an affair seemed less scary than talking openly with their partners. As often as not, the scary part about open nonmonogamy was the idea that their partner might also want another partner. In other words, they cheated because they wanted to have additional partners but didn't want their partner to.

Sometimes, when caught in this situation, people are tempted to say, "We can start a polyfi triad with the person I was cheating with!" This can feel to the cheated-on partner like a solution that lets the cheater go on having the affair, sometimes with a "side helping" of watching their committed partner and their previously illicit partner getting it on with each other, but without the fear of having their committed partner explore other relationships. As you can guess, we view this fantasy very skeptically. For starters, a person who has already shown a willingness to cheat in a monogamous relationship may well cheat in a polyfi relationship. The same factors that led to the affair may still be present. Moreover, it's difficult to sympathize with the notion that "we'll be polyfidelitous so I can keep my illicit partner, but you can't have one."

Finding the path from cheating to nonmonogamy requires everyone to actively buy in, and building fairness means *not* starting from the assumption that the cheated-upon person will never have other partners in the future, even if they can't imagine wanting them now. If you're trying to move from cheating to nonmonogamy, be prepared to question *everything* about your relationship. It's also reasonable for the cheated-upon person to need time. Expecting someone who's just been cheated on to embrace nonmonogamy immediately after learning of the infidelity is excessively optimistic. For a functional nonmonogamous relationship to arise overnight from the ashes of an affair is highly unlikely.

Even when a relationship does move from cheating to nonmonogamy, you don't always get to stay with the person you cheated with. First of all, often *they* won't be okay with this. Even if they are, the person you cheated on may never be okay with you staying with someone who's already shown a reckless disregard for their needs and boundaries. And when we say finding the path requires the active participation of everyone involved, that includes the third person. For the relationship to transition to nonmonogamy with the same cast of characters, that person is going to need to feel included, empowered and welcomed. Yes, welcomed. Like we said, it won't be easy.

In most cheating situations, couples counsellors recommend that a person caught in an affair cut off all contact with the third person. Obviously, if the goal is to create a working nonmonogamous relationship, that's not going to be good advice. But you can't have it both ways. Relationships tend to work when everyone feels empowered. A nonmonogamous relationship isn't likely to succeed if the third person is simultaneously treated like a partner and a resented outsider. As uncomfortable as it may be, if you want to go forward with nonmonogamy that includes them, including them in counselling might be a good idea.

During this transition, it might help for each person to consider what they want the new relationship to look like, and then negotiate for that. After infidelity, you're essentially creating an entirely new relationship. Being willing to start from first principles and build something that reflects the needs of everyone involved is going to be necessary.

Of course, not all cheating is the same. Different people have different ideas of where the "cheating" line is. To some, cybersex chat with strangers is cheating; to others it's their partner's harmless fun. The point is, there are levels of cheating and differences of opinion about it. Generally speaking, if you're doing something you can't tell your partner about, you're probably cheating.

Because there are gradations of cheating, some violations are easier to recover from than others. For example, it will probably be easier to recover from an illicit kiss than from months or years of furtive sex in the back of your car. In any case, talking to your partner and coming clean will almost certainly be easier if you do it sooner rather than later.

QUESTIONS TO ASK YOURSELF

If you're thinking about transitioning from a monogamous relationship into nonmonogamy, you're not alone, but you're in for some pretty big changes. Here are some questions that may be helpful:

- What assumptions do I have about what my relationships "should" look like? How are these assumptions influenced by the cultural narratives about monogamy, and how much are they truly mine?
- What parts of my relationships are most important? How can I preserve those elements while knowing that my relationships will change over time?
- What guarantees do I want from my relationships? Are they realistic?
- How much space do I have to devote to new relationships right now?
- As I seek new relationships, what assurances can I offer my new partners that I will make space for them, listen to their needs, and be able to change to accommodate these new relationships? Am I ready to maintain these commitments with integrity?
- Where does my sense of security come from in my relationships? What am I willing to do to help my partners feel secure?
- How do my explorations in nonmonogamy intersect with other things, such as experiences in swinging, BDSM or queer subcultures? Do I need any specific support to navigate these intersections?

In a healthy environment, conflict and diversity offer opportunities for everyone to learn a little bit better how to love.
DANYA RUTTENBERG

17 Mono/Poly Relationships

Few things put the amatonormative idea that "true love conquers all" to the test more than major incompatibilities in core values or the kind of life you want.

Differences in religion, political views, a desire (or lack thereof) for children, and more can all be showstoppers depending on their importance and how willing or able the people involved are to budge. One significant point of incompatibility, of course, is when one person desires exclusivity and the other does not.

When people know they have specific deal-breakers, most will do their best only to connect with people who want the same things they do. But hearts have a way of pole-vaulting over even the most well-defended barriers, and sometimes people do find themselves in deep connection, but misaligned on their approach to exclusivity. Or one person in an established partnership—whether open or closed—may realize the current structure isn't working for them, and they need to ask for change. Or someone is in a secure monogamous partnership, but finds themselves falling in love with another person, while their love for their original partner remains undiminished. In cases like these—where one person in a dyad wants nonmonogamy and one doesn't—a decision must be made: Either you go your separate ways and each seek out the life you want, or you choose each other and try to make it work. Welcome to the mono/poly relationship.

For some people, a good mono/poly relationship is possible. But getting there is hard. In fact, it is among the most difficult nonmonogamy structures to navigate in a way that promotes and respects the well-being of everyone involved. These relationships require patience, persistence, flexibility and compassion. They require careful communication and a willingness to do some deep soul-searching. The people in them must be willing to work together, and the nonmonogamous person's other partners, if there are any, also need to be willing to show sensitivity and kindness to the needs of the monogamous person.

Defining monogamy

The concept of monogamy is more complicated than it seems. Some people consider themselves monogamous because *they* want only one partner, but they're okay if their partner has other lovers. Others identify as monogamous because they want a relationship in which their one partner is also exclusively faithful to them. Also, different people have different ideas about what constitutes fidelity. Some swingers self-identify as monogamous; for them, sex without emotional attachment doesn't count. Other people consider even a platonic relationship that has emotional depth, or even an unrequited crush, to be a profound betrayal of monogamous agreements.

As you might imagine, a nonmonogamous relationship with a monogamous partner who only wants one partner, but is okay if you have other relationships is going to be a lot easier than a nonmonogamous relationship with someone who really wants it to be just the two of you. Mono/poly relationships also follow a different course when the monogamous person falls in love with a nonmonogamous person who already has other partners than when a couple start a relationship together and the door to nonmonogamy opens later.

The monogamous person could also be "solo monogamous," meaning they don't want an escalator-style relationship, but they don't have a desire for more than one partner themselves, and they don't mind if their partner has other relationships. Such an arrangement may not pose too much difficulty if it's what everyone truly wants—in such cases, the nonmonogamous person might even have a nesting or escalator relationship with another (monogamous or nonmonogamous) partner. The monogamous person may be asexual and want just one queerplatonic life partner, but be happy for that person to have intimate relationships with others. Or they could be post-nonmonogamous, meaning in this context (there are others!) that they've spent time living nonmonogamously and have transitioned back to wanting only one partner. These folks may have already done the work of unpacking mononormativity, and may have had healthy nonmonogamous relationships in the past. So assuming they didn't leave nonmonogamy thinking "Well, that sucked—I'll never try that again!" but have other reasons, such as time or resource limitations or just a lack of interest, a post-nonmonogamous person also may not struggle too much with having a nonmonogamous partner.

Likewise, as we discussed on page 16, nonmonogamous folks have different relationships to their nonmonogamy. For some, it's essential to who they are—they could never consider an exclusive relationship. Others are more adaptable, and would be fine with limiting their connections with others for the right person. The latter kind of person is likely to be able to be far more flexible in how they accommodate a monogamous partner.

Since there is so much variation in how people came to and practise both monogamy and nonmonogamy, not all mono/poly relationships will present special challenges beyond those covered in the rest of this book. The rest of this chapter focuses on pairings where there's an uncomfortable degree of difference in what people want their relationships to look like, or even a philosophical divide over the relative importance of monogamy and nonmonogamy, as this tends to be where special support is needed.

You won't change each other

Nonmonogamous folks have heard this story a million times: Two people have been together a couple of years. One's nonmonogamous, one's not—in fact, the very thought of nonmonogamy exhausts them. But the nonmonogamous partner believes the monogamous one will someday "wake up" to nonmonogamy's advantages, while the monogamous partner believes their beau will eventually "settle down" to monogamy. They're in love, and each is prepared to patiently wait for the other to change...as long as it takes.

There's a word in the nonmonogamy world for monogamous people who knowingly pair up with a nonmonogamous person, hoping to change them: cowpokes (or cowgirls, or cowboys). They ride up alongside a nonmonogamous crowd and try to "rope one out of the herd." There's no special nickname for the nonmonogamous person who hopes to change their mono partner, but there should be. Both are setting themselves up for long-term pain and thwarted dreams.

The cowpoke story usually goes like this: The monogamous person has internalized the narrative of mononormativity—that nonmonogamy is just a phase, that when the person they want meets The One (who is, of course, the monogamous person), they'll settle down. The nonmonogamous person, meanwhile, believes the monogamous person will come around once they feel secure, or starts to want variety, or sees other nonmonogamous relationships working, or just sees the light.

Each *says* they accept the other's nature. The monogamous person may even agree to an open relationship in theory—just not yet, not until the relationship is stable. And the nonmonogamous person offers that time. And more time. And whenever they talk about opening the relationship, there's some reason not to (see the section on pocket vetoes on pages 236–238). Maybe there's some external stressor, or there's something wrong with the person the nonmonogamous partner wants to date. And after a lot of time has passed, and the two are deeply bonded, and the nonmonogamous person seriously falls for someone new...well, of course that person is seen as a threat, because the nonmonogamous person wants to change the now-long-established default.

Note that we're not referring here to the kind of arrangement that Jessica Fern and David Cooley refer to in *Polywise* as a temporary vessel. Temporary vessels—a specific period of relationship closure—can offer valuable guardrails when a relationship (or person) is going through a rough patch. But temporary vessels are time-limited, usually have specific expectations about how the time within the vessel will be used, and often don't involve cutting off other existing partners, just not looking for or starting new relationships.

The problem we're talking about is when two parties entered, or continued, a relationship on the assumption that one would eventually change the other, when the other person has not (freely) agreed they want to change. For many people, nonmonogamy and monogamy aren't things they can simply change; they are fundamental. Mono/poly relationships only work when each person wholeheartedly embraces who the other is, allowing them to live the way that's most authentic for them, without judgment. Intimacy comes from accepting and loving others for who they are.

Choosing your path

If two people with a major relationship incompatibility decide to try to move forward together, at least one of them is going to have to give something up. To make it work, one person may have to change religions, or give up the idea of having children, or move to another country. When a monogamous person and a nonmonogamous person pair up, they will, of course, have to decide together whether the relationship will be monogamous or nonmonogamous, for how long, and what that will look like. The solution to this puzzle will look different for everyone, and there should be no assumptions from the outset about what it will be—but it will go much better, and set you up for longer-term success, if you go into the negotiation without assumptions about who holds a moral high ground.

It can be all too easy for a monogamous partner to reach for mononormative messages from the surrounding society to try to shame their partner into agreeing to exclusivity. It can be all too easy for a nonmonogamous partner, especially in certain subcultures, to try to shame their monogamous partner into an open relationship with arguments that nonmonogamy is more enlightened, or that the monogamous partner is just insecure and needs to work on themselves. Please don't do this—or let a partner do this. If you're going to go forward together, you both need an opportunity to freely choose.

A monogamous partner may try to agree to a nonmonogamous relationship while essentially viewing the nonmonogamy as a problem to be managed, rather than a source of joy and wholeness for a loved one. They may find it difficult to recognize that nonmonogamy isn't a flaw or a failing; it's a different, entirely valid way of seeing relationships. The nonmonogamous person, for their part, may see a monogamous partner's needs as obstacles to be worked around, or as unreasonable expectations to be dealt with. They may feel that if the monogamous person would just *get with the program,* these needs would fall by the wayside.

Exclusivity is not an imposition—it's a valid, healthy and reasonable way to conduct romantic relationships. The monogamous partner isn't unevolved, unenlightened or selfish. There is nothing wrong with wanting one exclusive partner. It's a totally valid option for a mono/poly couple to decide to have an exclusive relationship, if the nonmonogamous partner doesn't feel that means sacrificing something core to who they are.

And, as much as it might hurt, it's also a totally valid option to decide to go your separate ways if you can't find a relationship structure that feels genuinely safe and authentic for both of you. But this is a book about nonmonogamous relationships, so the rest of this chapter is about the third option: having a nonmonogamous relationship where one of the partners is monogamous.

Confronting assumptions

Communication about assumptions and expectations is especially vital in mono/poly relationships, because when you don't talk openly about something, the default social norms tend to dominate. Some of the assumptions monogamous partners make may include ideas like "If you truly loved me, I would be enough for you" and "If I am not enough for you, something is wrong with me." They may react to a new flirtation by asking, "Why aren't the partners you have enough?" or "What's missing from your life that you need to go out and look for something more?" (To be fair, even staunchly nonmonogamous folks can be plagued by these kinds of doubts, too.)

One of the most difficult hurdles to overcome can be an assumption that a person is nonmonogamous because something is missing in a relationship. Sometimes nonmonogamy *does* offer an opportunity to satisfy an unmet need; for example, some nonmonogamous people are interested in BDSM but have a partner who isn't, or have an asexual partner while they themselves are allosexual. But even in those situations, nonmonogamy isn't a reflection of the deficiencies of the monogamous person, it's just a recognition of a difference.

Nonmonogamy can even be a benefit to the monogamous partner. For example, some people feel guilty over not being able to provide their partners with something, such as if they are not interested in bondage but their partner absolutely loves it. When the bondage-lover starts dating a new partner who is also enthusiastic about bondage, the vanilla partner might feel intimidated at first—is this going to be the end? But after time goes by and that doesn't happen, they might no longer feel guilty about not being able to provide the bondage-lover with what they want.

From the perspective of a monogamous person, nonmonogamy may look like a licence to behave indiscriminately. It can be difficult to shake the notion that commitment and exclusivity are the same thing. This can lead to thoughts that a nonmonogamous person can't or won't commit, and therefore must be unreliable or wildly promiscuous. A better way to think about it is in terms of openness to intimate connection, not too different from the way most people are open to making new friends, but to a degree that goes beyond the lines usually inscribed by mononormativity.

Social recognition can also be a big issue in mono/poly relationships. A monogamous person in a nonmonogamous relationship often wants the social recognition that comes with being conventionally partnered, and they may feel uncomfortable with public signs of partnership that involve others. Placing restrictions on public affection with other partners, though, is likely to create resentment—the nonmonogamous person may feel forced into fakery or shamed about their other partners or relationships. Sometimes this is just an issue that people need time and space to work through. Sometimes it can be dealt with by planning inclusive public activities together. This is a place where working to unpack mononormative stories can be really helpful.

Cultivating trust

Mono/poly relationships require special commitment to trust and communication, because it's hard to trust someone whose motivations you don't fully understand. When someone's motivations don't make sense to you, you will find it difficult to predict what choices they might make. When two people don't see eye to eye, it's easy for a tiny seed of doubt to blossom into a full-blown breakdown of trust.

Being willing to take a leap of faith that a nonmonogamous partner is dedicated to your relationship, even if you don't understand their motivations, is especially important for the monogamous partner. On the other side, as the nonmonogamous person, when opportunities to build trust arise, you really have to behave with integrity. If you've made promises to your monogamous partner, keep them. If those promises create real problems for you or others, don't break them: renegotiate them. Cultivate trust by demonstrating that you can be trusted.

Finally, for the monogamous person, trust in yourself—in your self-efficacy—is as important as trust in your partner. Many people find that sticking with it and getting through those early struggles gives them confidence that they can get through future struggles. Even if you're terrified at the beginning of your relationship, when nonmonogamy is a complete unknown, with time and a trustworthy partner who builds security with you, you can build confidence that if hard times come back, you can get through them and be okay.

Transparency is important. The nonmonogamous partner may hesitate to tell the monogamous person about new interests for fear of hurting them. The monogamous person might not want to talk about their fears or insecurities for fear of upsetting the nonmonogamous partner. But relationships live or die by the quality of the communication in them. It's vital that both people talk openly, even when talking openly is difficult.

If you're the monogamous partner

Being content as a monogamous person in a mono/poly relationship means finding a way to make the relationship work for you. If you see nonmonogamy as a problem to be worked around, you're less likely to be happy than if you find a way to make it benefit you too. That doesn't necessarily mean you have to have multiple relationships yourself; it might mean nonmonogamy gives you the opportunity to explore other interests or hobbies. (We talk more about this later in this chapter.) If you know there's something you can't offer a partner, it might take stress off you when your partner finds someone else who can. If you're introverted and your partner is extroverted, nonmonogamy might let you spend time doing things you want while your partner is socializing with others.

Remember, there is nothing wrong with you. Your partner is nonmonogamous because they are nonmonogamous. No matter who you are, no matter what you could be or do, they would still be nonmonogamous. If you have a friend and you decide to make another friend, it probably isn't because there's something wrong with the first friend. It's about bringing more love, companionship and intimacy into your life. Nonmonogamy extends that familiar philosophy to intimate relationships.

You don't have to make peace with this all at once. It's okay to need time. Nonmonogamy is a radical change, and sometimes it takes awhile to process change. You may feel jealous or insecure at times. That's okay. It doesn't mean you're doing something wrong. It's also okay to ask your partner for help when this happens. Not help as in "I need you to dump you other partners," but help as in "I need your reassurance and support here." There's nothing wrong with asking your partner to show you why you're valued. (Remember HEARTS from page 112.)

There's also nothing wrong with being monogamous. If you don't want other partners, don't try to force yourself to have them. If you want to explore what it's like, that's one thing, but you don't have to in order to be with a nonmonogamous person! There's nothing wrong with being who you are. And there's nothing wrong with your partner for being nonmonogamous. It isn't a moral failing. It isn't because nonmonogamous people can't commit—that's important to keep in mind, too. Suggesting that nonmonogamy is a problem or that there's something wrong with your partner is unlikely to make your relationship better.

Your partner's other partners are human beings. It can be hard at times not to resent them. It can be tempting to tell yourself they have no right to be there. That's not true. Nonmonogamy is a valid relationship model, and the people involved in a nonmonogamous relationship have a right to be there, just as you do. Your partner's other partners are not your enemies. They don't necessarily have to be your family, or even your friends, but respecting them and treating them kindly as people your partner loves, and who add value to your partner's life, will definitely help your own relationship run smoothly.

As we like to emphasize, people are not interchangeable. It may seem that if your partner has another partner who is similar to you, or likes the same things you do, then they don't need you anymore. But remember, they're nonmonogamous and don't think or feel that way. They love you for who you are. Doing something with you is an entirely different experience from doing the same thing with someone else. And if your partner has a partner who's very different from you, it's not a covert way of saying that the different things about you aren't good, wonderful or valuable, or that they want you to be like someone else.

In any nonmonogamous partnership, it's common have a situation where someone is off with one partner while another person is home alone. In a mono/poly relationship, it's likely to happen even more often. But some folks just can't handle that—they need to be with their partner every night, or know that they are always available. If you know that is true for you, then you might not be able to manage a mono/poly relationship without abandoning yourself. If it's something you want to be okay with, you will benefit from developing a rich life separate from your partner. Hobbies, social activities and other interests can be really helpful. (Of course, this is true for monogamous relationships too!)

You need to have people—preferably outside the relationship—with whom you can talk and process your emotions. But finding such support can be difficult. Ideally such a confidant(e) won't just point to nonmonogamy and say "See, here's the problem!" Yet if your relationship background is entirely monogamous, you might not have friends to confide in who are friendly to or versed in nonmonogamy. We strongly recommend finding a nonmonogamy discussion group in your area, if you can—try an online search for nonmonogamy in your area. Many discussion groups will have some members who are in mono/poly relationships, and having other such people to turn to can be an invaluable source of support.

If you're the nonmonogamous partner

As a nonmonogamous person with a monogamous partner, you're asking a partner to believe, in the face of overwhelming social messages to the contrary, that you're not looking to replace them; that the reason you're open to other partners is not because there's something wrong with them; that you're not asking for permission to cheat; and that you don't have one foot out the door. You're asking them to accept that having other lovers isn't just a way for you to move from one relationship to the next. Make sure that's true. Make sure you are worthy of that trust.

You can't turn a lifetime of expectations around on a dime. Give your partner space and time. They may also need to spend some time mourning the loss of the kind of relationship they expected. Allow them room to experience their emotions and to get through to the other side. Be compassionate.

Being nonmonogamous is not a licence to do whatever you want. There will be times when your partner struggles and needs your support. Be there. Be supportive. Be willing to hold their hand when things are tough. Be willing to go the extra mile to talk about what you value in them, why you love your relationship with them, and why you want to be with them.

Time management is important in any nonmonogamous relationship, but especially in a mono/poly relationship. Your partner may not be accustomed to spending time alone. Be transparent about your plans and intentions. Communicate openly about your schedule. Work with your partner to apportion time in a way that works for both of you.

Your partner may never want to explore other relationships, and that's okay. Avoid starting from the idea that it's fair for you to be nonmonogamous if your partner is "allowed" to have multiple relationships just like you. If your partner doesn't want them, the opportunity to have them isn't a benefit. Don't assume that your partner will suddenly become nonmonogamous as soon as they discover how wonderful it is.

Finding your bottom line

Mono/poly relationships require flexibility, negotiation and willingness to compromise. They also require a good understanding of your personal boundaries, and the things you can't compromise on. When people have radically different ideas about what their ideal relationship should look like, they will be especially tempted to make compromises that, over time, bargain away more than they intended. When negotiating a mono/poly relationship, ask yourself, "What are the essential things I must have? At what point will my needs no longer be met? What are my values? What must I have in order to act with integrity?" Don't compromise on those answers. If you negotiate away your integrity, ethics or agency, you are no longer a full and equal participant in the relationship.

You must also be aware of your partner's boundaries, and not ask (or expect) them to compromise past those points. Talk about what they need to have a healthy, fulfilling relationship, and where those needs overlap with yours. Be careful, too, not to compromise on behalf of other people who aren't even present yet. Sometimes when you're trying to find a way out of an impasse, you may be tempted to make compromises that affect others—especially when those others are still hypothetical. It can be tempting to try to ease stress by bargaining away their agency in advance, such as by agreeing to rules that will apply to future partners (see chapter 10). When you do this, you are using the agency of other people as bargaining chips.

Instead, focus on practical things your partner does have control over. If you need more time with them, say "I need more time with you," not "I don't want you spending so much time with other people." Be concrete about the things that are bothering you—schedules, chores, responsibilities, time with the kids, fun time together—and negotiate for those things specifically.

Your relationship is a choice

The relationship escalator narrative doesn't dwell much on the notion of choice; it can seem that once you fall in love, you're on that ride whether you want to be or not. It can be surprisingly easy to lose track of the fact that you do, in reality, have choices, even if they're difficult.

In a mono/poly relationship, it is especially important that the people involved feel they are agreeing to the relationship on purpose, because they each see value in the other that makes the relationship a positive choice for both of them. In contrast, when one or both partners believe that they must keep the relationship at all costs, it becomes difficult to give meaningful consent.

Remember that no matter how much you love each other, you are not obligated to be in a relationship with each other. You have a choice. If it doesn't work, if one of you is hurting too much, it's okay to let it go. The fairy tale is wrong: True love doesn't necessarily conquer all—except perhaps in the sense that sometimes the most loving thing you can do is let someone go to pursue the life they want.

QUESTIONS TO ASK YOURSELF

Mono/poly relationships offer some unique challenges and require careful negotiation if they are to succeed. Before embarking on a mono/poly relationship, here are a few things to consider.

If you are the monogamous partner:

- Why do I identify as monogamous? Is it because I only want one partner for myself, or because I want my partner to be only with me, or both?
- Do I enjoy time to myself or without my partner? Do I have hobbies I enjoy alone or with others, and a social life that does not rely on my partner? Can I develop these if I don't have them already?
- Am I prepared to face uncomfortable feelings such as jealousy, insecurity and fear about my partner's loyalty, and to put in the work required to overcome them?

If you are the nonmonogamous partner:

- Am I prepared to give my monogamous partner time and space to process their feelings about nonmonogamy?
- Am I prepared to make concessions in my relationship to help the monogamous person work through their feelings?
- What limits do I have on the concessions I will make, either in terms of what I will agree to or the time span of the agreement?

For both partners:

- Do I fully understand my partner's choice to be monogamous or nonmonogamous, and am I able to accept my partner for who they are?
- Can I build a relationship that respects both my partner's agency and my own, as well as the agency of others who are (or will be) involved?
- Does this feel like a choice I am freely making, or do I feel resentful, angry or under duress?

I fall in love with myself, and I want someone to share it with me.
EARTHA KITT

18 Finding Partners

"How do I find partners?" is one of the top questions people ask when they're new to nonmonogamy. And there are certainly unique concerns: finding nonmonogamous partners, choosing partners who are compatible with you and your nonmonogamy style, and disclosing your nonmonogamous relationships are all things to think about. We'll get into those concerns in depth in a minute, but we'll start with some basic principles.

First, try not to make every social encounter about your search for a partner. There are tropes about the new-to-nonmonogamy couple cruising local events imagining they'll just show up and run into their ideal third, or that one single dude who hits on every person he meets at the book club. It can get so distracting that a lot of groups have rules specifically prohibiting using them to look for dates. The more you do this, the more desperate (and clueless) you appear, and the more people will avoid you—except the kind who find desperate-seeming people attractive, and these are often not the kind with whom you'll be able to form a healthy relationship.

Next, be out—if you can. For dating purposes, in the broad sense, it's a lot easier to meet fellow nonmonogamous people if you're at least somewhat out about being nonmonogamous. While there are, of course, situations where coming out might be too risky, treating nonmonogamy like it's a shameful secret can be off-putting to other nonmonogamous people and can send the wrong message to potential dates who might not yet have figured out how they feel about nonmonogamy. Also, the more out you are, the more likely potential partners may already know you're nonmonogamous, which makes the initial conversations much simpler.

Third, network with other nonmonogamous folks. If you're already involved in a queer or BDSM/kink/Leather community, you may already be surrounded by nonmonogamy. If you're not, you may want to try going to nonmonogamy-related groups or events. And on a related note: Don't be afraid to expand your social horizons. If you don't know any nonmonogamous folks in your social group, look for or build new social groups. Hang out with other nonmonogamous people even if you don't want to date them. Make friends. Get to know people as people before sizing them up as dating material.

Should you date only nonmonogamous people?

You can avoid a lot of problems from the outset if you choose only partners who are already nonmonogamous. Choosing partners who are already nonmonogamous means they already know it's what they want, have probably at least done some reading about it, and may already have developed some skills navigating it. Some dating apps are better than others for finding nonmonogamous folks, but the recommended ones shift as years go by and vary from place to place, so rather than list them, we'll simply recommend that you go looking to see what the current go-to apps are in your area and what kind of crowd each one attracts. Sometimes you can just sign up and see what's out there. If the app is favoured by queer folks, offers nonmonogamy as a filter or allows linking of profiles, or if you see people specifically mentioning nonmonogamy in their profiles, then you've probably found a good one.

On the other hand, making this choice really does narrow the dating pool. The situation isn't as dire as it was even ten or twenty years ago, but even so, if you're part of a local nonmonogamy-focused community and consider that to be your dating pool, it can begin to feel real small, real quick. This is another reason why so many nonmonogamous people engage in long-distance partnerships and meet people at larger gatherings such as conferences and retreats.

If you opt to start a relationship with someone who's new to nonmonogamy but open to it (as opposed to someone who's committed to being monogamous but open to dating you, which is what chapter 17 was about), be prepared for a lot of discussion and negotiation. It can be helpful to check out websites, read books, listen to podcasts and engage with other resources about nonmonogamy together. Talk about what nonmonogamy means to each of you, and how your visions of it mesh. Trying to "convert" a person to nonmonogamy is a bit of a mixed bag.

Some people take to nonmonogamy naturally as soon as they discover it. Others find that, no matter how hard they try, they can never become happy with it. Starting a relationship with a person who's unsure but willing to try may mean painful renegotiations later, and possibly a choice between the end of the relationship or the curtailment of your life as a nonmonogamous person.

Telling a prospective partner about nonmonogamy

So you're on a hot date, maybe with someone you met online or at a party—outside of a nonmonogamous context. Things are looking good, you're feeling chemistry...so when do you bring up nonmonogamy?

That's a trick question! Because if you're already on a first date with them, since you've got a policy of complete honesty, you've already told them. Maybe you put it in your online dating profile, or maybe you brought it up as soon as they asked you out. Either way, they were fully informed before you made dinner reservations. Right?

A few people will hold out: "Not until you're sure you want a relationship." But if you avoid bringing up the subject early for fear of scaring off a prospective partner, you're not giving them the full set of basic information they need to know to decide if they want to date you. And in any case, if someone isn't okay with nonmonogamy, it's best to know right away so you don't waste each other's time. Putting off the conversation will make an incompatible partner feel like you pulled a bait and switch, especially if you already have any other partners; you deprived them of the chance to give informed consent to being on a date with you at all. Hiding or talking obliquely about your partner, your spouse or your relationship-anarchy approach to dating is really not going to impress your date—at least not in a good way. You may occasionally get lucky and find someone who'll be unfazed—but it's a roll of the dice, and rolling a natural twenty doesn't mean you weren't still taking a big risk with someone else's consent.

Treating nonmonogamy like bad news that needs to be broken gently also isn't a great approach. People take their cues about how to respond to something from the way you present it. If you treat nonmonogamy as if it were an unfortunate medical condition or a guilty secret, that's how they'll see it. If you treat it as a straightforward truth about yourself and how you approach relationships, you can start on an honest footing with them.

Start simply. "I'm nonmonogamous." Explain, in brief, what that means to you and what your current situation looks like. Ask questions, such as "Are you open to nonmonogamy?" or, if you know your prospective partner is nonmonogamous, "What kind of nonmonogamy do you practise? What does that look like for you?" Approaching a potential new partner with integrity means being transparent about your relationship expectations.

The importance of partner selection

The notion that people don't choose their relationships is surprisingly widespread. Compatibility, shared vision, mutually negotiated relationships—none of these things matter in the face of true love, says the fairy tale. When you fall in love, you are obligated to start a relationship. And once you're in it, the love is the fuel that makes it go. As long as you're in love, you will be happy.

If you accept the idea that people do not choose their partners, you may find yourself in relationships by default, not design. You may end up with partners who are a poor match, because you may not think to ask questions that might tell you how well matched you are.

You do have choices about your intimate life. Andrea often refers to something they call the "50-40-10" rule: 50 percent of the key to successful nonmonogamy is working on yourself, 40 percent is picking the right partners, and 10 percent is the technical stuff (communication skills, time management and so on). You can skip right over vast quantities of relationship problems by exercising good partner selection skills at the outset. While you may not always have control over your feelings, you do have control over what you do about them—and that includes choosing whom you will enter a relationship with. Love, of and by itself, is not enough to guarantee a good relationship.

One part of the skill of partner selection is knowing your deal-breakers—what would make someone a poor choice as a partner for you. Sexual incompatibility is one common deal-breaker; different takes on using drugs or alcohol is another. So is a history of violence against past partners. You may not want to partner with someone who votes in a direction you find abhorrent, buys into conspiracy theories, or holds radically different spiritual or religious beliefs than you. None of these are deal-breakers for everyone, of course (though we suggest a history of violence should be unless the person has done extensive work on those behaviours, with real evidence of change); it depends on what matters to you. But a misalignment of important values predicts problems. You may want to avoid dating people who have developed a troubling reputation in the communities they're part of, though rumours can be misleading gossip or they can be effective warning systems, so listen to what's out there and then use your discernment. If you are a woman who dates cisgender men, however, we do recommend giving strong weight to any warnings of abusive behaviours from a man's past partners, as these reports are very likely to be true, and abusive men are very good at convincing new partners that their past partners are crazy, lying bitches.

Many other signals that someone may not be a good match for you are more subtle. For example, if you work best at night, partnering with a morning person might be just fine—but it might not be, if the morning person thinks you're an irresponsible party animal because of your preferred hours, or if you think they're kinda dull for going to bed early, or if you'd both simply feel ditched when your person can't join you for your preferred activities (sunrise yoga or 3 a.m. stargazing!). If it's too early to have a deep discussion about values, you can look for small tells about their values and personality: Do they treat customer service workers with respect? Do they take good care of their pets or plants? How do they react when small bad things happen, like if they step in something gross with their new shoes, the show is starting half an hour late, or you miscommunicated about what street corner to meet on? If they make an error, are they able to apologize?

One factor that can be very revealing is how a prospective partner talks about ex-partners. In an ideal world, everyone would be able to stay good friends with their exes. Sometimes, things are just too tender for that, or the relationship may have been toxic. Don't judge someone by these criteria alone, but do listen to how they speak about former intimates. Is every ex automatically a monster to them as soon as the relationship is over, or are they able to show some nuance? Are they a victim in every relationship they have been in? Do they express contempt for past partners? Are they able to show awareness of and remorse for their part in any past toxicity? And especially: Do they use past relationships as an excuse to mistreat you?

Look at a date's current relationships, if any. Do they seem turbulent or generally smooth? Do you like the way this person treats their current partners? Does your date speak positively and respectfully about these people, and honour their agreements? If so (or not), they will likely do the same with you. Similarly, what are their friendships like? Consider quality over quantity, but do take note if a person appears to have no friends at all, or so many they can't keep track. All these things add up to a picture of the person you're considering getting involved with. Do you like what you see?

When selecting a partner, you can end up in a strange state of limbo: a person doesn't display any particular red flags or deal-breakers, but you don't feel really enthusiastic about them, either. If you make choices based on whether or not someone hits any of your deal-breakers, you might plow ahead with a relationship without considering whether or not that person has the qualities you *want* in a partner.

One policy for partner selection is "'fuck yes." This policy, first articulated by writer Mark Manson, is based on the idea that it makes no sense to invest time and romantic energy with someone you're not that excited to be with, or who isn't excited to be with you. If the idea of dating someone doesn't prompt an enthusiastic "fuck yes!" for you, then the answer is no. This kind of policy works well if you tend to keep dating people you think you really *should* be attracted to, even if the chemistry is just blah. The requirement of a "fuck yes" can jolt you out of settling for someone who looks good on paper but just isn't a great match in real life.

That being said, sometimes love grows slowly. For some people, such as demisexuals, attraction only really arises when they're already in a solid friendship with someone. For others, attraction may sneak up on them unawares, until they one day realize they've gradually been falling in love with a friend or acquaintance. This can be especially surprising if you're not accustomed to the "slow burn" approach!

It's also worth trying to stay open to possibilities you might not have seen coming. Don't go against your intuition or your values, of course. But if you require your potential partners to meet a rigid set of superficial criteria, you may end up missing out. And if you require your relationships to take a specific shape, finding someone who will fit that exact shape is especially difficult, as described in chapter 16. Looking instead for good *people,* not for good role-fillers, leaves you open to connection even if it takes a form you didn't expect.

Kittycat lessons

A kittycat lesson is what we call a situation where people generalize poorly from their experiences or learn a lesson that works against them. Anyone who has lived with cats knows that they can be highly intelligent, but very much do not see the world the way people do. This means that when they learn, they often don't learn the specific lessons their people want them to. For example, Eve once had a cat who started trying to wake her people up at 5 a.m., which in the cat's opinion was breakfast time. The humans responded to this by putting the cat out of the bedroom as soon as this started to happen each morning. Instead of learning, "I should stop trying to wake my people up because it gets me kicked out of the room," the cat learned, "I need to make as much noise as possible when they put me out of the room, because that at least gets them out of bed. No food for me, no sleep for them!" This did not, however, serve the cat's ultimate goal of acquiring breakfast at 5 a.m.

One kittycat lesson we have both seen many times involves strategies for finding new partners. People who feel threatened by nonmonogamy often try to manage risk by placing rigid limitations on new partners. Yet people with experience in nonmonogamy often avoid restrictive relationships. So the people who opt in to such relationships are more likely to have little experience in nonmonogamy and few skills. When problems happen and the relationships end, the people who placed the restrictions may decide they were not restrictive *enough*, and then try to limit new partners even more. This becomes a self-fulfilling prophesy: People with experience in nonmonogamy avoid such folks even more, which increases the likelihood they will only find partners with limited experience in nonmonogamy or poor boundaries, which increases the odds of trouble.

There's no easy solution to all this—after all, your takeaway follows logically from your experience, so it can be hard to catch yourself in kittycat-lesson mode. This is one reason it's so valuable to have friends, communities and support systems that are nonmonogamy-friendly. The right person might be able to offer some insight or wisdom to help you notice if you're heading down an erroneous path like this.

What are you offering?

When it comes to seeking partners, people often think about what they want, but don't put as much thought into what they've got to offer. This isn't so much about writing up an appealing online profile or picking the most flattering profile pic—although those things can go along well with some of the deeper thinking. Mostly it's about trying to mentally step outside your situation and look at it the way someone new might.

Put yourself in a potential partner's shoes:

- What would it be like for them to get involved with you?
- What kind of partner are you? What values do you bring to your relationships?
- What are you offering in terms of time, relationship skills and enrichment of their life?
- How much space do you have in your life? Are you asking them to be squeezed into time slots between a dozen other commitments, or do you have availability to give them?
- Are you inviting them into a messy, difficult situation, or a relatively stable and secure one?

You don't have to have a perfect life and zero problems to be nonmonogamous. But it does help to make sure you're actively solving or doing good maintenance on the problems that come as part of the current "you" package. Some examples include taking care of your health, both physical and mental; maintaining any established partnerships you've got; and having in place adequate support for your life, such as a therapist, a reliable time management system, predictable child-care arrangements, or whatever else helps you stay up to date on life's obligations. It's also handy to be able to tell someone what the next six months of your life are probably going to look like: you're expecting a heavy work schedule on weekdays but should be fairly open on weekends, you're just starting a new school program and so will have exam periods and papers to write, you've got plans for travel or major surgery, and so on. Nobody can predict the future with perfect accuracy, but you can usually offer some general ideas, which can help someone decide whether they want to sign up to be part of that journey.

What situation are you entering?

Any time you start a relationship with a person who is already partnered, there will probably be responsibilities, expectations and commitments already in play. The same is true of unpartnered people—very few people lead lives that include blank spots just waiting to be filled by a partner. They tend to fill their time with friendships, hobbies, side hustles and other pursuits. Learn about them.

Talk directly to your partner about what effects their other relationships and commitments may have on you. What time constraints and energy commitments on their part will affect you? Is your partner out or closeted? Are they in a hierarchical relationship, and will you be considered a secondary partner? Are there veto arrangements? Do they have expectations about how you will relate to your metamours? What information will your new partner want to have about other relationships you might want to start in the future, and at what point do they want to hear about the presence of new people in your intimate life? If you're already partnered as well, how do they feel about meeting your established partners?

A cautionary note on couple-centrism

The nonmonogamous world is, unfortunately, filled with people who have been terribly hurt by well-meaning but inexperienced couples. When two people have only each other as partners, they often fall into a pattern of sharing everything, committing all time and resources to the relationship. So when one decides to open their heart and life to a new person, the other often feels that they are losing something—time, focus, energy—and often that's true.

Imagine you have planted an oak tree in your garden and tended exclusively to that tree for many years. The tree grows big and strong, forming a beautiful canopy that expands over the entire garden, shading everything beneath it. You love that tree and the shade it gives and have spent many long summer days beneath it, looking up into its branches.

Then one day you find a tiny plant. It intrigues you. You don't know what it's going to grow into, but you want to find out. You want to plant it in your garden...but you don't have any sunny spots left. Your beloved oak tree is shading everything. You don't want to harm your oak tree, so you just plant the new thing in a shady spot, thinking, *Maybe it will be something, a nice fern perhaps, that likes the shade.* Sometimes that's what happens. The relationship that gets planted beneath the old relationship naturally thrives in the shade. But when that happens, it's sheer luck.

Most intimate relationships, and romantic ones in particular, do not naturally stay small and inconspicuous. Eventually, there will be a conflict: Either the new relationship will wither, or the older relationship must be trimmed a bit to allow sunlight for the new one to grow. Many couples go through this process, and many survive it with healthier relationships as a result. But it can be painful, particularly for the partner who feels like their relationship is being "pruned." Uninterrogated mononormativity can allow the couple to shift the brunt of the conflict onto the new partner, who shoulders shame and blame as the interloper.

Many closely coupled people are indeed available for deep intimacy with others, maintain autonomy over their relationship decisions, and gracefully make room in their lives to honour both their existing commitments and new ones. How do you identify such people? If you're the newcomer, take some time to get to know the couple and observe whether they have strong, independent identities apart from each other or appear completely enmeshed. Do they have individual hobbies, friendships or other pursuits? Are all their online photos of them as a couple, or do they appear also as separate entities? Are they attached at the hip at social events, or do they give each other space to mingle and then circle back and reconnect?

QUESTIONS TO ASK YOURSELF

When you're interested in a new person, considering these questions alongside the others in this chapter may help you decide whether they are a good choice for you as a partner:

- Am I excited by the prospect of being with this person? Are they a "fuck yes!"? If not, does it feel more like a slow burn that still gives me a clear yes?
- Does this person have relationship values similar to mine? If not identical, are they compatible?
- Do I understand the person's current relationship situation and overall life saturation, and do I understand how all that will affect my relationship with them?
- Am I being asked to give up anything to be in this relationship? If so, do I feel that what I will get in return is worth the price?
- Is this person available to give me what I think I want in the relationship—in terms of time, emotional intimacy and freedom for the relationship to grow?
- Is there anything about this person that I'm hoping will change? Realistically, how likely is it that the change will happen? If this person stayed forever exactly as they are right now, would I want to be with them?
- Does this person bring out the best version of myself? Or do they leave me feeling insecure, uncertain or otherwise unclear on what's going on? Do signs point to any habits or patterns that I know to be harmful to me?

Asking the following questions of a potential partner can help you figure out whether your values and approaches will mesh well in a relationship:

- How do you feel about nonmonogamy? If you practise nonmonogamy, what kind do you practise? Do you have experience with nonmonogamous relationships, and what does that look like for you?
- What restrictions, if any, do you (or your partners) expect to be able to place on other partners?
- What kind of relationship do you envision me having with your other partners? Do they have expectations of the kind of relationship I will have with them?
- Do you have any expectations or hopes about the role I will play in your life?

Loving all of you only strengthens
my love for each of you.
CHARLIE JANE ANDERS

19 Life in the Polycule

Once you've wound up in a nonmonogamous situation of some kind, you'll find yourself in one of three positions: You may have multiple partners, you might be involved with someone else who has multiple partners, or both.

The common ground here is that regardless of what specific position you occupy in your configuration, you will be navigating a new kind of relationship category: the one between metamours. A metamour is a partner's other partner. If you're the pivot or hinge in a vee, your two partners are metamours to each other. If you're involved with someone who already has partners, those partners are your metamours. And you get a bonus prize if you're doing both at once! (It's in the mail, we promise.)

The entanglement spectrum

As you might expect, relationships between metamours are diverse, and you can never really know ahead of time how they're going to turn out—they can evolve over time, from distant to close or the reverse. (Your metamour may even become your partner at some point!) But at any point in that journey, they tend to fall into a few broad categories: *parallel*, *networked* and *kitchen table*.

Parallel relationships are treated as very separate. Metamours may know of each other, at least in general terms, but don't have any particular relationship with each other beyond dating the same person, and may never meet unless there's a specific reason to. It also means the polycule doesn't tend to hang out as a group—or at least, that the specific people in the polycule who prefer a parallel style of relating may not be that keen on group polycule events. This does not mean that the metamours are *required* to be distant. One nice thing about nonmonogamy is it allows you to meet other cool people, and as we mentioned, relationships between metamours can shift over time. Of course, even in parallel relationships, it's very helpful for everyone, when they do run into each other, to be *friendly*, even when they are not friends.

Networked relationships are those where metamours enjoy meeting one another and generally get along. Members of the network may plan group outings or events, or a person might invite some or all of their partners to social functions. The people who share a partner are often open to building friendships with one another if the fit is right. Some folks call this approach to metamours *garden party* or *birthday party polyamory*.

Kitchen table polyamory is the term some people use for a network in which the people prefer to have close relationships, and may even consider each other chosen family (some people may even refer to their polycules as *polyfamilies*). The name invokes the idea of sitting down together at a family dinner. Kitchen table polycules can happen organically, when the people a person dates happen to quite like one another. Or they can be prescriptive, where there's a stated expectation that dating one person means being part of the group—or in extreme cases, as we talked about earlier, even dating and having sex with that person's other partners.

In the prescriptive sense, the kitchen table ideal can seem like a way to short-circuit problems with jealousy, time division or fear of abandonment. Unfortunately, it's hard to mandate that two people be close to one another just because they are intimate with the same person. Prescriptive kitchen table polycules tend to have coercion hiding in their closets, either because they make access to a critical intimate relationship reliant on having a specified relationship with others, or because they make access to the support network contingent on continuing an intimate relationship.

Kitchen table polyamory and polyfamily work much better when they happen organically, by inclination and affinity rather than obligation and expectation. And if you're already part of a kitchen table polycule, bear in mind that the weight of expectation to join can be off-putting to anyone new. Slow your roll! Give everyone some breathing room and let their relationships evolve naturally. This is part of what it means when we say that the people in the relationship are more important than the relationship.

Writer Laura Boyle has a great, in-depth series covering the range of polycule styles, from DADT to kitchen table, on her blog *Ready for Polyamory*.

THREE PEOPLE EQUALS FOUR RELATIONSHIPS

Triads and vees can start in any number of ways. (Same with larger multi-person configurations centred on a hinge.) Sometimes several singles come together. Sometimes a couple takes up with a third for some steamy sex and they all realize they want more than just the Saturday-night kind of fun. Sometimes one member of a couple gets involved with someone, and the vee eventually morphs into three-way love. Sometimes a larger nonmonogamous formation is whittled down by breakups, and what's left is three people who remain connected. Regardless of how a triad or vee forms, but especially if it's not a spontaneous collision of three solo people, it's important to keep in mind that each new person you add to the mix changes the terms of the entire equation.

This is most relevant in the couple-plus-one version of triad or vee formation—a common path into the shape, but one that often creates the illusion that somehow the original couple remains unchanged and enduring but with an extra added bonus. But that's rarely how things actually work. You haven't just added a third person to a pair; you've created three new relationships on top of the one pair dynamic you already had. You've now got person A's relationship with the new person, person B's relationship with the new person, and the relationship that happens with the three of you all together. This is true even when the two points of a vee don't (yet) have contact, because they almost inevitably occupy some space in one another's minds by virtue of each showing up in the life of the person (hinge) with whom they're involved.

This whole process can't help but change the way person A and person B relate to each other. Relationships change you. That's just what they do. So the original dyad, if there is one, should expect that and communicate about it accordingly.

Zero-sum and inclusive relationships

People new to nonmonogamy often fear that embarking on this road means giving up time: Every minute that your partner's other partner gets is a minute that you don't get, right? That is often true, but isn't always—depending on how well you and your metamours get along. When you can spend time with your partner together with your metamours, every minute given to your metamours does not necessarily mean a minute taken away from you.

Time management issues can be eased (though never completely solved), or can be exacerbated, depending on how comfortable you all are spending time together as a group and whether you can get some of the same things from group time as you can from dyad time. That is, how much time in your relationship needs to be one-on-one, and how much can be shared activities? Is your time a zero-sum affair, to be carved up among your different partners and other commitments, or are you able to experiment with a more inclusive approach, where parts of your relationships and time are shared?

There is no right answer, though you often hear people forcefully arguing for one approach or another. Each approach has benefits and trade-offs, and some people are simply better suited for one than another. Watch out if you end up in relationships with people who are suited to different approaches—the styles often don't mix well. And even in the closest of polycules, dyad time is important for building intimacy and giving each other focused attention (more on that shortly).

If you assume that your relationships *have* to be inclusive, one of your partners may find themselves spending a lot of time in the presence of someone they don't much care for, or simply aren't drawn to become close with, in order to be with you. This is similar to how sometimes monogamous couples assume that every time one of them receives an invitation, it automatically includes their spouse. This mindset is notoriously hard on friends, family and others who treasure one-on-one time with their loved ones but don't want to say "Can you ditch your partner for one night?" Sometimes, you just need to order pizza and really talk with a bestie, no spouses allowed!

Each person needs to be able to set boundaries without blame. As much as you may crave inclusive relationships, it's not okay to force them. It's also not okay to try to shame or threaten your partners into liking each other, even when you really really really want them to get along. If an important relationship is contingent on any other relationship, this can introduce a strain that is not just about getting along, but about feeling like something deep in you is being violated—a loss of consent. If your partners are to be free from coercion, then separate time, or even complete separation, needs to remain an option.

Of course, there are consequences of such zero-sum relationships. Intimacy will be affected, and you may have to grieve for what is lost when those boundaries are set. Those losses may even include one or more of your relationships. This can be truly heartbreaking. But don't blame. It needs to be okay, in every moment, for your partners to set boundaries—with you, and with each other.

At the other end of the spectrum, metamours may end up on the higher end of the connection scale with one another: a vee that begins to develop a lot of closeness, a full triad, or similar kinds of entwinement. Especially if you started out with a couple-plus-one situation, or any other situation in which two members of a polycule know each other better or have been in each other's lives longer than the new member, it's a good idea to bear in mind the discrepancies in relationship history between each dyad and make communication choices accordingly. So, for example, it's not wrong to reminisce about that awesome vacation the original couple had three years ago, but if you're going to do that, you might want to bring out the photos and make an evening of showing them to the newer person in a way that creates connection rather than making them feel excluded. While you're at it, let that be a good way to start the conversation about the fabulous trips you'd like to take all together, if applicable. Likewise, use your existing in-jokes and habits as pathways into new intimacies with a new person, rather than turning them into shorthand for territoriality over a shared past. This isn't about denying or downplaying history; it's about making sure that history is not used for the purposes of exclusion or one-upmanship, especially since that can happen unintentionally.

Benefits and challenges of metamours

In the best of circumstances, metamours enhance partners' lives, helping them learn and grow in ways they might otherwise not. They provide an extra source of support and strength for your partners, and sometimes for you. They can help negotiate solutions to problems you may not have found an answer for on your own. And they can even end up being people you love very much—up to and including long past the end of the hinge relationship that brought you together in the first place. Your relationships with them can also be complex, painful and fraught in unique ways. The possibilities are pretty much endless, and mononormative society has no words for these relationships. The good news—and the bad news—is that you and your metamours get to make them up entirely by yourselves.

Another of nonmonogamy's invented words is *compersion*. This refers to the happy feeling many people experience in seeing their partners take joy from another relationship. Some people use the word *frubbly* to describe this feeling (as a noun: *frubble*). Different people experience compersion differently: For some it's just a warm glow, while for others, it can be almost as euphoric as being in love. And some people don't experience it at all. It's normal to experience compersion, and it's awesome if you do, but it's also normal never to experience it. Not experiencing it doesn't mean you're deficient, or that you can't still benefit from having metamours in your life.

That said, sometimes people just don't like each other. Columnist Dan Savage has said that all relationships have a "price of admission." The perfect partner doesn't exist. Everyone has some quirk, habit or trait that becomes annoying once you get involved with them. It might be something as simple as leaving dirty socks on the coffee table. Whatever it is, there's always an annoyance or three that you need to be able to get over if you want to be with someone for long.

In the nonmonogamous world, sometimes a person's other partner might be that price of admission. Occasionally, someone you love very much will love someone else very much whom you love not much at all. The best guidelines we can offer are to behave, to the best of your ability, like a reasonable adult when you're around people you don't particularly like; to understand that these people add value to the lives of those you care about; and to seek to be supportive and compassionate toward those your partners love, even if it is not reciprocated.

Nonmonogamous people can sometimes act as though metamour relationships are free. That is, you invest in relationships with your partners, but don't often think of the investment required to maintain relationships with *their* partners. In fact, these relationships can require considerable effort to build and maintain, especially for people who have very busy lives or tend to be introverted. An expectation of close relationships, or even family ties, among your metamours is essentially an expectation that someone will be willing to invest significant time and emotional energy in other people just to be with you.

WHEN METAMOURS MEET

Unless you're very strictly parallel, sooner or later metamours will likely meet. *When* is largely a matter of personal preference. Some people, especially those who prefer kitchen table–style nonmonogamy, like their partners to meet potential new partners right away, before any relationship begins to grow—and many people, likewise, want to meet the established partners of someone they're considering becoming involved with. Others—often people with a more parallel style—prefer to wait until a relationship is taking root, when they're fairly certain that a new person is going to be important in their or a partner's life, before expending the time and energy to meet other partners—particularly if the polycule is large or far-flung. There's no single optimal strategy for when or how (or even if you should) meet your partners' other partners (or their partners, or...). Ask a dozen nonmonogamous folks their approach to meeting metamours, and you'll likely get two dozen answers.

If you're the hinge, you have a few things to consider. First, you can't (and shouldn't) *stop* your partners from meeting, even if you don't feel ready. Trying to dissuade your partners from having contact raises an instant red flag among many nonmonogamous people that something dishonest may be going on, even if it isn't, and lays the groundwork for mistrust. If your partners want to meet, ask for whatever support or setup you need, but if at all possible, don't get in the way. Introducing a new partner to an established partner, or to the rest of your network, is also a meaningful ritual for some. It shows that you value your new partner and consider them important. So it's good etiquette for the hinge to take the initiative and ask the others if they would like to meet. If one of your partners expresses an interest first in meeting the other, be the one to make it happen—whether that means connecting them to each other so they can meet up one-on-one, or organizing a group activity if that's their preference—and make it clear that the meeting matters to *you*, too. How you introduce a new partner to your network can make all the difference in how welcome they feel.

If the first meeting is in a group, be mindful of power dynamics, especially if one relationship is much more established than the other. If you share a home with one partner, will it feel nice to the new partner to be invited for dinner—or will it feel awkward and overwhelming for them to meet your established partner for the first time in the space you share together, and isolating if they have to leave afterward, while you and your established partner stay home? If you're meeting somewhere else, will one dyad be arriving together or leaving together, and how might that feel for everyone involved? How might each of the metamours feel about seeing the hinge be affectionate with the other? Some people don't care about any of these things—and some care a lot. Take the time to find out. Depending on each person's comfort zone, some of these things can be addressed with careful logistical planning, but some might point to the wisdom of the two metamours getting to know each other one-on-one first and letting those emotions settle a bit before trying out a group dynamic.

If a new situation is long-distance and you share a home with a partner, check in with them about whether it's okay for a first meeting to be combined with a romantic tryst at the shared home. Maybe it'd be better to book a hotel for the visit so that nobody has to overhear anyone else having sex in the next room. Some people would be fine with that right away, others might get there once everyone's gotten comfortable with each other and built some trust, and for still others, it might never be okay. Having a new long-distance metamour stay somewhere else could also create more low-pressure one-on-one opportunities for the metamours—but for some people, it could feel excluding. Talk about it!

While a group meeting may sound nice, and may work out fine for some people, sometimes a relaxed coffee between metamours—no hinges allowed—can be the best way to start off on the right foot. And yes, hinges, that means your partners will be meeting without you—and probably talking about you, too! If your partners are going to have a relationship, this is something you'll have to get used to. Hopefully you trust everyone to act in good faith (and if you don't, use your discernment to try to figure out why). But be careful about trying to manage the relationships among your partners. You have enough on your hands already, and after all, they're grown-ups and can take care of themselves. And remember, their relationship is very much not about you, nor does it exist *for* you. There may end up being benefits for you, sure, but try to leave room for them to create the relationship that works for them, too, without expectation or judgment.

If you're an established partner, you may feel a particular kind of trepidation or insecurity about meeting the shiny new person that your partner is into. But remember, you hold a lot of power. You're likely to be more intimidating to that new partner than they are to you. While you see NRE and the excitement of budding intimacy, they see a shared history that is not accessible to them. A new relationship is a time of intense vulnerability for you *and* the new metamour. Treat that vulnerability with kindness and compassion.

If you're a new partner, you may feel your own kind of worry and insecurity about meeting the person your partner has already committed to and invested in. You may want to make a good impression, fear being judged or just not know what to expect. Think about your wants and needs, and talk about them with your partner. They can't guarantee a good first meeting, but they can certainly help put into place the conditions for success based on what they already know about each of you!

Expectation management is key to helping a relationship with a metamour get off to a strong start. Don't expect that because you're both into the same person, the two of you will feel some kind of instant bond. Don't expect immediate intimacy, don't expect to just "get" each other right away, and don't expect instant "family." Your shared partner likes you both, but is that because of your similarities, your differences or both? Will your differences and similarities make you click, or cause you to feel alien to each other? A first meeting may be weird or awkward. Your shared partner may be able to help ease the discomfort, or maybe you and your metamour will bond by making gentle jokes at your shared partner's expense ("Do they always forget to compliment your new haircut, too?"). Either way, do your best to be open and friendly, while paying attention to your metamour's cues. You can't predict how things will go, but you can offer your best efforts. In practical terms, this means seeing your partner's other partner as a person, not a projection of your own fears and hopes. The best approach is the same you might take with a friend of a friend: be open and welcoming, look for shared interests, ask questions. Take the time to get to know them, but without being pushy or intrusive. Make a warm and welcoming space for them, but don't try to force them into it.

Hinge life: When you have multiple partners

When you have more than one partner, at some point you may face the unique joys and challenges that come with being the person in the middle, between two partners. *Pivot* used to be the more common term for this role, but the word *hinge* is more widely used now, so that's mostly what we're using here—although we do switch between them a bit in this book.

There are two main varieties of hinge existence. You may be the person in the middle of two partners who are also partners with one another—a full triad (in which case each one of you is a hinge!). Or you might be the midpoint of a vee, and if that's the case, your partners can range from being (or becoming) good friends to being total strangers, or even—though hopefully not—antagonistic. You may also shift between these two forms: a triad in which one dyad breaks up but the other two remain together turns into a vee, and a vee in which the two points end up partnering with each other turns into a triad. If you're in a vee, the relationship between the metamours may shift over time depending on how open everyone is to becoming closer, and whether there's any natural chemistry and compatibility to work with. Your strategies will of course need to be different according to your situation, so as with anything, when it comes to the thoughts we're sharing here, your mileage may vary!

Triads and vees are in some ways the simplest form of nonmonogamy, but of course you can extrapolate from them to any other configuration that involves one person in the middle: one person with three partners, one person who's part of a triad and also has another partner, and so on. Of course, all of these groups can be part of larger polycules, but for this discussion, we're simplifying to talk about the immediate neighbourhood of the hinge.

In some ways, in being a hinge, you're living the nonmonogamous dream: You get all the benefits of partnership, times two! And you might be having fantastic threesome sex on top of it all! Entire porn genres have been built around the life you are now living. Amazing, right?

Yes! Actually, yes, it is amazing. We're not gonna shoot that down. But while cultural fantasies about threesomes (and moresomes) abound, as with any fantasy, living it out in reality also comes with a hefty dose of, well, reality. The French expression *ménage à trois* is often used in English to refer to threesome sex, but the word *ménage* actually means household (or housekeeping). Indeed, maintaining an actual three-person household or even simply doing the everyday "housekeeping" of maintaining a three-person connection involves lots more than hot sex. Also, of course, not every three-person configuration involves group sex! None of this is necessarily negative, but it is worth talking about what the reality can look like: the unique difficulties that can come up, ways to do preventative maintenance, and so on.

The waters here can be turbulent. Your partners may have contradictory needs, or want the same thing from you at the same time, or end up in conflict with each other. You may find it difficult, when this happens, not to feel pulled in two directions.

Even when your partners are involved with each other in an intimate relationship of their own, there will be times when you're stuck in the middle. Maybe they'll both want your attention, but in different ways or for different reasons. Maybe each has different plans for the day and wants you to participate. This will happen, sure as night follows day. It helps to be prepared.

Of course, this situation isn't unique to nonmonogamy, as anyone with more than one child can tell you. When you're asked to care for, support and cherish two (or more) people who have different ideas and needs, life can be a balancing act. The difference in nonmonogamy is that you're not the boss. You're dealing with self-determining adults, which means "Because I said so!" is not a workable fallback argument. (It's not ideal with kids, either, but that's a different book.) You'll be asked to make decisions that are responsible and that follow your ethical principles while respecting the autonomy of each of your partners.

WHO OWNS YOUR CHOICES?

People talk so much about communication and negotiation in nonmonogamy that it can be easy to forget that the hinge actually holds a great deal of responsibility for *making decisions.* And make them you must. Negotiation is important, but it's also important not to lose sight of the purpose of a negotiation, which is ultimately to make a choice. A choice that upholds your commitments and honours the needs of everyone affected, but a choice nonetheless. Gather data, certainly. Discuss, negotiate, listen and empathize. But then make a decision.

Nearly everyone who's been a hinge has probably done this at least once: running back and forth between your partners, trying to please everyone but rarely making a choice (or worse, making decisions that only last until you see your other partner). It's an easy pattern to fall into. But if it becomes chronic, it will wear you and your partners down and damage trust among all of you.

Shifting responsibility for your choices onto your other partners is cowardly. If your partners buy into this—and many will, because they trust you—you will be able to deflect their unhappiness onto each other instead of you. However, this ploy serves you poorly in the long term, for a couple of reasons. One, taking responsibility for your choices is a sign of integrity, which helps build trust. Shifting that responsibility will, over time, undermine not just your partners' trust in each other, but their trust in you. Two, even if your partners never become close, it's in your interest for them to trust each other and feel safe communicating with one another. Deflecting tensions from their relationship with you onto whatever friction they may have with each other can easily create much more confusion and conflict over the long term.

Your choices are always yours, regardless of whether they make you or your partners happy or unhappy. Own up to them. If you use phrases such as "Blake won't let me," or "Rowan made me," or even "The rules say I have to," you are shifting responsibility. There are certainly more subtle ways of doing this, too, such as hinting to one partner about dire consequences if you displease another partner, or complaining to the first partner about how difficult it is to bring things up with the second—which also invites them to step into a role of rescuer. Overt or covert, the effect is the same. And make sure to refer back to the section on triangulation on pages 131–133.

WHO OWNS YOUR TIME?

One of the assumptions that many people learn from mononormative culture is that in a long-term relationship, especially when you live with a partner, your partner's time becomes "yours" by default. So when they choose to do something social that's independent of you, it can feel like they're taking away something that rightfully belongs to you.

An intimate relationship, even one designated "primary," does not confer ownership of another person's time. When someone gives time to their partners, it is just that—a gift. While promises can certainly be made, and should be honoured, gifts of time in the absence of promises do not constitute entitlements for similar gifts in the future. People can (and should) express their needs and wants, and a skilled hinge will take these into account when choosing how to schedule their time.

Such an approach can benefit you and your partners in a few ways. First, if you start from the premise that you are an autonomous adult responsible for your own allocation of time, your partners will be less likely to see you as a commodity to be fought over. Second, if you start from the assumption that your time is yours until it's shared with someone, this reduces (but doesn't eliminate) the possibility that one partner will see time shared with another as a personal loss.

That said, over time you will probably develop patterns and expectations in a relationship—remember the R, rituals and routines, in HEARTS (page 112)—and it is normal and okay for someone to come to rely on them, as well as on a certain (established and negotiated) level of access. It's also understandable for them to be hurt and confused if those patterns and level of access dramatically change without warning. It's impossible to build a secure relationship (if that's what you're going for) if there is no baseline someone can rely on, or if a partner's availability shifts with the wind. Past patterns can be renegotiated, of course, but—especially depending on the attachment styles of the people involved—it's often kindest to introduce changes gently and with warning, and to allow space for other people to have their feelings about them. At the same time, it's not inherently a betrayal to ask for change in a pattern of relating, and while it's okay for others to feel and express things like surprise, hurt and loss, it's not okay for them to shame or punish you for exercising your agency. As with so many things, it's a balancing act.

INVEST IN EVERY DYAD

Each dyad within a triad or vee (or larger group) needs care. If you're in a full triad, care means that you don't get so wrapped up in your triad that you forget to spend quality time nurturing the relationships you have with each individual person. Triads can be intoxicating: Classic NRE is often exponentially multiplied, and that multiplication can last way past what you might traditionally expect. (Someone should study this, chemically speaking.) If you're in a triad and can't remember the last time you had a one-on-one date, chances are you're coasting on the triad energy but neglecting two dyads.

It's important to make sure that each dyad is actually communicating. Don't assume that if you mention something to one person, it gets magically conveyed to the third. Even if that happens and works well at first, it means you're placing a double burden of communication on one person, a strategy that is bound to occasionally fail (hey, communicating well in just one relationship is challenging enough!), and it means you're essentially relegating the third person to the last spot on the priority chain of information-sharing. Even if you end up repeating yourself on occasion, better to err in that direction than make someone feel like they're always finding things out after the first two, or like you couldn't be bothered to tell them something directly.

Create strategies that work for you. If you're in a vee with partners who are not strongly connected to one another, come up with ways to make sure that you convey important information to each person. For example, when some people tell one partner, "I'm on a business trip for the last two weeks of January," they mentally check the "told partner" box...and forget to tell the other partner as well. This can result in both hurt feelings and logistical snags!

And don't forget about yourself in the process. As a hinge, with all this relationship-nurturing time, it's all the more essential to keep your wits about you and remember that sometimes you need some solitude, too. Spending time on your own, whether that means alone or with friends or colleagues who are not your partners, is an opportunity to breathe, integrate, let everything settle and remember who you are when you're not in the company of one or more partners. Do the "you" things you've always done, just do them with a bigger grin on your face.

Respecting boundaries

Boundaries are important no matter what position you hold in your nonmonogamous configuration. You'll likely encounter three major categories: boundaries for you as a metamour, boundaries for you as a hinge, and boundaries when you're in a larger network and conflict arises that doesn't directly involve you.

BOUNDARIES FOR METAMOURS

If you're in the metamour role, part of treating a partner's other partner as a person rather than as a blank slate for your own fears means respecting some basic boundaries. Intimate relationships provide ample opportunity for you to be invasive and intrusive. We encourage you not to take advantage of these opportunities. Here is a list of some things that will likely be seen as intrusive:

- Spying on your partner or their interactions with your metamours, such as reading their email, logging into their social media accounts, reading their text messages or listening to their phone calls.
- Eavesdropping on other aspects of your partner's other relationships, for example by checking up on your partner's whereabouts or monitoring their activities.
- Calling, texting or otherwise interrupting whenever your partner is on a date. Emergencies happen, and many people like to prearrange check-ins so they know their partners are safe. But beyond that, a habit of constant contact with a partner who's with someone else can quickly become intrusive.
- Oversharing or asking inappropriately intimate questions of a metamour. *Appropriate* is a relative term, and different people have different boundaries around their personal lives. Still, it's good form to pay attention and back off if you're starting to make your metamour uncomfortable. Don't expect a metamour's emotional intimacy with your hinge to automatically transfer to you.
- Copying a metamour in any way that's not invited or consensual, such as adopting their style of dress, makeup or fragrances, giving similar gifts, or doing similar activities with a partner (if you're doing it *because* that's what your metamour did, not because that's something you too enjoy and have always done).
- Turning up uninvited to places you know your partner will be with your metamour.
- Expecting to be included in all their activities, especially intimate ones.
- Disclosing intimate details of your relationship with your hinge without establishing whether that's welcome.

You can't control how your partners' other relationships develop, but you can control how you allow them to intersect with and affect your life. You are allowed to set boundaries on your personal space and time, too. If a metamour is pushing on these boundaries, you may be in a tough position. Depending on the situation and the degree of closeness you have with your metamour, you may be able to deal with them directly without even involving your hinge; you may need to have a three-way conversation with your hinge in the room; or you may need to have a private conversation with just your hinge. The array of possibilities is endless, so we can't advise on every situation, but it's wise to ask yourself not "What would be easiest for me here?" but rather, "What course of action is most likely to produce a successful outcome?" For that, of course, you need to define what "success" means for you. In all cases, avoid triangulation as much as possible—the more direct you can be, the better. And always return to your values and your ethical system.

BOUNDARIES FOR THE HINGE

If you're a hinge, successfully navigating your role requires good boundaries too. When your partners have competing needs or desires, if you don't have good boundaries you can become a prize to be fought over, rather than an autonomous person with decision-making capability and needs of your own. This can happen even when everyone is acting in good faith.

When faced with tension between your partners, the first thing to do is to ask yourself, "Does it involve me directly?" If not, don't assume it's your job to fix the situation, but do understand that you may have a role to play. Check in and see what that role should be! In some cases, metamours can sort things out on their own. In other cases, you really need to be part of the discussion.

An important question is, what do *you* want? When people you love have different ideas or opinions, the question of what you want can easily get lost in the struggle to please others. Moreover, if you're focused on trying to please your partners rather than taking responsibility for your choices, it becomes easy for your partners to focus on *each other* as the reason you're not doing what each of them wants. Advocating for what *you* want when you're being pulled in different directions is a powerful tool to help resolve conflict, contrary to what you might imagine.

Boundaries around communication are another important part of balancing your role as a hinge. We already talked on page 342 about using triangulation to avoid taking responsibility for your choices, but there's another way you can invite triangulation as a hinge. If your partners are in conflict, it's easy to slip into the role of trying to play the mediator, or of "translating" them to each other, especially when they're not both in the room. This is dangerous ground, because you're not allowing them to speak for themselves, and as someone with skin in the game too, you're likely to try to steer them toward an outcome that's best for you, but not necessarily for them. Attempting to mediate can end up estranging them from each other and eroding their trust in you. Their conflicts are theirs to solve—though you're certainly within your rights to sit them both down together and explain how their conflict is affecting *you*, and ask for some boundaries around that.

Part of setting good boundaries as the hinge is to speak only for yourself, not for your partners, as much as possible. In a vee with more distant metamours, you may need to do some of this translation work, but keep a close eye on it so you don't end up preventing a possible connection from forming when you could have enabled one.

BOUNDARIES DURING CONFLICT

If you're nonmonogamous long enough, at some point you may have two or more metamours through one hinge who aren't getting along. This will likely cause pain to the hinge. When that happens, it can be very hard not to want to intervene or take sides.

When people you care about are embroiled in conflict, it's tempting to try to mediate. Maybe you think you can offer some special insight, or that you have enough distance to help everyone see everyone else's point of view. If you have rock-solid relationships with everyone involved, and if you are a skilled negotiator—and able to keep your own emotions in check—you may decide to wade into those waters to try to bring peace to your polycule, and you might actually do some good.

However, maybe you're not an objective mediator; maybe you think someone is right and someone else is wrong. In truth, maybe one person is indeed being unreasonable, even obstinate or manipulative. Maybe your hinge can't see this. Should you share your observations with your hinge, or try to make the unreasonable metamour see the light, or stand by the wronged metamour—taking sides?

We won't say no, but we will say you should tread very carefully here. Taking sides in a conflict between your metamours—or between a metamour and a partner—can amplify rather than attenuate the problem. Your investment in the situation raises the stakes (which may already feel or be quite high), and the metamour you're opposing is likely to become even more entrenched and defensive, lowering the possibilities for a successful resolution. It's also possible that someone is engaging in triangulation, trying to create a "drama triangle" in which they are the victim, you are the rescuer and the third party is the villain. If you are going to be involved at all, it's useful to think about how you can act as an attenuator.

When part of your network is embroiled in a conflict that doesn't directly involve you, probably the most useful thing you can do is listen. We discussed active listening in chapter 7; it's useful here. Offer empathy, without analyzing, fixing or blaming. Many people remain embroiled in conflicts because they desperately need to feel heard. You can help by hearing them. There's also a gotcha here, though. If you're helping your metamours (or partners) by actively listening to them, you may be tempted to start carrying messages between them. After all, they're not hearing each other, right? Maybe they just need some translation help? No! Resist the temptation! If you begin playing messenger, you are likely to *increase* the distance between them rather than decrease it. If they start to rely on you as their interlocutor, it will become harder and harder for them to communicate with each other.

What you *can* do is encourage them to speak directly to one another. If one of them asks for insight about what the other is thinking or feeling, resist the urge to answer, and instead suggest they ask the other person directly. If their conflict is going to be resolved, *they*, not you, will resolve it.

Time management

Time management can be one of the toughest parts of having multiple relationships—for some folks, it's harder than issues like jealousy and insecurity. It also doesn't come naturally to many people.

As with many other nonmonogamy skills, effective time management really comes down to communication. Good communication about time includes being clear about what time commitments you are available for, how much time you need in each relationship (including how much needs to be dyad time, as opposed to group time), how much you need for yourself, and what time commitments you already have. It also includes being very clear about what you are committing to and with whom—which can be harder than it sounds.

Figuring out all the specifics of when you're going to be where and with whom can be a real puzzle. But it can help to see it not as an onerous chore but as a chance to demonstrate care, consideration and creativity.

A wise person once taught Andrea the concept that "logistics is love." If you can see every scheduling conversation as a reaffirmation of your relationship, an occasion for co-creation and a way to make sure each person gets to enjoy quality time with their partners, it can make the operation feel less burdensome. If your polycule leans toward the kitchen table variety, you may even want to make an event out of it: Sit down as a group once per season, let's say, with good snacks and whatever scheduling tools work best for you. Online calendars are convenient, but for some folks, it's all about the cute stickers, highlighters and planner pages! Sketch out the regular commitments that show up routinely every week (classes, child care, date nights) and then address the exceptional stuff (trips, special events, medical appointments, big work deadlines). You might find unexpected synergies—turns out that time-sensitive errand one partner is struggling to squeeze in is right next to another partner's monthly book club meeting! You might also find conflicts that require some care to sort out, but it's certainly better to know well ahead of time whenever possible instead of scrambling to fix it in the moment with frazzled people and hurt feelings.

Many nonmonogamous people set up regular date nights with specific partners. For people who are into scheduling, this is a good tool to help let everyone know what to expect—though, as with everything else, you need to be somewhat flexible. Life isn't always tidy, and should a conflict come up, or a partner become ill or injured, it's reasonable to be able to rearrange the schedule without causing undue grief. As with anything, use judgment: If a long-distance partner comes into town for a week every six months, it's reasonable to expect date night to get rescheduled. Be aware, too, that schedules may need to change permanently to accommodate a new relationship.

Regular date nights are a great way to help nurture any relationship, even live-in ones. They create a setting where the people involved can get back in touch with the intimate part of the relationship, free of distractions like chores, housework and kids. Sometimes nonmonogamy makes this easier; when you have more than two people involved, it becomes easier to trade off one person taking care of the little things that always need taking care of while two others spend time alone together. As long as the same opportunities are available to everyone, and everyone treats one another compassionately and without resentment, scheduled, focused time with each partner helps all the relationships thrive. (It's important, of course, that this not become a "service secondary" issue, as discussed in chapter 11.) You can also get creative here: Perhaps once a month on a rotating basis, one partner plans a surprise date for the other two, or two partners are in charge of making the third person's birthday celebration happen.

Google Calendar has become tremendously popular among non-monogamous people for time management. It's so popular because, unlike a paper day planner or similar tools, it's also a *communication* tool: Calendars can be shared among multiple people, with different levels of access, and several people's calendars can be viewed simultaneously. You can pull up six or seven calendars at once to look for opportunities for dates, shared time and so on.

Google Calendar is so powerful that it requires careful negotiation before you start to use it. Failure to set explicit expectations about the purpose and use of the calendar can lead to serious misunderstandings and hurt feelings. What are your boundaries about what you are willing to share, and how you want your partners to interact with your calendar? Do you want them to see only free or busy times, have read-only access or have editing access? You can schedule private events, which can only be viewed by those with owner-level permissions on your calendar—so even if someone has read or edit access, you can keep some of your life private. When scheduling shared events, do you prefer to have the event added directly to your calendar, or sent to you as an invitation that you can accept or decline?

Shared calendars can also pose a couple of special problems in nonmonogamy. If a person doesn't feel their needs are being met, but sees on their partner's calendar the time they are spending with other partners (or doing other things), this can trigger jealousy. Some people also find it easy to slip into feeling that a partner's unscheduled time should be theirs—it can be easy to forget that time for oneself is just as (or more) important, and is not a snub.

Different people have very different boundaries around sharing calendars and assumptions about what sharing means. For some it's a deeply intimate exchange, while for others it's just a logistical convenience. Folks who practise parallel or solo poly, especially, may be inclined not to share their calendars at all, negotiating dates case-by-case as they would with friends or business associates. Discussing these expectations and boundaries can help avoid misunderstandings and heartache. And you're definitely not required to share with anyone.

TYRANNY OF THE CALENDAR

Some nonmonogamous people treat their calendars like games of Tetris, seeing how much they can pack into a day, week or month. They're scheduled to the hilt. Among nonmonogamous people, you'll often hear complaints like these:

> "I feel like I have to make an appointment to be with my husband."
> "I wish I could be more spontaneous."
> "Sometimes I just really feel like I need to be with Quin, but I have to keep my date with Ari."
> "I'm exhausted. I don't have any time for myself."

Nonmonogamous folks tend to have lots of commitments—not just relationships, but work, projects, volunteering, social lives. You might sometimes end up feeling like all your time is allocated to other people—even like you've lost control over your life. This is another reason why it's important, as we've stressed so many times, to remember that your time is yours, to remember to take time for yourself and to be intentional about whether you really have space for new people.

That said, part of personal integrity is showing up and meeting your commitments. In the flush of a new relationship, it's normal to crave the presence of a new partner almost constantly. Or when you're going through a breakup and are heartbroken, maybe all you want to do is hide in your room watching *Sense8* and eating pints of Ben & Jerry's. It can be difficult to balance your desire to be with someone when your calendar says you need to be elsewhere. Blowing off dates with your long-standing partners—or your kids—to go running through a sunbeam-filled meadow with your new shiny person isn't going to win you points in the integrity department.

And when you're with someone, work on being present with them. They will feel it if you're not, and if it happens enough, it will damage your relationship with them. Maybe someone (or something) else is on your mind, but the person you've committed your time to is in front of you right now.

QUESTIONS TO ASK YOURSELF

Problems between metamours can be as corrosive as problems between partners in nonmonogamous relationships, so they bear careful thought. Here are some questions to ask yourself about your approach to your metamours:

- Do I want to meet my metamours? If so, how and at what point in my relationship with the hinge?
- What kind of support do I want from my partner as I meet my metamour or metamours?
- What are my expectations of my relationships with my metamours? What will I do if I don't get along well with a metamour?
- What would I consider good metamour principles and behaviours to be? What skills do I need to develop or what support do I need to ask for if I want to embody those principles and behaviours?

If you're a hinge, being able to set good boundaries for yourself and advocate for your needs, while also being considerate of your partners, can feel hard. As you build the skills to do this, here are some questions to ask yourself:

- When my partners have competing desires, how do I express what *I* need? How do I make sure my own desires aren't lost in the shuffle?
- How can I best take responsibility for my choices, and make sure I'm not expecting my partners to make them for me?
- What does *fairness* mean to me? How does this affect the way I make choices and interact with my partners?
- What do I value most in each of my relationships? How can I demonstrate this to my partners?
- What mix of group time and dyad time do I prefer? How do my partners feel about that? How do I respect their other time commitments?
- What boundaries do I set for myself in relation to each of my partners?
- How can I best support my partners' relationships with one another in ways that respect their agency and right to choose their level of intimacy?
- What do I do if one of my partners doesn't get along well with another of my partners?

For a moment she saw the two of them as Heaven might: two briefly embodied human spirits, brushing together for a moment during the long dark journey of their life and death and life again.

SHELLEY PARKER-CHAN

20 Sex, Pleasure, Risk and Health

What is sex? It's a notoriously difficult question to answer, and in the context of nonmonogamy, it's...actually not all that important. By all means, explore the theoretical complexities of this question on your own or with your partners if that floats your boat!

The topic of sex is endlessly fascinating to many people, and this one question can lead to rich conversations. (Is masturbation sex? How about kissing? Going to a strip club? Wearing hot shoes? Cuddling naked?) But for the purposes of managing the choices you make within your relationships, it's usually more effective to be able to talk about specific desires, risks, strategies and acts. And that requires a much bigger vocabulary and a much broader set of concepts and questions. That's what we explore in this chapter.

This chapter is *not* going to do a few things.

First, we're not going to teach you sexual techniques. You can find a gazillion how-to guides out there depending on what sorts of things you're into, as well as countless workshops, retreats, online learning platforms, and much more. We'd encourage you to seek out learning from reputable sources, such as the resources offered at your local feminist and queer-friendly independent sex shop. And just as you wouldn't try to learn how to swing from a trapeze by watching a Cirque du Soleil show, we'd discourage you from learning how to have sex by watching porn—not that porn can't be wonderful, but remember, it's designed for entertainment, not instruction.

Second, we're not going to prescribe any particular kind of sex, or frequency, or anything else of the sort. The right kind of sex life is yours to figure out, on your own and with your partners.

Third, we're not going to give you a comprehensive sexual health education. We do raise some key topics and concepts for you to think about, but mostly we just want to convey that it's important for you to take your sexual health seriously. That means turning to trusted sources to find out how to best manage the kinds of risks you're likely to encounter depending on what you like to do in (and out of) bed. This is partly for your own health and well-being, and partly so you can avoid putting your lovers at risk.

Let's talk about sex!

When you don't want sex

Let's make something extremely clear as a baseline: You should never have to have sex when you don't want to. Not to save a relationship (or have access to intimacy at all), not to show you care, and not to get any of your other needs met—financial (note we're not talking about sex work here), emotional or social. Not desiring someone physically isn't a sign that you don't love them. Or that you want to hurt them. Or that there's something wrong with you. It's not even a sign that you're not a compatible partner with them. It just means that, for whatever reason, your body isn't responding to them. And if you don't want it, definitely don't do it.

Mononormative and patriarchal culture instills a number of toxic beliefs about sex and relationships, including:

- You owe sex to someone you're in a relationship with.
- Sexual desire is something that can be offered or withheld at will.
- A lack of sexual desire is, at best, a sign of something wrong in the relationship. At worst, it's a sign of malice.

These beliefs are part of a system of social pressures. One of those pressures is known as amatonormativity, which we discussed in the introduction. Another is allonormativity: the belief that everyone desires sex and experiences sexual attraction, or should. Other "norming" pressures can come into play too, such as heteronormativity (the belief that everyone is or should be heterosexual, or that penis-in-vagina (PIV) is the only "real" kind of sex) and various flavours of gender normativity that pressure everyone to conform to toxic standards of binary gender ("a real man always wants sex," "a wife always gives it to her husband if she wants to keep him around," and so on).

But desire isn't a button you can push. No matter how much you may care for someone, no matter how much you may want to meet their needs, if sexual desire or attraction is not there, it's not there. Yes, some people can work on it, and many couples can work through reduced desire—but many can't, and there's nothing wrong with them. Sometimes you just don't want it—and sometimes you just don't want the person you think you're supposed to want. (And sometimes, of course, you don't even *want* to want it—if it weren't for the social pressure, you'd actually be just fine not feeling sexual desire at all.)

There are two main situations in which people don't want sex. One is when a person is on the asexuality spectrum. The other is when a person is allosexual, but their libido has waned in a specific set of circumstances. That may be because of high stress, illness or some other external context, or it may be a compatibility or relationship issue between specific people. When this comes up in the context of a partnership, it's referred to as desire discrepancy.

We're going to look at each of these situations in turn.

ASEXUALITY

Some people who self-identify as asexual or aromantic find nonmonogamy attractive because it allows them to form intimate, loving bonds without the fear that they'll experience sexual pressure or deprive their partners of the opportunity for a pleasurable and fulfilling sex life. Emotional closeness, support, love, touch and cuddling can all exist independent of sex. Intimate and even romantic relationships without sex are not "merely" friendships. They can and do include passionate emotional intimacy, living together, shared goals and dreams, and lifelong plans.

When an asexual person partners with one or more fellow aces, they may have an easier time negotiating the issue of sex. But due to sheer numbers, it's pretty common for ace people to be in relationships with allosexuals, in which case both or all partners need to take care to negotiate relationship parameters that work for all concerned. Some asexuals are totally sex-averse, meaning they don't want sex of any kind ever at all, while some are willing to have (and even enjoy!) certain kinds of sex under certain circumstances. Whatever understandings you come to, it's crucial that the allosexual partner or partners place no pressure on the ace person to be sexual.

DESIRE DISCREPANCY

Mismatched libidos are pretty common in relationships. Desire discrepancy can come up for a few reasons. Asexuality is one, of course. But it happens even among allosexuals of all genders. Quite commonly, in fact!

A lot of people (across all genders and sexual orientations) have a flawed understanding of how desire works. Far from being a problem that can be solved by taking a pill, low levels of desire are often related to living in stressful contexts where a person's arousal "brakes" are constantly primed and their arousal "accelerators" hard to reach. This can be true at any relationship stage, but it may be particularly noticeable in long-term relationships. In any multi-year partnership, you're going to end up dealing with the sometimes draining and unpleasant realities of everyday life, which are often not so sexy (brakes!), without the counterbalance of all the fresh and exciting hormones that show up in the early stages of sexual relationships (accelerators!). Also, Western society has normalized the idea of spontaneous desire as the only real kind, whereas for a large percentage of people, desire operates in a more responsive way—meaning, context matters a lot. Moreover, people's emotions, desires, fantasies and bodies change over time, especially as they age. Sometimes, a thing you used to love in bed just doesn't do it for you anymore. Sometimes, you discover a new turn-on where you least expect it. Figuring out what you want and like, sexually, is not just a project for young people—it's lifelong.

All this to say that discrepancies in desire are common, in both long-term and newer relationships. And many people, maybe even most people (yes, even the super kinky and adventurous ones!), need to unlearn some of the notions they've absorbed and learn new ones. A fresh perspective and new conceptual tools about sex can work wonders in a relationship if everyone involved is willing to put in the time and effort. A great place to start is Emily Nagoski's fantastic book, *Come As You Are*, which discusses brakes and accelerators and other useful concepts, and her recent follow-up, *Come Together*, which focuses on sex in long-term relationships. Nagoski's explanations of how desire works are based on sexuality research that was largely ignored until her first book brought it to light when it was published in 2015. It's really worth your time to check out her work—it is truly revolutionary.

Desire discrepancy is something you can work on with a partner. You may be able to find workarounds and new ideas to help you deal with "outside" situations such as illness or stress. You may be able to deal with the accelerators and brakes, come up with creative solutions for sexual connection when you're dealing with the limitations of your bodies at this time, even redefine and expand what "sex" means to you altogether. However, desire discrepancy can also come up because of eroded or broken trust, communication problems or other relationship issues. In these cases, lack of desire is a symptom of something deeper that might need other kinds of work, for example in a therapist's office rather than in bed. Each situation is different, and we believe it's worth digging in to find out what yours in particular is all about before you try to "spice up your sex life" with new toys or adventures. If it turns out that all you need is a vacation and a vibrator, great! But you might also, or instead, need to prioritize a lot of talking and tenderness, process unresolved conflict or heal festering emotional wounds, or develop and practise new communication skills.

It is also possible, sometimes, for someone to find they are not attracted to their partner at all—either because they never really were, or because of some physical, chemical or hormonal change that caused a once-strong attraction to go away. Long-term conflict or relationship toxicity can also permanently extinguish attraction. In that case, still another kind of conversation is in order, concerning whether the relationship should become nonsexual or transition out of partnership completely.

Is nonmonogamy a solution for desire discrepancy?

In monogamy, a romantic partner and a sexual partner are, almost by definition, the same person. Emotional intimacy and physical intimacy are so tightly entwined that some self-help books speak of "emotional infidelity" and encourage married couples not to permit each other to become too close to their friends. Advice columnists and television personalities will speak gravely of the dangers that "emotional affairs" pose to a monogamous marriage and ask, "Is emotional infidelity worse than sexual infidelity?" Monogamy can leave surprisingly little room for close friendships, much less for nonsexual romances or other kinds of intimacy.

This creates problems for asexuals and for couples whose members are no longer sexually attracted to one another or have mismatched libidos. If your romantic partner is also expected to be your only sexual partner, and furthermore you are expected to want sex automatically as part of wanting romance, what happens when sexual compatibility isn't there? What do you do when one person is unwilling or unable to be sexual with the other? In cases like this, monogamy struggles. It seems on the face of it absurd to tell another person "I'm not okay with you having your sexual needs met by anyone but me, and I won't meet your sexual needs," but that's precisely what happens. The monogamous person with unmet sexual needs faces a set of choices: pressuring, coercion, cheating or celibacy.

Even when a good monogamous relationship is nonsexual through mutual choice, it is often treated dismissively, if not derisively. "You and your spouse haven't had sex in two years? Oh, I'm so sorry. That must be awful! What's wrong?"

One of the advantages of nonmonogamy is that it does not mean hitching all your sexual wagons to a single star. It allows room for change that would threaten the existence of many monogamous relationships. An emotionally satisfying, deeply committed, loving open relationship between two people who are, or have become, sexually incompatible can still flourish. However, the situation demands a careful approach. Sometimes, nonmonogamy can present solutions, for instance by creating space for partners with higher desire levels to explore without placing pressure on lower-desire partners to join in or keep up. At the same time, it's important to not default to the "if the relationship isn't working, just add more people!" approach, which can do a lot of harm to everyone concerned. As we discussed in the last section, desire discrepancies within a relationship can be a signal not that naturally occurring difference is rearing its head, but that something particular to that relationship needs work. Even when two people bring their natural differences to a relationship, discrepancies can still often be bridged if both people take the time to understand each other's needs and figure out how to create the right contexts for desire to flourish. So if you simply throw your hands in the air and say "Our desires are just too different, guess we better stop trying!" you can end up turning away from a sexual relationship that could have been deeply satisfying if you'd only made the effort.

Alternatively, you may stay in relationships that really should come to an end, distracting yourself with new and shiny people while letting your existing partnership starve to death instead of dealing with problems head-on. The further danger is that you may end up treating new partners like sex toys or desire-fulfillment machines. You might start hopping from adventure to adventure, or gorging yourself on all the happy hormones that come with NRE. In cases like this, nonmonogamy can end up looking a lot like serial monogamy, just with some overlap time during which one relationship withers on the vine while the next one gets all the water and sunlight.

Remember, too, that needs aren't necessarily transitive. What you need from one partner can't necessarily be given by someone else. For some people, sexuality is an expression of intimacy and love; such people may need to be sexual or romantic with all their intimate partners, and if that expression isn't available, it may damage a relationship.

Another painful situation can arise when a couple thinks they have mismatched libidos, but after opening their relationship, they discover that one of them just wasn't that attracted to the other—because they may actually have a very high libido with another person or other people. That can be extremely hurtful for the person who had previously been viewed as the higher-libido partner but was in fact, it turns out, just undesired. This situation plays into a common fear that opening a relationship will result in a breakup because someone "better" comes along. The truth is, this same issue can come to a head in monogamous relationships that haven't opened up: A supposedly low-libido partner may suddenly find themselves wildly desirous of someone else at any point. They may then cheat, or they may simply end their current relationship and pursue a new one. Or they may keep it to themselves and suppress it to stay in their established relationship—which can sometimes be okay, but often will simply create tension and disconnection. Becoming nonmonogamous can be a catalyst for this problem to come to light, but it's rarely the sole cause. Regardless of how they got to this point, the couple may have some tough choices to make about whether to stay together or part ways in light of this new information.

So if you're in a partnership where there's a discrepancy in desire, is nonmonogamy the solution (or part of the solution)? Possibly! But we'd encourage you and your partner to take a long and careful look before leaping in so that you don't find yourselves just compounding your difficulties.

Emotions

Sex can bring up powerful emotions—both negative and positive. There can be enormous vulnerability in baring your body, touching another person and being touched, and allowing yourself to explore the unknown or be seen as you experience pleasure. In its best moments, sex can elicit feelings of satisfaction, closeness, silliness, fun, excitement, release, catharsis, even transcendence. In its more difficult ones, you can feel awkward, anxious, uncomfortable, disconnected, sad, angry, ashamed or fearful. You can also map a lot of meaning onto sex. It can symbolize security, love, desirability, worth, competency and much more, which means a lot is riding on it going well.

This intensity and complexity of emotion (to say nothing of sensation!) can be one of the big reasons people are drawn to having sexual encounters and relationships, but it also brings with it a level of risk—partly for yourself, and partly for the person or people you're having sex with. A great deal of ink has been spilled on the topic of sex, and distilling it all here would be an impossible task. Mostly we want to emphasize that regardless of what emotions and meanings sex brings up for you, whether you're an experienced sexual adventurer or really new at a lot of things, it's worth giving yourself and your partners a lot of gentleness, compassion and time as you explore them.

You may discover that you have a lot of curiosity or want to learn new things—skills, techniques, approaches. This may be for your own reasons or because you find yourself interested in or partnered with someone who has a really different outlook on sex, or a different set of experiences or preferences, than you do. Learning about sex can be a rich and exciting project, and a lifelong one. And nonmonogamy does attract some people with above-average appetites for sexual adventure, including kink, group sex and more. Just remember that while nonmonogamy might expose you to new paths and pleasures, you're not obliged to follow or partake in all of them. Nonmonogamy is not only for the adventurous. Explore at will, but remember that it's okay to just not be interested in some things. In the kink world, there's the concept of the "squick"—meaning a kink that totally grosses you out, but that you're not judging to be bad. It's a handy concept for all kinds of sex that aren't kink, too. Just because you don't enjoy a thing doesn't mean there's anything wrong with you, or that you're against others enjoying it. It just means you don't want to do it, whether for now or forever, with a specific person or with anyone at all.

You may also realize that sex brings up some troubling emotions for you. If so, we encourage you to seek out healing in whatever form feels the most accessible and right for you, whether that's self-exploration, classic therapy, sex therapy specifically, new kinds of exercise or physical self-care, or any other kind of work that helps you heal.

Two of the most common difficulties that can come up when exploring sex and sexuality are shame and trauma triggers.

SHAME

According to sex therapists Lauren Fogel Mersy and Jennifer A. Vencill in their book *Desire*, sexual shame is "the worry that some part of us is unacceptable, wrong, or bad in the eyes of others," and the feeling that something about us will make others reject us. They say there are two major sociocultural roots for this kind of feeling. The first is a lack of adequate sex education—which is sadly all too common today in most countries. Despite the wealth of research and knowledge available, many school jurisdictions provide inadequate sex education or none at all, mostly for political or religious reasons. As far as the United States is concerned, Mersy and Vencill blame religious-right purity culture for much of this, but the problem extends well past the realm of evangelical influence. Around the world, sex ed curricula (when they exist at all) are often shaped by values that have nothing to do with scientific accuracy or an imperative to set young people up for a lifetime of sexual health and well-being and consensual pleasure. They also frequently exclude queer and trans people from the materials entirely, leaving tons of young people ashamed and in the dark even compared to their peers' limited learning. As a result, lots of people end up feeling scared of sex, ashamed of their bodies, unaware of how to experience pleasure or communicate clearly about their limits and desires, and set up with inadequate or inaccurate information about safer sex.

If that describes your own experience of sex ed as a teenager, you are not alone! The good news is that there are tons of resources available for you to learn from. The slightly less good news is that it's entirely up to you to seek out this knowledge and challenge yourself to rethink (or unlearn) the things you learned early on. Check out the resources at the back of this book for a few starting points, or pay a visit to your local sex-positive, feminist sex shop to see what they recommend.

The second factor that gives rise to shame, according to Mersy and Vencill, is "an inability to speak openly and honestly about sexual health topics." Which of course ties in directly to the first factor. If you're not taught about sex in a shame-free, accurate way, especially if you're also told it's bad and wrong, then it may be really intimidating to say anything about it—even when talking with someone you're having sex with! Getting comfortable with talking about sex is a really great step toward taking good care of your own health and the health of the people you have sex with. It might be terrifying at first, but it's worth working on. If you're new to this, or just want to improve your sex conversations, you may want to check out the book *Sex Talks* by Vanessa Marin with Xander Marin (it's not geared for nonmonogamous people, but it's still got good tips), or work with a coach or sex therapist, alone or with one or more partners.

TRAUMA

Statistics tell us that half of all women and nearly a third of men have experienced some kind of physical sexual violence in their lifetime. In addition, trans, gender-nonconforming and queer people are subjected to atrocious levels of violence, much of it gender-based or sexual in nature. Not every experience of violence leads to long-term physical or emotional trauma symptoms, but given these high numbers, it's not surprising that a lot of people's experiences of sex and sexuality are shaped by trauma. And that's not even counting the common experiences of sexual harassment, stalking, catcalling and general objectification that many people are subjected to, especially but not only women. Or the additional levels of violence and discrimination experienced by people with disabilities, Black people, Indigenous people and people of colour, as well as the many people who live at the intersections of multiple oppressions.

What does all this mean, practically speaking? A lot of things, but two in particular stand out.

First, you, yourself, may have trauma (sexual or otherwise) that affects how you engage in sexual relationships and how you have sex. In their book *Cultivating Connection*, therapist Sander T. Jones explains that post-traumatic stress disorder (PTSD) "results in real, physical changes in brain structure" which are "in some ways beneficial and adaptive when a person is living in a dangerous environment." They write,

> The resulting symptoms—hypervigilance, hyperarousal, avoidance, and multiple forms of dissociation—help a person survive, function, and avoid additional trauma when living in an ongoing trauma-inducing environment [but] when we leave traumatizing environments and move to safer environments, symptoms that were once adaptive [...] can be maladaptive and become additional sources of pain.

For this reason, they encourage healing in a way that involves "developing peace, happiness, and functionality that doesn't attempt to deny the powerful changes of our life experiences."

If you have trauma, you may already have done a lot of healing, or you may be at the beginning of your journey. We can't prescribe a course of action for you, but we do want to say that you're worth the time and effort it takes to heal. Nonmonogamy can reopen old wounds, but it can also provide additional support and care as you undertake or continue this work, whatever it may be for you.

The second thing is that even if you don't have sexual trauma yourself, there is a good chance that at some point in your journey, you may partner or have a sexual encounter with someone who has. So it's worth learning more about how trauma affects people's emotions, bodies and communication, and how to be a sensitive partner to someone who manages trauma triggers. Some great places to start are Jessica Fern's book *Polysecure*, Jones's *Cultivating Connection*, or JoEllen Notte's *The Monster Under the Bed* for a great discussion of how mental health concerns can affect sex.

Consent, boundaries and communication

Sex is the erotic experience or exchange that happens within all participants' boundaries and subject to all participants' consent. You may communicate about it a lot or not very much, and you might enjoy it a lot or not very much—sex can be a messy affair in which you make mistakes, learn about yourself and others, and figure out how to make the best of things when they go wrong. Bodies are messy and leaky, furniture can break, sex toys can go on the fritz, safer sex supplies can fail, and you might run out of lube or get a phone call from one of the kids at exactly the wrong moment. You might also encounter a boundary or trigger you didn't know was there, in yourself or someone else, and have to navigate that in the moment with as much care and sensitivity as possible. But if everyone involved communicates clearly and respects each other's boundaries and consent, it tends to reduce the potential for damage and boost the potential for pleasure and connection, even when life interferes.

CONSENT

A lot of people aren't familiar with this legal definition of consent. It's a lot stricter than many might expect! For that reason alone, we think it's worth setting it out here.

In Canada, the law is very clear in stating that sexual activity requires an affirmative, voluntary agreement to be considered consensual. That means consent is active, not silent or passive, and not just a failure to say no. The law also makes it clear that consenting to one act doesn't mean you're consenting to everything else someone might want to do with you. It also says that if you don't have the full capacity to give consent—say, if you're drunk or high or asleep, or your judgment is otherwise impaired—then your consent isn't considered valid. It also doesn't count as consent if the other person uses their position of power or authority to coerce you into a yes.

But legalities aren't the only important thing. Among other things, they tend to be based on the idea that everyone holds equal negotiating power, except in cases where someone is in a position of official power or authority over someone else (say, a teacher and a student). This is what might be called a "liberal" notion of equality under the law. This legal framework, robust as it may be, fails to account for differences along the lines of social privilege: for instance, if one person is physically disabled and another not, or if one person is more sexually experienced or better known in a given community. You can think critically about these kinds of power differences and negotiate with them in mind; you can do better than just respecting the law. Finally, the legal framework does not address the murky areas of misunderstandings, activity that was consented to (even enthusiastically) but that caused harm anyway, and re-evaluation of your experiences as you grow and learn. As A.V. Flox writes:

> In a legal model, even one that attempts to expand our understanding of consent like affirmative consent does, there is no space for people to reflect on what they've done and honor the evolution of their feelings about it or their partner in a wider context. This is because the legal model of consent is one that primarily focuses on whether static rules are being broken, rather than one that centers on the individuals, who are by nature dynamic.

Robin Bauer, a scholar who studies dyke and queer BDSM communities, calls for people to establish what he calls critical consent. He defines this as "an active, ongoing collaboration for the mutual benefit of all involved, helping to establish and maintain each participant's own sense of integrity." A critical consent approach, as he explains it, comes with a heightened sense of responsibility, the willingness to be accountable for the consequences of your actions, and a sense of increased sexual agency that's not based on pretending that social hierarchies and norms don't exist. Rather, he calls for people to work together on critical consent practices, "for instance through the insight that, for consent to be valid, actors do not need to be equal (which is practically impossible), but do need to be able to access negotiating power in that particular situation."

Practically speaking, that means you need to acknowledge the power differentials between yourself and the partners you're having sex with, and then negotiate in full awareness of those differences. So you're not just going for a yes-or-no kind of conversation, or even a "yes to this, no to that" one. Instead, you're looking to notice, speak out loud about and work with your differences. You might try to have conversations about what kind of setup and activities would make an inexperienced person feel safest when having sex with a more experienced person, establish a safe caller (someone to check in with at a specific time during or after a date) and other agreements for a person who's about to go home with a stranger, or have explicit discussions about race or gender as they affect what you want to do with each other in bed. You might discuss intentions, types of touch, roles, or what sort of feelings you're hoping to experience: "I'm having a sad day but I'd really like to have some skin time with you, so let's make this a gentle and soft experience," for instance, or "People treat me with kid gloves because of my disability, but I'm quite strong and want my partners to see and feel that aspect of me, so it would feel great to go rough!"

BOUNDARIES AND COMMUNICATION

We've discussed boundary-setting in several chapters of this book, including chapters 2 and 3. We won't repeat all the general concepts here, but of course sex is another place where boundaries come up. Those boundaries may be emotional, such as needing certain accommodations for trauma triggers or checking in before certain kinds of touch, or physical, such as asking that your partners use condoms or gloves for certain acts or respect your physical limitations around pain or disability. And just as anywhere else, your boundary is about what you will permit to happen—not about controlling another person's behaviour. So for example, you can say "I won't have PIV sex with you if you're having unprotected PIV sex with others," because that's about your own risk tolerance. But it's no longer boundary-setting when you say "You're not allowed to have PIV sex with anyone but me"—that's crossing the line into imposing rules on others' behaviour.

To set sex-related boundaries, it helps to know what you like and don't like, and to be able to tell a sexual partner about those things. But how do you figure out what you like and don't like? Do people come preprogrammed with that knowledge? In some cases, yes, in the sense that you can feel disgust or desire toward a particular act (or person) without having direct experience to back it up or confirm it. A great example is sexual orientation. People often know, even in childhood, that they're drawn to others of a certain gender presentation, and this knowledge is valid and real. That doesn't mean what you like is always stable and never changes, but it does mean that some major features of your desires may be clear to you long before you confirm them through direct experience.

But in a lot of cases, you find out what you do and don't like by trial and error. This is the beauty and magic of sex: It's an opportunity to take a leap of faith, extend trust to someone, and experience things, whether for the first time or the three thousandth, without ever being able to fully predict what it's going to be like. It's also part of what makes sex emotionally and physically risky. And it's part of why any advice on how to communicate about sex needs to take into account the things that you might simply not be able to know going in. There always needs to be room for everyone to say, "Yikes! That doesn't feel the way I thought it would; I need a time-out!" or the equivalent.

That means that good communication about sex needs to happen before, so that you can establish boundaries and desires together; during, so that all involved have the ability to keep each other in the loop about what's going on while sex is happening; and after, to whatever degree is appropriate to the relationship.

Gaining strong communication skills is a long-term project. You might want to work with a coach or therapist, read self-help books and practice techniques, or even take classes, such as for active listening or other approaches. You might learn techniques and concepts from the kink world, such as speed negotiation, safewords and other tools. You might seek out knowledge about body language and start asking your partners things like "I'm noticing that you're holding your breath—is that a good thing, or does it mean you're not enjoying this?" (Body language does not trump a verbal yes or no, but it does give you more information to work with.) And you can definitely benefit from doing self-exploration, because the more in tune you are with your own needs and desires, the more likely you are to be able to express them accurately.

Another kind of sex-related boundary is that everyone has a right to privacy about the details of the sex they have. There's no hard-and-fast line that clearly separates one person's right to be informed from another's right to privacy; setting these boundaries requires compassion and negotiation. Certainly, you have the right to know about your partner's sexual activities with other people in general terms, especially to the extent that it could affect your sexual health, but at the same time, the details of sexual acts are things that your partner and their partners can reasonably expect to keep to themselves if they don't want to share them.

As with anything else, talk about privacy with everyone you're involved with. People can have remarkably different ideas about what privacy means and how it should be respected, and trust can easily be broken if there's a misunderstanding. Proactive conversation is a good idea! Refer back to the discussion on privacy on pages 266–267.

Bodies: What kind and how many

Sex is real no matter what kind of body you have, and no matter how many people are doing it. All bodies are good bodies! Fat and skinny, disabled and nondisabled, tall and short, old and young, of every race and ethnic background, and across the entire spectrum of gender: People in all these groups have sex. You don't need to look a certain way or be a certain type of person to enjoy sex.

Of course, desire is political. People in marginalized groups often report that they get fewer matches, hookups and dates than people from more privileged groups, and are more often fetishized for their attributes instead of seen as whole human beings. People's specifications on dating apps may be racist, transphobic, ageist or fatphobic. And because of all this, people in some groups aren't encouraged to even see themselves as sexy or potentially desirable at all. If that describes some of your experience, you're not alone. You may want to read some tailored guides or other resources, listed at the back of this book, or take part in a supportive sex-positive community that's focused on your particular intersections of experience. As well, women (trans and cis) are subjected to unrealistic beauty standards and impossible dichotomies (you're either a prude or a slut!), while men (trans and cis) often must grapple with the ideals of toxic masculinity holding them to their own unrealistic standards of appearance and telling them they're not supposed to have emotions, be gentle, feel responsive rather than spontaneous desire, or feel anything erotic anywhere but their genitals. No book is going to solve these many intersecting problems, but it's still worth noting that taken together, pretty much everyone is subjected to one or more of these harmful frameworks. And yet, as that terrible early '90s song goes, people are still having sex. You might be one of them—or you could be!

Solo sex, i.e., masturbation, is a great way to get to know your own body and what feels good. It can be entirely for your own pleasure, but it's also very handy (ha!) for figuring out how to show or tell a partner what you like. You may also explore written or visual erotica or porn to help figure out what turns you on, or use sex toys to experience sensations that you can't get from just your hands.

Partnered sex with one other person can involve a huge range of practices. Maybe you're doing long-distance sex when your partner isn't in the room with you (sexting, phone sex, video calls or more). Maybe you're in person, but masturbating across the room from each other or connecting through a shared fetish or kink activity that doesn't require you to take your clothes off. Or maybe you're naked and touching each other, which may include mutual masturbation, oral sex, penetration of various orifices or any number of other fun things. *It all counts.* Unfortunately, a lot of people are taught that the only "real" sex is the kind that involves a penis going into a vagina. That's totally untrue—just for starters, that definition excludes many kinds of sex that queer people have!—and it can really get in the way of pleasure. For example, if a cis man is not able to get an erection, does that mean he can't have sex? Not in the least! He can stimulate his partner in tons of other ways (fingers, hands, mouth, toys) and receive pleasure too. Similarly, if a person who likes to be penetrated isn't able to for whatever reason (temporary or chronic pain, disability, symptoms of illness or menopause, and so on), that doesn't mean the end of sex. It just means they need to find workarounds and get creative.

None of this is particular to nonmonogamy, of course. But when you're nonmonogamous, it does help to expand your idea of what sex is, and what it can be to you, because the presence of more than one partner in your life may present you with new sexual situations that don't follow the patterns you're familiar with. Also, we're all only temporarily able-bodied, and we're all aging, so our bodies can and will change over time. To maintain robust and enthusiastic sexual connections over time, we can all stand to do a little rethinking of what counts, and what we can do to give and receive pleasure.

Group sex is, in some ways, the classic nonmonogamous sexual experience. Justin Lehmiller from the Kinsey Institute surveyed over four thousand people for his book *Tell Me What You Want* and found that the single most popular fantasy was multi-partner sex, whether threesomes, foursomes or more. In fact, at least 85 percent of his respondents said it was one of their fantasies! So if this is something you're interested in, you've got plenty of company. But of course, that doesn't in any way make it mandatory just because you're exploring nonmonogamy. It might not be your thing at all, and that's okay! Group sex works best when everyone's into it—which shouldn't need to be said, but unfortunately, sometimes one partner really wants to experiment with it and another one goes along to please them. That can work out, but it can also be disastrous. If you're looking to engage in group sex with an established partner, it's worth having some pretty in-depth conversations ahead of time about your fears, desires, expectations and boundaries so that you can best enjoy the experience. Of course, you'll want to negotiate the basics with the additional person or people you engage with, too. There are some really cringey (and shockingly homophobic) threesome guides out there, but Stella Harris's book *The Ultimate Guide to Threesomes* is a good one if you're looking for an overview.

No matter what kind of sex you're having or want to have, it helps to know your boundaries and communicate clearly with your partners about your desires and how you want to manage the risks that come with your chosen activities.

Risk assessment

Fact: You are terrible at objectively assessing risk. So are we, and so is everyone you're likely to meet. Our brains are poor at evaluating real risk vs. perceived risk. We fear riding in airplanes, but get into cars, which are a more dangerous way to travel, without a second thought. Our emotional assessment of risk is strongly skewed toward spectacular but unlikely scenarios (sharks!) and biased away from situations where we feel a sense of control (lighting a match). Our brains are also terrible at understanding probability, which leads us to irrational decisions. For example, if you drive 15 kilometres to buy a lottery ticket, you are far more likely to be killed in a car crash getting there than to win the lottery. Furthermore, research has demonstrated that our perception of risk is collective; it relies more on the particular social group we are part of than on the actual level of risk.

This inability to assess risk applies just as strongly to sexual health as to anything else in our lives. We fear AIDS but not hepatitis, even though hepatitis is more common and kills more people worldwide every year. Add to that the stigma associated with sexual health, and it's no surprise that realistic assessment of sexually transmitted infection (STI) risk is difficult. We tend to treat someone who has had gonorrhea very differently than someone who has had strep throat, even though both are bacterial infections that are sometimes antibiotic-resistant, sometimes dangerous, but generally treatable.

Many people react with horror to a disclosure that someone has something common like herpes. Many people say, "I would never even consider a partner with herpes!" even though, ironically, perhaps half (or more) of the people who say that actually have herpes themselves and just don't know it. Depending on where you live in the world, anywhere from 50 to 90 percent of the population has HSV-1 (typically oral herpes) or HSV-2 (typically genital herpes), but the vast majority of those people are not aware they have it. Many of these people are asymptomatic or have one outbreak, easily missed, and never have an outbreak again.

In another example of perceptions versus reality, people often see kink as being a grab bag of high-risk practices—so much so that BDSM communities over time, in their own defense, have evolved a strong emphasis on teaching and promoting risk awareness, safety techniques, communication tools (such as safewords) and political messaging to mitigate the stigma associated with the idea that kink is dangerous. While BDSM practices come with real risks that must be taken seriously, many of the most popular ones aren't high-risk at all. For instance, you would have to work very hard to do major physical damage to a person with a spanking, a flogging or a boot worship scene, or by wearing most fetish gear. Such practices don't come with risks of STI transmission or pregnancy; they're not even as dangerous as most team sports. You might experience some bruising. Meanwhile, penis-in-vagina sex comes with the risk of both STI transmission and pregnancy, each of which can have lifelong consequences or even, in some cases, lead to death—but how often do you hear people suggest that anyone who's into PIV sex is a dangerous weirdo who should be avoided?

In a third example, choking is a practice that kink communities recognize as quite dangerous, so much so that it's been the source of acrimonious debate for decades with no clear resolution. Some BDSM educators say it should never be done at all, while others insist that taking a harm reduction approach is better than simply banning it at kink gatherings. Few deny that it's one of the ways a person can quickly kill or injure someone by accident, even if they're being watchful. (In Victoria, Canada, where Eve works as an emergency sexual assault response volunteer, choking is one of very few scenarios in which a visit to the hospital is mandatory.) But in the last decade, choking has become a stock element in mainstream porn, and from there has made its way into hookup culture and college-age dating—one article refers to it as a "Gen Z hookup trend." And even when both participants agree that it was consensual, they acknowledge it's often done without any negotiation beforehand, or any knowledge at all about safety or risk.

On top of our skewed perceptions about the risks of specific practices or of specific STIs, our emotional perception of risk makes us likely to rate risk higher when we have no direct benefit from it than when we do. This means that you're likely to feel more afraid when a partner has other sexual partners than when you have other sexual partners yourself, even if the risk profile is the same, and even though you have an extra degree of separation from your partner's sexual partners.

Like driving a car or climbing a ladder, there is no way to guarantee sex will be absolutely safe. Even if previously celibate people start a totally monogamous relationship, that is not a guarantee. Many nominally sexually transmitted infections, including herpes and human papillomavirus (HPV), are often transmitted nonsexually as well. For example, more people contract herpes 1 (often expressed as oral cold sores) by nonsexual means than by sexual means, usually during childhood. And by far the riskiest infection today, in terms of prevalence and likelihood of long-term damage, is COVID-19, which is transmitted in a wide variety of social (and sexual) situations, and which, regrettably, few people anymore take even the most nominal measures to prevent or negotiate around.

Given that sex carries some degree of risk, the real question isn't "How can we be totally safe?" but rather "What level of risk is acceptable?" Different people have very different answers.

Negotiating risk tolerance

When talking about safer-sex boundaries and risk tolerance, remember there's no one right answer. Everyone's threshold of acceptable risk is different, and people use different metrics for assessing risk. For example, if you have a compromised immune system, you might be very conservative with risk-taking concerning sexually and nonsexually transmitted infections. The same might be true if you're a single parent or living on a low income and have to reduce the likelihood of getting ill as much as you possibly can, because you don't have much of a financial cushion or the ability to take time off work. Or maybe you've had a previous experience of being seriously ill and have vowed to never repeat it if you have any say in the matter.

Everyone must decide on the degree of physical risk they are willing to accept in their own sex and relationship lives. This decision is an important part of acting with agency. Each person is responsible for protecting their own health, and that includes making decisions about what risks they will accept. Part of that decision will be emotional, and that's okay.

Just as you have the right to choose your own level of acceptable risk, so do others. Shaming other people for their choices is not good behaviour. This includes shaming people for making choices that are not only more conservative than yours, but also less conservative. It's fine to choose not to be involved with someone whose risk threshold is higher than yours, but that doesn't make such a person untrustworthy, reckless or foolish. When you contribute to the stigma surrounding sexual choices and STIS, it's actively harmful. Shame is one of the key factors that prevents people from seeking out testing and treatment, so the less shaming you do, the more likely people around you will take better care of their health.

Fluid bonding: It's not a thing

One idea you're likely to come across in nonmonogamous circles is that of the fluid bond. Essentially, the idea is that once you've all shared STI test results and discussed risks and so on, you might agree to have unbarriered sex with one or more partners (meaning you don't use condoms, dental dams or gloves), creating a "bond" that allows you to share bodily fluids without worry among yourselves. To maintain that worry-free zone, you all agree to use protection with others with whom you are not fluid bonded.

Unfortunately, while it's a popular concept, fluid bonding is not a *scientific* concept. Why? A bunch of reasons! To begin with, it's based on the kind of advice that doctors often give to patients based on assumed monogamy: the idea that once you've settled down in a stable partnership, you're only dealing with two people's bodies, fluids and behaviours. But even monogamous people transmit STIS to each other. Even if two people who've never had sex before decide to become a monogamous pair and stay that way for life, they may each bring in viruses that are transmissible by sexual means. And how many of us show up in a monogamous relationship with zero previous sexual experience? It's vanishingly rare today.

Next, many STIS are transmitted in ways that don't involve bodily fluids. For example, genital warts spread via skin-to-skin contact, so using barriers offers only partial protection unless those barriers cover the entire genital area—which condoms and dental dams don't. In another example, mpox also spreads via skin-to-skin contact, often around the genitals, but also any other skin. When mpox outbreaks began to occur in North America in 2022, they hit gay men's communities in particular—but some guys contracted it without having sex, simply from spending time at bars where people brushed against each other in close quarters. Outbreaks occurred in elementary school classrooms for that same reason.

Third, getting a slate of negative STI tests doesn't guarantee that you have zero STIs. Your doctor will likely recommend what to test for based on what "risk groups" you belong to—and even if you ask, some insurance won't cover certain tests outside those risk groups. For example, in many places it's not recommended to test for HPV in people under 30 or who don't have a cervix, in part because HPV is common and often goes away on its own. There is also a range of less common STIs, as well as ones for which tests are not routinely conducted or for which testing is not always of great practical use. For example, a herpes swab might (but won't always) tell you if a sore you have is caused by a herpes virus, but that doesn't help if you don't have any sores; many people are asymptomatic. You can get a herpes blood test, which might (but won't always) tell you if you've been exposed to the virus, but the blood test can't tell you if a specific sore you have is caused by herpes, and you can transmit the virus even if you never have a sore anywhere.

Lastly, fluid bonding doesn't take into account the three elements involved in STI transmission: the virus in question, the bodily fluid in question, and the specific behaviours you engage in. For example, the insertive and receptive partners in anal sex are at very different degrees of risk for HIV transmission. And it's easier to transmit hepatitis C through blood than through sexual fluids, meaning you're more likely to catch it from borrowing someone's razor than from engaging in oral sex with them—but razor-sharing isn't usually part of the fluid bonding discussion.

Beyond all this, consider also that fluid bonding won't protect you from other kinds of viruses that also transmit between people in close contact—everything from the common cold to COVID-19, which you can share by breathing each other's air. As we well know at this point, common airborne viruses can inflict lasting harm and even be deadly. It's entirely possible to fully respect a fluid bond, but still pick up a virus at the grocery store that can have devastating consequences for your whole polycule.

None of this is meant to discourage you from coming up with agreements about safer sex that make sense between you and your partners. Rather, we want to encourage you to get really comfortable researching the risks involved in your practices, asking your doctor about them, getting the right tests for you, and coming to agreements with your partners armed with a full slate of information (more about all this shortly). That includes not only discussions about safer sex, but also about safer practices with regard to airborne viruses and anything else that could affect your health as a pair or as a group.

Beyond that, we also think it's important to acknowledge that no matter how thorough and careful you are, there's still a chance you'll be surprised by an unexpected diagnosis. Viruses don't judge, they just replicate. It feels really personal when you're sick, but it's totally not personal to them—not laden with value judgments, and not targeted because of anyone being "bad" or "good." The more you and your partners can take a cue from them and simply try to deal with the reality that we all coexist with viruses, the better you'll be able to protect yourselves and each other without judgment, and take care of each other with kindness when your best efforts fail.

Wonderful and worrying developments in the STI world

The last ten to fifteen years have seen some radical new developments in the world of STI prevention and treatment. Here are a few major examples.

- The HPV vaccine, which prevents multiple strains of genital warts, was first released in 2006. Originally it was recommended for girls and young women up to age 26, but today it's also recommended for boys and young men in that same range, and is available and considered worthwhile for everyone up to age 45. Since its release, the vaccine has reduced the instance of the HPV types that cause most HPV-related cancers and genital warts by over 80 percent among teen girls and young women. These same vaccines prevent over 70 percent of head and neck cancers.
- A new class of hepatitis C medicines known as direct-acting antivirals was introduced in 2011. Today, these medications can cure more than 90 percent of people in a span of eight to twelve weeks, without the debilitating side effects of the older types of treatments. From its discovery in 1989, hepatitis C now holds the distinction of being the fastest viral disease ever to be identified

and cured. It is also the only chronic viral illness that can be completely cured.

- In 2016, the U = U campaign was launched by an international organization known as Prevention Access Campaign, or PAC. U = U stands for "undetectable = untransmittable," and it refers to the fact that when someone who is HIV positive is taking appropriate treatment, their viral load can become so low that it's undetectable on a test, and at that point, it's also not possible for them to transmit HIV.
- Pre-exposure prophylaxis (PrEP), an HIV preventative medication that can be taken orally or by injection, has become widely available. Post-exposure prophylaxis (PEP) has also become widely available. This is a month-long, anti-HIV preventative emergency medication regime that must begin within 72 hours (three days) after possible HIV exposure. Both are effective at preventing HIV infection.

These developments are astonishing, and have saved countless lives. The news isn't all good, though. Just for starters, access to these preventative medications and vaccines is, of course, not universal. Inequities in health care access remain entrenched in many areas of the world, including the United States and Canada. For example, some vaccines are only available if you pay out of pocket, and costs can be prohibitive for some people. Here are some other negative developments:

- In 2022, the World Health Organization (WHO) reported that the United States and Canada, among others, have seen an increase in at least three STIS: syphilis, gonorrhea and chlamydia.
- The WHO further noted increasing outbreaks of "non-classical STIS," meaning illnesses that are spread by a range of means including sexual contact, such as *Shigella sonnei*, hepatitis A, *Neisseria meningitidis*, Zika and Ebola. The WHO also reported a re-emergence of what they call "neglected STIS," such as *lymphogranuloma venereum* (LGV) and *Mycoplasma genitalium*.
- Also in 2022, there was a sudden new spread of mpox outbreaks in major North American cities, chiefly but not exclusively among men who had sexual contact with one another.
- The WHO is also concerned about increasing antimicrobial resistance in *Neisseria gonorrhoea* and *Mycoplasma genitalium*,

meaning that treatment options may become less effective and more limited.

- And again, let's not forget COVID-19, which is among the many illnesses transmitted in ways well beyond sexual contact but that certainly include sexual contact. Acute infection is still dangerous, particularly to people who haven't kept up with vaccinations. Today, nearly 12 percent of the Canadian population is coping with long COVID symptoms, meaning symptoms that endure three or more months after infection, and many thousands of people are dealing with severe, life-altering disability. COVID-19 isn't considered an STI, but it certainly affects a lot of people's sex lives!

Considering how quickly STI information can change—whether we're talking about new forms of prevention and treatment or new or resurgent STIs to be concerned about—we don't feel that it makes sense to give you a detailed rundown of STI-related information in this book. (Most of the developments above have happened in the ten years since the first edition of this book was published. Who knows what will happen in the next ten!) Instead, we urge you to take a proactive approach to your health in three ways: keeping up to date on the latest scientific research, working with your health care provider to make sure you get appropriate vaccinations and tests based on your practices and the risks that come with them, and practising safer sex with your partners based on ongoing conversations with them about your practices and their associated risks.

STAYING UP TO DATE

When we advise you to do your own research, we don't mean going down conspiracy-theory rabbit holes based on social media memes. Rather, we're talking about making a habit of checking a few trusted websites regularly. In Canada, a good source of STI information is CATIE (catie.ca), essentially a clearinghouse for the latest research that aims to disseminate information to health care providers and the general public. You can also check searchable government databases of disease prevention and treatment information, such as the Public Health Agency of Canada (canada.ca/en/public-health/services/diseases.html) and others. Planned Parenthood (plannedparenthood.org) and Scarleteen (scarleteen.com) are also great sources of sexual health and wellness information more generally. Your local sexual health clinic may have an informative website, too.

You don't need to become a researcher or start reading medical journals (unless you want to!). But trust that a lot of progressive organizations are on a mission to help people make good choices about their sexual health and are doing incredible work to get information out there in a way that's accessible and useful for the general public. All you have to do is seek it out.

WORKING WITH YOUR HEALTH CARE PROVIDER

Accessing good health care is becoming increasingly difficult in Canada, and has long been a challenge in the United States. Whether it's underfunded and short-staffed public health services or overpriced private ones, sometimes the barriers may seem insurmountable. It's also been clearly established that marginalized people are often treated very poorly in health care settings—including Black people, Indigenous people, people of colour, people with disabilities, people with addictions and mental illnesses, queer people, poor people, fat people, women, kinky people, sex workers, and anyone with invisible disabilities or rare or episodic symptoms. The specific flavours of mistreatment vary from group to group, but in all cases, members of these groups encounter barriers that more privileged people do not. It's also an especially scary and difficult time for trans people, who are often misgendered, denied care or even criminalized for seeking it in some jurisdictions these days. If you experience any of this when you need health care services, all we can say is that's rotten, and lots of people are fighting hard to make it better. In the meantime, your self-education and prevention efforts—and the support of your partners—are all the more crucial, and you may want to make an extra effort to seek out health care services that are tailored to your specific needs and advertise themselves as friendly to nonmonogamous people as well as to people belonging to your specific demographics.

If you have a family doctor or other regular health care provider, great! But even then, it's no guarantee that they're as open-minded as you might need them to be when it comes to your sexual practices, the number of partners you have and your needs for STI testing. This can play out for nonmonogamous people in many ways. Some health clinics, particularly in small towns, have been known to shame people who seek regular STI testing. Many nonmonogamous people do regular screening, yet there is a perception even among some health care professionals that testing is unnecessary for people in stable relationships. Organizations that focus on HIV and sexually transmitted and blood-borne illness education tend to have mandates centred on harm reduction, and have been fighting hard to dismantle stigma and shame for decades now, as well as to stop the criminalization of HIV non-disclosure. But it is an ongoing struggle despite major advances in the prevention and treatment of many STIS. You may need to get pushy to get your needs met.

We believe it's important to be open with your health care professional about being nonmonogamous, but at the same time, we recognize that some people in the medical community are prejudiced and judgmental about nontraditional relationships, so proceed with caution. You want to strike the balance between being open enough to get good advice and services, and holding whatever boundaries you need in order to feel emotionally safe in your doctor's office.

Wherever possible, if you encounter stigma or shaming from health care professionals, speak up. Tell them directly that their behaviour is inappropriate. If possible, consider filing a formal complaint, switching health care professionals, or both. The resources section of this book includes information on finding a nonmonogamy-friendly health professional.

TALKING WITH YOUR PARTNERS AND PRACTISING SAFER SEX

In nonmonogamous circles, it's common for people to be screened for STIS regularly, usually annually and whenever they are considering starting a new sexual relationship, and to talk about test results with a potential new partner before any activity that might involve fluid exchange.

This approach makes a lot of sense in the context of dating and establishing new relationships. But if you're involved in other types of sexual encounters, like casual hookups or bathhouses, you may need to lean more heavily into using barriers or being choosy about what acts you'll engage in, and less toward having extensive discussions about sexual history, which don't fit as easily into the available space and time or the degree of investment between any two people involved. You may also be a good candidate for PrEP. Your local HIV organization or sexual health clinic may provide good advice on safer sex in the context of hookups.

Just as some people are too embarrassed or ashamed to seek STI testing, some people see asking others about it, or being asked, as a mark of distrust. But it just means that you value your own health and the health of your partners highly as part of the way you love yourself and them. If you're new to these kinds of conversations, it's worth doing some work to get more comfortable with them, whether with a therapist, by practising with a friend, or just by taking a deep breath and diving in. It can be scary—but you can do it!

Talk about what you've learned through your research and from speaking with your health care provider. Talk about what you like doing sexually already, what you want to try and what risks you think you might need to plan for. Talk about what feels like reasonable risk levels for everyone involved, and aim to accommodate the person who has the lowest tolerance.

If you keep the door open to ongoing dialogue about STIs, sexual health and sex more generally, it nourishes trust between you and your partners and also helps you take better care of your own and each other's health.

Pregnancy, the other risk

Conversations about safer sex usually revolve around mitigating the risk of STIs, and it's surprising how many nonmonogamous people don't talk about pregnancy. It is a fact of nature that anytime sex involves putting sperm in potential contact with an egg, pregnancy sometimes results—even, occasionally, when using contraception. This is about cells, so it's true regardless of the participants' gender identities and sexual orientations. In fact, sometimes queer people who are accustomed to same-sex sexual partners can forget that certain types of sex can lead to pregnancy—so if you're queer and exploring your attractions to people with different plumbing than you, you may need to consider factors you're not used to when it comes to risks.

In all cases, it pays to talk with your partners about pregnancy risks and contingencies. What happens if someone accidentally becomes pregnant?

How do you all feel about abortion? Let's be super clear that the ultimate decision about whether or not to have an abortion belongs solely with the person who is, or could become, pregnant. However, this is an emotionally charged topic that many people have strong feelings about, and major disagreements here can be relationship-breakers. It's best to have the conversations ahead of time so that you aren't dealing with both a surprise pregnancy and a surprise conflict or breakup at the same time. It's also possible that partners may agree on the abortion question, but not on how to proceed once the decision has been made. Some people consider an abortion to be a routine health procedure and have no particularly intense feelings about it, whereas for others it's a very emotional experience and they need a lot of support. Especially if you live in a place where you're likely to encounter loud protestors, distressing imagery or laws that require health care providers to discourage you from aborting or provide you with inaccurate medical information, it can be a traumatic experience. Having a loving partner or partners at your side can make a huge difference. Last but not least, abortion is not always easy to access. In some states, it's illegal or as good as illegal, and in some places in both the United States and Canada, abortion providers are few and far between. So while in some places it's as simple as booking an appointment, in other places getting an abortion may involve secrecy, expensive travel, time off work and out-of-pocket costs for the procedure itself, which may not be in the budget for everyone. If you could impregnate someone and you live in a place where abortion is hard to access, you may want to consider getting a vasectomy—a procedure that is usually reversible and nearly painless. If you could get pregnant, you may want to consider taking extra contraceptive precautions, such as getting an IUD or taking birth control pills, and having mifepristone at hand (you can order it online) in case of a condom break. Stacking your contraceptive methods can add extra layers of protection in case one should fail.

Alternatively, would you see an accidental pregnancy as a happy occasion? If so, are all the affected partners in agreement on how they would proceed, what their respective roles would be, and so on? If there is more than one possible impregnator, does it matter who it was? For example, if a person gets pregnant as part of a casual encounter, would they want to raise the child with their nesting partners? As another example, in a triad made up of a cis woman and two cis men, everyone involved may feel it's important to know who the biological father is, or they may deliberately *not* want to know, because they'd like to raise the child as a three-parent unit no matter whose cells were involved in conception. Kinship is a choice, after all. Whatever the specifics of your situation, having a baby is no small undertaking, and it's worth being deliberate about it if you possibly can.

No matter what discussions you have, you're probably going to feel some pretty strong emotions if pregnancy occurs. Pregnancy is a big deal and likely to be disruptive for everyone. Give yourselves time to process your feelings and talk about it together. Don't postpone the discussion until it's too late. For more about these issues, how to have these conversations, and how to prepare to raise kids in a nonmonogamous family, see Jess Mahler's book *Polyamory and Pregnancy,* listed in the resources.

QUESTIONS TO ASK YOURSELF

Whatever your relationship to sex might be, nonmonogamy is likely to present you with new opportunities and new challenges. We wish you learning, healing and pleasure along the way—however you define all these things.

Here are some questions that might help you figure out where to start or continue your journey!

- How would I describe or define my sexuality—my orientation, desires and experiences thus far? What are my likes and dislikes?
- Is there an area related to sex where I could use some care or healing work? What is it, and what strategies could I pursue to feel better? What kinds of resources or help do I want to seek out?
- What new things would I like to explore sexually or learn about sex? What would I hope to get out of those explorations?
- What skills do I want to gain or improve in the realm of communication, negotiation and consent? How can I pursue this learning?
- What are a few sexual boundaries that are important to me?
- What approach do I take to risk in the area of sex, STIs and pregnancy? What do I want to know about a prospective partner before we have sex? What safer sex measures do I want to take? How would I approach a surprise pregnancy? What conversations do I want to have with my partners about these questions?
- What are my strategies for staying up to date on sexual health information and taking care of my sexual health? Do I need to revisit or amend them?
- How do I want to approach sex in the context of nonmonogamy? How does my nonmonogamous situation affect my answers to the other questions in this list, or vice versa?

One thing you can always count on is that hearts change.
HAYAO MIYAZAKI

21 Relationship Transitions

People are living, dynamic organisms; you grow or you die. (Actually you die, period; growth is optional.) You will change. Your partners will change. Your relationships will change. This is a fact, something you must try to accept gracefully.

If you fear change, if you cling too tightly to what your relationships are now and insist that they must always be this way, you risk breaking them. Yes, sometimes relationships change in ways you don't want, and people grow in ways that pull them apart rather than bring them together. That's the risk you accept when you get involved in this messy, complicated business of intimate relationships.

The things you value in your relationship now may not exist in the future. The things you want now, you may not want in the future. The things you see in your partner now may not be there in the future. And that's okay. Adopt a flexible and resilient idea about the way your life will look, keep in touch with your changing needs and those of your partners, talk to your partners about these things openly and without fear, and you can build relationships that grow as you grow. If you do not, your relationships can become brittle and shatter.

Allowing change with grace, without expecting to control how the change happens, is a key skill for people who want to create strong, resilient nonmonogamous relationships. Be clear on what your relationship needs are, be willing to advocate for them, and accept that things are going to change. That way, at least to some extent, you'll be ready.

Nonmonogamy makes space for types of relationship transitions that are less commonly understood in a mononormative framework. In some cases, these transitions are pretty much the same as in a monogamous model, but nonmonogamy has more language for them, or a different view of what they mean. In other cases, the structure of nonmonogamy creates possibilities for kinds of shifts that simply don't exist when only two people are involved.

Re-evaluating long-term relationships

In long-term relationships, usually a time arrives when the two new people you've become over the years stand there looking at each other and ask, "Whatever we believed or wanted a few years ago, do the people we are now belong in an intimate relationship together?" Sometimes the answer is yes, these two new people still want to be together. And then you move forward, perhaps stronger than before.

But sometimes the answer is no, it doesn't make sense anymore. This is normal and okay, even though it can be painful to realize. Not only do people change, but every relationship has a natural ebb and flow. Relationships can come and go and come again with the same person. When you acknowledge that, and allow space for changes to happen, you create relationships that can weather almost any storm.

Since people change all the time, you can debate whether it even makes sense to make lifelong commitments, at least in the way society encourages people to. Many people are taught that marriage should mean your relationship never changes, rather than meaning you can be family for life but the shape the family takes can change. Instead of the idea of "breaking up," where the presumption is that you'll stay in a relationship until something makes you leave it, perhaps you should sit down every year or few and say, "Okay, who are we now? How is this relationship working? Do we like the way it's going? Should we change something? Do we even still like each other that much? Does it make sense to continue?" If you think of this as renewing the relationship every now and again, then even if the answer to the last question is no, the result does not necessarily have to be a breakup. To use the widespread nonmonogamy term, it's a *transition*.

The best way to evaluate whether a relationship is a good one, regardless of what form it takes, is to think about the things you need and want in the relationship, and evaluate whether it gives you those things. It's not the shape of the relationship that's important; it's whether it meets your needs. Another good technique is to interrogate your feelings. When you think about the relationship ending, what is your first response? If it's a sense of relief, maybe it's time for the relationship to end.

Of course, part of the fairy tale is the idea that relationships only succeed if they last until someone dies. This is, if you think about it, a strange metric for success. If you manage to find one another's company pleasant enough for long enough, someone dies, and then the surviving partner can claim success. Relationships are often measured in terms of longevity; if they end before the death of one of the partners, people call them failures.

In his book *The Commitment*, columnist Dan Savage described his grandmother's unhappy marriage, which ended in her suicide. He commented:

> The instant my grandmother died, her marriage became a success.
>
> Death parted my grandparents, not divorce, and death is the sole measure of a successful marriage. When a marriage ends in divorce, we say that it's failed. The marriage was a failure. Why? Because both parties got out alive. It doesn't matter if the parting is amicable, it doesn't matter if the exes are happier apart, it doesn't matter if two happy marriages take the place of one unhappy marriage. A marriage that ends in divorce *failed*. Only a marriage that ends with someone in the cooler down at Maloney's is a success.

Longevity is a seductive idea, because the idea of "forever" can feel like the equivalent of "safety." In practice, when people subscribe to longevity as a value, they often end up remaining in partnerships that are joyless, loveless, even abusive—situations that are far from safe if you consider the long-term effects of constant misery. This commitment to longevity often comes along with the idea that the "failure" entailed in splitting up is shameful. In some cultural, religious and social contexts, that's true, in which case it can take a great deal of courage to contravene the community norms that insist you should remain in an unhappy partnership.

If you stop thinking in terms of "happily ever after" and start thinking in terms of how you want to write the story of your life, chapter by chapter, then relationships that end are not failures, because they still contributed to your story. And you get to keep writing it, fondly remember the good stuff, learn from the mistakes, and make meaning of the whole experience.

We propose a different metric for the success of a relationship. Relationships that help you be the best versions of yourself and that help you create meaning in your life are successes. Those that don't are not, regardless of how long they last. A ten-year relationship that ends in friendship is more successful than a lifetime relationship of misery. That doesn't mean good relationships always make the partners happy; in fact, if we return to Carrie Jenkins's argument, the purpose of having intimate relationships isn't necessarily to make you happy at all, but to be "collaborative works of art"—to support you in having a meaningful life, filled with the full range of human emotions.

Of course, you shouldn't bail at the first conflict or trouble. All relationships have their ups and downs; it is not reasonable to expect otherwise. But on the whole, good relationships promote the long-term well-being of the people involved; when that no longer becomes possible, and there's no clear path to making it possible, then it might be time for the relationship to end.

Nonmonogamous breakups

Nonmonogamous breakups are both easier and harder than monogamous breakups. They're easier in the sense that when you have more than one partner, you may have more support to help you through the loss. You may also not have to experience some of the things like skin hunger or endless nights alone that can cause so much pain after monogamous breakups. However, this support doesn't actually make the pain of loss go away—though some insensitive people believe that having more than one partner means you must not grieve when a relationship ends. No matter how many relationships you may have, breakups still cause pain.

Nonmonogamous breakups pose special challenges because the breakups can involve more people, and can create ripples of ambiguity and uncertainty throughout a whole network of relationships. Your partner's breakup may also affect you very seriously, even if you're not dating the same person. When two people share a partner in common and one of those relationships ends, the pain is greatly magnified.

There can be a lot of strange carryover effects when a nonmonogamous relationship ends. One common situation arises when a close, nesting partner or primary-style relationship ends—say, for example, a married couple divorces or a live-in relationship breaks up. People who are less entwined can feel a pull to fill the void, even if they don't want to, and even if the pull is not intentional on the part of the person navigating the breakup.

Conversely, less entwined partners may have an expectation that if a close, domestic relationship ends, their relationships are now eligible for "promotion" to a closer, more entwined status, even if that isn't the most natural form for them to take, or if the person experiencing the breakup doesn't want that. Even without a "promotion," when a relationship that formerly occupied a great deal of a person's time and attention ends, some of their remaining partners might assume that this time is now available to them.

We can't give an exhaustive analysis of how nonmonogamous breakups work because each situation is so different. For example, if an abusive relationship ends, everyone who was affected by it might be relieved. If a casual partnership comes to an amicable close and everyone remains friendly, it might not make a major difference in the overall situation at all. The partners not directly involved in the breakup may feel anxious about what it means for their relationships, but afraid to ask out of fear of making a partner's pain about them. This anxiety and uncertainty is normal, though, and deserves to be addressed. To prevent misunderstandings and avoid sliding into situations while you're in the midst of grief and transition when you wouldn't otherwise have chosen them, it can help to sit down with your remaining partners and talk about what, if anything, the breakup means for those relationships. Regardless of where you're positioned in a nonmonogamous structure, express your feelings, tell your partners about your needs, and try to extend compassion and care to each other. A breakup between two people can imply a lot of reorganization, a shift in the baseline of how people's lives are set up—everything from living arrangements to figuring out whether the whole polycule will still go to games night every second Tuesday with the quad down the street. Don't assume. Instead, discuss: ask questions, set boundaries, be kind.

Grief

Even when it transitions into a different kind of relationship, the end of an intimate relationship is hard. It's normal to feel hurt. It's also normal to mourn the loss of a partner, and the loss of the goals and dreams you shared.

Psychologists say the five stages of grief (denial, anger, bargaining, depression and acceptance) apply to grief over a lost relationship as much as they apply to terminal illness. It takes time to grieve the loss, even when you want to preserve a friendship on the other side. Ending and transitioning relationships with dignity and grace means knowing the emotional storm is coming and being prepared to weather it.

There's no easy way to deal with the pain you experience when relationships end. Make space for your feelings, but don't let them take charge of you. Turn to your support networks and coping mechanisms, and opt as much as possible for pain-easing solutions that do minimal harm (bingeing a TV show) over ones that carry higher risk (bingeing a case of beer). Eat nutritious food, move your body, try to get enough sleep. Do things that help you feel all your feelings, and do things that help keep you functional, too. Wait, and let time do its job. Thinkers, poets, scholars and therapists have written a great deal about the grieving process and how to navigate it; seek out their voices and advice, learn what you can and discard what doesn't work for you.

One aspect of grief that comes up a lot in nonmonogamy is the experience of holding multiple emotional states at the same time. In monogamous relationships, you're generally feeling things about one relationship at a time. Even in the case of overlapping emotional states—such as grieving a divorce while also starting a new relationship—you're typically in just one relationship actively. In nonmonogamy, you can be heartbroken and grieving about one person while at the same time in the midst of NRE with another, perhaps while also securely attached and comfortable in yet another relationship. Sometimes these overlaps can cause odd emotional states—a muddy mix or a bizarre clash of feelings. Be gentle with yourself if you're experiencing this kind of cognitive and emotional load. It's normal to find it challenging. With experience, you may develop an emotional skill set to manage this kind of weirdness when it comes up.

Another aspect of grief that's common in nonmonogamy is that when one relationship ends, you have to figure out how much you can lean on the partner or partners you're still with to get support in your heartbreak. Do you have boundaries around what you want to share with them? Do they have boundaries around what kind of support they're able to provide you? Ideally, your needs and abilities are compatible, but it's not a guarantee, particularly if the breakup also affected them in some way and they have their own feelings about it. Maybe you can be mutually supportive, or maybe you'll need to turn to other supportive people, or some combination of these strategies. Talk about it with your partners and come up with an approach that works for everyone involved.

What have you learned?

When a breakup happens, often you just need to get through it: Deal with the big feelings and the logistical upheavals while still trying to maintain the rest of your life and fulfill your obligations. But once the initial phase has passed and you're adjusting to the new reality, it can be worth taking some time to assess what happened and what you can learn from it. In serial monogamy there's usually a built-in transition period between relationships where, hopefully, some self-reflection occurs. When one of multiple relationships end, it can be easy to try to just skip over that messy, uncomfortable bit. While that may feel easier in the short term, you—and your future partners—might lose out over the long run. Avoid the temptation to use your other relationships, existing or new, as distractions from both the grieving and growing processes, or to look to them for vilification of your ex and validation that you were blameless.

We all come up with the stories of our relationships—how we met, what set us on a path together, who did what and why it ended. What part did you play in the ending? Do you need to take accountability for any mistakes you might have made? Do you need to do things differently in future (or current) relationships based on what you've learned? Do you need to refine your criteria for choosing partners or update your mental list of red flags or signs of incompatibility? Maybe you need to set new boundaries with partners going forward or engage in some kind of healing work. What resources would you need to marshal, or what skills would you need to develop, in order to prevent or avoid whatever problems arose this time? What were the good things about the relationship that you'd really like to experience again in some way? What are you grateful for? What are you angry or hurt about? With any luck, each relationship that ends leaves you with useful lessons that you can carry with you to the next ones you pursue.

You can do this process of reflection in a concerted way over a short period of time, but people often learn in spirals, deepening their understanding as they revisit a topic over time. As long as you're not dragging yourself down with endless rumination, it can be worth thinking about the end of a relationship at multiple points in the months and years after a split, to see how your own perspective shifts.

When you have kids

Children are often affected in nonmonogamous breakups, since many people find themselves forming close relationships with the children of their partners. As mentioned in chapter 15, it's even common to have multi-parent live-in households. The implications of breakups in these arrangements are similar, of course, to situations that can arise when blended families split up.

Regardless of the particulars of your situation, when a kid is involved, remember that they're in a formative phase, and cutting off their attachment-based relationships can cause a great deal of emotional hardship for them for the rest of their lives. As you figure out your plans for handling a breakup, consider their needs as a high priority. Do your best to make sure the kids continue to feel safe and loved, with some kind of stability and ongoing access to the adults who have been important parts of their lives so far.

The law generally does a much better job of protecting the interests of children when their (two) legal parents split up than it does when a family situation is more complex. This means that nonmonogamous people have to put in the time and the work to navigate unfamiliar waters for the child's best interests, with no guidance along the way. You may need to get creative together—which can be super difficult when you're splitting up and full of big emotions! Seek support if you need it, and get creative about that too. For example, if two adults find it too painful—at least for a time, as is common—to stay in close contact, metamours who are still connected to the child may be able to help facilitate a relationship with the former partner.

Above all, don't use kids as chess pieces. When a breakup becomes acrimonious, it can be tempting to drag children into the fray. Hold onto your values here and remember that treating other people as real isn't just a principle for intimate relationships—it applies to kids, too.

Ambiguous endings

Sometimes, among nonmonogamous people, we see what we call Schrödinger relationships:* relationships that are near-over in practice,

* After the "Schrödinger's cat" thought experiment, in which people are asked to imagine a cat that is simultaneously alive and dead.

but have fallen into a pattern of comfortable non-contact or non-intimacy. It's easy for nonmonogamous people to let such non-relationships linger a long time, because when you have multiple partners, there's often not as much incentive to formally end a relationship in order to "move on"—and it can feel easier to drift apart than to have a tough conversation. This can be quite painful, though, if both partners are not aware of what's happening, and one partner thinks of the relationship as "on" and the other thinks of it as "off." Everyone deserves clarity about the nature and standing of their relationships, and retreating into muddy communication isn't fair or kind. What one person is viewing as "going with the flow" might actually come across, to another person, as avoidance, manipulation or ghosting. Don't put someone in the unhappy position of having to ask, "Hey, have I been dumped?" Respect them, their feelings and their dignity enough to be direct about what's going on.

Other members of the network can suffer too when the two partners involved in the breakup are not clear with each other, or with their other partners, about what is happening. At the very least, metamour relationships can become awkward if you don't know whether you're really relating to a metamour. And as counterintuitive as it may seem, many people need to grieve their partners' lost relationships too. Letting a relationship drift off into the ether without closure can make this process much harder. Clear conversations about relationship transitions can be important for *everyone* affected.

That said, many solo poly people and relationship anarchists do prefer to have much more fluid, undefined relationships that slip between friendship and romance. If this is the case for you, then clarity and "define that relationship" conversations may be much less important for you and your partners. Hopefully, however, you will have had early conversations with them about how the sort of fluidity you prefer in your relationships works for you—and can work for them.

De-escalating

One kind of transition that's really tough to manage is de-escalation. In some ways these are even more difficult than breakups, and not infrequently, that's where they end up.

A de-escalation refers to what happens when you move a relationship to a lesser degree of closeness while still remaining intimate. Maybe you're on the relationship escalator and heading toward marriage and kids when you realize that isn't what you want—but you don't want the relationship to end, either. Maybe you realize your partnership works way better when you don't share a bedroom or don't live together at all. Or maybe, once the NRE wears off, you realize that the sexual chemistry is great but you don't have enough in common to build a deeper relationship and should stick to booty calls and threesomes at sex parties. (We also discuss the reverse, where relationships become non-sexual but remain close, in chapter 20.)

Unless it's entirely mutual, there are likely to be some hurt feelings in the mix when one person brings up a de-escalation. There's no recipe for managing this well aside from trying to be compassionate, kind and graceful as you talk about it. It is especially difficult to do this when your life is very entwined—it's hard to say "I love you and I want to stay together, but could you move out?" Brace yourself: The answer might be, "I can leave, but for me that means this is the end."

There aren't a lot of models for de-escalating relationships. The relationship escalator model is powerful and pervasive, and de-escalation flies in the face of all the considerable social pressure to constantly be moving "up." It can feel like failure if someone tries to turn off the machine or go back down the steps. The person being asked for a de-escalation might feel ashamed or rejected, or simply not be able to envision anything other than steadily increasing closeness over time.

Be as gentle with each other as you can. A relationship can thrive in a new shape, but only if everyone is on board.

Opportunity shift

Relationships take shape in the interplay between the spaces you create for them and their own inherent inclinations. For example, a long-distance relationship might thrive on a visit once per season with a weekly phone call in the interim—if that's the level of closeness and contact that feels right for that relationship. That same situation could be unbearably painful if the people involved craved daily togetherness but simply couldn't have it because of physical distance.

This range of possibilities is true for the example of long-distance relationships, but it also holds true for other outside circumstances that limit how often people can see each other: a demanding job or school program, a relationship configuration that takes up a lot of someone's focus, even a health problem that places limits on a person's energy or availability.

So when your relationship has grown in the shape of the space it's permitted, what happens when that space changes? This can go in one of two directions: toward more or toward less. When a long-distance partner suddenly has a job opportunity in your city, you may be faced with the question of how much time you really want to spend together, now that distance will no longer present a built-in limit on that time. Maybe you'll both jump at the chance to deepen your relationship. Or maybe you'll realize that actually, a fairly infrequent, comet-style connection still works best for you even if you could, in theory, hop on the subway and meet up for dinner with them twice a week. Either way, now you have to talk about it, because being three provinces apart is no longer doing the job for you. On the other end of the spectrum, maybe the person you've been seeing twice a week for three years suddenly has to move away to care for an ailing parent in another province. This may present an occasion for you both to realize you want more—the thought of being parted might be the catalyst you needed to decide you actually want to live together. Or maybe the move will serve as a gentle push toward a distancing that might have been coming anyway.

Opportunity shifts like these can be enlightening. They can help show you what you really want; they can jolt you out of complacency. You might not always like what you learn. It can feel crappy to realize you don't really mind that someone's suddenly unavailable—you maybe should have noticed months ago that you just weren't really into them anymore. It can be shocking to figure out that you're actually deeply attached to someone only when suddenly faced with the possibility that they might not be around as much. These shifts can also be painful, particularly if they catalyze one person in one direction ("I want to follow you!") and take the other person in the opposite direction ("Well, I guess this is goodbye…").

It takes some grace and care to navigate these situations, which can be delicate enough between just two people. You may need to express what you want and need in a whole new way, and depending on the circumstances, you may not get it. Also, when opportunity shifts happen, they can be disruptive to the structures of your larger nonmonogamous networks, particularly if they cause a cascade of changes: Grey moves to town, so Shen starts spending way more time with them, which makes AJ realize they want a nesting partner, which makes Jazz realize they need to break up with AJ…and so on.

The important thing is to be honest with yourself and with your partners about what you want and what you don't want. While it's good to recognize the impact that circumstances have—on what you do and on what you even consider to be possible—don't let the circumstances do the work of making your relationship decisions for you. They shouldn't be used as excuses; don't say "We can't keep dating if you live so far away!" when what you really mean is "I don't think I'm willing to invest in a long-distance relationship with you." And don't let them artificially limit you any more than strictly necessary, either. Sometimes a stumbling block really can be a stepping stone—maybe instead of suffering through a 14-hour time zone difference, moving to Australia for a year while a partner is on sabbatical there is actually just the shakeup you need.

Opportunities can shift due to circumstances totally beyond your control. But that doesn't mean you have no power to shift them yourself. Instead of seeing opportunity shifts as random acts of nature to which you are helplessly subjected, let them remind you that you can have a hand in creating them on purpose.

Staying friends with your exes

There's a saying among many nonmonogamous people: "Relationships don't end, they just change." It's a noble idea, and one that society in general could probably benefit from. In a mononormative worldview, it's quite common to see ex-partners as potential threats to a relationship, and many people don't want to maintain friendships with exes (or, more to the point, don't want their partners to maintain friendships with exes).

Ceasing all contact with exes is easier to do when a breakup just means you each disappear back into the roiling mass of undifferentiated (monogamous) humanity from whence you emerged. It's a lot harder in smaller communities, including queer, kink and nonmonogamy-focused circles, because it's harder to avoid socializing with former partners. The same is true if your dating pool tends to be focused on niche hobbies or subcultures, or if you live in a place with a small population, such as an island, small town or rural area.

But staying friends with your exes is not just something you might be semi-forced to do by dint of proximity. Provided a relationship isn't ending because of grievous betrayal, the intimacy and knowledge that partners have built up together over time can serve as a really solid and beautiful foundation for a friendship (or, if you're a relationship anarchist, another variety of more-ship). A former metamour of Eve's uses the word *retromour* to refer to past partners who are still in her life, acknowledging the unique nature of friendships that are shaped by past intimacy. This is another reason why nonmonogamous talk of "transitioning" a relationship rather than just "breaking up" is often an accurate description, not a euphemism. In mononormative culture, the idea of ending a romance and becoming "just friends" is often treated as a joke, or a promise meant to alleviate guilt but that's never really followed through on. In the world of nonmonogamy, it's often entirely real and valuable.

Resuming contact may take a while; breakups are painful and raw, and a cooling-off period of no contact is often advisable, possibly for weeks or months (or even years). But time mellows all things, and nonmonogamous exes often eventually find that they can build a lasting friendship—up to and including becoming long-term chosen family to each other. In queer circles, this is incredibly common, to the point of being a sort of cultural in-joke. When you start asking people at a backyard Pride barbecue how they know the host, chances are you'll discover half of them are their exes.

Exit strategies

Some folks advocate for creating an "exit strategy" early on in a relationship to help ensure friendly transitions. You may not want to think at the beginning about how things could end, but that's exactly the point: it's better to talk about (and commit to) how you want to treat each other when you're still seeing the best in each other and more inclined to be generous, than when you're in conflict and pain. It's also better to try to avoid potentially hurtful surprises and discuss incompatibilities, such as when one person wants a long no-contact period and one wants a smooth transition into friendship, when they're still hypotheticals.

An exit strategy for a non-escalator relationship might not look much like a mononormative prenup, and you can't anticipate everything that might happen, but it could include things like how you would want to make the decision, how you want it communicated, whether you want to try relationship counselling first, if you'll want a no contact and for how long, what your hopes and intentions are for staying in each other's lives, how you prefer to handle mutual friendships and shared events, and more. You can also revisit it as your relationship changes—but ideally not when a possible transition is actually near. The goal of an exit strategy should be to help create a sense of safety and security, not to create anxiety that you're about to break up. It's more about discussing what kindness looks like to you, and committing to it in specific ways that matter to your partner before you're experiencing the emotional pressures that might make it hard.

When a partner's other relationship ends

At some point, you are likely to find yourself involved with someone who has another relationship that's falling apart. This can put you in the complex position of needing to be supportive while also, quite likely, having your own feelings about the breakup. As a baseline, it can be hard to see someone you love in pain, when often you can do little other than be a shoulder to cry on and a place of refuge if needed. This is one of the downsides to nonmonogamy; the odds are good that, sooner or later, someone else will hurt somebody you love, and there's not a lot you can do about it.

More complicated cases are common, too. For example, maybe you're secretly (or not-so-secretly) thrilled that a toxic relationship is finally ending, so that your beloved partner can heal. Maybe you're angry at them for staying so long while it was clearly not working, and in fact may have been harming you as well as your partner—you might have a case of the "I told you sos" that you'll need to rein in if you want to be properly supportive, or you may be angry at your partner's poor judgment. In another register of emotion, sometimes your metamours have become vital parts of your life: trusted friends and confidants, delightful co-conspirators, even cherished chosen family. You may form attached relationships with them in your own right, even if they remain totally platonic, including major life entwinements such as living together. And you may be romantically involved, such as in a triad, where a breakup between two people reconfigures the structure into a vee. In cases like these, your partner's breakup affects you directly, and it can be devastating—even sometimes totally destabilizing to the relationships that remain. To make matters worse, if you don't have a lot of nonmonogamous friends, it can be hard to find people to talk to who are able to understand and mirror the complex mix of emotions you could be experiencing. Go easy on yourself, and know that no matter how weird and isolated you might feel right now, what you're going through is normal. Many others have been where you are.

In other cases, particularly if you are a relatively new partner and your metamour has been in relationship with your partner for longer than you have, you may be cast as the villain who "stole" your partner from your metamour. You may even worry about this yourself! It can feel terrible to show up with only the best of intentions only to find that your presence disrupts a long-term relationship to the point where it can't be saved. If you're in this scenario: Remember that as long as you act with integrity and recognize your partner's right to make choices, without controlling or manipulating them or trying to undermine their other partnerships, you are not responsible for their relationships with their other partners. You are not to blame simply because you have added value to another person's life.

QUESTIONS TO ASK YOURSELF

Mononormativity offers few models for relationships that transition—there's either breaking up or staying together, and not much else. You may not face all the different kinds of transitions we've discussed in this chapter, but you'll almost certainly have to deal with at least one or two of them. Here are some questions that can help you navigate various transitions:

- How do I want to approach the end of my relationships? What principles, resources and ways of thinking do I feel strongly about when it comes to how I handle breakups?
- Who can I turn to for support if I'm grieving a breakup? What other resources would help—books, therapy, art, movement...?
- How do I feel about staying friends with my exes? What steps do I need to take to ensure this happens?
- If a relationship within my nonmonogamous network ends, what does that mean for everyone else in the network? What does it mean for people in our lives who aren't intimate partners, such as kids, friends or others? How can we communicate about this?
- How would I feel about an opportunity shift with one or more of my partners? If we realize that an opportunity shift would radically change our relationship, is there something we can choose to change deliberately, instead of waiting for circumstances to do it for us?
- What kinds of things would I want to address in an exit strategy? What kinds of commitments would I want to make to my partners about how I will handle transitions?

Transform yourself to transform the world.
GRACE LEE BOGGS

The Future of Nonmonogamy

When we started working on this book together, we had a conversation that went something like this:

"What do we see as being the purpose of this book? What are we trying to accomplish?"

"Well, it's kind of an *everything* book."

"Right. Okay, that sounds easy. Let's get started!" (Cue gales of terrified laughter.)

Nonmonogamy has always been one of those places where micro and macro meet—where the intimate choices we make in our everyday lives intersect with social currents and global realities that are bigger than any of us. It might be hard to see how a quiet conversation with someone you love ("So, sweetheart, I've been curious about open relationships...") could have anything to do with, say, the impact of colonization on how land was distributed hundreds of years ago, and from there, how we understand family structures and kinship. It might not be intuitive to understand how sharing a kiss with a stranger at a sex party connects with the ways capitalism has informed our notions of love and desire or how attachment theory and trauma research could help us make better choices.

Of course, no one book can be an "everything book," but we have tried to keep coming back to those big macro questions: Why do we see love, relationships, sexuality, family and commitment the ways that we do? How did we get here? Is this where we want to be? Is it serving us and bringing us health, joy, connection and meaning? What would we like to change? How can we do that?

At the same time, we've tried to avoid floating off into pure theory-land. We have tried to stay grounded in the concrete realities of our bodies, our lives, the individual people we connect with and care about, and the day-to-day responsibilities on which we place importance. And that leads to a different range of questions: How do we balance honesty and respect for others' privacy? How do we navigate the currents of power that come up between any two or more people when we're trying to balance connection and freedom, safety and kindness? How do we take care of ourselves and be good to others? (Whose turn is it to make dinner, and did they get that list of everyone's dietary restrictions?)

Does this all sound way bigger than just "nonmonogamy"? Well, it is, but that's only because the reality of nonmonogamy is a lot bigger than the way it's often portrayed. Nonmonogamy isn't about getting lost in the fancy jargon, going to certain kinds of parties and conferences, or getting laid in exciting new configurations—though it can certainly include all of those things.

Nonmonogamy gets at one of the scariest questions we have to face today: How do we survive, thrive and love each other in a world that's rapidly changing? Some people answer that question by clamping down, investing in exploitative relationships and rigid approaches, making fear-based decisions, and having control-based dreams. Nonmonogamous people aren't any less scared of the future or any less worried about maintaining our relationships—and we're not immune to the bad habits, problems and challenges that are part of being human. We just consider the possibility that the solutions might lie in being open to the possibility of more love, doing the hard work of figuring out how to be kind, learning to set boundaries while still being generous and compassionate, and putting our energy into growth and connection rather than isolation and disconnection.

Nonmonogamy invites us to think in new ways and proposes new possibilities. But nonmonogamy is just one of the many ways people are shifting the way they relate and create and care—away from old models and toward something more adaptable, more in tune with the way our lives work in this millennium. It's not the only way, and that's why our goal isn't to promote nonmonogamy per se. We believe that thinking carefully about all these questions is beneficial for just about all of us, whether or not you end up deciding that nonmonogamy is part of how you want to shape your life. And for those who do decide to go ahead, we've tried to make our own small contribution to helping you get a sense of what's out there, what kind of work you might have to do, what challenges you might face, and how to avoid some common pitfalls. We hope it's been useful.

We also hope that ten years from now, we'll look back at this book and think: Wow, so much has changed! We've learned a lot since then, so many new ideas and fresh thinkers have contributed to the conversation, and amazing people have made genius connections between ideas and asked crucial new questions to keep moving us all forward. Forward to what? Among other things, taking better care of ourselves, each other, our communities and the planet.

How do we try to enact the change we want to see in the world within our individual everyday choices? How do we love bravely while living in a world that sometimes seems so intent on turning ever more inhuman?

Loving *more* is one way, but ultimately, we hope people learn to love *better*.

Afterword

What is there to be said at the end of such a comprehensive book on navigating nonmonogamy as *The New More Than Two*?

When my dating life first began many decades ago, I moved unquestioningly into default monogamy. Lots of those relationships were at best unfortunate, at worst disastrous. Not because of monogamy! It was mostly, on both sides, things like poor communication skills, previous unaddressed trauma and lack of therapy. For my part, it was also my inability at the time to perceive all the choices I had—because who knew there were other relationship models?

But I am no longer that person. I've now been practising some flavour of nonmonogamy for almost thirty years. As I read *The New More Than Two*, I found myself nodding at familiar concepts, situations and analyses. My first thought upon reading it was, "Boy, I could have really used this information thirty years ago." My second thought was to be glad I have the opportunity to peruse this book now, because there was plenty of information in it that was new to me. I found myself having "aha!" moments, and in at least one case, scurrying to partners to say, "I just figured out what was really going on for me when I said/did X." I found confirmation for experiences I'd never put words to before. I found some of my own actions and convictions challenged (sigh). I found paths to resolution, restitution. To forgiveness of self and others. I found new ways of understanding, new frameworks. The book has helped me to finally tease apart why I gravitate toward some nonmonogamy practices and shy away from others. I suspect this will all serve me well as I navigate existing relationships and enter new ones.

I'm a published author in the speculative fiction genres that include science fiction and fantasy. I view speculative fiction as the literature of social and technological change. In spec fic, we can imagine the world as it currently is not. We can storify the negative consequences if we don't stop destroying the planet's resources. But we can also imagine, for instance, functional social systems in place of some of the ones we have now. As any artist does, I put my convictions into my art.

By the mid 2000s, I had been out to self and others for some time as being queer and nonmonogamous. My writing had become bolder as well. I went a lot further in depicting polyamorous relationships than I had before. My 2024 novel *Blackheart Man* was set in Chynchin, an imaginary Caribbean nation (I am originally from the Caribbean), in a past roughly analogous to the sixteenth through eighteenth centuries. In Chynchin, a standard marriage consists of three people—a troie—typically one woman and two men. Sex before marriage is a non-issue. Queerness is a non-issue, as is being nonbinary. Work is for the most part non-gendered, with a couple of exceptions. Veycosi, my protagonist, is betrothed in marriage to a man and a woman. Although the three don't all relate sexually to each other—there's no social expectation that they do—they are close friends. Sounds like the makings of Paradise, yes? My kind of Paradise, anyway.

But fiction is about what's going wrong, not an endless vision of harmony. The country of Chynchin is in danger, and that's big enough. But on an interpersonal level, Veycosi, though he loves his two betrotheds deeply, is at the beginning of the novel steadily undermining the trust they can have in him. *The New More Than Two* puts it succinctly: "Some people who are dishonest with their partners are trying to shape a partner's behaviour in a desired direction" (page 125). Veycosi lies by omission about the fact that he has become enamoured of someone else. He also harbours a secret scorn over a choice his female fiancée made when she was much younger. In his life in general, he does whatever he sees fit, without consulting other people who will be affected by his actions. And for the longest while, he refuses to be honest with himself about his own motivations and failings. His relationship, predictably, erodes, and all the while he's trying as best he can to do his (headstrong) part to help his nation, which is under siege from an outside power.

Since marriages of three people were the norm in my story, I was also able to briefly sketch successful, harmonious troies. However, I didn't go into much detail about what made those relationships successful. *Blackheart Man*, after all, is the plot-driven story of a flawed human in a nation being attacked on two fronts, by an army of the living and one of the dead. I had some action scenes to fit in!

If I had written an in-depth fictional exploration of nonmonogamy, I wonder how I would have tackled it? For those of us doing some form of nonmonogamy, there aren't many examinations or models out in the world about what our "normal" is, what we might expect from nonmonogamous relationship structures, or what it means for our relationships when they shift in nature and focus over time. In a world whose prevailing story is that nonmonogamy is pathological, it's easy to blame yourself. To suspect that you're doing this wrong. That you're a bad person. That nonmonogamy obviously can't work, and you've been deceiving yourself.

What a relief, for instance, to read in *The New More Than Two* that "It's common for connection to start out very large and exciting and shrink as a relationship deepens and stabilizes, or sometimes to start out small, grow to a peak and then wane. Commitment tends to start small and grow. People in long-term, very committed relationships may still struggle to maintain connection" (page 202). So not only are the shifts to be expected, but you and your loves may be able to reimagine or rebalance them. This is powerful stuff, empowering stuff. The frank, compassionate approach that Rickert and Zanin have taken throughout this book doesn't sugarcoat nonmonogamy or demonize monogamy. They're giving information, not trying to convince the reader. It's also wonderful to read practical advice such as where to look for community and potential partners.

Fact is, everyone, if they're lucky, has multiple relationships. They may be platonic or not, intimate or not, familial, collegial, friendship-based, the seven of you on the board of that community organization, your neighbours. Whether or not nonmonogamy is for you, I hope that you've also found insights between these pages that will lead you to your own "aha!" moments in all your varied relationships, and to stronger, more functional, more joyful connections with others.

Nalo Hopkinson
Vancouver, 2026

Glossary

Language evolves. We have defined the terms here as they are commonly used today, which may not reflect how they were used when originally coined.

2SLGBTQI+ An acronym standing for Two-Spirit, lesbian, gay, *bisexual*, *trans*, queer, intersex and more.

AMATONORMATIVITY The notion that it is the universal human experience to feel romantic love and to prosper best in long-term romantic relationships. Term coined by philosopher Elizabeth Brake.

ANCHOR PARTNER A partner with whom you share a close, long-term, committed connection. May or may not be a live-in partner with financial entanglements; relationship may or may not include an expectation of a significant time commitment.

ASEXUALITY A spectrum that includes a lack of sexual interest in or attraction to other people, or a lack of interest in sexual activity. Asexual people may refer to themselves as "ace" for short.

BDSM A triple acronym standing for "bondage and discipline," "dominance and submission," and "sadism and masochism." In practice, used as shorthand to refer to many kinds of kinky activities involving consensual engagement with power, pain (or intense sensation) and fetishism.

BISEXUAL A term used to describe someone who is sexually attracted to or sexually active with partners of more than one gender, though not necessarily equally.

CHEATING In a relationship, any activity that violates the agreements of that relationship.

CISGENDER A person who identifies as the same gender that was assigned to them at birth.

CISNORMATIVITY The notion that it is right, normal and expected for people to be *cisgender*; the assumption that everyone is cisgender and that being cisgender is the best way to be.

CLOSED GROUP MARRIAGE A polyfidelitous relationship in which all the members consider themselves to be married.

CLOSED RELATIONSHIP Any intimate relationship, such as a conventional monogamous relationship or a polyfidelitous relationship, that specifically excludes the possibility of creating new intimate connections with others.

COMET A person who occasionally enters your orbit as an intimate or sexual partner, passing through once in a while, but who is not a regular part of your everyday life. Often long-distance.

COMPERSION A feeling of joy you may experience when your partner takes pleasure from another romantic or sexual relationship.

CONSENSUAL NONMONOGAMY (CNM) A form of nonmonogamy done with the full and informed consent of everyone involved.

COUPLE PRIVILEGE External social structures or internal assumptions that consciously or unconsciously place a couple at the centre of a relationship *hierarchy* or grant special advantages to a couple.

COWPOKE, COWBOY, COWGIRL A monogamous person who engages in a relationship with a nonmonogamous partner with the hope or intention of separating the nonmonogamous partner from any other partners and bringing them into a monogamous relationship.

DEMISEXUAL A term used to describe a person who experiences only secondary sexual attraction—the kind of attraction that emerges as an emotional connection or attachment develops.

"DON'T ASK, DON'T TELL" (DADT) A relationship structure in which a person who is partnered is permitted to have additional sexual or romantic relationships on the condition that their partner does not know anything about those additional relationships and does not meet any of those other people.

DYAD The relationship between any two people, distinct from the connections either person has with anyone else.

ETHICAL NONMONOGAMY (ENM) A form of nonmonogamy done with the full and informed consent of everyone involved.

EXCLUSIVITY An agreement among two or more intimate partners not to have or seek other partners, either for a period of time or in perpetuity. See also *polyfidelity*.

FLUID BONDING 1. Practices that involve the exchange of bodily fluids from the genitals, such as barrier-free sex. 2. A set of boundaries, agreements or rules between two or more people who are engaging in unbarriered sex designed to protect the fluid-bonded status. (See chapter 20 for a discussion of problems with this notion.)

FRUBBLE, FRUBBLY (BRITISH) See *compersion*.

GENDER BINARY The notion that there are only two genders, men and women. Generally paired with the notion that these genders match up with the sex people are assigned at birth, so babies with penises become boys and men while babies with vulvas become girls and women, and intersex babies are assigned a gender based on doctor and parent preferences. Also generally paired with the notion that specific traits and behaviours are exclusively associated with each gender.

GROUP MARRIAGE See *closed group marriage*, *polyfidelity*.

HETERONORMATIVITY Assumptions and presumed social roles that promote the idea of heterosexual relationships as the norm and that equate biological sex, gender identity and gender roles.

HIERARCHY, HIERARCHICAL RELATIONSHIP An arrangement in which members of one relationship are subject to nonreciprocal control or rule-making by participants in another relationship. Usually involves *veto*; may also involve restrictions on activities, commitment, entanglement, time or emotions.

HINGE The person "in the middle," with two or more partners. See also *pivot*.

INTIMATE NETWORK The sum total of a person's partners, those partners' partners, and so on. Usually used to describe an open network. Usually includes smaller *molecules* such as *vees*, *triads* or *quads*. May also be called a romantic network.

INTIMATE RELATIONSHIP Any kind of relationship that the partners in question consider intimate, including both romantic and non-romantic relationships.

KINK See *BDSM*.

KITCHEN TABLE POLYAMORY A nonmonogamous network in which the people prefer to have close relationships and may consider each other chosen family (see also *polyfamily*). The name invokes the idea of sitting down together at a family dinner.

LIFE PARTNER A partner, usually but not always an intimate partner, with whom someone intends to have a long-lasting, intertwined, committed and supportive relationship.

LIMERENCE A state of romantic attraction characterized by intrusive thoughts of a person, overwhelming fear of rejection by that person, and a powerful, obsessive need for reciprocation. Not necessarily mutual. Coined by psychologist Dorothy Tennov in 1979.

METAMOUR A partner's other partner.

MOLECULE Used to describe a set or subset of nonmonogamous relationships, such as a *triad*, *vee* or *quad*, or a complete intimate network. See also *polycule*.

MONOGAMY The state or practice of having only one sexual partner or romantic relationship at a time.

MONONORMATIVITY The notion that it is normal, right and expected for people to be monogamous; the notion that the monogamous couple is an organizing unit of society and is the only acceptable form of relationship. Also known as compulsory monogamy.

MONO/POLY A relationship between someone who self-identifies as nonmonogamous and someone who self-identifies as monogamous.

NESTING PARTNER A partner with whom you share a living situation with some degree of entwinement, shared decision-making and life activities, etc. Partners living in non-entwined shared situations such as collectives or roommate arrangements may or may not also consider themselves nesting partners.

NEW RELATIONSHIP ENERGY (NRE) A strong, almost giddy feeling of excitement and infatuation common in the beginning of any new romantic relationship, which usually lasts for a few months but can last as long as several years.

ONE-PENIS POLICY (OPP) An arrangement in which a man is allowed to have multiple partners who are women (or who have vulvas), each of whom is allowed to have sex with other women (or people with vulvas) but may not have any other partners with penises.

OPEN MARRIAGE Any marriage whose structures or arrangements permit one or both of the members involved to have other sexual relationships, romantic relationships, or both. The term *open marriage* is a catchall for marriages that are not emotionally or sexually monogamous, and may include such activities as nonmonogamy or *swinging*.

OPEN NETWORK A relationship structure in which the people involved are free to add new partners as they choose.

OPEN RELATIONSHIP An intimate relationship in which there is an agreement that partners may seek or start additional relationships.

PARALLEL POLYAMORY A polyamorous style in which people's relationships are treated as very separate. Metamours may know of each other, at least in general terms, but don't have any particular relationship with each other beyond dating the same person and don't tend to spend time together as a group.

PIVOT See *hinge*.

POLY An adjective used to describe something that is polyamorous or related to polyamory: a poly relationship, a poly person, a poly discussion group. Also used as an identifier and hashtag by people who identify as Polynesian. To avoid confusion, many polyamorous people prefer to use the prefix *polyam*, especially in hashtags and titles, or to simply spell out *polyamory* in full.

POLYAM Variant of *poly*.

POLYANDRY One woman with multiple husbands, the less common type of *polygamy*.

POLYCULE An *intimate network*, or a particular subset of relationships within an intimate network, whose members are closely connected. Some people use *polycule* to refer to their entire intimate network. Also used to describe a sketch or visualization of an intimate network, as these drawings often resemble the depiction of molecules used in organic chemistry.

POLYFAMILY 1. A set of nonmonogamous people who live together and identify as part of the same family. 2. A nonmonogamous group whose members consider one another to be family, regardless of whether or not they share a home.

POLYFIDELITY An agreement among a group of people who are romantically or sexually involved with one another that they will not seek additional partners, at least without the approval and consent of everyone in the group. Also *polyfi* as an adjective.

POLYGAMY The state of having multiple wedded spouses at the same time, regardless of the gender of those spouses. Polygyny—one man with multiple wives—is the most common form of polygamy in societies that permit multiple spouses. For that reason, many people confuse the two.

POLYNORMATIVITY The notion that, if a person is going to pursue polyamory, they should or must follow the one normal, right and expected kind of polyamory for which *mononormative* society has made a little space. This type of polyamory starts with a couple opening up, is always hierarchical, involves a lot of rules, and—in terms of media representation—usually looks like a white, heterosexual-ish couple with a girlfriend on the side. Coined by Andrea Zanin in 2013.

POLYSATURATED A term that describes someone who is nonmonogamous but not currently open to new relationships or new partners because of the number of existing partners, or because of time constraints that might make new relationships difficult.

POST-NONMONOGAMY A state in which a person has had a meaningful experience of nonmonogamy and still believes in people's right to define and build their relationships as they see fit, including through nonmonogamy, but is currently not choosing to seek or be in multiple relationships, whether they are single or exclusively partnered. Coined by Andrea Zanin in 2023.

PRIMARY/SECONDARY A *hierarchical relationship* structure in which the partners who are higher in the *hierarchy* are referred to as "primary" and other partners are referred to as "secondary." Sometimes used to describe a non-hierarchical relationship structure in which partners are not equal to one another in terms of interconnection, emotional intensity or entwinement in practical or financial matters. (We discourage the latter use, which is becoming less common among nonmonogamous people.)

QUAD A nonmonogamous arrangement involving four people, each of whom may or may not be sexually or emotionally involved with all the other members. This arrangement often begins with two couples. Quads may also be part of a larger *intimate network.*

RELATIONSHIP ANARCHY (RA) A philosophy or practice in which people are seen as free to engage in any relationships they choose, spontaneity and freedom are valued, no relationship is entered into or restricted from a sense of duty or obligation, and any relationship choice is considered allowable. Relationship anarchists often do not make a clear distinction between "partner" and "non-partner."

RELATIONSHIP ESCALATOR The default set of social assumptions concerning the "normal" course of a relationship, usually proceeding from dating to moving in together to getting married to having children.

SAFER SEX An approach to sexual activity in which the people involved aim to reduce the risk of sexually transmitted infections by using barriers, agreeing on STI testing approaches, or agreeing to limits on types of activities.

SECONDARY See *primary/secondary*.

SEX-POSITIVITY The notion that sex and sexuality are a natural and healthy part of the human experience; a social movement that emphasizes the notion of personal choice in the realm of sex, *safer sex* practices and consent.

SOLO POLYAMORY A style of nonmonogamy in which a person is open to having multiple intimate relationships but maintains an independent or single lifestyle. They may not live with partners, share finances or want to pursue escalator types of relationships.

SWINGING The practice of having multiple sexual partners outside of an existing romantic relationship, most often engaged in by couples as an organized activity, and with the understanding that the focus of those relationships is primarily sexual rather than romantic or emotionally intimate.

TRANSGENDER/TRANS An adjective describing a person whose gender identity or gender expression is different from the one assigned to them at birth.

TRIAD A nonmonogamous arrangement in which three people are involved with one another. Occasionally applied to *vees*. Triads may also be part of a larger *intimate network*.

TRIGGER A specific thought, action, sight or event that sets off an emotion that is usually linked to past traumatic events.

UNICORN A hypothetical *cisgender* woman (usually *bisexual*) who is willing to be involved with both members of a couple (usually heterosexual) on their terms.

VEE A nonmonogamous arrangement involving three people in which one person is romantically or sexually involved with two partners who are not romantically or sexually involved with each other. Vees may also be part of a larger *intimate network*.

VETO A relationship agreement, most common in *primary/secondary* relationships, that gives one person the power to end another person's additional relationships, or in some cases to disallow some specific activity.

WIBBLE, WIBBLY (BRITISH) A feeling of insecurity, typically temporary or fleeting, when someone sees a partner being affectionate with someone else. Sometimes used to describe minor pangs of jealousy.

Notes

EPIGRAPH

vii **I am listening** adrienne maree brown, *Emergent Strategy: Shaping Change, Changing Worlds* (Chico, California: AK Press, 2017), 13.

xiii **Another world** Arundhati Roy, *War Talk* (Cambridge, MA: South End Press, 2003), 75.

xiv **Toronto Star** Kevin Donovan, "CBC Fires Jian Ghomeshi Over Sex Allegations," *Toronto Star*, October 26, 2014, https://www.thestar.com/news/canada/cbc-fires-jian-ghomeshi-over-sex-allegations/article_892cf877-a892-515b-b05f-7aa044c8eaa3.html.

xvi **founders of the system** "'Kill the Indian in Him, and Save the Man': R. H. Pratt on the Education of Native Americans," Carlisle Indian School Digital Resource Center, https://carlisleindian.dickinson.edu/teach/kill-indian-him-and-save-man-r-h-pratt-education-native-americans.

xvi **that talked about love** Matika Wilbur, Desi Small-Rodriguez, Adrienne Keene, Geraldine King and Jillene Joseph, "All My Loving Relations," May 17, 2021, in *All My Relations*, podcast, https://www.allmyrelationspodcast.com/podcast/episode/48f75f91/all-my-loving-relations.

xvii **global humiliation** Gustaf Kilander, "Johnny Depp Said Amber Heard Was 'Begging for Global Humiliation' After She Filed for Restraining Order," *The Independent*, May 25, 2022, https://www.independent.co.uk/news/world/americas/johnny-depp-amber-heard-texts-b2087471.html

xvii **typical account** See Michael Hobbes, "The Bleak Spectacle of the Amber Heard-Johnny Depp Trial," *Substack*, June 2, 2022, https://michaelhobbes.substack.com/p/the-bleak-spectacle-of-the-amber; and Katelyn Burns, Oliver-Ash Kleine and Michael Hobbes, "Deep Depp-ception," *Cancel Me, Daddy*, podcast, May 26, 2022.

xviii ***Parable of the Sower*** Octavia Butler, *Parable of the Sower* (New York: Four Walls Eight Windows, 1993).

xxiii **murdering eight** Wendy Gillis, "'Guilty.' Serial killer Bruce McArthur admits to first-degree murder in deaths of eight men," *Toronto Star*, January 29, 2019, https://www.thestar.com/news/gta/guilty-serial-killer-bruce-mcarthur-admits-to-first-degree-murder-in-deaths-of-eight-men

INTRODUCTION

1 **The universe is made** Muriel Rukeyser, *The Speed of Darkness* (New York: Vintage Books, 1968), quoted in Maria Popova, *Figuring* (New York: Vintage Books, 2019), 16.

11 **Who identify as Polynesian** See, for example, Kevin Patterson, *Love's Not Color Blind: Race and Representation in Polyamorous and Other Alternative Communities* (Portland, OR: Thorntree Press, 2018), 47.

1 CHOOSING NONMONOGAMY

15 **Every story is a love story** Alix E. Harrow, *The Ten Thousand Doors of January* (New York: Redhook, 2019), Kobo edition.

20 **Authors such as** See, for example, Sarah Carter, *The Importance of Being Monogamous: Marriage and Nation Building in Western Canada to 1915* (Athabasca, Alberta: Athabasca University Press, 2008); Kim TallBear, "Making Love and Relations Beyond Settler Sex and Family," in *Making Kin Not Population: Reconceiving Generations*, ed. Adele E. Clarke and Donna Haraway (Chicago: University of Chicago Press, 2018), 145–164; Stephanie Coontz, *The Social Origins of Private Life: A History of American Families 1600–1900* (New York: Verso, 1998); and Carrie Jenkins, *Sad Love: Romance and the Search for Meaning* (Cambridge, UK: Polity Books, 2022).

21 **inherently insecure** Jessica Fern, *Polysecure: Attachment, Trauma and Consensual Nonmonogamy* (Victoria, BC: Thornapple Press, 2020), 137–138.

24 **ancient biological machinery** Carrie Jenkins, *What Love Is: And What It Could Be* (New York: Basic Books, 2017), 82.

24 **intimacy as a mirror** Heidi Priebe, "How the Mirror of Deep Intimacy Will Either Destroy or Heal Your Attachment Relationships," YouTube (February 15, 2024), youtube.com/watch?v=v7gUXk8RyQI.

25 **access intimacy** Mia Mingus, "Access Intimacy: The Missing Link," *Leaving Evidence* (blog), May 5, 2011, https://leavingevidence.wordpress.com/2011/05/05/access-intimacy-the-missing-link.

26 **kinship and relationships** TallBear, "Making Love and Relations," in Clarke and Haraway, *Making Kin Not Population*, 156.

27 **instead of or alongside** Jenkins, *Sad Love*; Jenkins, *Nonmonogamy and Happiness* (Victoria, BC: Thornapple Press, 2024); Wendy-O Matik, *Redefining Our Relationships: Guidelines for Responsible Open Relationships* (Oakland, CA: Defiant Times Press, 2002); Rhaina Cohen, *The Other Significant Others: Reimagining Life with Friendship at the Center* (New York: St Martin's Press, 2024).

28 **In an interview** Jessica Fern, Eve Rickert and David Cooley, "Jessica Fern, David Cooley and Eve Rickert Discuss *Polywise*," YouTube (September 27, 2023) https://youtu.be/Odbv1WA_-dY?si=MEsVA9QkrUS6KJGV.

2 FINDING YOUR COMPASS (OR, DON'T BE MEAN)

31 **What are we sowing** Kelly Hayes and Mariame Kaba, *Let This Radicalize You: Organizing and the Revolution of Reciprocal Care* (Chicago: Haymarket Books, 2023), 4.

32 **On a different note** Claire Louise Travers, "Why You Should Drop the 'E' in Ethical Non-Monogamy," *Medium* (blog), May 28, 2021, https://clairelouisetravers.medium.com/why-you-should-drop-the-e-in-ethical-non-monogamy-32069e129df1.

34 **Over the course of this book** Kate Bornstein, *Hello, Cruel World: 101 Alternatives to Suicide for Teens, Freaks and Other Outlaws* (New York: Seven Stories Press, 2006), 95–96.

35 **rooted in disconnection** Jess Housty ('Cúagilákv), "Kinship," in *Spirits of the Coast: Orcas in Science, Art and History*, ed. Martha Black, Lorne Hammond, Gavin Hanke and Nikki Sanchez (Victoria, BC: Royal BC Museum, 2020), 180.

35 **capitalism requires** Mia Mingus, "Transformative Justice & Pod Mapping," January 19, 2019, in *Beyond Prisons* podcast, https://www.beyond-prisons.com/home/transformative-justice-amp-pod-mapping.

36 **emergence** brown, *Emergent Strategy*, 15.

36 **fundamental unit of change** Sage Crump, Mia Herndon and adrienne maree brown, "Host Favorites: Relating During the Pandemic with Autumn Brown (2021)," February 9, 2023, in *The Emergent Strategy Podcast*, podcast.

36 **shape that change** Octavia Butler, *Parable of the Sower* (New York: Grand Central Publishing, 2019), Kobo edition.

37 **Your values are** Barbara Carrellas, *Ecstasy Is Necessary: A Practical Guide* (Carlsbad, CA, and New York: Hay House, 2012), 30.

37 **I'm not a big believer** Kai Cheng Thom, *I Hope We Choose Love: A Trans Girl's Notes from the End of the World* (Vancouver, Canada: Arsenal Pulp Press, 2019), 84.

39 **A boundary on my own behavior** Sander T. Jones, *Cultivating Connection: A Practical Guide for Personal and Relationship Growth in Ethical Non-Monogamy* (Cast Net Books, 2023), 113–114.

39 **The East Coast is kind** Jordan K. Green (@jordonaut), Twitter, January 21, 2021, 2:11 p.m. https://www.twitter.com/jordonaut/status/1352363163686068226.

40 **But it was my integrity** Alan Moore, *V for Vendetta* (New York: DC Comics, 1988), 156.

44 **Love is the perception of individuals** Iris Murdoch, "The Sublime and the Good," *Chicago Review* 13, no. 3, (1959): 42–55 (p. 51), quoted in Maria Popova, "What Love Really Means: Iris Murdoch on Unselfing, the Symmetry Between Art and Morality, and How We Unblind Ourselves to Each Other's Realities," *The Marginalian* (blog), January 8, 2022, https://www.themarginalian.org/2022/01/08/iris-murdoch-the-sublime-and-the-good.

45 **Much harm is caused** Danya Ruttenberg, *On Repentance and Repair: Making Amends in an Unapologetic World* (Boston: Beacon Press, 2022), 174.

50 **As Nora Samaran writes** Nora Samaran, *Turn This World Inside Out: The Emergence of Nurturance Culture* (Chico, CA: AK Press, 2019), Kobo edition.

51 **Kitty Stryker summed up** Kitty Stryker, "'Radical Self-Reliance' Is Killing People," *Hack Grow Love* (blog), November 4, 2015, https://medium.com/hack-grow-love/radical-self-reliance-is-killing-people-c980eb05b867.

52 **a conformist agenda** Ratna Kapur, "There's a Problem with the LGBT Rights Movement – It's Limiting Freedom," *The Conversation*, September 17, 2018, https://theconversation.com/theres-a-problem-with-the-lgbt-rights-movement-its-limiting-freedom-101999.

3 ABUSE

58 **Never be cruel** *Dr. Who*, season 10, episode 13, "Twice Upon a Time," directed by Rachel Talalay, written by Steven Moffatt, aired December 25, 2017.

59 **In Canada** Natalie Rech, "#MeToo Movement in Canada," *The Canadian Encyclopedia*, January 31, 2019, last edited May 22, 2020, https://www.thecanadianencyclopedia.ca/en/article/metoo-movement-in-canada.

59 **England and Wales** Ciara Nugent, "'Abuse Is a Pattern.' Why These Nations Took the Lead in Criminalizing Controlling Behavior in Relationships," *Time*, June 21, 2019, https://time.com/5610016/coercive-control-domestic-violence.

61 **In her book** bell hooks, *All About Love* (New York: HarperCollins, 2001), 4–6.

62 **I want to encourage** Kitty Stryker, *Ask Yourself: The Consent Culture Workbook* (Victoria, BC: Thornapple Press, 2023), 9–10.

63 **Canada's House of Commons** Carmen Gill and Mary Aspinall, *Submission to the House of Commons Standing Committee on Justice and Human Rights: Study on Bill C-247: An Act to amend the Criminal Code (controlling or coercive conduct)*, February 2021, https://www.ourcommons.ca/Content/Committee/432/JUST/Brief/BR11085796/br-external/Jointly1-e.pdf.

63 **In the *Globe and Mail*** Molly Hayes, Elizabeth Renzetti and Tavia Grant, "Coercive Control Can Be a Life or Death Issue in Relationships. But Few People Even Know How to Recognize It," *The Globe and Mail*, March 13, 2022, https://www.theglobeandmail.com/canada/article-coercive-control-can-be-a-life-or-death-issue-in-relationships-but-few.

64 **by any means necessary** See, for example, Gavin de Becker, *The Gift of Fear: Survival Signals That Protect You from Violence* (New York: Back Bay Books, 2021), and Lundy Bancroft, *Why Does He Do That? Inside the Minds of Angry and Controlling Men* (New York: Berkley Books, 2003).

65 **tactics of their abusers** Connie Burk, "Distinguishing between Violence and Abuse," in *Creative Interventions Toolkit: A Practical Guide to Stop Interpersonal Violence* (Creative Interventions, 2012), 524–533, https://www.creative-interventions.org/wp-content/uploads/2020/10/CI-Toolkit-Final-ENTIRE-Aug-2020-new-cover.pdf

67 **situational and characterological violence** Daniel Joseph Friend et al., "Typologies of Intimate Partner Violence: Evaluation of a Screening Instrument for Differentiation," *Journal of Family Therapy* 26 (2011): 551–563.

68 **missing stair** Cliff Pervocracy, "The Missing Stair," *Pervocracy* (blog), June 22, 2012, https://pervocracy.blogspot.com/2012/06/missing-stair.html.

69 **As Freyd writes** Jennifer J. Freyd, "What Is DARVO?" accessed May 12, 2024, https://dynamic.uoregon.edu/jjf/defineDARVO.html.

69 **sense of victimization** Bancroft, *Why Does He Do That?*, 96–99.

72 **dying by suicide** Cheng Thom, *I Hope We Choose Love*, 42–46.

72 **As Kai Cheng Thom writes** – Kai Cheng Thom (@kaichengthom), "Any ideology..." Instagram, April 2, 2024, https://www.instagram.com/p/C5RLCz7O4j7/?img_index=1

72 **a sort of inversion** Shea Emma Fett, "Abuse in Polyamorous Relationships," *Medium* (blog), November 22, 2014, https://medium.com/@sheaemmafett/abuse-in-polyamorous-relationships-d13e396c8f85.

73 **some cult theory** See Alexandra Stein, *Terror, Love and Brainwashing: Attachment in Cults and Totalitarian Systems* (London, UK: Routledge, 2016), Kindle edition.

73 **their biggest ally** Bancroft, *Why Does He Do That?*, 282–284.

74 **himpathy** Kate Manne, *Down Girl: The Logic of Misogyny* (New York: Oxford University Press, 2017), Kindle edition.

74 **a reserve army** Barucha Peller, "Polyamory as a Reserve Army of Care Labor," *Anarcha Library* (blog), March 13, 2013, https://anarchalibrary.blogspot.com/2013/03/polyamory-as-reserve-army-of-care-labor.html.

74 **your polycule is your family** Fett, "Abuse in Polyamorous Relationships."

80 **having a hard time deciding** Lundy Bancroft, *Should I Stay or Should I Go? A Guide to Knowing if Your Relationship Can—and Should—Be Saved* (New York: Berkley Books, 2011); Mira Kirshenbaum, *Too Good to Leave, Too Bad to Stay: A Step-by-Step Guide to Help You Decide Whether to Stay In or Get Out of Your Relationship* (New York: Plume, 1997).

80 **safety planning** The Network/La Red, "Safety Planning," https://www.tnlr.org/en/safety-planning.

83 **her book *Stop Signs*** Lynn Fairweather, *Stop Signs: Recognizing, Avoiding, and Escaping Abusive Relationships* (Berkeley, CA: Seal Press, 2012), 83.

86 **To whom would I turn** For one in-depth approach to figuring out who you'd turn to if you either experienced harm or harmed someone, see Mia Mingus, "Pods and Pod Mapping Worksheet," *Bay Area Transformative Justice Collective*, June 2016, https://batjc.wordpress.com/resources/pods-and-pod-mapping-worksheet.

4 TENDING YOUR SELF

89 **It is a fault** Simone Weil, *Gravity and Grace* (London, UK, and New York: Routledge, 2022), quoted in Maria Popova, "Simone Weil on the Paradox of Friendship and Separation," *The Marginalian* (blog), August 24, 2015, https://www.themarginalian.org/2015/08/24/simone-weil-friendship-separation.

92 **shame researcher Brené Brown** Brené Brown, *Daring Greatly: How the Courage to Be Vulnerable Transforms the Way We Live, Love, Parent, and Lead* (New York: Gotham Books, 2012), 231–238.

98 **courage by couraging** Mary Daly quoted in Brené Brown, *The Gifts of Imperfection: Let Go of Who You Think You're Supposed to Be and Embrace Who You Are* (Center City, Minnesota: Hazelden, 2010), 7.

101 **growing pain and shrinking pain** Heidi Priebe, "Growing Pain Versus Shrinking Pain: How to Tell if You're Moving Forward," YouTube, July 23, 2023, https://youtu.be/iWEB3jfeBzc.

107 **intimacy scarcity** Heidi Priebe, "Fearful-Avoidant: How Intimacy Scarcity Keeps You Codependent (and How to Change It)," YouTube, February 12, 2024, https://www.youtube.com/watch?v=TLiZDks_vlU.

108 **Sara Maitland** Sara Maitland, *How to Be Alone* (London: MacMillan, 2014).

5 NURTURING YOUR RELATIONSHIPS

111 **The longer I live** Maria Popova, "The Light Between Us," *The Marginalian* (blog), January 31, 2022, https://www.themarginalian.org/2022/01/31/james-baldwin-nothing-personal-love.

112 **the acronym HEARTS** Fern, *Polysecure*, 173.

114 **generative conflict** Jessica Fern and David Cooley, *Polywise* (Victoria, BC: Thornapple Press, 2023), 149–162.

114 **trust and faith** The Loving Avoidant (@thelovingavoidant), "Trust vs. Faith," Instagram, February 15, 2023, https://www.instagram.com/p/CosyteqPRDL.

118 **Ginny Brown** Ginny Brown (@ginnymoonbeam), "The values shield: ethics as defense," Tumblr, May 13, 2024, https://www.tumblr.com/ginnymoonbeam/750404680582037504/the-values-shield-ethics-as-defense.

6 COMMUNICATION PITFALLS

122 **We are not obliged** Rabbi Abraham Joshua Heschel, *God in Search of Man: A Philosophy of Judaism* (New York: Farrar, Strauss and Giroux: 1976), 401–3, quoted in Ruttenberg, *On Repentance and Repair*, 60.

134 **four horsemen** Fern and Cooley, *Polywise*, 99–104.

7 COMMUNICATION STRATEGIES

137 **power over the story** Salman Rushdie, "One Thousand Days in a Balloon," speech at Columbia University, December 11, 1991, quoted in Sabrina Hassumani, *Salman Rushdie: A Postmodern Reading of His Major Works* (Vancouver, BC: Fairleigh Dickinson University Press, 2002), 104.

146 **the goal of the conversation** Shea Emma Fett, “10 Things I Wish I'd Known About Gaslighting,” *Medium*, July 5, 2015, https://medium.com/@sheaemmafett/10-things-i-wish-i-d-known-about-gaslighting-22234cb5e407.

152 **as Kate Abramson discusses** Kate Abramson, *On Gaslighting* (Princeton, NJ: Princeton University Press, 2024).

8 BEFRIENDING THE GREEN-EYED MONSTER

155 **a monster is** Kai Cheng Thom, *Falling Back in Love with Being Human: Letters to Lost Souls* (Toronto, ON: Penguin Canada, 2023), 102.

157 **a useful framework** Jessica Fern, unpublished interview by Eve Rickert, August 11, 2023.

158 **primal panic** Fern, *Polysecure*, 145.

159 **Fern says** Jessica Fern, email to Eve Rickert, May 22, 2024.

159 **justice jealousy** Fern and Cooley, *Polywise*, 106–114.

159 **Fern refers to as** Jessica Fern, email to Eve Rickert, May 22, 2024.

159 **Jenkins noticed** Carrie Jenkins, unpublished interview by Eve Rickert, July 6, 2023.

160 **parts exercises** Fern and Cooley, *Polywise*, 76–92.

160 **Fern says** Fern, unpublished interview by Rickert, August 11, 2023.

162 **re-storifying** Jenkins, unpublished interview by Rickert, July 6, 2023.

9 BOUNDARIES

167 **daring to set boundaries** Brené Brown, "3 Ways to Set Boundaries," *Oprah.com* (blog), no date, https://www.oprah.com/spirit/how-to-set-boundaries-brene-browns-advice

169 **author Nora Samaran** Nora Samaran, “For Men Who Desperately Need Autonomy,” (blog), July 21, 2016, https://norasamaran.com/2016/07/21/for-men-who-desperately-need-autonomy-make-it-dont-take-it.

171 ***The Tree Who Set Healthy Boundaries*** Topher Payne, *The Tree Who Set Healthy Boundaries: A Parody Alternate Ending for Shel Silverstein's The Giving Tree* (n.d.), https://www.topherpayne.com/giving-tree.

177 **reassert a no** de Becker, *The Gift of Fear*.

180 **Alyssa Gonzalez's book** Alyssa Gonzalez, *Nonmonogamy and Neurodiversity: A More Than Two Essentials Guide* (Victoria, BC: Thornapple Press, 2023).

181 **decades of trauma study** Gabor Maté and Daniel Maté, *The Myth of Normal: Trauma, Illness and Healing in a Toxic Culture* (Toronto, ON: Knopf Canada, 2023).

181 **sex, depression and interpersonal support** JoEllen Notte, *The Monster Under the Bed: Sex, Depression, and the Conversations We Aren't Having* (Victoria, BC: Thornapple Press, 2020); and *In It Together: Navigating Depression with Partners, Friends, and Family* (Victoria, BC: Thornapple Press, 2023). See also her essay “Sex and Love When You Hate Yourself and Don't Have Your Shit Together,” in *Ask: Building Consent Culture*, ed. Kitty Stryker (Victoria, BC: Thornapple Press, 2017), 9–14.

10 RULES AND AGREEMENTS

184 **the lifeblood** Kirshenbaum, *Too Good to Leave, Too Bad to Stay*, Kindle edition.

188 **novel situations** See, for example, Timothy D. Wilson and Daniel T. Gilbert, "Affective Forecasting," *Advances in Experimental Social Psychology* 35 (2003): 345–411.

199 **an inverse relationship to trust** Andrea Zanin, "The Problem with Polynormativity," *Sex Geek* (blog), January 24, 2013, https://sexgeek.wordpress.com/2013/01/24/theproblemwithpolynormativity.

11 HIERARCHY AND PRIMARY/SECONDARY POLYAMORY

201 **People like certainty** Sarah Marshall, "Juvenile 'Justice' with Josie Duffy Rice," March 13, 2023, in *You're Wrong About*, podcast, https://www.buzzsprout.com/1112270/12433925-juvenile-justice-with-josie-duffy-rice.

208 **mononormative culture** See Zanin, "The Problem with Polynormativity."

212 **as the couple's nanny** Goddess of Java, "Ask the Misanthrope: Cover Story," *The Polyamorous Misanthrope* (blog), December 8, 2008, archived at https://web.archive.org/web/20120207174523/http://www.polyamorousmisanthrope.com/2008/12/08/ask-the-misanthrope-cover-story.

214 **motte-and-bailey doctrine** Nicholas Shackel, "The Vacuity of Postmodernist Methodology," *Metaphilosophy* 36, no. 3 (April 2005): 295–320. https://doi.org/10.1111/j.1467-9973.2005.00370.x

218 **In her memoir** Louisa Leontiades, *A World in Us: A Memoir of Open Marriage, Turbulent Love and Hardwon Wisdom* (Portland, OR: Thorntree Press, 2017), 176–177.

12 VETO ARRANGEMENTS

226 **The trouble with human happiness** Hannah Arendt, *Love and Saint Augustine* (Chicago: University of Chicago Press, 1998), quoted in Maria Popova, "Hannah Arendt on Love and How to Live with the Fundamental Fear of Loss," *The Marginalian* (blog), February 25, 2019, https://www.themarginalian.org/2019/02/25/love-and-saint-augustine-hannah-arendt.

13 EMPOWERED RELATIONSHIPS

240 **The most vital right** Emma Goldman, "The Tragedy of Woman's Emancipation," in *Anarchism and Other Essays* (New York & London: Mother Earth Publishing Association, 1911), 219–231.

243 **a fog over a meadow at evening** Samuel R. Delany, *Tales of Nevèrÿon* (Middletown, CT: Wesleyan University Press, 1993), 63.

243 **not showing up fully** See, for example, Heidi Priebe, "The Biggest Blindspot of People with Low Self-Esteem (& How to Keep It from Ruining Relationships)," YouTube, February 19, 2024, https://youtu.be/HFUIV2YXRjw.

244 **keenly aware of power dynamics** Heidi Priebe, "10 Signs You May Have a Fearful-Avoidant Attachment Style," YouTube, January 16, 2022, https://youtu.be/5jk7PAa8D1o.

250 **seen this experiment** Frans de Waal, "Moral Behavior in Animals" (TedX Peachtree, Atlanta, Georgia), November 2011, video, https://www.ted.com/talks/frans_de_waal_moral_behavior_in_animals.

14 PRACTICAL NONMONOGAMY AGREEMENTS

253 **I've worked really hard** Lauren Bacon, "The One Question You Must Ask (or, The World's Shortest Bucket List)," *LaurenBacon.com* (blog), June 18, 2013, https://laurenbacon.com/the-one-question-you-must-ask

15 HOW NONMONOGAMOUS RELATIONSHIPS ARE DIFFERENT

273 **we can change** Terry Tempest Williams, *When Women Were Birds: Fifty-Four Variations on Voice*, quoted in Maria Popova, "The Bird in the Heart: Terry Tempest Williams on the Paradox of Transformation and How to Live with Uncertainty," *The Marginalian* (blog), January 24, 2024, https://www.themarginalian.org/2024/01/26/when-women-were-birds

277 **coined the term limerence** See Dorothy Tennov, *Love and Limerence: The Experience of Being in Love* (Lanham, MD: Scarborough House, 1998).

290 **educate a teacher** Ashley Speed, *Nonmonogamy and Teaching: A More Than Two Essentials Guide* (Victoria, BC: Thornapple Press, 2023).

291 **all over Canada** Canada's Polygamy Laws Upheld by B.C. Supreme Court, *CBC*, November 23, 2011, https://www.cbc.ca/news/canada/british-columbia/canada-s-polygamy-laws-upheld-by-b-c-supreme-court-1.856480.

291 **child they were raising together** Michael McDonald, "3 Adults in Polyamorous Relationship Declared Legal Parents by N. L. Court," *CBC*, June 14, 2018, https://www.cbc.ca/news/canada/newfoundland-labrador/polyamourous-relationship-three-parents-1.4706560.

16 OPENING FROM A COUPLE

294 **life has taught us** Antoine de Saint-Exupéry, translated by Lewis Galantière and Stuart Gilbert, *Airman's Odyssey* (San Diego, CA: Harcourt, Brace & World: 1967), 195.

303 **Marcus McCann's book** Marcus McCann, *Park Cruising: What Happens When We Wander Off the Path* (Toronto, ON: House of Anansi Press, 2023).

304 **Kinky folks might want** Lee Harrington and Mollena Williams, *Playing Well with Others: Your Field Guide to Discovering, Exploring and Navigating the Kink, Leather and BDSM Communities* (Emeryville, CA: Greenery Press, 2012); Raven Kaldera, ed., *Power Circuits: Polyamory in a Power Dynamic* (Hubbardston, MA: Alfred Press, 2010).

17 MONO/POLY RELATIONSHIPS

309 **in a healthy environment** Danya Ruttenberg, *On Repentance*, 24.

310 **post-nonmonogamous** See Andrea Zanin, *Post-Nonmonogamy and Beyond: A More Than Two Essentials Guide* (Victoria, BC: Thornapple Press, 2024).

312 **temporary vessel** Fern and Cooley, *Polywise*, 42–48.

18 FINDING PARTNERS

321 **I fall in love with myself** Eartha Kitt, interviewed in *All By Myself: The Eartha Kitt Story*, directed by Christian Blackwood (New York: Michael Blackwood Productions, 1982).

325 **abusive men** see Bancroft, *Why Does He Do That?*, 282–284.

325 **to mistreat you** See Bancroft, *Why Does He Do That?*, 97.

326 **fuck yes** Mark Manson, "Fuck Yes or No," *Mark Manson* (blog), July 8, 2013, https://markmanson.net/fuck-yes.

19 LIFE IN THE POLYCULE

332 **loving all of you** Charlie Jane Anders, *Promises Stronger Than Darkness* (New York: Tor Teen, 2023), Kobo edition.

333 **writer Laura Boyle** Laura Boyle "Kitchen Table Polyamory and Parallel Polyamory: Introduction," *Ready for Polyamory* (blog), March 18, 2020, https://www.readyforpolyamory.com/post/kitchen-table-and-parallel-polyamory-part-2-extreme-kitchen-table-1.

20 SEX, PLEASURE, RISK AND HEALTH

353 **For a moment she** Shelley Parker-Chan, *She Who Became the Sun* (New York: Tor Books, 2021), Kobo edition.

356 **A great place to start** Emily Nagoski, *Come As You Are: Revised and Updated: The Surprising New Science That Will Transform Your Sex Life* (New York: Simon & Schuster, 2021); Nagoski, *Come Together: The Science (and Art!) of Creating Lasting Sexual Connections* (New York: Ballantine Books, 2024).

361 **the worry that some part of us is unacceptable** Lauren Fogel Mersy and Jennifer A. Vencill, *Desire: An Inclusive Guide to Navigating Libido Differences in Relationships* (Boston, MA: Beacon Press, 2023), p. 36

362 **results in real, physical changes** Jones, *Cultivating Connection*, 182.

363 **for a great discussion** Notte, *The Monster Under the Bed*.

363 **In Canada** Consent Comes First Toronto Metropolitan, "Understanding Consent," Toronto Metropolitan University, https://www.torontomu.ca/sexual-violence/education/laws-of-consent-in-canada/

364 **As A.V. Flox writes** A.V. Flox, "The Legal Framework of Consent is Worthless," in Stryker, *Ask: Building Consent Culture*, 15–25.

364 **access negotiating power** Robin Bauer, *Queer BDSM Intimacies: Critical Consent and Pushing Boundaries* (London, UK: Palgrave Macmillan, 2014), 106.

367 **tailored guides** Joan Price, *Naked at Our Age: Talking Out Loud About Senior Sex* (Berkeley, CA: Seal Press, 2011); Nillin Lore, *How Do I Sexy? A Guide for Trans and Nonbinary Queers* (Victoria, BC: Thornapple Press, 2024); Hanne Blank, *Big Big Love: A Sex and Relationships Guide for People of Size (and Those Who Love Them)* (Berkeley, CA: Celestial Arts, 2011); Reece M. Malone et al., eds., *An Intersectional Approach to Sex Therapy: Centering the Lives of Indigenous, Racialized, and People of Color* (New York: Routledge, 2022)(it's not just for therapists!); Miriam Kaufman, Cory Silverberg, and Fran Odette, *The Ultimate Guide to Sex and Disability* (San Francisco, CA: Cleis Press, 2007).

368 **Justin Lehmiller of the Kinsey Institute** Justin J. Lehmiller, *Tell Me What You Want: The Science of Sexual Desire and How It Can Help You Improve Your Sex Life*. (New York: Hachette Go, 2018), 14.

369 **There are some really cringey** Stella Harris, *The Ultimate Guide to Threesomes* (San Francisco, CA: Cleis Press, 2021).

370 **Gen Z hookup trend** Julia Pugachevsky, "Choking without Consent is a Gen Z Hookup Trend. Even If It Doesn't Bother You, It Can be Extremely Dangerous," *Business Insider*, November 9, 2022, https://www.businessinsider.com/choking-gen-z-sex-hookups-consent-assault-2022-10.

373 **even if you never have a sore anywhere** Valerie Johnson, "Why Can't I be Tested for ALL Sexually Transmitted Infections?" *Planned Parenthood of the St. Louis Region and Southwest Missouri* (blog), May 19, 2020, https://www.plannedparenthood.org/planned-parenthood-st-louis-region-southwest-missouri/blog/why-cant-i-be-tested-for-all-sexually-transmitted-infections.

374 **head and neck cancers** "HPV Vaccine Age Limit: You Might Not Be Too Old — What You Should Know," *Memorial Sloan Kettering Cancer Center* (blog), February 8, 2023, https://www.mskcc.org/news/think-you-re-too-old-get-hpv-vaccine-prevent-cancer-maybe-not.

375 **completely cured** International Federation of Pharmaceutical Manufacturers and Associations, "Hepatitis C: Discovery to Cure in 25 Years," https://50years.ifpma.org/in-focus/hepatitis-c/

375 **transmit HIV** Prevention Access Campaign, https://preventionaccess.com/

375 **preventing HIV infection** HIV.info and National Institutes of Health, "HIV Prevention: Post-Exposure Prophylaxis (PEP)," last updated February 6, 2024, https://hivinfo.nih.gov/understanding-hiv/fact-sheets/post-exposure-prophylaxis-pep.

375 **syphilis, gonorrhea and chlamydia** World Health Organization, "STIs in 2022: Emerging and Re-Emerging Outbreaks," September 2, 2022, https://www.who.int/news/item/02-09-2022-stis-in-2022-emerging-and-re-emerging-outbreaks.

376 **months after infection** Statistics Canada, "Experiences of Canadians with Long-Term Symptoms Following COVID-19," *The Daily*, December 8, 2023, https://www150.statcan.gc.ca/n1/daily-quotidien/231208/dq231208a-eng.htm.

21 RELATIONSHIP TRANSITIONS

382 **hearts change** *Howl's Moving Castle*, directed by Hayao Miyazaki (2004; Tokyo: Studio Ghibli).

384 **In his book** Dan Savage, *The Commitment: Love, Sex, Marriage and My Family* (New York: Penguin, 2005), 113.

385 **collaborative works of art** Jenkins, *Sad Love*, 81.

THE FUTURE OF NONMONOGAMY

397 **Transform yourself** Grace Lee Boggs quoted in brown, *Emergent Strategy*, Kindle edition.

Resources

There's a lot out there on nonmonogamy, as well as the skills—such as communication and cultivating healthy self-esteem—that are useful in relationships of all kinds, including nonmonogamous ones. There's also a wealth of information on the history and philosophy of nonmonogamy, as well as some (though not as much as we'd like) about mononormativity and amatonormativity. With the list below, we've tried to present a few of the standouts in each category, organized by date of publication, with the most recent resources listed first.

ETHICS

Ask Yourself: The Consent Culture Workbook, Kitty Stryker (Thornapple Press, 2023). A guide to take you through an introspective process that can help you understand what consent means to you in your life and help you build consent culture in your world.

Let This Radicalize You: Organizing and the Revolution of Reciprocal Care, Kelly Hayes and Mariame Kaba (Haymarket Books, 2023). A practical and compassionate guide to grassroots political organizing, this book also offers a wealth of insight on how to build community and be in good relationship with one another.

I Hope We Choose Love: A Trans Girl's Notes from the End of the World, Kai Cheng Thom (Arsenal Pulp Press, 2019). Reflections on love, care and heartbreak in queer communities.

Turn This World Inside Out: The Emergence of Nurturance Culture, Nora Samaran (AK Press, 2019). A thoughtful and compassionate call to remake your communities and your culture on models of care and accountability.

Love's Not Color Blind: Race and Representation in Polyamorous and Other Alternative Communities, Kevin A. Patterson (Thornapple Press, 2018). A book that applies to all kinds of alternative communities but unpacks the race dynamics of many nonmonogamous communities specifically, and offers strategies for creating more inclusive spaces.

Emergent Strategy: Shaping Change, Changing Worlds, adrienne maree brown (AK Press, 2017). Meditations on transforming your relationships and the worlds you can imagine as the basis for transforming the world.

Braiding Sweetgrass: Indigenous Wisdom, Scientific Knowledge and the Teachings of Plants, Robin Wall Kimmerer (Milkweed Editions, 2015). Through a blend of memoir, scientific anecdotes and traditional knowledge, Kimmerer offers reflections on how you can live in reciprocal relationships with other people and the natural world.

SELF

Falling Back in Love with Being Human: Letters to Lost Souls, Kai Cheng Thom (Penguin, 2023). Poetic letters to people who are socially constructed as monsters, with suggestions for deep kinds of self-care and reconnection for all those who have felt rejected or harmed.

The Gifts of Imperfection: Let Go of Who You Think You're Supposed to Be and Embrace Who You Are, Brené Brown (Hazelden, 2010). A small but life-changing, evidence-based book on confronting insecurity, believing in your own worthiness and living what Brown calls "wholehearted" lives.

Hello, Cruel World: 101 Alternatives to Suicide for Teens, Freaks and Other Outlaws, Kate Bornstein (Seven Stories Press, 2006). A powerful list of 101 alternatives to suicide, rated by how dangerous they are and how effective they are, from a deeply kind trans writer who's been there.

RELATIONSHIPS

Cultivating Connection: A Practical Guide for Personal and Relationship Growth in Ethical Non-Monogamy, Sander T. Jones (Cast Net Books, 2023). A therapist's guide to working on yourself, understanding boundaries, handling triggers and establishing good communication in relationships, with a particular focus on nonmonogamy.

In It Together: Navigating Depression with Partners, Friends and Family, JoEllen Notte (Thornapple, 2023). A practical guidebook for people with depression and those who love them or are part of their communities.

On Repentance and Repair: Making Amends in an Unapologetic World, Danya Ruttenberg (Beacon Press, 2022). A new look at atonement, forgiveness and repair from harm, including both interpersonal and larger cultural issues.

Sad Love: Romance and the Search for Meaning, Carrie Jenkins (Polity, 2022). A philosophical argument against the pursuit of happiness in love and toward the pursuit of a meaningful life, in part through the idea of eudaimonic love—collaborative, creative and dynamic.

Daring Greatly: How the Courage to Be Vulnerable Transforms the Way We Live, Love, Parent, and Lead, Brené Brown (Penguin, 2012). About expressing courage in all your relationships and throughout your life by daring to be your most authentic self.

The Dance of Connection: How to Talk to Someone When You're Mad, Hurt, Scared, Frustrated, Insulted, Betrayed, or Desperate, Harriet Lerner (HarperCollins, 2009). Excellent techniques for high-stakes communication in any kind of relationship and in emotionally charged situations.

All About Love: New Visions, bell hooks (HarperCollins, 2001). Wisdom about the nature of love. Focused on monogamous heterosexual relationships, but some insights are broadly applicable.

Too Good to Leave, Too Bad to Stay: A Step-by-Step Guide to Help You Decide Whether to Stay In or Get Out of Your Relationship, Mira Kirshenbaum (Plume, 1997). A set of 36 yes-or-no questions to answer to help you decide whether to stay or go. Focused on cishet relationships and presumed monogamy, but applies more broadly.

The Dance of Intimacy: A Woman's Guide to Courageous Acts of Change in Key Relationships, Harriet Lerner (Harper Perennial, 1989). A classic book, geared at women but useful for everyone, on maintaining clear boundaries and a strong self while building intimacy in relationships.

ABUSE

On Gaslighting, Kate Abramson (Princeton University Press, 2024). A philosophical breakdown of what gaslighting is, how it works, and why it's a special kind of terrible.

Creative Interventions Toolkit: A Practical Guide to Stop Interpersonal Violence, Creative Interventions. (AK Press, 2021). Filled with practical exercises, worksheets and examples, this is a comprehensive guide to preventing and responding to abuse within communities.

The Gift of Fear: Survival Signals That Protect Us from Violence, Gavin de Becker (Back Bay Books, 2021). Insightful examination of how your instincts work to warn you of danger, how to better listen to and act on them, and how to notice the ways you are already making choices toward your safety instead of blaming yourself if you fall victim to violence.

Terror, Love and Brainwashing: Attachment in Cults and Totalitarian Systems, Alexandra Stein (Routledge, 2021). Describes the psychological mechanisms behind interpersonal systems of control, explaining how survivors of abuse, especially in groups and cults, can be manipulated into belief systems and behaviour that seem inexplicable from the outside.

Beyond Survival: Strategies and Stories from the Transformative Justice Movement, edited by Ejeris Dixon and Leah Lakshmi Piepzna-Samarasinha (AK Press, 2020). An anthology of real-life ideas, stories and strategies from people working to address interpersonal violence at the community level.

Disrupting the Bystander: When #MeToo Happens Among Friends, A.V. Flox (Thorntree Press, 2019). A guide to responding to abuse specifically written for friends and community members of the survivor.

Stop Signs: Recognizing, Avoiding, and Escaping Abusive Relationships, Lynn Fairweather (Seal Press, 2012). Practical and compassionate insights about abuse and what to do if you're being abused. Focused on cishet women and presumed monogamy, but much of it applies more broadly.

The Revolution Starts at Home: Confronting Intimate Violence Within Activist Communities, edited by Ching-In Chen, Jai Dulani and Leah Lakshmi Piepzna-Samarasinha (South End Press, 2011). Case studies showing different approaches to addressing interpersonal harm in communities. Note that this book is controversial in many circles, as some of the case studies are viewed as enabling or compounding harm. Worth reading, but with a critical eye.

Why Does He Do That? Inside the Minds of Angry and Controlling Men, Lundy Bancroft (Penguin Group, 2002). Widely recognized as the most essential text on recognizing, understanding and addressing misogynistic abuse.

Emotional Blackmail: When the People in Your Life Use Fear, Obligation, and Guilt to Manipulate You, Susan Forward and Donna Frazier (William Morrow, 1998). A primer on recognizing and dealing with emotional manipulation and blackmail in romantic relationships.

The Network/La Red, https://www.tnlr.org/. Survivor-led support for people experiencing intimate partner abuse. Kink-, queer- and nonmonogamy-friendly.

NONMONOGAMY

The Other Significant Others: Reimagining Life with Friendship at the Center, Rhaina Cohen (St Martin's Press, 2024). An examination of various ways people are building their lives around attached relationships with people who aren't romantic or sexual partners.

A Polyamory Devotional: 365 Daily Reflections for the Consensually Nonmonogamous, Evita "Lavitaloca" Sawyers (Thornapple Press, 2023). As the title says, 365 short reflections on a wide range of issues in nonmonogamy, from jealousy to metamour relationships to commitment and self-care.

Polywise: A Deeper Dive into Navigating Open Relationships, Jessica Fern and David Cooley (Thornapple Press, 2023). Insights into the paradigm shifts that commonly occur when people enter nonmonogamy and how to navigate them. Focused on the opening of previously coupled relationships.

The Anxious Person's Guide to Nonmonogamy: Your Guide to Open Relationships, Polyamory and Letting Go, Lola Phoenix (Jessica Kingsley Publishers, 2022). A realistic and practical guide focused on the emotional experiences of nonmonogamy.

Polysecure: Attachment, Trauma and Consensual Nonmonogamy, Jessica Fern (Thornapple Press, 2020). A groundbreaking book applying attachment theory to the context of nonmonogamous relationships.

"Making Love and Relations Beyond Settler Sex and Family," Kim TallBear, in *Making Kin Not Population: Reconceiving Generations*, edited by Adele E. Clarke and Donna Haraway, 145–164 (University of Chicago Press, 2018). An exploration of an Indigenous perspective on (and beyond) nonmonogamy and how it lines up with Indigenous ways of life and concepts of kinship.

It's Called Polyamory: Coming Out About Your Nonmonogamous Relationships, Tamara Pincus and Rebecca Hiles (Szymborski) (Thornapple Press, 2017). Just what it says on the tin: a comprehensive guide all about coming out, written by two nonmonogamous therapists.

Playing Fair: A Guide to Nonmonogamy for Men into Women, Pepper Mint (Thornapple Press, 2017). A short and sweet handbook specifically for men seeking nonmonogamous relationships with women.

Stepping Off the Relationship Escalator: Uncommon Love and Life, Amy Gahran (Off the Escalator Enterprises LLC, 2017). Presents the idea of the relationship escalator, how it works, and what ways people are choosing to step off it and into other kinds of relationship models.

What Love Is (and What It Could Be), Carrie Jenkins (Basic Books, 2017). A philosophical exploration of the need to reimagine your views and expectations of romantic love. Focused on nonmonogamy as a test case for what people think love can be.

Polyamory and Pregnancy and *The Polyamorous Home*, Jess Mahler (independently published, 2013 and 2017). Short, practical guides covering all the details of bringing a new baby into a polycule and exploring the options and practicalities of living arrangements among polyamorous folks.

Redefining Our Relationships: Guidelines for Responsible Open Relationships, Wendy-O Matik (Defiant Times Press, 2002). A tiny manifesto on abandoning the relationship escalator and creating intentional, honest nonmonogamous relationships.

The More Than Two Essentials series, various authors (Thornapple Press, ongoing). A series of bite-sized books focused on topics in nonmonogamy, including neurodivergence, happiness, sex work, death and many more. Listed at morethantwo.ca.

SEX, CONSENT AND PLEASURE

Come Together: The Science (and Art!) of Creating Lasting Sexual Connections, Emily Nagoski (Ballantine Books, 2024). More great science-backed advice, this time on long-term sexual relationships.

How Do I Sexy? A Guide for Trans and Nonbinary Queers, Mx. Nillin Lore (Thornapple Press, 2024). A guide for trans and nonbinary queers struggling to find their sexual selves in a landscape rife with misogynistic, transphobic and homophobic ideals and expectations.

Desire: An Inclusive Guide to Navigating Libido Differences in Relationships, Lauren Fogel Mersy and Jennifer A. Vencill (Beacon Press, 2023). A thorough examination of how desire works, why desire discrepancy arises in relationships and what to do about it.

Park Cruising: What Happens When We Wander Off the Path, Marcus McCann (House of Anansi Press, 2023). A poetic and political exploration of the gay park cruising subculture, its beauty and value, and the places it intersects with police repression and social opprobrium.

An Intersectional Approach to Sex Therapy: Centering the Lives of Indigenous, Racialized, and People of Color, edited by Reece M. Malone, Marla Renee Stewart, Mariotta Gary-Smith and James C. Wadley (Routledge, 2022). Fresh perspectives on sex and sexuality (it's not just for therapists!). Kink-, queer- and nonmonogamy-inclusive.

Refusing Compulsory Sexuality: A Black Asexual Lens on Our Sex-Obsessed Culture, Sherronda J. Brown (North Atlantic Books, 2022). A scholarly argument for making space for asexuality as a key element of a consent-based culture.

Come As You Are, Revised and Updated: The Surprising New Science That Will Transform Your Sex Life, Emily Nagoski (Simon & Schuster, 2021). Crucial information, delivered in accessible prose, about desire discrepancy, arousal nonconcordance, sexual "accelerators" and "brakes," and the effects of stress on your sex life.

The Ultimate Guide to Threesomes, Stella Harris (Cleis Press, 2021). Practical advice on how to become "a threesome person" and navigate the joys and challenges of group sex.

The Monster Under the Bed: Sex, Depression, and the Conversations We Aren't Having, JoEllen Notte (Thornapple Press, 2020). A heavily researched and deeply compassionate book that confronts assumptions about relationships and mental illness and offers a way forward for those struggling with depression and their partners.

Queer BDSM Intimacies: Critical Consent and Pushing Boundaries, Robin Bauer (Palgrave Macmillan, 2014). A scholarly exploration of how consent works in queer BDSM communities, with a focus on the concept of critical consent.

Ecstasy Is Necessary: A Practical Guide to Sex, Relationships and Oh So Much More, Barbara Carrellas (Hay House, 2012). How to recognize ecstasy and how to cultivate it in your sexual life and relationships, but also in your everyday, mundane experiences of moving through the world.

Big Big Love, Revised: A Sex and Relationships Guide for People of Size (and Those Who Love Them), Hanne Blank (Celestial Arts, 2011). A fabulous guide to sex for fat folks.

Naked at Our Age: Talking Out Loud About Senior Sex, Joan Price (Seal Press, 2011). A shame-busting practical sex guide for seniors.

The Ultimate Guide to Sex and Disability: For All of Us Who Live with Disabilities, Chronic Pain, and Illness, Miriam Kaufman, Cory Silverberg and Fran Odette (Cleis Press, 2007). An unsurpassed guide to sex for people with a range of disabilities.

CATIE (catie.ca). A key resource on the latest research about STIS.

Public Health Agency of Canada database of disease prevention and treatment information (canada.ca/en/public-health/services/diseases.html). Huge database of information on a long list of illnesses.

Consent Comes First Toronto Metropolitan, "Understanding Consent." (Toronto Metropolitan University, https://www.torontomu.ca/sexual-violence/education/laws-of-consent-in-canada). Accessible overview of consent law in Canada.

Planned Parenthood (plannedparenthood.org). Sexual health and wellness information on a wide range of topics.

Scarleteen (scarleteen.com). Sexual health and wellness information on a wide range of topics, targeted at teens but useful for anyone.

KINK

Hurts So Good: The Science and Culture of Pain on Purpose, Leigh Cowart (PublicAffairs, 2021). A journalistic-slash-personal exploration of why and how people seek out the experience of pain, including BDSM but also well beyond it.

Paradigms of Power: Styles of Master/Slave Relationships, edited by Raven Kaldera (Alfred Press, 2014). A thought-provoking book on M/s relationships featuring a wide range of writers, each describing their particular style of M/s.

Building the Team: Cooperative Power Dynamic Relationships, Raven Kaldera and Joshua Tenpenny (Alfred Press, 2013). An overview of how to engage in a mutually beneficial, collaborative partnership that happens to be based in chosen inequality.

Leading and Supportive Love: The Truth about Dominant and Submissive Relationships, Chris M. Lyon (CreateSpace, 2012). Lays out the basics of how chosen power dynamics work and describes the general personality types of those who engage in them in a healthy way. Suggests potential problem areas and gentle solutions, and above all, validates the great potential for these relationships' strength and durability.

Playing Well with Others: Your Field Guide to Discovering, Exploring and Navigating the Kink, Leather and BDSM Communities, Lee Harrington and Mollena Williams (Greenery Press, 2012). A tour of the many types of kink communities and events that exist out there, and tips on how to navigate them with grace.

The Ultimate Guide to Kink: BDSM, Role Play and the Erotic Edge, edited by Tristan Taormino (Cleis Press, 2012). A diverse collection of voices covering an astonishing range of kinks not often seen between the covers of a single book. Thorough!

Conquer Me: Girl-to-Girl Wisdom about Fulfilling Your Submissive Desires, Kacie Cunningham (Greenery Press, 2010). By-and-for submission advice about day-to-day living in a full-time power relationship. More human-to-human than girl-to-girl.

Power Circuits: Polyamory in a Power Dynamic, edited by Raven Kaldera (Alfred Press, 2010). The only book out there to address this topic in any depth, even though it is hugely relevant to a very large percentage of the people who do D/s and M/s relationships.

Partners in Power: Living in Kinky Relationships, Jack Rinella (Greenery Press, 2003). A thoughtful 101-level exploration of the nature of kinky relationships, how to meet people and how to get what you want.

The Seductive Art of Japanese Bondage, Midori (Greenery Press, 2002). Beautiful pictures and clear diagrams for the beginning bondage-lover.

Sensuous Magic: A Guide to S/M for Adventurous Couples, second edition, Patrick Califia (Cleis Press, 2001). A classic introduction to BDSM for beginners by a well-respected queer and trans veteran of the scene.

MEMOIR

A Part of the Heart Can't Be Eaten, Tristan Taormino (Duke University Press, 2023). Memoir of a trailblazing nonmonogamous queer feminist pornographer and sex educator.

Open: An Uncensored Memoir of Love, Liberation, and Non-Monogamy, Rachel Krantz (Harmony, 2022). Part memoir, part journalism, this story of exploring nonmonogamy for the first time also takes a hard look at dark sides of nonmonogamy such as coercion and gaslighting.

This Heart Holds Many: My Life as the Nonbinary Millennial Child of a Polyamorous Family, Koe Creation (Thorntree Press, 2019). The first memoir written from the perspective a second-generation nonmonogamous person.

Living My Life, Emma Goldman. Originally published in 1931 and 1934, it's now available in a variety of formats, including free online at theanarchistlibrary.org/library/emma-goldman-living-my-life. The autobiography of the famed anarchist includes her explorations with nonmonogamous relationships and her ideas about "free love."

HISTORY

The Importance of Being Monogamous: Marriage and Nation Building in Western Canada to 1915, Sarah Carter (Athabasca University Press, 2008). A discussion of the ways in which the colonial ideal of monogamous marriage was used as one of many tools to disrupt Indigenous cultures and families and implement social control.

The Social Origins of Private Life: A History of American Families 1600–1900, Stephanie Coontz (Verso, 1998). A historical exploration of the diversity of family types among different racial and cultural groups and social strata beginning with the early settlement of North America, and the economic and political forces that shaped the modern ideal of the monogamous nuclear family.

FICTION

Blackheart Man, Nalo Hopkinson (Simon & Schuster, 2024). Veycosi is inconsiderate and full of himself, but brilliant and good-hearted. In his quest to make his mark on society as he prepares for his hoped-for marriage, he accidentally resurrects a mythical monster. *Blackheart Man* isn't about nonmonogamy, but it is set in a society where the standard partnership arrangement is two co-husbands and a wife. Like all great fantasy, it helps us imagine a different way our world could be.

Sense8. A two-season science fiction drama TV series created by Lana and Lilly Wachowski and J. Michael Straczynski for Netflix (2015–2018). Follows the adventures of a multinational ensemble of characters (queer and straight, cis and trans) whose senses and perceptions become interconnected across time and space, resulting in a strange (and very sexy) sort of polycule.

The Fifth Season, N. K. Jemisin (Orbit, 2015). This first book in Jemisin's Broken Earth Trilogy includes a very well done nonmonogamous plotline.

The Marketplace series, Laura Antoniou (Circlet Press, various). A cult favourite among kinksters, this multi-book series explores an underground society based on consensual ownership. Too plot- and character-driven to be simple erotica, too erotic to be regular old fiction. Nonmonogamous by default.

SOCIAL MEDIA AND PODCASTS

In the last decade there has been an explosion of channels on YouTube, TikTok and Instagram, as well as podcasts, focused on nonmonogamy. The list changes rapidly and we certainly don't have a comprehensive view of everything out there, but as of the first printing of this book in 2026, a few worth looking at are Antimononormative, Evita "Lavitaloca" Sawyers, Polyamorous Black Girl, Ready for Polyamory, PolyaMarla and Chill Polyamory (on Instagram and Tiktok); Mainely Mandy on YouTube; and the podcasts *Making Polyamory Work*, *Playing with Fire* and *Non-Monogamy Help*.

Index

Page numbers in **bold type** refer to terms defined in the glossary.

More Than Two Essentials

More Than Two® Essentials is a series of books by Canadian authors on focused topics in nonmonogamy. Learn more at morethantwo.ca.

Nonmonogamy and Defying a Paradigm

Nonmonogamy and Betrayal

Nonmonogamy and Queer Inclusivity

Nonmonogamy and Group Dynamics

Nonmonogamy and Happiness

Post-Nonmonogamy and Beyond

Also from Thornapple Press

Thornapple Press is a Canadian publisher of thoughtful books on love, sexuality and relational ethics. Learn more at **thornapplepress.ca**.

Carry On: Unpacking Your Internalized Transphobic and Queerphobic Baggage

Mx. Nillin Lore, with a foreword by Andrew Gurza

"An affirming, nurturing, generous-spirited handbook that will help many queer people navigate brutal political times."

—Dr. Kit Heyam, author of *Before We Were Trans: A New History of Gender*

A Polyamory Devotional: 365 Daily Reflections for the Consensually Nonmonogamous

Evita Sawyers, with a foreword by Chaneé Jackson Kendall and illustrations by Tikva Wolf

"Vita doesn't pull any punches with her raw and deeply personal perspective. A year of her daily takes is definitely a learning experience that all of us can get something from."

—Kevin A. Patterson, M.Ed., author of *Love's Not Color Blind*

Polywise: A Deeper Dive into Navigating Open Relationships

Jessica Fern, with David Cooley

"In *Polywise*'s expansive and eye-opening exploration of the possibilities of nonmonogamous life, Jessica Fern invites us to examine our individual and societal beliefs about love and offers an indispensable guide for newly opened couples' transitions to their next chapter. If you are ready to think more deeply about communication, codependency, conflict, and repair in your most important relationships, *Polywise* is required reading. I am looking forward to recommending this guide to clients and students."

—Alexandra H. Solomon, PhD, author of *Love Every Day* and host of *Reimagining Love*

About the Authors

Eve Rickert is a white, Gen X, queer, solo polyamorous, relationship anarchist, neurodivergent cis woman living as a settler on unceded W̱SÁNEĆ and Lekwungen territory on the west coast of the place currently known as Canada. She is the curator of the More Than Two Essentials series and the nonmonogamy resource site morethantwo.ca, the founder and publisher of Thornapple Press and CanScience Books, and the founder and mastermind of the science communications firm Talk Science to Me.

Andrea Zanin, MA, is a white, nonbinary, middle-aged queer writer who lives in Tkaronto (Toronto, Ontario), on the traditional territory of the Mississaugas of the Credit, the Anishnabeg, the Chippewa, the Haudenosaunee and the Wendat peoples. Andrea's writing focuses on nonmonogamy and BDSM/Leather. Andrea has written for the *Globe and Mail*, *The Tyee*, *Bitch*, *Ms.*, *Xtra*, *IN Magazine*, *Outlooks Magazine* and the *Montreal Mirror*. Their scholarly work, fiction and essays appear in a variety of collections. Andrea blogs at sexgeek.wordpress.com, where they created the 10 Rules for Happy Nonmonogamy and coined the term "polynormativity." Their first book, *Post-Nonmonogamy and Beyond*, is also available from Thornapple Press.

Dr. Kim TallBear (Sisseton-Wahpeton Oyate) (she/her) is Professor and Canada Research Chair in Indigenous Peoples, Technoscience and Society, Faculty of Native Studies, University of Alberta. She is the author of *Native American DNA: Tribal Belonging and the False Promise of Genetic Science*. In addition to studying genome science disruptions to Indigenous self-definitions, Dr. TallBear studies the roles of the overlapping ideas of "sexuality" and "nature" in the colonization of Indigenous peoples and lands.

Nalo Hopkinson has published seven novels and three collections of her short fiction, including her novel *Blackheart Man* and her short story collection *Jamaica Ginger and Other Concoctions*. She has received the John W. Campbell Award and the Nebula Award, and has thrice won the Sunburst Award for Canadian Fiction of the Fantastic. Nalo is a professor of Creative Writing at the University of British Columbia in Vancouver, Canada.